Plinio Corrêa de Oliveira

Prophet of the Reign of Mary

Plinio Corrêa de Oliveira

Prophet of the Reign of Mary

by

Roberto de Mattei

Preface by
Bishop Athanasius Schneider

Translated by José Aloísio Aranha Schelini

Preserving Christian Publications
Boonville, New York
2019

English translation by José Aloísio Aranha Schelini
© 2019 Copyright by the Foundation for a Christian Civilization, Inc.

Published by Preserving Christian Publications, Inc. through special arrangement with the Foundation for a Christian Civilization, Inc.

Preserving Christian Publications Inc.
P.O. Box 221
Boonville, New York 13309
Tel: 315-942-6617
info@pcpbooks.com
www.pcpbooks.net

ISBN: 978-0-9840139-8-2

CONTENTS

INTRODUCTION

Who was Plinio Corrêa de Oliveira, familiarly known as "Dr. Plinio"[1]? Why does a veil of silence still surround this extraordinary figure twenty years after his death, which took place in São Paulo, Brazil, on October 3, 1995?

I believe the real and profound reason for this lack of recognition should not be sought in his thinking and activities, which stand out with crystal clarity on the background of our dark age, but in the intellectual and moral confusion that surrounds contemporary man, devoid of those criteria of discernment that would enable one to recognize men sent by Divine Providence in dramatic times of history.

In 1996 I tried to raise this veil with a biography dedicated to Plinio Corrêa de Oliveira, *The Crusader of the 20th Century*.[2] In that book I tried to situate the Brazilian thinker in relation to his time: a century of revolutions and genocide that has been called the bloodiest and most destructive in history.[3]

Plinio was born in the last years of the *Belle Epoque*, when the catastrophe of the First World War was taking place. He grew up and was formed in a society that still reflected the way of being and ancient Christian manners being extinguished in Europe.

From an early age he began a fervent Catholic militancy that led him to become president of Catholic Action in São Paulo, congressman at the Brazilian Constituent Assembly, editor of the weekly *O Legionário*, inspirer of the monthly *Catolicismo*, a leading figure in the Marian Congregations and the Third Carmelite Order, and finally, in 1960, founder of the Brazilian Society for the Defense of Tradition, Family and Property (TFP). His public life was a continuous and consistent cultural and moral crusade against the hedonism of liberal society, the pseudo National Socialist mysticism, the socialist-communist egalitarian utopia, and the self-destructive frenzy of Catholic progressivism.

---

[1] Throughout this work I will often refer to Prof. Plinio using the abbreviated term "Plinio" for easier reading.

[2] ROBERTO DE MATTEI, *Il crociato del secolo XX. Plinio Corrêa de Oliveira*, prefaced by His Eminence Alfonso Maria Cardinal STICKLER, S.D.B., Piemme, Casale Monferrato, 1996. After this first Italian edition, this work was translated into Portuguese (1997), Spanish (1997 and 2010 in Peru), French (1997), English (1998), Polish (2004), and German (2004).

[3] Cf. MARCO REVELLI, *Oltre il Novecento. La politica, le ideologie e le insidie del lavoro*, Einaudi, Torino, 2001, pp. 5 & ff.; ROBERT CONQUEST, *Reflections on a Ravaged Century*, W.W. Norton & Company, New York-London, 2001.

But this political and cultural crusade is only one aspect of the Brazilian author's historical mission. He was also the founder of an intellectual current and a spiritual school that, inspired by his thinking, now continues his work around the world.

What are the characteristics of this school and to what degree can Plinio Corrêa de Oliveira's lesson help us deal with the crisis of our time? That is the subject of this new book that I dedicate to the great Brazilian thinker and man of action, as a logical continuation of the preceding work.

I personally knew "Dr. Plinio" and met with him several times between 1976 and 1995. Those talks produced a durable and profound influence on my soul and decisively contributed to shaping my intellectual and spiritual personality. The following pages result from those conversations but also from reading thousands of published and unpublished pages taken from his books and articles, and from hundreds of lectures, meetings, and interviews faithfully transcribed by his disciples.[4]

I will try to expose his thought in an organic fashion by selecting from this huge doctrinal collection only some of the most expressive quotations concerning various topics. I will also fit them within Catholic tradition, if only to defend him from some unjust accusations that have been made about his orthodoxy.

A caveat, however, is necessary. Corrêa de Oliveira was not a bookish author, based on other authors. The historical, philosophical and theological quotations that I will use to show his teaching's compliance with the Church's doctrine do not necessarily refer to authors he read or knew. What I want instead is to demonstrate that the originality and creativity of his teaching stand in absolute continuity with Catholic Tradition.

The Brazilian thinker is the living proof of how Tradition is not the repetition of stereotyped formulas, but progress and development. "Tradition and progress," Pius XII taught, "complement each other so harmoniously that, just as tradition without progress would be a contradiction in terms, so progress without tradition would be a foolhardy proposition, a leap into darkness."[5]

---

[4] Most of this work is based on transcriptions of lectures, meetings and recorded conversations of Prof. Plinio Corrêa de Oliveira and have not been revised by him, which explains their colloquial style, which the author of this study chose to preserve. Many of the texts were extracted from compilations by Enrique Mario Loaiza.

[5] PIUS XII, Speech to the Roman Patriciate and Nobility of June 19, 1944, *Discorsi e Radiomessaggi*, V (1943-1944), p. 180.

The most original part of the thought of Plinio Corrêa de Oliveira is his theology of history, but before expounding upon it, it is necessary to show its philosophical foundations and spiritual roots. This explains the need for a first part of this work that may seem arduous to some readers because of the metaphysical nature of certain topics. In it I will try to show that from the philosophical standpoint, the Brazilian thinker was certainly Thomist, but just as Saint Thomas had made a great synthesis between Plato and Aristotle, so also in the twentieth century Dr. Plinio presents himself as a point of confluence between the legacy of the Angelic Doctor and the still unexplored legacies of Saint Bonaventure and the Victorians.

His spirituality of a "contemplative in action" was that of an authentic son of Saint Ignatius, but had nothing to do with the "manualist" tendency the Society of Jesus experienced between the 1800's and 1900's. Plinio takes up again and develops that fertile contemplative tradition in which Saint Ignatius meets Saint Teresa of Avila and Saint John of the Cross.

As a philosopher and theologian of history, Corrêa de Oliveira is the heir to the counter-revolutionary thought of the nineteenth century, which has extraordinary merits but also limits, and which in the twentieth century tends to lose its metaphysical and supernatural spirit. He broadens it and develops its perspectives, not only by meditating on the crisis of his age, but by pointing out concrete and fruitful ways to react. One should particularly emphasize Plinio's interest in that area, as vast and important as it is poorly studied, which he calls "Ambiences, Customs, Civilizations," and which constitutes a privileged battleground of the struggle between the Revolution and the Counter-Revolution.

It is important to keep in mind that he was not what is currently called an intellectual. The figure of modern intellectuals developed mainly with the French Revolution and was born from the Cartesian split between the intellect and reality, between thought and action. In Plinio the two aspects are in perfect harmony, forming the unity of his personality. It is for this reason that the philosophy of history was the aspect of philosophy that interested him the most, as he stated: "In view of it I find the connection between the two kinds of activities to which I have dedicated my life: study and action."[6] The Plinian view of the universe is neither separated from history nor from the effort and struggle which man carries out in history. "The fight is man's great interlocutor, and it is within it and in function of it that he thinks and affirms himself."[7]

---

[6] *Plinio Corrêa de Oliveira's Philosophical Self-Portrait,* at http://www.tfp.org/tfp-home/plinio-corrca-dc-olivcira/philosophical self portrait-plinio-correa-de-oliveira.html.

[7] MNF, 14 December 1981.

Plinio Corrêa de Oliveira was not only a man of learning and action: he was first and foremost a man of prayer. His inner life is the secret of his diverse intellectual activity and inexhaustible apostolate. Father Garrigou-Lagrange commented that, just as Descartes had separated philosophy from theology, so also in the modern era intellectuals separated the life of study from the interior life.[8] Likewise, one could say that among Catholic men of action, the apostolate has been dissociated from contemplative life as if the two were incompatible dimensions. Harmony between contemplative and active life characterized the life of Dr. Plinio, who was rightly called "a fighter while contemplative, and a contemplative while fighter."[9]

Like my previous book, this work may arouse misunderstanding and even loathing from some, but I deem it my duty to do justice to a figure to whom I owe so much, and, above all, to render a service to all men of good will who are now disoriented and confused and who can find, in Plinio Corrêa de Oliveira's counter-revolutionary school, spiritual solace, intellectual light, and greater vigor in action so as to better correspond to Divine Grace, on which hinges the fate of our souls and of the whole world.

It is necessary to emphasize that I deliberately kept biographical references on Plinio Corrêa de Oliveira to a minimum, as they have already appeared in *The Crusader of the 20th Century.* Nor do I deal with the work he founded – the TFP – which deserves a volume in its own right. My sole intention is to expound the main lines of the spiritual thinker and man of action's intellectual and spiritual legacy.

The Brazilian Master always said he wanted to submit his every sentence, line and word to the judgment of the Church, of which he proclaimed himself, even to his last breath, a faithful and most devoted son.[10] Allow me to make the same disclaimer. The following pages are intended to be a faithful echo not only of the thought of Plinio Corrêa de Oliveira, but also of the Magisterium of the Church, infallible guardian of faith and morals, to whose judgment I submit each and every line.

---

[8] REGINALD GARRIGOU-LAGRANGE OP, *Perfection chrétienne et contemplation*, Desclée, Paris, 1923, vol. II, p. 636.

[9] Cf. FERNANDO ANTUNEZ ALDUNATE, "Plinio Corrêa de Oliveira, a Contemplative," *Catolicismo,* no. 658 (October 2005), pp. 40-43.

[10] Prof. Plinio Corrêa de Oliveira always insisted that this note be inserted into all transcriptions of his texts: "A Roman and Apostolic Catholic, the author of this text submits himself to the traditional teaching of Holy Church with filial ardor. And he immediately and categorically rejects anything in it which, through some oversight, should be found at variance with that teaching."

Bio-Bibliographical Note

Plinio Corrêa de Oliveira was born in São Paulo, Brazil, on December 13, 1908, the son of attorney João Paulo Corrêa de Oliveira (1874-1961) and Mrs. Lucilia Ribeiro dos Santos (1876-1968), from the ancient aristocracies of the states of Pernambuco and São Paulo, respectively. He completed his secondary studies at the Jesuit *Colégio São Luis* and graduated from the metropolis's Law School. As he started his professional and public career, he became a major leader of the Catholic youth of São Paulo. At age twenty-four, in May 1933, on the slate of the Catholic Electoral League he was elected congressman to the Constituent Assembly, of which he was the youngest member and the candidate most voted for across the country. Shortly afterward he assumed the chair of History of Civilization at the Law School of the University of São Paulo and later at the Sedes Sapientiae and São Bento Colleges, both of the Pontifical Catholic University of São Paulo. He was one of the founders of São Paulo Catholic Action and the first president of its Archdiocesan Board.

From 1933 to 1947 he was director of *Legionário*, which he turned from a parish bulletin into the country's largest Catholic weekly. Around the paper he formed an intellectual current that gave a strong boost to the Catholic movement as a whole. From 1951 to 1995 he was the inspiration behind the cultural monthly magazine *Catolicismo,* published in Campos, state of Rio de Janeiro. He also wrote for Brazilian dailies from 1968 to 1993, especially a weekly column in *Folha de S. Paulo.*

In 1960 he founded the Brazilian Society for the Defense of Tradition, Family and Property (TFP), devoting himself body and soul to presiding over that association. Legally independent associations inspired by his thought were also founded in subsequent years not only in the Americas but throughout the world. He personally oriented the various TFPs when producing many of the books they published, which number over a hundred. The legacy of all this activity translates into over twenty thousand recordings of lectures, training sessions and talks in study commissions, now gathered in the Archives of the Plinio Corrêa de Oliveira Institute (IPCO).

Plinio Corrêa de Oliveira died on October 3, 1995 in São Paulo at nearly eighty-seven years of age, comforted by the sacraments of the Catholic Church and after receiving the papal blessing.

About him, in addition to *The Crusader* (*op. cit.*), see: *Half a Century of Epic Anticommunism*, The Foundation for a Christian

Civilization, Mount Kisco, NY, 1981, 459 pp.; BRAZILIAN SOCIETY FOR THE DEFENSE OF TRADITION, FAMILY AND PROPERTY, *A Man, a Life Work, an Epic Saga – Homage of the TFPs to Plinio Corrêa de Oliveira*, Edições Brasil de Amanhã, São Paulo, 1989; TFP STUDY COMMISSION, *Tradition Family Property – An Ideal, a Motto, an Epic Struggle: The Twentieth Century Crusade*, Artpress, São Paulo, 1990; VARIOUS AUTHORS, *Plinio Corrêa de Oliveira Ten Years Later,* ASSOCIAÇÃO DOS FUNDADORES DA TFP, São Paulo, 2005; MASSIMO INTROVIGNE, *A Battle in the Night. Plinio Corrêa de Oliveira and the Crisis of the Church in the 20th Century*, Sugarco, Milan, 2008; MATHIAS VON GERSDORFF, *Begegnung mit Plinio Corrêa de Oliveira. Katholischer Streiter in stürmischer Zei,* Patrimonium, Frankfurt, 2015; and numerous doctoral theses defended in Brazil such as LIZANIAS DE SOUZA LIMA'S *Plinio Corrêa de Oliveira: A Twentieth Century Crusader*, Universidade de São Paulo, 1984; GIZELE ZANOTTO'S, *It is Chaos!!! Plinio Corrêa de Oliveira's Anti-Land Reform Struggle*, Universidade Federal de Santa Catarina, Florianópolis, 2003; RODRIGO COPPE CALDEIRA, *Ultramontane Influence in Brazil: The Thought of Plinio Corrêa de Oliveira*, Universidade Federal de Juiz de Fora, Juiz de For a, 2005; LUIS FELIPE LOUREIRO FORESTI, *The Herald of the Counter-Revolution: The Conservative Thought of Plinio Corrêa de Oliveira (1968-1976)*, Pontifical Catholic University of São Paulo, 2013.

LIST OF BIBLIOGRAPHICAL ABBREVIATIONS

AAS   (before 1909): *Acta Apostolicae Sedis*, Typis Vaticana, Vatican City, 1909–.

Calmness   *Calmness and its Gentle Superiority*, Excerpts of the thought of Plinio Corrêa de Oliveira, gathered by LEO DANIELE, Editora Artpress, São Paulo, 2014.

Chivalry   *Chivalry Does Not Die,* Excerpts of the thought of Plinio Corrêa de Oliveira, gathered by LEO DANIELE, Brasil de Amanhã, São Paulo, 1998.

A-IPCO   Archives of the Plinio Corrêa de Oliveira Institute (São Paulo, Brazil).

Looking for Souls with a Soul, Excerpts of the thought of Plinio Corrêa de Oliveira, gathered by LEO DANIELE, Brasil de Amanhã, São Paulo, 1998.

BELLOCCHI: *Tutte le encicliche e i principali documenti pontifici emanati dal 1740*, edited by UGO BELLOCCHI, 13 vols., Libreria Editrice Vaticana, Rome, 1994-2008.

BENEDICT XVI *Insegnamenti: Insegnamenti di Benedetto XVI*, 16 tomes in 9 volumes, Libreria Editrice Vaticana, Vatican City, 2005-2013.

CJC   *Codice di Diritto Canonico*, Unione Editori e Librai Cattolici Italiani, Roma, 1997.

COD   *Conciliorum Oecumenicorum Decreta*, edited by Istituto per le Scienze Religiose, bilingual edition, EDB, Bologna, 2002.

DBI   *Dizionario Biografico degli Italiani*, Istituto dell'Enciclopedia Italiana, Roma, 1960 ff.

DDC   *Dictionnaire de Droit Canonique*, Letouzey et Ané, Parigi, 1935-1958 (7 vols.).

DENZ-H   HEINRICH DENZINGER, *Enchiridion Symbolorum definitionum et declarationum de rebus fidei et morum,* edited by PETER HÜNERMANN, bilingual edition, EDB, Bologna, 1995.

Ten Years Later, Various authors, *Plinio Corrêa de Oliveira Ten Years Later*, Associação dos Fundadores da TFP, São Paulo, 2005.

DGWE   *Dictionary of Gnosis and Western Esotericism, edited* by Wouter J. Hanegraaff, Brill, Leiden, 2006.

DHGE   *Dictionnaire d'Histoire et de Géographie Ecclésiastiques*, Letouzey et Ané, Paris, 1912 ff.

DHCJ   CHARLES E. O'NEIL, S.J. & JOAQUÍN M. DOMÍNGUEZ, S.J. (edited by), *Diccionario histórico de la Compañia de Jesús*, 4 vols., Institutum Historicum, S.J. – Universidad Pontificia Cornillas, Roma-Madrid, 2001.

DM   GABRIELE M. ROSCHINI, OSM, *Dizionario di Mariologia*, Edizioni Studium, Roma, 1961.

DSP   *Dizionario Storico del Papato*, Bompiani, Milano, 1996 (2 vols.).

DSp   *Dictionnaire de Spiritualité*, Beauchesne, Paris, 1937-1994 (16 vols.).

DTC   *Dictionnaire de Théologie Catholique, edited* by A. A. VACANT and E. MANGENOT, Letouzey et Ané, Paris, 1909-1972 (33 vols.).

EC   *Enciclopedia Cattolica*, Sansoni, Florence, 1949-1954 (12 vols.).

EE   *Enchiridion delle Encicliche*, bilingual edition, EDB, Bologna, 1995-1999.

EF   *Enciclopedia filosofica*, edited by Centro di Studi Filosofici di Gallerate, Epidem, Roma, 1979.

ENCH: CONC. *Enchiridion dei Concordati. Due secoli dei rapporti Chiesa-Stato*, EDB, Bologna, 2003.

EP   *Enciclopedia dei Papi*, vol. III, Istituto della Enciclopedia Italiana, Roma, 2000.

JOHN XXIII, *Discorsi: Discorsi, messaggi, colloqui di Giovanni XXIII*, Libreria Editrice Vaticana, Vaticano & ff., Città del Vaticano 1960-1967.

JOHN PAUL II, *Insegnamenti: Insegnamenti di Giovanni Paolo II*. Libreria Editrice Vaticana, Città del Vaticano 1980–.

Imbroglio, détraction, délire: Imbroglio, détraction, délire. Remarks on a report about the TFPs, 2 vols., Tradition, Famille, Propriété, Asnières, 1980.

La Chiesa   in *Insegnamenti Pontifici*, edited by the Benedictine Monks of Solesmes, Paoline, Roma, 1971 (2 vols.).

LTK   *Lexikon für Theologie und Kirche*, Herder, Friburgo in Brisgovia, 1957-1965 (10 vols.).

MANSI   GIOVANNI DOMENICO MANSI, *Sacrorum conciliorum nova et amplissima Collectio*, edited by LOUIS PETIT and JEAN-BAPTISTE MARTIN, Paris-Arnhem-Leipzig 1901-1927 (53 vols.).

Nobility and Analogous Traditional Elites in the Allocutions of Pius XII, prefaced by H.R.I.H. Prince Luiz of Orleans and Braganza; English translation: Hamilton Press, USA, October 1993.

Idealism: Nobility of Soul Fitting to All, Excerpts of the thought of Plinio Corrêa de Oliveira, edited by LEO DANIELE, Brasil de Amanhã, São Paulo, 2010.

The Universe Is a Cathedral: Excerpts of the thought of Plinio Corrêa de Oliveira gathered by LEO DANIELE, Brasil de Amanhã, São Paulo, 1997.

PAUL VI, *Insegnamenti*: Tipografia Poliglotta Vaticana, Città del Vaticano 1963-1978 (16 vols.).

PASTOR: LUDWIG VON PASTOR, *Storia dei Papi dalla fine del Medioevo*, Desclée & C., Roma, 1926-1963 (16 vols.).

PG   *Patrologiae Cursus Completus, Series Graeca*, edited by JEAN-PAUL MIGNE, Paris 1844-1864 (221 vols.).

PIUS XII   *Discorsi e Radiomessaggi*: Tipografia Poliglotta Vaticana, Città del Vaticano 1959 (21 vols.).

PL   *Patrologiae Cursus Completus, Series Latina*, edited by JEAN-PAUL MIGNE, Parigi 1844-1864 (226 vols.).

PRECES   *Preces pro opportunitate dicundae*, The Foundation for a Christian Civilization, York (Pennsylvania), 1993.

Revolution and Counter-Revolution: PLINIO CORRÊA DE OLIVEIRA, Spring Grove, Pennsylvania: The American TFP, 2002; http://www.tfp.org/

Summa Theologica: Saint Thomas Aquinas, http://www.newadvent.-org/summa/

The Crusader of the 20th Century: ROBERTO DE MATTEI, *The Crusader of the 20th Century: Plinio Corrêa de Oliveira*, with a preface by His Eminence Alfonso Maria Cardinal Stickler, SDB (Herefordshire, England: Gracewing, Fowler Wright Books, 1998).

TRE   *Theologische Realenzyklopädie*, de Gruyter, Berlin-New York 1977 ff.

Bibliographic notes relating to Plinio Corrêa de Oliveira's verbal presentations follow the nomenclature used by the Plinio Corrêa de Oliveira Commission of the Plinio Corrêa de Oliveira Institute (IPCO), responsible for the transcription, digitization and preservation of this data:

ALM   Informal conversation with friends during meals.

AMC   Sporadic meetings with a Commission of Studies on the United States.

AMP   Meetings and conversations with different groups about varied topics, during stays for study or rest at a farm in the city of Amparo (SP)

BCM   Weekly meeting on Saturday mornings between 1964 and 1967, with directors from São Paulo and other state capitals on public opinion topics.

COM   Compilations of excerpts from lectures dealing with the same topic, prepared by the Plinio Corrêa de Oliveira Commission.

DES   Daily working dispatch with his secretary, Mr. Fernando Antúnez Aldunate, or other aides.

MEC   Sunday afternoon meetings with a study commission initially made up by physicians and later opened to other people fit for those studies; it dealt with a great variety of doctrinal topics.

SNC   Saturday night conversations in his apartment, with a small circle of close friends.

EVP   Sunday conversation after dinner at the TFP's social headquarters, with a small circle of close friends.

EXT   Occasional meetings or spiritual conversations with a group of disciples.

MNF   Regular meetings (three times a week) with a study commission on philosophical topics.

PUB   Public speech or lecture.

NOR   Until the end of the 1960's, daily evening meeting (after dinner) at the association's auditorium open to directors from São Paulo and the interior, and to visitors from similar or friendly associations abroad.

RRR   Weekly meeting analyzing news clippings from daily papers and magazines.

RST   In the 1950's, Saturday afternoon meeting on topics of the spiritual life with São Paulo directors of the Marian Congregation founded by Fr. Walter Mariaux, S.J.

SD   In the 1960's, an evening daily meeting open to all volunteers, commenting on the life of the saint celebrated on that day. The meeting was later held on Wednesdays and Friday evenings, on the most varied themes.

SSD   Weekly Saturday evening meeting for younger volunteers on topics of interest for the youth.

SEF   Lectures during Specialized Weeks of Anticommunist Formation. They would usually be given at the opening and closing of those seminars.

Because of the adaptations they have undergone, citations from Plinio's meetings in this work cannot be considered literal versions and do not affect the original texts provided by the Commission or engage the Plinio Corrêa de Oliveira Institute. Likewise, their doctrinal interpretation is the sole responsibility of the author of this work.

PREFACE

At the most difficult times in the history of the Church, Divine Providence has always brought forth exceptional men who have vigorously and selflessly defended Catholic truth against the recurrent attacks of the powers of darkness.

`One can certainly count among these men Plinio Corrêa de Oliveira, who was born in São Paulo in Brazil in 1908, and died in this same city on October 3, 1995.

Roberto de Mattei, who published in 1996 the first biography of the Brazilian thinker and man of action, under the title *The Crusader of the 20th Century: Plinio Corrêa de Oliveira,* twenty years after this publication and the death of one who passed familiarly into history under the name of "Doctor Plinio," publishes a second study, devoted to the spiritual and doctrinal legacy he left to the men of the twenty-first century.

The first volume had a laudatory preface by His Eminence Cardinal Alfonso Maria Stickler. I have the pleasure in turn of presenting this second work by Professor de Mattei, whose critical rigor and deep Catholic spirit I appreciate.

The author rightly insists on the "Romanitas" of Plinio Corrêa de Oliveira, that is to say, his love for the Holy Catholic, Apostolic and Roman Church, of which he was a very devoted son to the end, writing in his testament: "*The persons, institutions and doctrines I have loved throughout my life, and which I still love, I have loved only because they were or are in conformity with the Holy Church, and to the extent that they were or are in accordance with Her. I have likewise never fought institutions, people, or doctrines except insofar as they were in opposition, and to the extent that they were in opposition, to the Holy Catholic Church.*"

The inscription, which can be read on the tomb of Dr. Plinio, in the Cemetery of Consolation in São Paulo, expresses the meaning of his life and his mission: *Vir totus catholicus and apostolicus plene romanus.* To be Catholic, apostolic and Roman means to be inflamed with the love of the Church, the Mystical Body of Christ, and thus to offer unconditionally one's own life, to the holocaust of oneself, for Our Lord, so that He reigns, in Heaven and on earth, through Mary: *"per Mariam ad Jesum!"*

The great ideal of Plinio Corrêa de Oliveira can be summed up in the formula of the Reign of Christ through Mary: *"Regnum Christi per Mariam."* This was the pivot of the doctrine and apostolate of St. Louis Marie Grignion de Montfort, of whom Professor Corrêa de Oliveira can call himself a great successor in the twentieth century. To spread ever more in souls and in human society the Kingdom of Christ through Mary: this was the heart of his life and activity.

One of the most effective spiritual means to promote the Kingdom of Christ through Mary is total consecration to Our Lady, according to the method of holy slavery taught by Saint Louis-Marie Grignion de Montfort. Holy Marian slavery was the foundation of the spiritual life of many saints who, at the school of the Immaculate Heart of Mary, learned to love God and to do His will. We must mention St. John Vianney, St. John Bosco, St. Dominic Savio, St. Therese of the Child Jesus, St. Gemma Galgani, St. Pius X, St. Maximilian Maria Kolbe, St. Pio of Pietrelcina and many other extraordinary figures who saw in the total consecration to Mary not a "devotion of any kind" or "another devotion," but a perfect devotion, this devotion dear to Jesus and requested by Him to make each of us an indefectibly faithful son of His Most Holy Mother.

Plinio Corrêa de Oliveira not only lived this holy slavery with fidelity, but became a true apostle of its diffusion. One cannot understand the public and social action of Professor Plinio unless one starts from his spiritual foundation. The consecration to Mary, lived in a total coherence, leads Mary to reign in the soul of her devotees. The reign of Mary in souls is therefore the beginning of the realization of the Kingdom of Christ in society. Plinio Corrêa de Oliveira has foretold an epoch of spiritual and visible radiance of the Church, which will correspond to the triumph of the Immaculate Heart of Mary announced by Our Lady at Fatima in 1917, and it is for this triumph that he fought until his last breath.

Those who reap the spiritual and cultural heritage of Plinio Corrêa de Oliveira, and Prof. De Mattei is part of this, participate in the same mission, that of leading souls to the light of Jesus and of Mary in the darkness of the contemporary world.

By encouraging the reading and the diffusion of this book, I wish to make mine also the program which it transmits to us:

"Cor Jesu adveniat Regnum Tuum, adveniat per Mariam!"

+ Athanasius Schneider
Auxiliary Bishop of the Archdiocese of
Most Holy Mary in Astana, Kazakhstan

PART ONE

THE PHILOSOPHICAL SYSTEM

CHAPTER I

REALISM OF THE PHILOSOPHY OF BEING

Faith and Reason: A Necessary Integration

The whole thinking and action of Plinio Corrêa de Oliveira are based on two pillars: reason, which is the noblest faculty of every human being, and the Roman Catholic and Apostolic Faith. His teaching follows an itinerary, which, starting from the foundations of reason, reaches the pinnacles of faith. In an era of the death or atrophy of reason,[11] Plinio's whole work seeks to restore the role of human intelligence. The philosophical system is the foundation of his theological and spiritual horizon.

An authentic philosophical system is a well-founded and coherent worldview: a *Weltanschauung*, as the Germans say, or *cosmovisión*, to use a Spanish expression. While few people rationally make their cultural perspective explicit, everyone has a conception of the world that inspires him. Most people think and judge according to the intellectual rules of the society in which they live.

In 1965, Plinio stated:

> "The philosopher, the sage, is a man who has a global notion of the universe thus constructed, be it true or false; and who communicates it to others and lives, not on a day-to-day basis, with the stupid improvidence of men without superior thought, but develops for himself a philosophy of life which the Germans would call a '*Weltanschauung*,' and he knows how to live accordingly."[12]

Philosophical thought is formed through reason and should not be confused with the deposit of faith entrusted to the Church, to which reason submits. The First Vatican Council, in the Constitution *Dei*

---

[11] Cf. For example, MARCEL DE CORTE, *L'intelligence en péril de mort,* Club de la Culture Française, Paris, 1969; MICHELE FEDERICO SCIACCA, *L'oscuramento dell'intelligenza*, Epos, Palermo, 2000.

[12] MNF, 30 March 1965.

Filius,[13] solemnly declared that "the doctrine of the faith that God has revealed has not been proposed to human intelligence as a philosophical system to perfect, but as a divine deposit, entrusted to the Church, the bride of Christ, to be faithfully preserved and infallibly proclaimed." [14] The same constitution defined the existence of a necessary harmony between faith and reason by stating that "although faith is above reason, there can never be any real discrepancy between faith and reason: because the same God who reveals the mysteries and communicates the faith has also placed the light of reason in the human mind." [15]

Faith is above reason but cannot contradict it because it is founded on reason. People today have lost the true notion of faith by reducing it to emotional experience, forgetting that it is an act of reason, which has the truth as its object. Although it is not a philosophical system, the Catholic faith needs rational premises to exist. Thus one must guard against two errors: rationalism, which absorbs faith into reason, and fideism, which dissolves reason into faith. Saint Thomas Aquinas's thinking in this regard gives us a perfectly balanced model.

In all his teaching, Plinio fights fideism and reiterates "the rational homage" that intelligence must pay in the act of faith:

> "I believe that the word 'love' is contained in the *obsequium.* It would be worthwhile to take a careful look at the meaning of the word *obsequium* in Latin. For I think that *obsequium* here is a reverence, an inclination; it is therefore the taking of a stand by the will; it is an act of love."[16]

The act through which reason submits to the faith is triggered, as every human act, by the will, which loves the truth to which it adheres.

"I Am a Convinced Thomist"

Plinio Corrêa de Oliveira begins his *Philosophical Self-Portrait,* written in 1976, with these words: "I am a convinced Thomist. "[17] With this statement he aligns himself to the Magisterium of the Church, which has always indicated the thought of Saint Thomas Aquinas[18] as the surest way in the fields of philosophy and theology.[19]

---

[13] 1st VATICAN CONCIL, 3rd Session, April 24, 1870, *Constitutio dogmatica de fide catholica,* in DENZ-H, nos. 3000-3045. Cf. also John Paul II, Enc. *Fides et Ratio,* of September 14, 1998; AAS 91 (1999), pp. 5-88.

[14] DENZ-H, No. 3020.

[15] DENZ-H, No. 3017.

[16] MNF, 24 March 1989.

[17] *Philosophical Self-Portrait,* http://www.tfp.org/tfp-home/plinio-correa-de-oliveira/philosophical-self-portrait-plinio-correa-de-oliveira.html.

[18] For an introduction to Saint Thomas Aquinas, cf. R. GARRIGOU LAGRANGE, O.P., *Synthèse thomiste,* Desclée de Brouwer, Paris, 1947; SANTIAGO RAMIREZ, O.P., *Introducción a Tomas*

However, Plinio Corrêa de Oliveira is not a mere repeater of Saint Thomas, but an original thinker who develops and deepens many points of Aquinas's thought. He can be called a great representative of the realist philosophy of being that comes neither through bookish or "existential" routes, but only after powerful philosophical speculation.

His way of thinking and expressing himself was always firmly anchored to what may be called the "philosophy of common sense," a profound sense of reality that he acquired since childhood through careful observation of men, ambiences, and historical facts. In his later years he developed this philosophy, which would be better defined as a method of thought, particularly in meetings with closer disciples at MNF,[20] a study commission with which he sought to form, even more than a philosophical school, a school of prudential wisdom having as its object concrete reality.[21]

> "MNF," he explained, "does not seek a pure, abstractive knowledge of the principles governing the order of the universe, but something richer than that, which is the following. The normal object of man's knowledge is not principles, but the reality he has before him and the principles contained in that reality, which are the best that reality contains, but are all implanted in reality. While it is true that pure speculative reason can know principles, it is through fidelity to the sense of being that one obtains knowledge of reality, which is principle plus everything else in which it is implanted. So cognition does not truly exhaust itself in the principle, but is completed in this sense of being. And this is why the MNF, like scholastic philosophy, which is the philosophy of common sense, seeks to explain that sense in the eyes of reason and prevent an overly abstract and theoretical reason from 'brutalizing' it. On the other hand, it aims to protect that sense against all kinds of sophistry and also against itself by showing it the way of truth and the path of duty. This

---

de Aquino, BAC, Madrid, 1975; IGNACIO ANDEREGGEN, *Introduzione alla teologia di san Tommaso,* Edizione Dehoniane, Roma, 1996; CORNELIO FABRO, *Introduzione a San Tommaso. La metafisica tomista e il pensiero moderno*, Ares, Milan, 1997; LOUIS JUGNET, *La pensée de Saint Thomas d'Aquin*, ed. revue et corr., Nouvelles Editiones Latines, Paris, 1999.

[19] At the end of the 19th century, the Encyclical *Aeterni Patris* of Leo XIII, of August 4, 1879 (ASS, 12 (1879), pp. 97-115) set in motion a rebirth of Thomism. Cf. edition of the encyclical commented by F. Ehrle (1880) and republished in an edition curated by F. PELSTER (Edizioni di Storia e Letteratura, Rome, 1954).

[20] On the occasion of the publication of *Revolution and Counter-Revolution*, a commission was established called "Manifesto" (abbreviated as MNF) to deepen the fundamental theses of that work. Prof. Corrêa de Oliveira would chair a MNF meeting three times a week with the participation of some of the oldest TFP members such as Dr. Adolpho Lindenberg, Dr. Paulo Corrêa de Brito Filho and Dr. Arnaldo Vidigal Xavier da Silveira. Younger members later joined those veterans, such as Prince Bertrand of Orléans-Braganza (cf. F. ANTUNEZ ALDUNATE, "A Day with Plinio Corrêa de Oliveira," *Catolicismo*, No. 562 (October 1997), pp. 23-24 (23-26).

[21] MNF, 30 March 1965; 22 November 1965.

would be the doctrine on sense, and common sense would be the good quality of that sense. And it is in this sense that scholastic philosophy is the philosophy of common sense." [22]

The starting point of any theological, philosophical, historical, but also purely human study, is the establishment of an intellectual method based on the use of reason. Plinio identifies this method with philosophical realism, which adheres to objective data offered by reality.[23] Man is made not only for an empirical but also a metaphysical knowledge of the concrete; because it is from the concrete that he rises to the abstract, grasping being in its concreteness.

> "The reason why an essential definition is enriched by the study of the concrete is that philosophy aims at the knowledge of being. The essential definition gives us only the abstract. And the abstract only *is* when it exists in concrete reality. And the very knowledge of the abstract is authentic only as it exists in the concrete."[24]

When studying a problem in universities and academic circles, they start from scratch. It is the Cartesian *tabula rasa*. You cannot start thinking if you still have not read everything that has been written on a given subject. Bibliography thus becomes the first condition for reflection. This approach is antithetical to the Plinian one, in which references are useful but only as instruments to support one's thought along the way. Thought has its own rules, which do not come from books, but from reality. The being of things precedes human knowledge. This is why reading is important, but thinking is even more so.

> "I have thought a lot more than I have read. I would never be a man who reads more than he thinks because that would be the same as eating more than digesting. It is an unhealthy phenomenon, which I reject. Man must think more than he reads or at least as much as he reads.[25] I would almost say that a little-read but very intelligent man is worth more than a well-read and very intelligent man."[26]

Precisely for his realism, Plinio proposes a "living philosophy" that develops in discussion, controversy, fight. Incidentally, many great works of Christian literature were born from the need to confront the theses of adversaries. The whole thought of Saint Augustine was formed through his memorable polemics against Manichaeans, Pelagians,

---

[22] MNF, 23 December 1965.

[23] Cf. JOSEPH GREDT, OSB, *Elementa philosophiae aristotelico-thomisticae*, 2 vols., Herder, Barcelona, 1951; ETIENNE GILSON, *Le réalisme méthodique*, Pierre Téqui, Paris, 2007 (1935); L. JUGNET, *La pensèe de Saint Thomas d'Aquin*, op. cit.

[24] MNF, 10 May 1965.

[25] RRR, 18 February 1968.

[26] RRR, 4 December 1976.

Donatists, and other heretics of his time. This explains the words of our author:

> "Within this process, studying is more an element to fight better than to get to know the truth better. This is not something done in an office, *in vitro*, studying in a test tube, but it is done in the clash, in the fight, in battle, thinking about it and studying what is needed to carry it out. That is how our thought moves forward."[27]

Logic as a Science of Reason

Thinking has rules established by a discipline known as logic. The object of logic, as Saint Thomas explains, is the activity of reason.[28] Logic is the science of *logos*, i.e., discourse, regarded as an expression of thought.[29]

Thought is developed through an orderly transition from principles to conclusions.[30] Logic is an analysis of thinking processes in order to grasp their structure and laws at the various stages. Plinio Corrêa de Oliveira states:

> "Therefore, order in the human mind is for it to have an intellect that proceeds according to the rules of logic; in which there is a will docile to that intellect and which imposes itself on the person's experiences, impressions, inclinations of the moment, and guides human behavior according to the intellect."[31]

When they asked him what virtue he appreciated most in a man, he answered: "consistency." He was referring particularly to consistency with the truth and the good, and thus eminently consistent with the Catholic faith. But one cannot have consistency in faith without rational coherence; and "logic" is the name of the intellect's consistency. Consistency is an immediate consequence of the principle of non-contradiction: its application to a set of elements considered from a logical standpoint.[32] To be consistent means to take logic to its ultimate consequences by making an entirely objective judgment about things. Logic, Plinio explains,

> "Is the natural order of the mind; and upright human intelligence delights in logic and rests on logic. This is also why an upright mind today feels a tremendous malaise in this profoundly illogical humanity, in which all things take place away from the straight path, from the path of

[27] RRR, 29 September 1974.

[28] ST. THOMAS AQUINAS, *In Anal. Post.*, I lect. 1.

[29] SOFIA VANNI ROVIGHI, *Logica*, EF (1979), cols. 163-178.

[30] ST. THOMAS AQUINAS, *In V Metaphysicorum lect.*, 1, no. 759.

[31] AMP, 8 March 1972.

[32] MSGR. ANTONIO LIVI, *Il principio di coerenza*, Armando Editore, Roma, 1997, p. 33.

duty and consistency; in which people have a kind of voluptuousness in contradiction, in not facing their duty head on, and in not taking things to their final consequences."[33]

However, it is not possible to preserve logic without the help of grace, just as it is not possible to stably keep the Ten Commandments without supernatural help.

"Then one needs grace, which enlightens man's intellect and strengthens his will so that, with supernatural help, he is able to do what his nature is incapable of. This is the principle.

"Although human intelligence is logical by nature, a man never manages to be entirely logical without the help of grace. This happens for two reasons: First, because the human intellect is not infallible. An entirely logical man, always able to find a logical solution to things, would be infallible. Second, because man has a thousand inner obstacles against logic.

"What are these inner obstacles? Logic often points out unpleasant truths and arduous duties, so the person tries to avoid logic. This is the most natural thing in the world. He tries to escape and to close his eyes to logic." [34]

For this reason, a logical man has a relationship of submission to the truth:

"For him to be logical, he cannot have whims or foolish illusions; he has to be a slave of the truth, looking for reality at every moment whether he likes it or not, and accepting it as it is in order to serve an objective truth, which in the final analysis is God Our Lord. This entails a dispossession of self. In order to be entirely logical, man often reaches conclusions and does things he does not want. In other words, a man who is a slave of truth, that is a logical man." [35]

Champion of the Principle of Non-Contradiction

Reason is the noblest faculty of the soul by which man knows, judges and speaks. This is why, according to Cicero, "we are superior to beasts."[36] In philosophical language, reason is distinguished from the intellect. The two terms are often used interchangeably, but Saint Thomas specifies their meaning: "Although intellect and reason are not different powers, they receive their name from the diversity of their acts:

---

[33] SSD, 12 February 1970.
[34] Idem.
[35] SSD, 18 March 1970.
[36] CICERO, *De legibus*, I, 10, 30.

the name intellect derives from an intimate penetration of the truth; the name reason, from research and from speech."[37]

The intellect immediately and directly intuits the first principles obvious to all, which underpin every rational discourse, while reason carries out the task of drawing consequences from the premises and judging a particular case in the light of a universal rule.

That first form of intuitive and direct knowledge is provided by the senses, through which the human intellect, through facts and individual experience, ascends to universal knowledge and to the actual formulation of the first principles.

Saint Thomas teaches that all knowledge begins from the senses.[38] At first, our intellect figures that something exists. We call this first known reality, being. Being, from the Latin *ens*, present participle of the verb *to be*, indicates a determined being that constitutes reality. Being, Saint Thomas says, is that which *is*.[39]

Saint Thomas distinguishes between external and internal senses[40] and divides them into two groups: formal senses (common sense and imagination) and the intentional senses (cogitative and memory).[41] Father Cornelius Fabro observes that the cogitative is the key faculty of the Thomistic glossary.[42]

The being of sensible things is the object of reflection of our intellect in opposition to non-being. The affirmation of a being's reality is expressed by the *principle of identity*, which tells us that "every being is one and the same": "*est, est, non, non.*" The negative form of the principle of identity is the *principle of non-contradiction*, according to which "something cannot be both true and not true at the same time when dealing with the same context."[43]

In the *Metaphysics*,[44] Aristotle sees the principle of non-contradiction as the necessary and primeval law of thinking and being, without which all certainty would crumble. More precisely, the principle of non-contradiction is the logical expression of the metaphysical principle of identity.

On the metaphysical level, the principle of identity precedes that of non-contradiction, but on the logical and psychological level it is through

---

[37] *Summa Theologica,* II-IIae, q. 49, a. 5 ad 3.

[38] *Summa Theologica,* I, q. 5, a. 2.

[39] SAINT THOMAS AQUINAS, *De ente et essentia,* 1.

[40] External senses are those whose organs are located on the periphery of the nervous system, while the internal senses have the brain as their central organ (JOSEPH GREDT, O.S.B., *De cognitione sensuum externorum,* Desclée, Romae, 1924, p. 14).

[41] *Summa Theologica,* I, q. 78, a. 4.

[42] C. FABRO, *Introduzione a S. Tommaso,* pp. 80-82.

[43] R. GARRIGOU-LAGRANGE OP, *La Synthèse thomiste,* pp. 63-64.

[44] ARISTOTLE, *Metaphysics,* 1. IV, cc. 3, 4.

non-contradiction that one arrives at identity. In the order of reason, this is a first truth that finds its eminent counterpart in the supreme metaphysical truth: "I am Who am."

God alone is absolutely equal to Himself in being and in acting. In what falls under our senses, there can be opposition between being and non-being, truth and error, good and evil, and in this regard the logical process sometimes shows contradictions, as happens in every man's life.

Plinio affirms that we must be champions of the principle of non-contradiction both in our life of thought and in that of action:

> "It is necessary to awaken the principle of non-contradiction in the typically broken man of our time through images, speeches, comments, and explicitations." [45]

Plinio's political and social doctrine, but also his whole counter-revolutionary action, has the principle of non-contradiction as its logical and metaphysical foundation.

> "To think seriously is above all something that requires a huge effort, for it is to think in terms of ultimate ends, to think in terms of the highest reasons. Therefore, we need to know how to delve deeper, deeper and deeper until we have that feeling – which is the peace of the intellect – that we have touched the core of the problem and that our intellect rests on the ground where the problem is solved. And thus it rests in anticipation of the problem's solution." [46]

No teacher needs to teach a child the principle of non-contradiction, the first logical and metaphysical principle thanks to which we are able to use our reason and know the reality that surrounds us. From early childhood the child nags us with his "why is that?" – instinctively searching for the cause and end of each thing. Everything that exists has a meaning because there is an order in the world; and a reflection of this order is engraved in the rational nature found in every man. This order is governed by natural laws: laws of matter, of the spirit, and of thought.

Common Sense as the Foundation of Certainty

In philosophical language, the expression *common sense* can designate both the faculty that has as its object data coming from the external senses, unifying them, and more commonly, the universal consensus of men on a given set of notions based on the original and innate apprehension of being common to all.[47] This is the meaning Father Garrigou-Lagrange gives in his now classic study dedicated to *Le sens*

---

[45] NOR, 10 June 1976.
[46] RST, 23 April 1964.
[47] Cf. P. FAGIOTTO, *Senso comune*, EF (1979), cols. 611-814.

commun.[48] Common sense is a certain number of obvious principles or notions on which everyone bases his conduct. It is the organic whole of factual certainties and principles that are common to all men and from which all human knowledge proceeds. "Equally true for all and known by all, these principles are immutable as such and for us...indelibly engraved in human reason."[49]

On these principles, which are as it were the original substance of rationality, are founded other universal primary certainties: man's freedom, the spirituality and immortality of the soul, the existence of God, without a need for faith or complex reasoning.[50] Without them there can be no certainty, and Plinio, following this line of thought, admits the existence of a *common sense* as the starting point of any philosophical discourse. More important in intellectual activity is to clearly know the first principles on which all reflection is based.

> "One who clearly knows the fundamentals can easily see, later, what is deduced from them. He who does not know the fundamentals clearly, does not deduce anything; his mind becomes cloudy, he gropes about with his own ideas, and stumbles over his own impressions."[51]

> "Intellectual life requires clear and easy inherited principles to which one's reason adheres, and which are the starting point. A man born in an unprincipled environment is as poor from the standpoint of his inner formation as one born in a desert hut. Because the function of every generation, in the world of ideas, is not to discover everything over again, differently from earlier generations, break down what they did and build a little something the succeeding generations will tear down. This is not the way the intellect operates. In science, there is progress. It should also exist in ideas."[52]

> "Certainty is the intimate and objective conviction that something is true. That conviction should be as safe and firm as to exclude any doubt."[53]

---

[48] R. GARRIGOU-LAGRANGE, O.P., *Le sens commun, La philosophie de l'être et les formules dogmatiques*, Nouvelle Librairie Nationale, Paris, 1926. Cf. also A. LIVI, *Il senso comune tra razionalismo e scetticismo (Vico, Reid, Jacobi, Moore)*, Massimo, Milano 1992; revised in *Filosofia del senso comune. Logica della scienza e della fede*, Edizioni Leonardo da Vinci, Roma, 2010 (Ares, Milan, 1990).

[49] R. GARRIGOU-LAGRANGE, *Le sens commun*, pp.116-117. JÉSUS GARCÍA LÓPEZ, *Doctrina de Santo Tomás sobre la verdad*, Eunsa, Pamplona, 1967, shows how the first principles shape the indispensable logical premises of a philosophical system. Cf. also DARIO SACCHI, *Evidenza e interpretazione (Argomenti in una riflessione sulla struttura del sapere)*, Vita e Pensiero, Milan, 1988.

[50] Idem, p. 131.

[51] NOR, 9 June 1972.

[52] NOR, 21 January 1999.

[53] RRR, 2 November 1990.

The need for certainty is inscribed in the human soul, and only in certainties does it find its perfection.

"The human soul attributes conclusive force to reasoning because, once reasoning is done, it has a sense of certainty. The soul also has a sense of certainty when facing obvious things. This sense of certainty, which somehow we could call the instinct of truth, is an excellence of the intellect by which it attains its own end, which is knowledge and understanding. In other words, the intellect is excellent to the degree that it attains knowledge.

"We could compare the human soul to eyesight. The purpose of intelligence is to know and understand. Now, in the face of a known and understood thing, the human soul has a sense of certainty that matches that of human sight. In other words, a well-functioning human eye gives the person the certainty that he is seeing the thing as it is; a certainty that excludes any doubt. A physician may say what he wants, but his patient sees it and disagrees, resisting all evidence to the contrary.

"This excellence of the human soul is not only an excellence but something without which the intellect becomes useless."[54]

The System of Explicitations

In this intellectual process we should not be limited to analyzing only what is rationally explicit, but must try to grasp also what is implicit and subjacent to the intellectual *humus*, that which is more a part of an intellectual atmosphere than of a logical reasoning. The purpose of the intellect is to possess the truth, but reasoning makes explicit a truth that is latent in the human soul. And the human soul recognizes the value of reasoning precisely because it knows that of itself it leads to certainty. The rules of logic in the human spirit are implicit. All that logic does is to make these rules explicit for man.

"The highest truths are either very evident or very hidden. In both cases man has enormous difficulty in knowing them; for when they are very evident he is unable to explicitate them, and when very hidden, he cannot find them."[55]

Plinio Corrêa de Oliveira attached great importance to this intellectual process that consists in making explicit the world of subconscious certainties contained in the human soul.

---

[54] BCM, 5 March 1966.
[55] RRR, 29 December 1974.

"There is a world of certainties within every man, which are not entirely valid in his mind because he has not made them explicit. They linger lazily, like a treasure at the bottom of a well. This happens in everyone. What naturally happens is that some have greater treasures than others in the well, but the treasures necessary for their soul are there, the question is to make them explicit. The human soul easily grasps things; the problem is to bring them from that grasp all the way to explicitation." [56]

Human thought incessantly proceeds from principles to consequences and from consequences to principles. [57] In their concreteness, facts are more useful to explicitate the truth than books; and the highest way to know facts is to understand what the value judgments are underlying them.

"When a fact happens, it is only fully understood when you understood the doctrine underlying it." [58] Conversely, "a concrete fact sets doctrine in palpable ways, in shapes more easily retained in memory because everyone can identify with it more than with a pure doctrinal exposition." [59]

Plinio's philosophy is never "bookish" but always "alive" precisely because he delves into being and explicitates its truth and certainties.

"The conquest of the truth begins as a slow explicitation of what the person already knows, not from a book. It is an ordination of the new things one gradually learns, but according to this fundamental common sense, these primary data.... The conquest of the truth is more or less a progression *de proche en proche*. I do not jump right away from the truths I know to the ultimate truths, but modestly make my way to closer truths. And from these I march on to others even though I may have already intuited the ultimate truth; for many people often happen to intuit the ultimate truth.

"I build a demonstration *de proche en proche*. But I build it without apparatus or fuss, humbly, solidly, organically, without agitation. And in this regard I maintain that we are by far our own best book. We are not a book; each of us is a library that contains immensely more than libraries with books. Never has anyone ever written all that can exist in a person's mind....

"What does the book do? It helps me harvest some data I need, gives me someone's well thought out idea, but never in the Cartesian way of pouring it into my head. Never! The book is a warehouse of materials for

---

[56] BCM, 5 March 1966.
[57] Cf. JUAN JOSÉ SANGUINETTI, *Introduzione alla filosofia*, Pontificia Università Urbaniana, Rome 1992.
[58] RRR, 18 July 1987.
[59] RRR, 23 September 1973.

my construction. Hence one does not need to read everything or to learn all its arguments. What you need is to have a basic, solid, fundamental notion, which at times a person may not even know how to substantiate in an argument.

"What is the test of certainty? It is the consonance between what was said and the data provided by the good sense that everyone has. I maintain that certainty is born from this process, for it is an initial certainty that develops *de proche en proche,* slowly but surely. But deep down this certainty is nothing but a projection of the sense of good and evil and the native sense of truth and error that are enhanced and gradually become ever more rigorous." [60]

Hypotheses and Predictions

Reasoning begins with a question posed by the intellect. Not all questions are meant to find an answer, but posing a problem, even without succeeding to solve it, already places you on the right path: "It is better to encounter a problem we do not solve than not to suspect that it exists."[61] After placing the problem one must raise hypotheses, for "without making hypotheses one does not think."[62]

The Plinian method is never apodictic. It consists in building hypotheses to be verified by experience and reason, while remaining always ready to challenge them.

"Hypotheses are useful as a method to explore reality. They are either true or false. If true they will be confirmed by reality. If false, they will help analyze reality and find the truth."[63] "Every intellectual progress begins with hypotheses and is propelled by them. Without a very great ability to make hypotheses, there is no such possibility.[64]

Formulating hypotheses is a research method.[65]

"The French say, 'he who does not know what he's looking for, does not know what he finds.' He who does not have a hypothesis to research, has nothing to research. What is he researching?"[66] "You only find something when you really look for it in earnest. The truth is preceded by researching hypotheses. There is no research without hypotheses. All research begins with a hypothesis." [67]

---

[60] BCM, 12 February 1966.
[61] RRR, 17 October 1987.
[62] RRR, 9 April 1973.
[63] RRR, 18 June 1988.
[64] DES, 2 January 1989.
[65] RRR, 12 January 1975.
[66] RRR, 5 September 1992.
[67] RRR, 11 May 1991.

Making hypotheses means making predictions, and he proposed "practicing the art of making hypotheses, that is, the art of making predictions."[68]

Plinio always had a 'preferential option' for the more pessimistic hypothesis. However, he defined himself not as a pessimist but a 'pessimologist,' a scholar of the awful things that unfortunately surround us.[69]

> "Preparing for the worst hypothesis makes man strong to fight if the not-so-bad hypotheses come true. Predictions of very bad things turn us into athletes to overcome things that are not as bad." [70]

> "A principle I invariably adopt in the question of hypotheses is this: When a person has two hypotheses to study about the same fact and both are probable but unequally probable, one is more likely than the other but the latter is worse than the former, we should give priority to study the worst hypothesis, rather than the most likely. For by studying the worst, even if it does not materialize, it is easier to improvise a solution to the less serious one than the other way around, that is, to study the least bad and have to improvise a solution to the worst if it emerges. So it is wiser, more regular to prioritize the worst hypothesis. But if the difference in probability is very great and the lighter hypothesis is more likely we should give preference to the lighter hypothesis. In this case it would be a mistake to spend time and gray matter studying the worst."[71]

Blunting the *Lumen Rationis*

One of the manifestations of today's cultural and moral crisis is the gradual decline of what Plinio Corrêa de Oliveira, in the wake of Saint Thomas, defined as *lumen rationis*.

Lumen rationis, of which the First Vatican Council also speaks in the Dogmatic Constitution on the Catholic Faith,[72] is a natural light of the intellect that allows us to know and possess those first, obvious and non-provable principles that are the common patrimony of all men at all times. Saint Thomas explains: "First principles become known through the natural *light* of the agent intellect, and they are not acquired by any process of reasoning but by having their terms become known." [73]

---

[68] RRR, 21 August 1991.

[69] LEO DANIELE, "Pessimologist," *Catolicismo*, No. 658, October 2005, p. 35.

[70] RRR, 16 December 1989.

[71] RRR, 21 September 1992.

[72] 1st VATICAN COUNCIL, chap. IV.

[73] ST. THOMAS AQUINAS, *In IV Metaphysicorum*, lect. 5, no. 599 (http://dhspriory.org/thomas/Metaphysics4.htm#5). *Lumen rationis* is what characterizes man's natural knowledge; in ordinary supernatural knowledge it is perfected by the *lumen fidei*; in extraordinary supernatural knowledge it is strengthened by the *lumen sapientiae* (Msgr.

Blunting of the *lumen rationis* is manifested in the weakening of intellectual faculties and the atrophy of reason, consequently increasing the rate of mental illnesses, starting with depression but more generally causing imbalance in the faculties of the soul, a typical phenomenon of the contemporary age.

Decline in the exercise of the *lumen rationis* marks the demise of the intellectual revolution which, starting mainly from France in the seventeenth and eighteenth centuries, claimed to illuminate the darkness of medieval civilization. The "light of reason" of Descartes and the Enlightenment has nothing to do with the *lumen rationis* of perennial philosophy. Indeed, it is its antithesis.

Descartes' starting point is expressed by the famous formula, *cogito ergo sum*: thought comes before being and is its foundation. The main characteristic of the rationalism he posits is to conceive thought as the foundation of being, reversing the realist conception by which knowledge is based on being, the act of being is the foundation of the act of knowing. However, modern philosophy affirms the primacy of knowledge over being, negating the transcendence of being with respect to consciousness. As Father Cornelio Fabro observes, realism means "consciousness's dependence (or being founded) on reality."[74] For modern philosophers, instead, the intellect knows itself before it knows being.[75]

The Cartesian roots of modern philosophy developed on the basis of the principle of immanence,[76] which makes being dependent on consciousness, the *sum* of *cogito*. For Descartes, the act of thinking is the essence of man.[77] Man is *cogitatio*,[78] thinking subjectivity, a thought with a body attached but always alien to it.

Plinio Corrêa de Oliveira vigorously refuted this view:

ANTONIO PIOLANTI, *La conoscenza sapienziale di Dio in S. Tommaso, Summa Theologica, II-IIae, q. 45*, Libreria Editrice Vaticana, Città del Vaticano, 1980, p. 4).

[74] C. FABRO, *Tomismo e pensiero moderno*, p. 428.

[75] "Descartes, 'the inventor of the Philosophy of Me,' placed within man the ultimate limit of intelligence and definitely closed for him the only road that leads to God. Descartes and Kant, founders of idealism, are great fallen intelligences; that is why the enemies of the Church so strongly acclaim them. In their school, modern philosophy and modern society have lost the notion of God; 'Patres comederunt uvam acerbam et dentes filiorum obstupuerunt' (Jer.)" (R. Garrigou-Lagrange, *Le sens commun*, p. 140).

[76] GIOVANNI DI NAPOLI, "Immanenza," EF 4 (1979), cols. 470-478, and "Immanentismo," idem, cols. 467-470; J. DE TONQUÉDEC, *Immanence, méthode d'immanence*, DAFC, II, cols. 579-612; idem, *Immanence. Essai critique sur la doctrine de M. M. Blondel*, Paris, 1933.

[77] "But what am I, then? Something that thinks. And what is something that thinks? It is a thing that doubts, that conceives, that affirms, that denies, that wants, that does not want, that also imagines and feels." René Descartes, *Discours de la méthode* (1637).

[78] R. DESCARTES, *Meditationes de prima philosophia* (1641), It. tr. *Meditazioni metafisiche sulla filosofia prima* in *Opere filosofiche,* op. cit, vol. II, p. 27.

"Descartes said: 'Cogito, ergo sum.' I abominate this. Allow me to employ a trivial expression to express all my hate: I vomit this. It is not *'cogito, ergo sum,'* but *'sum, ergo sum.'* I feel my being, therefore I am. In his *tabula rasa,* Descartes seeks not only to eliminate all previous concepts but also to eliminate from the order of thought this authentic life of being, which in its mystery is the fountain of my thinking. My thinking comes out of this mystery with all clarity because there is order in the mystery of my thinking. It is a highly ordered mystery whose order I do not know but apply. And this is the foundation of criteriology, of logic. And thus one understands the Gnostic character of Descartes."[79]

Hegel's maxim that "consciousness has its own measure within itself"[80] is a consequence of the Cartesian principle of immanence. The principle of immanence says that everything that presents itself to man's consciousness does not depend on an external reality but proceeds from the activity of his own consciousness. That absolute which is the Truth, the object of intelligence, is confined to the totality of subjective experience.

The Cartesian *cogito* replaces the philosophy of certainty with a philosophy of doubt that requires, as a starting point, thought without content; but as a Father Fabro notes,

"That absolute doubt which modern thought – from Descartes, Kant, Hegel, Marx, all the way to Sartre – seeks to set as a starting point is not entirely doubt but rather nothing; for doubt can only be an intermediate stage between an initial certainty and a darkness that appears. When you remove all content from the act of doubting, there is no longer any doubt because there is nothing left."[81]

As the philosopher Marcel De Corte observed, the intellect is no longer governed by reality but becomes the supreme legislator that imposes its rules on reality. However, if the intellect is emancipated from the being of things it is doomed to disappear because it is deprived of its natural object and begins, so to speak, to spin on itself. Modern thought, from Descartes to Kant and later Hegel, follows the route of a progressive destruction of all truth as such to exclusively establish the creative activity of reason. But once all truth is destroyed the intellect begins to doubt itself and is forced to recognize that the murder of *being* by *cogito* leads to the suicide of thought. The origins of many contemporary aberrations such as "gender theory"[82] are found in this emancipation of

---

[79] MNF, 3 June 1965.

[80] FRIEDRICH W. HEGEL, *Fenomenologia dello spirito*, It. tr., La Nuova Italia, Florence, 1963, vol. I, p. 74.

[81] C. FABRO, *Tomismo di domani*, "Aquinas" 1 (1966), p. 25.

[82] "Gender theory" brings together some of the most radical revolutionary currents that propose to destroy the family and radically desconstruct human nature. Cf. among others, GABRIELLA

the intellect from reality. If the intellect does not conform to the laws of reality but claims to recreate it, there is no longer anything defined and stable, not even an objective and immutable human nature.

If modernity, from Descartes to Hegel, has seen an apex of reason, postmodern thought – with Nietzsche, existentialism, structuralism and the so-called "weak" thought as its precursors – dissolves the rules of logic and the very substance of things. The human intellect believes it celebrates its triumph by affirming its self-sufficiency but marks instead the suicide of thought. Indeed, thought is considered incapable of understanding reality, or rather, can only understand it by self-destroying. "Wherever it works, thought means nothing," proclaims the "deconstructor" of language Jacques Derrida.[83] It is a path to unreason and insanity due to the loss of the supreme metaphysical and moral principles.

This path of self-destruction of the intellect, which has been called "nihilism,"[84] has spread from books of philosophers to the whole society. This intellectual virus has produced a social disease, moving from the theoretical to the psychological and existential levels. Plinio Corrêa de Oliveira analyzes this process, which has become a mass phenomenon in the West, by unveiling not only its ideological but also its psychological roots.

> "The extinction of *lumen rationis* is a gradual extinction of man's rationality. Contrary to what they say, it is not so much the extinction of man's ability to reason but of his disposition and willingness to reason. And this is not an ideological but a psychological phenomenon. It does not result from an ideology.... A person convinced of the emptiness of reasoning would no longer make use of the *lumen rationis* out of ideological conviction; an erroneous, stupid conviction, but ultimately ideological."[85]

People who are losing their *lumen rationis* do not realize the process they are undergoing. The weakening of reason – Plinio observes – causes them to lose an ordered vision of things, the nexus between relationships, which govern, for example, the world of memories. Without the *lumen*

KUBY, *Gender Revolution, il relativismo in azione,* It. tr., Cantagalli, Siena 2008; RODOLFO DE MATTEI, *Gender Diktat. Origini e conseguenze di un'ideologia totalitaria,* Solfanelli, Chieti, 2014.

[83] JACQUES DERRIDA, *Positions,* Editions de Minuit, Paris, 1972, p. 67. Cf. by the same author, *De la grammatologie,* Editions de Minuit, Paris, 1967.

[84] Cf. for example Emanuele Severino, *Essenza del nichilismo,* Milan, 1982; Gianni Vattimo, *La fine della modernità. Nichilismo e postmodernità nella cultura post-moderna,* Milan, 1985; Michel Foucault, *Dits et écrits, I (1954-1975) et II (1976-1988),* Gallimard, Paris, 2001.

[85] EVP, 18 March 1990.

rationis these relationships appear to us as confused and disordered notions bound to be dissolved.

> "Mnemonically speaking, that is, from the standpoint of memory, one of the things that helps memory to function well is to know the nexus and relationships of things among themselves. For by knowing that connection one gets to know things much better."[86]

In fact, the *lumen rationis* does not offer infallible certainty regarding different cognitive contents but enables man to form a reasonable vision of things considered as a whole.

> "I have been stressing for many years now that this reasonable view of things globally considered has been gradually extinguished. In other words, the number of partial aspects that man sees reasonably is diminishing. On the other hand, man becomes increasingly less sensitive to contradiction, nonsense, and even foolishness and the preposterous, which shows man's insensitivity to reason. The residues of the *lumen rationis* are ending, we find ourselves in an almost complete withering away of the *lumen rationis*."[87]

The extinction of the *lumen rationis* is a consequence of the extinction of principles. If you lose your principles, reason loses its object and almost atrophies, while instincts and the impulses of the lower powers of the soul become hypertrophied.

> "Contemporary man has no longer had principles for a long time. The extinction of principles largely predates the extinction of the *lumen rationis*, and principles are the foundation on which you have to put the famous lever of Archimedes. Principles are the foundation. If the person has no principles, the lever malfunctions. Later they gradually die without discussion to avoid confronting the value of reason, evidence that imposes itself in the eyes of everyone and no one dares to deny even today. A common man does not deny it."[88]

With the extinction of *lumen rationis* the way has been paved for "gurus," quacks and intellectual demagogues who appeal to people's feelings and to thoughtless motions of the human soul.[89]

The Evanescence of Reason

The fading of *lumen rationis* is a process Plinio Corrêa de Oliveira describes as "*evanescence.*" It is evaporation not only of reason but also

---

[86] MNF, 13 March 1992
[87] RRR, 3 December 1983.
[88] Idem.
[89] Idem.

of the will, which characterizes all epochs of decadence, but especially ours.[90] Everything seems to lose its vigor, wane, and fade.

> "Evanescence, a phenomenon that was possible even when there was the *lumen rationis*, takes up the space that the *lumen rationis* used to occupy. It fills the space the *lumen rationis* once took and produces this general staggering of humanity that makes it prey to all forces wishing to lead it."[91]

Plinio imagines that such evanescence will characterize the end of the world and is prefigured by the evanescence of our times.

> "Here it is reasonable to conjecture – it is not a proof or affirmation – that even the forces of nature will grow more tired; the sun will emit less light; the moon, less bright reflections.... As a result of this and other events the vitality of plants, animals and men will be less. Nights and days will perhaps wax longer, tending to perpetuate themselves, and the general course of nature will become tired, hulking, evanescent."[92]

When the intellect is eclipsed, darkness falls on the world. Plinio is dramatically clear:

> "*Tenebrae factae sunt.* There was darkness over the whole earth. It is over. Dusk has fallen upon the human mind."[93]

However, the extinction of the *lumen rationis* is not complete, for otherwise man could not even do evil.

> "There is a natural extinction of the *lumen rationis* that is worse than its complete extinction because it survives at the service of evil. Reason survives for evil, and no longer for what is upright."[94]

The causes of this phenomenon are not only natural but also preternatural. The fallen angel, who hates man, also affects his faculties, but

> "The devil prefers the loss of the *lumen rationis* to complete madness because it gives him more glory to be adored by a man who still preserves a modicum of reason.... It also gives him more glory to be worshiped by an entirely rational man than by one that suffered the loss of

---

[90] A French counter-revolutionary author, Antoine Blanc de Saint Bonnet (1815-1880), back in the nineteenth century saw the "weakening of reason" as "the cause of Europe's decadence" (*De l'affaiblissement de la raison de la décadence en Europe*, L. Hervé, Paris, 1854, 2nd ed., p. IV).

[91] RRR, 3 December 1983.

[92] Idem.

[93] RRR, 23 April 1993.

[94] Idem.

the *lumen rationis*. So why does he cause the loss of the *lumen rationis*? It is because he realizes that he will be unable to get all men to adore him in all his horror and so he hopes to obtain a lesser result in this alternate way." [95]

Plinio thus describes the process of extinction of the *lumen rationis*:

"The process begins very remotely as the keel of the ship of certainty is diverted from the certainties of the direction it should follow to a destination it should not. In other words, man is saturated with so many certainties and ends up by finding them trivial and setting out on adventures of the mind in pursuit of poetic forms, new literary forms, neologisms, etc. In this quest he searches for something that reason does not justify and which corresponds to inner desires, aspirations, dreams, a thousand such things. And this is obviously something that deviates somewhat the ship's keel from the port where it should arrive.

"This aggravates the situation because, by giving himself over to those delights man ends up understanding or thinking he understands that the world of delights is much more desirable than the world of truths, and that, while undoubtedly searching for truths one also needs to chase after delights. And the individual seeks the truth eagerly but laboriously while he flies in search of delights. This causes him to begin seeing many things poetically, thinking that poetry is a kind of rectifier of what is very arid and poor about the rational view of reality." [96]

Sense of Being and Sense of the Absolute

Logic and metaphysics are two distinct, but not separate, parts of philosophy. When well employed, both have in common the recognition of the primacy of being. Accordingly, the proper use of logic leads man to understand the great metaphysical truths derived from the order of being. [97]

"In this conception, the essence of life and of the *raison d'être* of human existence ends up being this: man exists to know the metaphysical order and to properly align himself with it. And everything that happens in human existence is destined for this." [98]

---

[95] EXT, 12 April 1992.

[96] MNF, 13 March 1992.

[97] Cf. GUIDO MATTIUSSI SJ, *Le ventiquattro tesi della filosofia di san Tommaso d'Aquino: approvata dalla Congregazione degli Studi*, Università Gregoriana, Roma 1947 (1917); R. GARRIGOU-LAGRANGE, *Synthèse thomiste*, cit.; LOUIS LACHANCE OP, *L'être et ses propriétés*, Les Editions du Lévrier, Montréal 1950; LEO J. ELDERS SVD, *La metafisica dell'essere di san Tommaso d'Aquino in una prospettiva storica*, Libreria Editrice Vaticana, Città del Vaticano, 1995.

[98] MNF, 9 March 1965.

The existential eclipse of the *lumen rationis* logically corresponds to the loss of the primacy of being through a sin of the spirit, which Plinio defines as "criteriological sin."

> "One does not lose the notion of being through a frontal metaphysical denial, but through a refusal of the mind that leads to slackening and denying the importance of the principle of contradiction and of the principle of identity."[99]

Being is what there is of most intimate but also most noble in everything. Being is what gives reality to what exists. "What I call being," Saint Thomas says, "is the most perfect of all things."[100]

> "The notion of being is composed of two elements, one of which is static – that which *is* – and the other dynamic – the inner movement of being. And this is why the word *being* is a noun and a verb: the noun indicates what *is*, and the verb indicates what acts or moves. The very word 'being' could not fail to be a nominalized verb and a verbal noun. These two elements constitute *being.*"[101]

For Plinio the first indirect evidence man has is that of his own contingency. Man perceives he is a finite, limited, contingent being. But he understands he is contingent because he has an implicit notion of the absolute. In the same glance he sees his being but also the contingency of his being and this allows him to properly grasp his metaphysical essence. This means that his mind already contains elements that enable him to think about the absolute. This first notion of being presupposes the notion of absolute being, "for being properly speaking is either absolute or it is nothing." [102] The foundational matrix of the absolute precedes the notion of one's own contingency.

> "A righteous, virtuous man, one who preserves or regains his innocence, has in the depths of his soul the notion of the absolute. According to Paul VI, 'the notion of the absolute is the presupposition of all thought.' He is right. With this notion of the absolute is born in man a fountain of conviction regarding the absolute truth: there must be an absolute truth, an absolute good, an absolute beauty in function of which all goods, truths and beauties must be judged. I search for absolutes with internal criteria that are in me, corroborated by the criteria of others that share the same innocence, the same aspirations, the same desires."[103]

---

[99] Idem.

[100] ST. THOMAS AQUINAS, *De Veritate*, q. 10, a. 8, ad. 12. Cf. also *Summa Theologica*, I, q. 4, a. 1, ad 3.

[101] MNF, 11 August 1965.

[102] MNF, 25 June 1976.

[103] RRR, 23 May 1981.

"I was almost as enthused reading the praise Scripture makes about the Prophet Daniel as over the praise Our Lord makes of Saint Bartholomew: 'Behold an Israelite indeed, in whom there is no guile.' He is an innocent man. Scripture says of the Prophet Daniel: 'Daniel pleased God because he was a man of desires' – *Desideriorum vir.* He was a man of aspirations, ideals, who wanted more, higher, purer and more beautiful and complete truths, etc. The movement of the men of desires throughout history is one. However little they may encounter one another, they constitute a collective opinion. I would almost say that they feel one another even when they do not know one another." [104]

The "sense of being" is rooted in this experience:

"The pure notion of being has at the same time something abstract and something experimental combined, for if I did not feel my own being I would not know what it is to be. It is such an immediate notion that it has something experimental...before it is abstract. Experience is the first element exerted to propel the notion of being." [105]

Act and Potency, Substance and Accident

The experience of the senses shows us not only that things exist but also that they are contingent and limited because they are subject to change. Therefore they are not perfect and immutable as the Being subsistent of itself necessarily is. But what man knows is only the being of things, never being as such. [106]

Along with the experience of being, man has that of the becoming of things. Greek philosophy is divided between the followers of Parmenides, who affirmed *being* as opposed to *becoming,* and those of Heraclitus, who supported *becoming* against *being.* Heraclitus claimed that in the general flow of all things, everything *became,* nothing *was.* "You never bathe twice in the same river" is the phrase attributed to him to express the fugacious becoming of things. On the contrary, Parmenides said that becoming is contradictory: only being *is,* and hence becoming is not: therefore, being is the one and only.

In order to reconcile the principle of being and that of identity asserted by Parmenides with the principle of becoming and of multiplicity stated by Heraclitus, Aristotle developed the doctrine of potency and act. This doctrine was deepened and further developed by Saint Thomas Aquinas.

---

[104] Idem.

[105] MNF, 26 October 1979. The sense of being (*Der Sinn des Sein*) is the underlying theme of the metaphysical work of Saint Teresa Benedicta of the Cross (Edith Stein, 1891-1942) in light of Saint Thomas Aquinas's *Quaestiones disputae de veritate.* Cf. EDITH STEIN, *Essere infinito e essere eterno. Per una elevazione del senso dell'essere,* Città Nuova, Roma, 1968.

[106] Cf. L. LACHANCE, *L'Être et ses propriétés,* pp. 30, 133, 230.

According to this doctrine, every material or corporeal being and likewise every finite being is composed of potency and act. Act designates all that is perfect, made, determined in its order, while potency indicates that which, being imperfect and incomplete, has an ability or aptitude to be realized.[107] Through the distinction between act and potency one can grasp the essence of becoming, which is the passage from indetermination to determination, from potency to act. God alone is pure act, eternal and infinitely perfect being. The creature is distinguished from God because, being limited, it is as it were composed of non-being and being, or, analogously, of potency and act.[108]

Another key distinction in the metaphysics of the created being is the one between substance and accident. Substance (from the Latin *sub-stare*) indicates the stable and permanent part of each individual being.[109] Conversely, accidents are the changing elements of being. The etymology of the word accident, which is Latin for arrive, occur, happen, gives out the precarious nature of the being, its inability to exist on its own. The substance exists in itself while the accident receives its being from the substance to which it is inherent.

It is easier for the human intellect to understand the distinction between substance and accident because the human mind knows first of all the accidents, and through them the substances. In numerous MNF meetings held since the early sixties, Plinio Corrêa de Oliveira adopts this doctrine of scholasticism stressing that "the excellence of a being is for it to possess to a fully defined degree all the accidents that its essence admits."[110]

Metaphysics of Essences

The distinction between potency and act corresponds to the fundamental one in Thomistic thought between essence and the act of being. Saint Thomas explains that created things have their own essence, distinct from the being that they receive. In a word, they are composed of being and essence: being comes from God, while essence specifies their way of being in the created world.

---

[107] ARISTOTLE, *Metaphysics,* IV, II, 170-185.

[108] "This is the boldest statement of Platonic, Aristotelian, and Thomistic metaphysics: there is a middle ground between being and pure nothingness, non-being and potency" (R. GARRIGOU-LAGRANGE, *Le sens commun*, p. 153).

[109] TOMAS TYN, O.P., *Metafisica della sostanza. Partecipazione e analogia entis*, Edizioni Studio Domenicano, Bologna, 1991; MARC HAUSMANN, *La sostanza nel Commento di san Tommaso alla Metafisica di Aristotele con particolare riferimento all'atto di essere,* Verlag St. Josef, Kleinhain, 2010.

[110] MNF, 26 January 1965.

Essence, Saint Thomas explains in the *De ente et essentia*, is the object of the definition of the thing, that which it actually is.[111] Everything that exists has its essence because it is distinct from and should not be confused with all that surrounds it. A being's essence is therefore its specific identity and unity, which distinguish it from the multiplicity of reality.[112] Being does not belong to created things of themselves, while essence is their specific perfection, that for which we say something is what it is.[113]

Essence and the act of being have a relationship of potency and act only because they make a possible entity come true. "Essence would be nothing if being did not make it such."[114] Thus there is an ontological primacy of being with respect to essence. However, if in an abstract philosophical exposition one must start from God, pure act and Being by essence, essences are always the starting point in man's concrete knowledge. And this is the path that Plinio follows, developing Saint Thomas.

He notes that the statement that God is pure act is certainly right but one needs to be careful not to instill any doubt that in God is the foundation of the existence of created potency. Indeed, potency is neither evil nor nothingness. There is a risk of making potency a purely negative entity, a reality opposite to act and almost anti-divine. One must not forget that if God is pure act, all that He created is a compound of act and potency and is good as such.[115]

> "We should say: if God is pure act there is in God, as pure act, a foundation for the existence of potency. It is in pure act that one should find the foundation for the existence of potency, which would be the mysterious matrix of relationship and multiplicity."[116]

What we are saying about act and potency may also extend to cause and effect.

> "God is the *causa causarum*. Who could cast that into doubt? But the very existence of the effect as such would not be possible if it lacked a mysterious foundation in God. Such are the foundations of distinction, of reason, that one sees obliquely but end up being necessary for an exact understanding of what we mean when we say that God is the cause of causes.

---

[111] ST. THOMAS AQUINAS, *De ente et essentia*, chap. II, no. 2.
[112] *Summa Theologica*, I, q. 11, a. 1.
[113] ST. THOMAS AQUINAS, *De ente et essentia*, chap. II, no. 5.
[114] ST. THOMAS AQUINAS, *De Potentia*, q. 3, a. 5, a. 2.
[115] MNF, 2 June 1965.
[116] MNF, 3 June 1965.

Also 'substance and accident,' the transcendentals, etc., purely on the creature's side have some foundation in God. This foundation is not in the accident or in something in God that is different from His substance. There is something in God's very substance that ineffably gives foundation for the existence of all of this. And the relationship of the divine substance with that in it which gives foundation to being, is the meeting point of contrasts and the matrix of relationship, of the dynamic, the various, and it is ineffable. Here we truly have, groping, a feeling of delight that tells us that something matches our primary notion of *unum*."[117]

Therefore, the primacy of being over essence should not lead us to overlook the importance of essence.[118]

"It is correctly said that essence is a principle of being that limits the *esse*. And that, were it not for the essence, the *esse* would be infinite of itself. This statement is very true and we should bear in mind, from beginning to end of the considerations now being made, that this statement is somewhat dangerous in that it seems to deny a counter-balancing buttress that we would explicitate as follows: While it its true that the essence limits the *esse*, it is also true that the created *esse* exists ordained to a determined essence. And it is not true that it would be infinite if it did not have essence, for if it had no essence it simply would not exist. Essence is for a positive element whereby it constitutes an individual, whereby it *is*. And essence has something positive and delimitating that gives us an idea of what is positive in the *various,* with all its inherent limitations, which are more evident than those existing in the *unum*. To give some image of this we should consider the limiting element in a plant. A plant produces a flower, which is a play of *esse* and essence and makes what is limited in the flower, whereby it is a flower, to be coupled with its positive elements in order to produce the flower. And here we would have to consider the essence as a factor that is also positive as such; which is co-created with the *esse* factor, and in whose co-creation *esse* and essence produce the constitution of being."[119]

Participation in the Divine Perfections

The concept of participation, which designates the nexus of sensible things with ideas, is of Platonic origin, as Aristotle demonstrated.[120] However, the philosophy of participation *par excellence* is that of Saint Thomas, founded on the principle that God, pure act and Being by essence, is "the perfection of all perfection." [121] For Plato there is a world of ideas distinct from the sensible world, and all that exists participates in

---

[117] Idem.
[118] MNF, 2 August 1965.
[119] MNF, 2 August 1965.
[120] ARISTOTLE, *Metaphysics*, I, 6, 987, b. 10.
[121] ST. THOMAS AQUINAS, *De Potentia*, q. 7, a. 2, ad 9.

the absolute perfections of the world of ideas. For example, all the beautiful things of the material world in which we live participate in the idea of beauty. However, Plato, like Aristotle, does not go so far as to formulate the notion of a God creator of all existing things and thus efficient cause of all reality.

The decisive contribution of Christian thought and particularly Saint Thomas is to explain the notion of participation in the light of the idea of Creation, and could be summarized in the following points: Finite and contingent beings participate in God's perfections inasmuch as they receive their being from Him. God alone is the most perfect Being; created beings possess in a finite and limited way the absolute and unlimited perfections of the Being by essence. All that is created is a caused "participant"; God alone, pure Act, infinitely perfect, receives nothing from any being.

In the second half of the twentieth century, some Neo-Thomist scholars such as Louis de Raeymaker[122] and Father Cornelio Fabro[123] deepened the concept of participation and of *actus essendi*. The Plinian school is close to the reflection of Father Cornelio Fabro, who sought to rescue the essence of Thomism by criticizing a certain tendency among neo-scholastics toward pure abstraction and loss of the concreteness of being.[124] The point in which the Plinian school is distinguished from Father Fabro, however, is its increased focus on the world of essences.[125]

Indeed, one should not forget that participation exists in the participant, and that the reality the intellect knows directly is not that of being but that of essences. The primacy of the *actus essendi* over essence certainly is an undeniable datum of Thomism. But the *actus essendi* of itself is too brilliant for created intelligence and cannot be the proper terrain of the philosophical speculation of man, whose first object is precisely the knowledge of "essences."

"This reality is not only one that exists extrinsically to things, which is the way Aristotle primarily considers it. But it is a reality existing

---

[122] Louis DE RAEYMAKER, *La problematica dell' 'esse' tomistico*, Aquinas, 2 (1959), pp. 194-225.

[123] C. FABRO, "La nozione metafisica di partecipazione secondo S. Tommaso d'Aquino: saggio di introduzione analitica al pensiero tomista," *Vita e Pensiero*, Milan, 1939; later published by EVI, Segni, 2005. Cornelio Fabro (1911-1995), ordained in 1935 in the order of Stigmatines, was a professor of philosophy at various universities, member of the Preparatory Commission and *peritus* at the Second Vatican Council and an internationally recognized philosopher; about him see, among others, ROSA GOGLIA, *Cornelio Fabro. Profilo biografico, cronologico, tematico da inediti, note di archIdemo, testimonianze*, Edivi, Rome, 2010.

[124] C. FABRO, "L'obscurcissement de l'être dans l'école thomiste," *Revue thomiste*, 58 (1958), pp. 443-472. ID., "L'actualité et originalité de l''esse' thomiste," *Revue thomiste*, 56 (1956), pp. 240-270; 480-507.

[125] MNF, 9 November 1966.

intrinsically in things and which has to be seen in conjunction with the concrete datum and as immanent in the concrete datum. This is the fact. So we have it that the system continues in a kind of *conversio ad phantasmata* [conversion to the phantasms][126] that results in this: I see the concrete and the universal as present in the concrete. And in this joint vision I see the universal itself. I cannot see the universal separated from the concrete." [127]

God sets the degree of perfection of beings and places them in a certain order or hierarchy through the degree of participation of their essences in being, whose supreme cause is His subsistent Being.[128]

Indeed, according to Saint Thomas,

"Everything is therefore called good from the divine goodness, as from the first exemplary, effective and final principle of all goodness. Nevertheless, everything is called good by reason of the similitude of the divine goodness belonging to it, which is formally its own goodness, whereby it is denominated good. And so of all things there is one goodness, and yet many goodnesses."[129]

From this variety and hierarchy of similarities with the Divine Goodness, Plinio deduces that created beings participate in the attributes of others that have them in greater degree, and thus serve as their archetypes. He thinks this support of creatures by their respective archetypes happens not only with the angelic and human worlds but even among irrational or inanimate beings.

"Therefore, whenever there is a predicate in a particular being, this predicate participates in a predicate of another, higher being. Let us say, for example, the color red. There is a whole gamut of reds, but there will be somewhere in creation a perfect and ideal red; the absolute, archetypal red which is the perfection of redness and in which all other reds participate. It is the king of reds."[130] "What sustains this red in its color is the fact that in the order established by God, there is a greater red in which all others participate. If it did not exist, the existence of lesser reds would become problematic."[131]

---

[126] Saint Thomas Aquinas states that the intellect knows particular things through the external and internal senses. The cogitative is man's internal sense by which his intellect operates the *conversio ad phantasmata*, that is, the universal return to the phantasms transmitted by his external senses in order to grasp the universal nature of specific entities (*Summa Theologica*, I, q. 84, a.7; q. 85, a 1 & 8; In II Super Sent., d. 23, q. 2, a 2; *De Veritate*, q. 10, 2 ad 7; etc.).

[127] MNF, 9 November 1966.

[128] C. FABRO, *Partecipazione e causalità secondo san Tommaso d'Aquino*, SEI, Torino, 1960, later Edivi, Segni, 2010.

[129] *Summa Theologica*, I, q. 6, a. 4, c.

[130] BCM 11 June 1966.

[131] *Primeval Innocence*, p. 123.

In *De Substantiis Separatis*, one of his last works, Saint Thomas Aquinas is explicit: "If someone considers the general order of things, he will always find that the maximum in any genus is the cause of all in that genus; as fire, which is the maximum of heat, is the cause of all hot things."[132]

Plinio comments:

"The same can be said of human qualities. Throughout history, humanity distills perfect types, especially when aided by the Church, which limits the effects of original sin and leads to the highest holiness men who respond to grace.

"Lesser perfections, born under the inspiration of a greater one, are sustained by it. Thus, the whole creation should be viewed as a series of types hierarchically placed relative to one another and whose apex is an archetype. In turn, this archetype has its highest achievement in an angel. The angels are purely spiritual archetypes of qualities existing in creation....For their part, some angels are archetypes of others and thus one arrives to God, the foundation of this whole hierarchy of analogies and participations because He is perfect, supreme, and uncreated. It is not correct to say that God 'has' qualities: He 'is' the qualities He has. And all qualities existing on Earth are participations in His qualities."[133]

---

[132] *Summa Theologiæ*, I, q. 6, a. 4, c.

[133] *Primavel Innocence*, p. 123. The type is the "ideal model gathering in itself the essential characters of a certain species of objects in their highest degree of perfection." The archetype is the "supreme type of which the objects we experience are nothing but copies: prototype, standard, original, model, paradigm" (PAUL FOULQUIÉ, *Dictionnaire de la Langue Philosophique*, PUF, Paris, 1962).

CHAPTER II

TRANSCENDENCE AND SACRALITY

The Hierarchical Principle of the Universe

Love of the concrete, the individual and "diverse" was a fundamental trait of Plinio Corrêa de Oliveira's thought. He made his own the fundamental principle of Thomism that the proper object of the human intellect is not the indefinite being but the *"quidditas rei sensibilis,"* the specific essences of corporeal reality. It is through the direct experience of specific essences that man can attain knowledge of the universal and his own formulation of the first principles. What we know first of all are essences, and with them not the totality, but the inequality of reality. More accurately, we get to know unity through multiplicity.

In philosophical speculation, the principle of identity is joined by that of difference or diversity, and that of distinction.[134] Identity and unity are determined by substance, essence, or nature. To the identical is opposed the different or diverse, just as the similar is opposed to the dissimilar and the equal to the unequal. The distinction and multiplicity of things – Saint Thomas explains – comes from God, Who "brought things into being in order that His goodness might be communicated to creatures, and be represented by them; and because His goodness could not be adequately represented by one creature alone, He produced many and diverse creatures."[135]

In order to be radically different, entities must be made ontologically different. An existing being, whatever it is, must exist in a determined way. Indeed, either there is only one being that contradictorily is all beings at the same time, or there are many beings, each made of its own act of being. As an entity, a being is never another being, for otherwise the two would form a single being.[136]

---

[134] ROBERTO BUSA, *Differenza e diversità*, in EF, 2 (1979), cols. 907-909 e *Distinzione*, idem, cols. 1012-1025.

[135] *Summa Theologica*, I, q. 47, a. 1.

[136] Cf. G. DI NAPOLI, *Essere*, EF, cols. 287-288.

Saint Thomas Aquinas presents as a finding that the universe does not give an impression of chaos but of order.[137] *Quaestio* 47 of Part I of the *Summa Theologiae* is dedicated to the plurality and diversity of things in general. Considered from the point of view of God, the created order is a "descending" ontological series in which the different species express the glory of God, each in its own way and at its own level.[138] Saint Thomas says that God produced many and varied creatures so that what one lacks to represent Divine Goodness is compensated by another; indeed, goodness, which exists in God in the state of simplicity and unity, is found in creatures in a complex and fragmented way. "So that the whole universe participates in and more perfectly represents divine goodness than any particular creature."[139] "A single creature," Prof. Plinio observes, "would not be impossible as such from the standpoint of *potentia Dei absoluta*.[140] But it would be abortive and, as such, impossible to *potentia Dei ordinata*."[141]

For Plinio, the order of the universe is not an abstract theory without consequences on the human mind. On the contrary, man draws his own order and interior balance precisely from the vision of this order.

> "The vision of the order of the universe implies a kind of ordination, by reciprocity, of the whole mind of the person considering it…. So that a person accustomed to considering the order of the universe may acquire an order inside his head that, as far as I know, is the only way to actually acquire an ordered mind; naturally placing the Catholic Religion, its doctrines, in short, the whole Catholic Church at the heart of this ordination as the paramount element in the order of the universe. This is not a naturalist attitude but can also apply to the whole natural order, temporal order, etc."[142]

---

[137] Cf. AMÉDÉE DE SILVA TAROUCA, "L'idée d'ordre dans la philosophie de saint Thomas d'Aquin," *La Revue néoscolastique de philosophie*, 55 (August 1937), pp. 341-384; ANTONIO FOSSATI, S.J., *Dialettica dei gradi secondo la filosofia di S. Tommaso*, Pont. Univ. Gregoriana, Gallarate, 1961; B. BENITO Y DURÁN, "La ordinación del universo según San Augustinus y San Bonaventura," *Augustinus*, 19 (1974), pp. 31-47: RENZO LAVATORI, "Unità nella pluralità. Il principio dell'ordine secondo Tommaso d'Aquino," *Divinitas*, XLV, 2 (2002), pp. 121-152; Id., "La quarta via di S. Tommaso d'Aquino secondo il principio dell'ordine," idem, XVIII (1974), pp. 62-87.

[138] On the order of things, cf. also L. ELDERS, *La metafisica dell'essere*, I, pp. 265-273.

[139] *Summa Theologica*, I, q. 47, a. 1.

[140] *De potentia Dei absoluta* v. *De potentia Dei ordinata*. Theological axiom that explains that God, because of His omnipotence (*de potentia dei absoluta*) can do everything that is not contradictory, but in His infinite wisdom He made them in a certain way (*de potentia Dei ordinata*). For example, God could have established the absolution of sins without the need for sacramental confession.

[141] MNF, 25 January 1965.

[142] MNF, 3 April 1991.

The Degrees of Perfection

We must start from a point that the First Vatican Council defined as an article of our faith: the possibility for human reason to reach certainty about the existence of God and believe in Him by following an itinerary that ascends to God through created things.[143] In the words of Saint Paul, "for the invisible things of him, from the creation of the world, are clearly seen, being understood by the things that He made" (Rom. 1:20).

Each of the five ways in which Saint Thomas proves the existence of God leads to the knowledge of an attribute of God starting from the created world.[144]

Among the classic "proofs" of the existence of God, Plinio Corrêa de Oliveira appreciated especially the "fourth way," the one in which Platonic appearance is more salient and consists in rising to God through the ladder of perfection of the created things.[145] However, rather than as an abstract philosophical syllogism, he understands it as a method of formation and a psychological process that shapes the human soul. In particular, Plinio sees the fourth way as a path not only to know God but also, and above all, to love Him.[146] It shows God not only as the efficient and final cause but also as the exemplary cause of Creation and contemplates the created order as a universe of harmony and beauty, a reflection of the uncreated Divine Beauty.

Saint Thomas says that God "also made the universe to be best as a whole, according to the mode of a creature; whereas He did not make each single creature best, but one better than another."[147] Hence in natural things, species seem to be arranged in degrees; …and in each of these classes there are species more perfect than others. Therefore, as Divine Wisdom is the cause of the distinction of things for the sake of the perfection of the universe, it is also the cause of inequality."[148] The fourth way leads to God, most perfect Being, through the perfections in which every created being participates, in different degrees.

Prof. Plinio develops the notion of "degrees" according to which the creatures are like steps of a ladder through which the human mind can rise to God. All things exist in God's mind even before being created.

---

[143] DENZ-H, Nos. 3004-3006.

[144] Cf. MARIO PANGALLO, *Il creatore del mondo. Breve trattato di teologia filosofica*, Editrice Leonardo da Vinci, S. Marinella (Roma), 2004.

[145] Cf. C. FABRO CPS, "Sviluppo, significato e valore della IV via," *Doctor Communis*, no. 7 (1954), pp. 71-109; ID., "Il fondamento metafisico della quarta via," *Doctor Communis*, no. 18 (1965), pp. 49-70, now together in *L'uomo e il rischio di Dio*, Studium, Rome, 1967, pp. 226-271.

[146] AMP, 23 October 1970.

[147] *Summa Theologica*, I, q. 47, a. 2, ad. 1.

[148] *Summa Theologica*, I, q. 47, a. 2, resp.

God conceives them *ab aeterno,* from eternity, wanting them to be, in varying degrees, a reflection of His perfections.

"The human intellect was created to gradually ascend – like the steps of a ladder – to the supreme Principle which is God."[149]

"A degree is that inequality that exists between act and potency, cause and effect, from substance and accident. We call that inequality degree. And whenever a relationship of this nature is established between two creatures, one is superior to the other as such. This is the innermost content of the notion of degree, and the content of the notion of number essentially has to stick to this.

"This requires a consideration. Since matter is indispensable to form in order to constitute a being, if we take the notions of matter and form, everything a being has which is indispensable to something else, is – because indispensable — superior as such to the other. However inferior matter is in relation to form, it is – *aliunde,* and in a secondary sense – nobler than form. And the relationship of inequality never is one of complete inequality. But it is an inequality, which, *simpliciter,*[150] is inequality in a certain line, but *secundum quid,* it is inequality in another line.

"In this sense, under some aspects, the people are more than the king. And hierarchy is a relationship between unequals, but not a relationship of unequals in everything; it is a relationship between unequals *simpliciter.* Or rather, in an aboslute sense the king is more than the people, who *secundum quid* are unequals in the reverse sense (from a certain point of view, the people are more than the king). And in some way this hierarchy is the overlapping of these two inequalities, not as a one-way street, but in two different directions, with two-way traffic." [151]

Analogy and Sacrality

Recognition and love of the existence of inequalities in Creation as made by God is the foundation of what our author defines as *sacrality.* To the sense of being, which makes us understand with immediate evidence the existence of reality, corresponds the sense of the sacral, which shows us how this reality, being contingent is created, being created is unequal, and, in its inequality, it is harmoniously ordained to God, source of all reality. Sacrality is a consequence of the correlation of analogy that exists in the created universe.

---

[149] ST. BONAVENTURE, *Breviloquium,* p. 2, c. 12 (V, 230 a).

[150] *Simpliciter v. secundum quid.* Distinction made by Scholastics, following Aristotle, between a statement made in absolute terms, without qualifiers (*simpliciter*), and one made from a partial standpoint (*secundum quid*).

[151] MNF, 25 May 1965.

Analogy is used to establish a parallel between essentially different realities that nevertheless have something in common. Unlike the univocal, in which one and the same term is applied to many subjects in an identical way, and the equivocal, in which it is applied in a totally different way, analogy consists in attributing the same term to different entities in a sense that is partially equal and partially different. Thus, the term "healthy" is properly and mainly applied to the body, but by analogy it also applies to food, the climate, or a face that express the health of the body. Similarly, it is said that truth is for the intellect what sunlight is for the eyes of the body.[152]

On the metaphysical level analogy is based on the participation of various entities in the same perfection. In fact, according to Saint Thomas, "a thing is said to be one not only numerically, specifically, or generically, but also according to a certain analogy or proportion. In this sense a creature is one with God, or like to Him."[153]

Plinio emphasizes inequality as one of the elements of analogy:

> "The state of sacrality is a state of analogy which, on the part of the lower being, is expressed thus: 'I love that being because of what it has in common with me.' The greater the analogy, the greater the love. The other side is: 'I love that being for what it has that is different from me, whereby it is superior to me.' The greater the superiority, the greater the veneration."[154]

> "The concept of analogy always brings a concept of inequality, for two different things are always necessarily unequal. Two things cannot be on the same plane when there is difference. Ultimately, one is more beautiful than the other, better than the other, or some difference like that."[155]

> "This analogy leads some things, as it were, to be reversed in others, reflected in others in a world of extraordinary transparencies that would be like a succession of crystals through which the sun passes. A soul that sees the analogy of minerals with plants, plants with animals, animals with men, men with the angels, Our Lady at the top of creation, and Our Lord Jesus Christ, and then goes on to make an analogy in the opposite direction, toward the devil, in my view that soul would be making a very profound prayer."[156]

---

[152] REGIS JOLIVET, *Dizionario di filosofia,* It. tr., Morcelliana, Brescia, 1966, pp. 21-22.
[153] *Summa Theologica,* I, q. 93, a. 1, ad 3.
[154] BCM, 22 April 1967.
[155] Idem.
[156] CSN, 27 May 1989.

The Way of Logic and the Way of Symbolism

The method of analogy is used above all by those who see reality as a set of symbols. There are two ways to the total knowledge of reality: the abstractive way and the symbolic way.

The abstractive way is the one through which one attains the truth by means of reasoning; the symbolic way attains it through the meaning expressed by things in their visible concreteness. Plinio traveled this way and suggested it because,

> "Even without logic, a symbol can give more life to a topic than can logic without a symbol."[157] "Symbols make us see reality as much as abstractive knowledge, but through another path. We must therefore develop both pathways and not just the one of abstractive knowledge."[158]

Although not a professional theologian, Plinio was a thinker whose reflection on the temporal order is theologically and philosophically substantial and innovative. His theological and philosophical process, however, soars from the temporal to the eternal, from the finite to the infinite, while the classical theological method proceeds from God and ends in the creature.

The symbolic way does not contradict that logic in any way but integrates and perfects it. Plinio states,

> "It is true that the human mind acts according to reasoning. Everyone knows how much veneration and enthusiasm I have for everything related to reasoning. But parallel to it is the whole world of symbols and the whole world of the sense of being, the Catholic sense, which harmoniously marries the world of reason and is not its enemy. They support each other reciprocally."[159]

Corporeal things do not exhaust the whole of reality for they refer to a higher dimension of creation, which is invisible but even more profoundly real than the visible. The symbol is a visible expression of this superior and immaterial higher reality of the universe. The symbol expresses the meaning, that is, the most profound reality of each being. The whole universe is a symbol of God.

> "The symbolic meaning is the bridge that connects the visible to the invisible. Men would be much more inclined to reflection if they perceived the symbolic value of things."[160]

---

[157] *Primeval Innocence,* p. 100.
[158] EVP, 26 December 1993.
[159] Idem.
[160] EVP, 12 December 1993.

Every symbol expresses a similarity between a certain concrete reality and its abstract or spiritual equivalent. With its form, a sword, for example, symbolizes the combative spirit, made of strength, righteousness, inflexibility.

"The similarity exists and is neither small nor fortuitous, for at a certain time in history the sword was the weapon *par excellence*. But the reason for it is that the fighting spirit is made of rectitude, inflexibility, an ability to hit and hurt. So that a person with a polemic spirit takes actions that the sword perfectly symbolizes... A symbol exists when there is similarity between a concrete object and something abstract or spiritual. Here the definition of symbol is perfectly characterized."[161]

"Saint Paul has this very typical phrase: 'If we do not love the creatures we see, how will we love God Whom we do not see?' The symbol, then, is something that makes visible what was invisible. And whenever we manage to connect an abstract idea to a symbol, it is as if a blind man was cured."[162]

The visible sky, studded with stars, narrates the glory of its Author because it is the symbol of the invisible heaven where the angels and the saints sing the glory of God in eternity. The universe is a metaphysical symphony that contains not only the real but also the world of the possible, the world of what could be but is not; a world that transcends reality and thus can be contemplated by the intellect and imagined by fantasy.[163] The song that rises from the earth to glorify God is the symbol of a celestial, metaphysical and spiritual music with which the whole universe of realities and possibilities glorifies God. The world's music is a sensible symbol of the harmony and spiritual order that govern the order of the cosmos.

"The whole universe, in one way or another, is a symbol of God. It is an immense symbolic building of which man is the highest part."[164]

The Medieval Universe of Symbols

For a Christian, and especially for a man with the spirit of the Middle Ages, nothing exists without meaning and everything that exists is made in order to awaken the thought and remembrance of God.[165]

---

[161] EVP, 28 November 1993.

[162] EVP, 12 September 1993.

[163] *Primeval Innocence*, cit., p. 157.

[164] Idem, p. 98.

[165] On medieval symbolism and aesthetics, cf. JACQUES MARITAIN, *Art et Scolastique,* Louis Rouart et Dils, Paris, 1927; EDGAR DE BRUYNE, *L'esthétique du Moyen Age,* Editions de l'Institut Supérieur de philosophie, Louvain, 1947; *Etudes d'esthétique médiévale,* 2 vols., Albin Michel, Paris, 1998; ERWIN PANOFSKY, *Architecture gothique et pensée scolastique,* Les

Omnia in mensura et numero et pondere disposuisti, reads the Holy
Scripture (Wis. 11:21). The Belgian philosopher Edgar De Bruyne
emphasizes the exceptional importance of this verse on which is based
what he calls the "sapiential" aesthetic of medieval man.[166]

In turn, Etienne Gilson observes:

> "Under whatever aspect you look at it there actually is only one
> medieval vision of the world, albeit it is at times expressed in works of
> art, at other times in philosophical concepts: the one that Saint Augustine
> masterfully outlined in his *De Trinitate,* which directly employs the words
> of the Book of Wisdom (11:21): *omnia in mensura, et numero, et pondere
> disposuisti.*"[167]

This is a theme famously cultivated by Church Fathers, Scholastics,
and by classical theology. It has its premises in the teaching of Saint Paul
(especially in his *Epistle to the Romans* and *Epistle to the Colossians*),
and is particularly developed in Saint Augustine's *De Civitate Dei* (with a
reflection on vestige and image) and the *De Divinis Nominibus* of
Dionysius the Areopagite (with the doctrine on the hierarchy of degrees
of perfection).

The Victorines[168] and Saint Bonaventure[169] were the authors who
developed this aspect of theology more profoundly in the Middle Ages.[170]

Editions de Minuit, Paris, 1975; MARIE-MADALEINE DAVY, *Il simbolismo medievale,* It. tr.,
Edizioni Mediterranee, Rome, 1988; OTTO VON SIMSON, *La cattedrale gotica. Il concetto
medievale di ordine,* It. tr., Il Mulino, Bologna, 1988; CATHERINE VINCENT, *Fiat Lux. Lumière
et luminaires dans la vie religieuse du XIII au XVI siècle,* Cerf, Paris, 2004,

[166] E. DE BRUYNE, *L'esthétique du Moyen Age,* p. 11.

[167] E. GILSON, *Lo spirito della filosofia medievale,* It. tr. Morcelliana, Brescia 1969, p. 126.

[168] The Canons Regular of the former abbey of St. Victor in Paris. Founded by William of
Champeaux in 1113, the abbey became extinct during the French Revolution. It is best known
for the number of scholars, mystics, and poets it produced, including Hugh of St. Victor (1096-
1141), Richard of St. Victor (d. 1173) and Walter of St. Victor (d. after 1180). Founded on the
left bank of the Seine River, the abbey was profoundly influenced by Cluny.
https://www.catholicculture.org/culture/library/dictionary/index.cfm?id=37099 and RAINER
BERNDT, *Victorins,* DSp, XVI (1994), cols. 559-562.

[169] Saint Bonaventure of Bagnoregio (1221-1274), known as the "Seraphic Doctor," was Master
General of the Franciscan Order from 1261 until his death. In his works he dealt with major
theological issues and Leo XIII, in his Encyclical *Aeterni Patris,* called him "prince" of
Scholastic theology, along with Saint Thomas Aquinas. "His doctrine marks the culminating
point of Christian mystics and is the most complete synthesis it has ever produced" (E. GILSON,
La philosophie de Saint Bonaventure, J. Vrin, Paris 1934, p. 472). Cf. also E. SMEETS, DTC, II,
962-986; E. LONGPRÉ, DSp, I, 1768-1843; L. DI FONZO, BSS, III, 239-278. His philosophical,
theological and spiritual writings are collected in a critical edition in nine large volumes
produced by Quaracchi Publishers (1882-1902).

[170] Cf. also ROBERT SAVELET, *Image et ressemblance au XII siècle,* Letouzey et Ané, Paris,
1967 ; J: M. BISSEN, O.F.M., *L'exemplarisme divin selon saint Bonaventure,* J. Vrin. Paris,
1929; V. C. BIGI, "La Dottrina della luce in St. Bonaventure," *Divus Thomas,* 65 (1961), pp.
495-442; CORNELIO B. DEL ZOTTO, *La teologia dell'immagine in San Bonaventura,* LIEF,
Vicenza, 1977; EFREM BETTONI, O.F.M. *San Bonaventura da Bagnoregio,* Biblioteca

Richard of Saint Victor writes, "Every visible body presents a resemblance to an invisible good."[171] And Hugh of Saint Victor says: "All visible objects are given (by God) to signify and manifest invisible realities, symbolically, that is, figuratively, teaching us through our eyesight."[172] Thus, every visible beauty is a symbol, sign, and image of the invisible beauty of God.[173]

Plinio called "Victorinism" that form of the metaphysical spirit by which an individual conceives, through the sensible, not only the abstract but also the archetype, the notion of how all things should be if they were perfect – a primeval and crystalline notion of the original perfection of all things, which is "the antechamber of the heavenly life."[174] But Victorinism is neither poetry nor preaches contemplation of an unreal universe; it requires effort, which Plinio defines as "an interior crusade against one's own Sancho Panza.[175] No one has the Victorinist spirit if he has no fighting spirit."[176]

The Plinian way is similar to St. Bonaventure's, who offers us a journey of the soul to God through signs of the sensible world, which, always under different and unequal characters, conveys to us a single Divine call. In addition to being the efficient and final cause of Creation, God is also its exemplary cause. "The splendor of the Divine Model is found in every creature....Thus, every being is a way that leads to the Model; it is a vestige of God's wisdom."[177]

In this sense, the created world is one that resembles God, its exemplary Cause. All creatures, according to their degree of perfection, are a vestige, an image or likeness of God. All reflect their Creator. For those able to see, all things without exception are made in order to awaken in us the thought and remembrance of God.[178]

The Word is the exemplary cause of every vestige, image or likeness of every being created by God. Finite realities are exemplifying realities, *i.e.*, imitating likenesses in relation to the imitated model. The human intellect rises from the example to the Exemplar.[179] As examples,

---

Francescana, Milano, 1973; *L'uomo in cammino verso Dio*, Biblioteca Francescana, Milano, 1978.

[171] RICCARDO DI SAN VITTORE, *Benjamin major*, PL, 196, col. 90.

[172] UGO DI SAN VITTORE, *In Dionisii Coelestem Hierarchiam expositio*, PL, 175, col. 978.

[173] UGO DI SAN VITTORE, *Didascalion*, P. L., 175, VII, cols. 948-949.

[174] MNF, 7 November 1983.

[175] Just as everyone has a fighting hero as an ideal model in his own spiritual combat, he also has some aspects of Sancho Panza, who represents his capital vice (translastor's note).

[176] MNF, 7 November 1983.

[177] ST. BONAVENTURE, *Hexaemeron*, cols. 12, Nos. 14-15.

[178] E. BETTONI, *San Bonaventura*, p. 130.

[179] LUIGI IAMMARONE, *Imago-Vestigium*, in *Dizionario bonaventuriano*, a cura di ERNESTO CAROLI, Edizioni Francescane, Padova 2008, p. 484.

finite realities, *i.e.*, similarities, thy lead man's mind towards his Exemplar. The rational creature must tend toward likeness to its Creator because it is an image of Him." [180]

Saint Bonaventure's *Journey of the Mind into God* is famous:

> "All creatures of this sensible world lead the mind of the one contemplating and attaining wisdom to the eternal God; for they are shadows, echoes, and pictures, the traces, simulacra, and reflections of that First Principle most powerful, wisest, and best; of that light and plenitude; of that art productive, exemplifying, and ordering, given to us for looking upon God. They are signs divinely bestowed which, I say, are exemplars or rather exemplifications set before our yet untrained minds, limited to sensible things, so that through the sensible which they see they may be carried forward to the intelligible, which they do not see, as if by signs to the signified. The creatures of this sensible world signify the invisible things of God [Rom. 1:20], partly because God is of all creation the origin, exemplar, and end, and because every effect is the sign of its cause, the exemplification of the exemplar, and the way to the end to which it leads." [181]

All that depends on God resembles Him, visibly reflects His invisible perfections and has its own degree of perfection because it is made in the likeness of the most perfect Being, who contains all perfections. It is this similarity between creature and Creator that allows us to lift up our minds to the things of God. [182]

All virtues and vices can be expressed by a symbol. Underlying the thought of Plinio Corrêa de Oliveira is a relentless pursuit of

> "ultimately finding a *verum,* a *bonum,* a *pulchrum* which is a reflection of God. And, in the opposite direction, finding a *falsum, malum et horrendum,* which is the devil. Therefore, underlying all the avenues of my thinking is God on one side and the devil on the other." [183]

Saint Thomas says that an imprint of the Holy Trinity is found in all creatures. [184] And Saint Bonaventure adds that "the creation of the world is like a book in which the creative Trinity shines, manifests itself and is

---

[180] ST. BONAVENTURE, *In I Sent.,* d. 6, a. un., q. 3, concl., 1, 26.

[181] ST. BONAVENTURE, *Journey of the Mind into God,* II, 11-12.

[182] As Etienne Gilson observes, this resemblance does not imply participation by things in the essence of God. "The real similarity that exists between Creator and creatures is a similarity of expression. Things are to God as signs of the meaning they express; they therefore constitute a kind of language, and the whole universe is nothing but a book where one reads the Trinity everywhere" (*La filosofia nel Medioevo. Dalle origini patristiche alla fine del XIV secolo,* It. tr., La Nuova Italia, Florence, 1973, p. 533).

[183] SNC, 27 May 1989.

[184] *Summa Theologica,* I. q. 47, a.7, c.

read in three degrees of expression, that is, as footprint, image, and likeness."[185]

Like Saint Bonaventure and the Victorines, Plinio is convinced that the universe as a whole and in every particular aspect reflects the Divine Trinity, which is the foundation of inequalities in the created universe, whose rule is not only the *reductio ad unum,* but also the *reductio ad trinum.*

> "It is *reductio ad unum* inasmuch as it is a *reductio* to the seed. But it is not *reductio ad unum* inasmuch as it is *reductio* to the content of the seed, which is triune. So it is not true as they say that the *reductio ad unum* is always the ultimate point of wisdom; in fact, *reductio ad unum-trinum* is the ultimate point of wisdom. This is the sapiential *unum* which is not that homogeneous *unum* but instead a *unum* in whose mystery dwells a *trinum,* which is something entirely superior."[186]

> "There are two orders of being. A first order of being is the Most Holy Trinity, unfathomable, perfect, superior to everything. Then, in a second order of being we see creatures. Between these two orders there is an abyss and at first sight there is no point of contact at all.

> "In the lower order of creatures, Our Lady is the highest of the highest, and in the merely created world she is the apex, center and pinnacle of all perfections. She is the personification, the highest standard of this order and contains all perfections in their respective hierarchy, and is thus the paradigm to which all angels and all men are turned. She is on the apex of everything.

> "Between her and God, above this abyss, there is a unifying link which is Our Lord Jesus Christ, God-Man. The idea of a God-Man is unfathomable, and if Revelation did not teach it, we could not imagine it. In only one Person He has both natures, the human and the divine, so He is that unifying link. Our Lady has such an elevated position because her body provided the matter for that Incarnation. Accordingly, She outdoes herself on the point that she touches Divinity: it was in Mary's flesh and blood that the Word of God became flesh and dwelt among us. Our Lord Jesus Christ is exclusively Her Son and not Saint Joseph's, and therefore the Flesh and Blood of the Lamb of God are solely and entirely Her flesh and blood.

> "God picked the most select, the most chosen and most perfect portion of the whole visible universe to unite Himself to her in an admirable way and establish this link with mankind. Mother of the Word, She also becomes Spouse of the Holy Ghost Who, in order to beget in her the most holy humanity of Our Lord Jesus Christ, united Himself to her

---

[185] St. Bonaventure, *Breviloquium,* 2-12.
[186] MNF, 27 May 1965.

through an operation not only physiological but with unfathomable impact on her soul. The intimate union of her soul with the Holy Ghost can only be gauged by considering the intimacy of that operation whereby He takes her flesh and blood to create and shape therein the body in which the Word of God will become incarnate.

"He who loves the order of the universe must become entranced, facing Her who was placed in the created universe in such a height as to have above herself only the One Who is Her body and blood. This is so high as to give you a little dizziness, which becomes palpable as you reflect about it before any statue of Our Lady with the Child Jesus in her arms: that Child, Who is God omnipotent and reigns above the cherubim and seraphim, is in her arms with all calmness, happiness and well-being as if He were in His Heaven. For God, Who is unfathomable, perfect and self-sufficient happiness to be in the arms of a simple creature with such well-being, joy, and also playing with her, you can imagine to what degree Our Lady is at the apex of everything. This apex attains such lofty heights of thought that one would say the word apex explodes, incapable of expressing all that we would like to say.

"Our Lady synthesizes the perfections of the order of the universe in such a splendid way that only Our Lord Jesus Christ is above her, and all the rest comes way below." [187]

"Just as in the supernatural order Our Lady is the compendium of the perfections of all angels, men and creatures, She certainly also encompasses the supernatural perfections of creatures created *ab aeterno,* because she has everything in the highest degree. So that if we saw her in her glory we would have the impression that she was created *ab aeterno* because of the supernatural glory that surrounds her."[188]

Principle of Immanence and Principle of Transcendence

Saint Pius X identified the core of modernism with the principle of immanence,[189] a philosophical conception that assumes experience as absolute and excludes all transcendent reality.[190] In his history of modern atheism, Father Cornelio Fabro profoundly analyzes the philosophical journey of this devastating error, from Descartes to contemporary philosophers.[191]

---

[187] EXT, June 1974.

[188] EVP, 2 January 1983.

[189] PIUS X, Encyclical *Pascendi dominici gregis* of September 8, 1907, EE, *Pio X* (1998), nos. 196, 208f., 220-223, 228. St. Pius X wrote, "The philosopher has declared: *The principle of faith is immanent*; the believer has added: *This principle is God*; and the theologian draws the conclusion: *God is immanent in man.* Thus we have *theological immanence*" (no. 208).

[190] C. FABRO, *Immanenza*, EC, VI, col. 1673 (cols. 1673-1680).

[191] C. FABRO, *Introduzione all'ateismo moderno*, Editrice del Verbo Incarnato, Segni, 2013 (1964).

On the theological plane, the philosophical principle of immanence corresponds to the anthropological deviation spanning from modernism all the way to Karl Rahner,[192] one of the authors who most influenced the Second Vatican Council.

On the spiritual level the principle of immanence corresponds to Maurice Blondel's method of immanence. In his work *L'Action*, published in 1893,[193] Blondel proposed a new form of apologetics that assumed the immanentist premises of modern thought. From that immanentist methodological assumption came the confusion, which essentially becomes assimilation, between the tendency to the infinite that man can have in himself and the infinite reality of God; the idea that man, following his desire for the infinite, can participate in the Divine infinite by identifying himself with it.[194]

The method of immanence aims to find and develop the truth of religion and the mysteries of the revealed faith starting from the needs, aspirations and requirements that emerge in man's subjective experience. The philosophical principle of immanence translates into an anthropological decrease of spirituality in which individual experience plays a decisive role.

By confusing his aspiration to the absolute with the absolute itself, man finds the answer to his metaphysical pursuit in himself. He replaces the search for the glory of God with the fulfillment of his (spiritual) needs. The essence of Christianity is reduced to "feeling" or "experience," which, as Saint Pius X noted, can add nothing to feeling "other than making it more intense."[195]

The method of immanence has a Gnostic and egalitarian substratum. For Saint Pius X,

> "Now the doctrine of immanence in the Modernist acceptation holds and professes that every phenomenon of conscience proceeds from man

---

[192] For a critique on Karl Rahner, cf. C. FABRO, *La svolta antropologica di Karl Rahner*, Editrice del Verbo Incarnato, Segni, 2011; *Karl Rahner: un'analisi critica. La figura, l'opera e la recezione teologica di Karl Rahner (1904-1984)*, prepared by Fr. SERAFINO M. LANZETTA; GIOVANNI CAVALCOLI, O.P., *Karl Rahner: il Concilio tradito*, Fede e Cultura, Verona, 2009.

[193] MAURICE BLONDEL (1861-1949), *L'Action. Essai d'une critique de vie et d'une science de pratique*, Alcan, Paris, 1893. The work was republished during its centennial by Presses Universitaires de France, Paris, 1993.

[194] This tendency to pantheism becomes obvious in the twentieth century in theologians like Karl Rahner and Henri de Lubac (cf. Card, GIUSEPPE SIRI, *Getsemani. Riflessioni sul Movimento Teologico Contemporaneo*, Fraternità della Santissima Vergine, Rome, 1980, pp. 51-100).

[195] St. PIUS X, *Pascendi*, no. 228.

as man. The rigorous conclusion from this is the identity of man with God, which means Pantheism.[196]

Plinio Corrêa de Oliveira meditated more profoundly than anyone on transcendence, the principle opposed to immanence, making it not only a *principle* but a *method* and a spiritual way.

The concept of transcendence is clarified only with the theoretical concept of God the Creator. The word transcendence, in opposition to the word immanence, expresses first of all the capacity of the human intellect to learn something distinct from itself. The notion of transcendence, which Saint Thomas places at the summit of metaphysical science,[197] thus implies the idea of distinction and overcoming. Plinio explains it clearly:

> "Any plant whatever transcends a stone, which is mineral by nature.... And just as a plant transcends a mineral, an animal transcends a plant; and man, a rational animal, transcends a mere animal....Thus, within this order of things, transcendence is that special superiority one thing has over another by the fact that it intrinsically has a totally different quality." [198]

From superiority to superiority, from transcendence to transcendence, one arrives at the transcendent Being par excellence that transcends us infinitely, which is God. If the principle of immanence confines us in the world separating us from God, the principle of transcendence allows us to rise to something absolute, that is, toward the idea of an absolute Being Who has all perfections in Himself.[199] Immanence secularizes reality, while transcendence reveals its sacrality, that is, orders it according to God.

Transcendence shines through in the universe because everything that is created reflects the infinite perfections of God. Plinio resolutely states:

> "The purpose of creatures and the universe is God, and He cannot be reached by means of a vast assembly of mutually articulated gears but through the likeness with Him that shines through being."[200]

Plinio also highlights the social impact of the principle of transcendence. In fact, God's relationships with man are repeated from creature to creature, from angel to angel, from angel to man, and from man to man.

---

[196] Idem.

[197] ST. THOMAS AQUINAS, *In Metaphy. Prooemium.*

[198] NOR, 15 September 1966.

[199] *Primeval Innocence,* p. 134.

[200] MNF COM, no. 38.

"For the Revolution, God is immanent in nature, for example, as light is present in the air; but this image does not quite give the idea of this immanence. Perhaps one could say that God would be immanent in nature like a blessing in holy water.

"If God is immanent in nature, He is immanent in all beings. If God is immanent in all beings, all beings are somehow immanent in all others, and equality is the good order in the relationship of all beings. Immanence places God at the same level as men. It is an attempt to give a religious garb to atheism, as it would be the same thing to say that 'there is no God' or that 'God is immanent in nature.' From these two diametrically opposed conceptions of God come two diametrically opposed conceptions of Church."[201]

While there are several degrees of transcendence,

"God alone is absolute transcendence. Only God absolutely transcends all creation."[202] "Transcendence is properly something that exists absolutely, that is, in God, and which at the same time is very similar to all that we know but entirely different from anything we know. Or, expressing myself better, it is entirely similar to the analogous thing and entirely different from the analogous thing."[203]

For example, contemplating a representation of Louis XIV, Plinio rises from the majesty shining from the Sun King to God's absolute majesty:

"When a man sees an extremely high degree of majesty, for example, the majestic soul of Louis XIV, he gets to have a livelier notion of absolute majesty than if he would read a treatise on morals....This leads to God Our Lord because we can say that a man is majestic, but of God we must say He is Majesty. In other words, God does not have qualities but *is* the qualities He has. With that which our eyes see one has something similar to the beatific vision. Something of God's majesty is imperceptibly seen in Louis XIV.... This is the way in which, through the fourth way, we get to see God."[204]

God is indeed everywhere, as Saint Paul said to the Athenians: in Him we have life, movement, and being: *"In ipso enim vivimus, movemur et sumus"* (Acts 17:28). There is a natural immanence of God in things (and especially in rational creatures) as the First principle, creator, preserver and cause of creation;[205] there is also a supernatural immanence when, through grace, a creature is allowed to participate in God's intimate

---

[201] RRR, 23 February 1985.

[202] EVP, 20 October 1974.

[203] EVP, 5 January 1975.

[204] NOR, 23 March 1973.

[205] *Summa Theologica,* I, qq. 44, 104, 105.

life; and finally, there is an immanence in God, fully proportional to their soul, in the life of the blessed in glory.[206] But in order to avoid confusion, it is better to speak of presence rather than immanence, as does Saint Thomas, devoting an entire question to *"praesentia Dei in rebus."*[207] "The term 'presence,' rather than 'immanence,' expresses the progress of the Christian concept, founded on God's absolute transcendence and freedom," Fr. Fabro explains.[208]

The spirituality of abandoning oneself to the present time, which Father Garrigou-Lagrange expounds in a profound work,[209] is a spirituality of the eminently sacred presence of God: nothing is alien to God in human life, in time and in society. There is not a single moment in our life or place in the universe from which God is absent.

To ignore this presence is to fall into what Plinio calls "minor atheism," no less corrosive than the major one, which frontally denies God.

> "Minor atheism is not the denial that God exists transcendently in relation to the world. It is the denial that He has this form of presence in the things of the world. It is the denial of this participation."[210]

The exercise of transcendence proposed by Plinio is a form of exercise of the presence of God in all things, but it develops the traditional method in a new way. Traditional spirituality starts from a reflection on the attribute of the immensity of God, present in all things by *essence* inasmuch as God gives being to all that exists; by *presence*, since nothing escapes His gaze; and by *power*, as all things are subject to His power.[211] This consideration leads us to behave as if God were always present. In turn, the Plinian exercise of transcendence starts from things in order to rise to God by degrees; in a word, it is more directly centered on God and makes the created universe into a tool for that end. Fr. Joseph Pollien notes that one word defines the created:

> "This word, whose scope is immense, is that creation is an instrument and nothing but an instrument."[212]

---

[206] C. FABRO, *Immanenza,* col. 1675.

[207] *Summa Theologica,* I, q. 8.

[208] C. FABRO, *Immanenza,* col. 1675.

[209] R. GARRIGOU-LAGRANGE, *La Providence et la confiance en Dieu: fidélité et abandon,* Desclée de Brouwer, Paris, 1932.

[210] EVP, 15 July 1973.

[211] A. ROYO MARIN, *Teologia della perfezione cristiana,* Nos. 473-477.

[212] Joseph POLLIEN, *La vita interiore semplificata e ricondotta al suo fondamento,* It. tr. Paoline, Roma, 1969, p. 75. Dom Joseph Pollien (1853-1936), in religion Francis de Sales, born in Annecy in 1884, joined the Great Charterhouse of Grenoble and led an exemplary monastic life, serving as superior in many monasteries until his death at the Charterhouse of Serra San

God is the only end of creation; creatures are but means, each in accordance with their own characteristics and specificities.

The Rules of Aesthetics of the Universe

Of all the divine perfections, beauty is the one that makes an exercise of transcendence easier and quicker. For Plinio Corrêa de Oliveira there is a set of rules that can help us understand the beauty of the created universe and elevate us to the uncreated beauty that is God Himself. The most fundamental of these rules is the "harmonious coexistence of unity with variety."[213] Instead of merely giving a cold enunciation of principles, Plinio shows us this rule in its visible expression beginning with a concrete example, that of the sea. Contemplating the sea, we observe that unity is one of the first elements of its grandeur.

> "All the seas of the Earth communicate with one another and constitute a huge body of water that spans the whole globe. On the seafront anywhere in the world, one of the most pleasant things one can do is to gaze at the liquid mass before us all the way to the end of the horizon and think that it does not end there but has successive immensities behind it, forming only one great, immense ocean that moves, lashes out and plays around throughout the surface of the Earth."[214]

But at the same time that the sea shows us this wonderful unity, it impresses us for the *variety* it manifests: from that variety we return to its unity.

> "Variety, first of all, in its movement. Now the sea presents itself tame and serene, appearing to satisfy all of our soul's longings for peace, tranquility and quietude. Now it moves discreetly and suavely, making us smile and relax considering the amenable and delightful realities of life. Now it finally shows itself majestic and wild, rising up in sublime movements, launching forth furiously against haughty rocks, and moving unfathomable masses of water from its own abysses, as if to submerge islands and invade continents. In this state, the sea seems dominated by overwhelming fury and roars with all the grandeur and might that exists in its depths, but which one could not imagine in its moments of gentleness

---

Bruno in Calabria. His masterpiece is *La vie intérieure simplifiée et reconduite à son fondement* (1894) published under the pen name Joseph Tissot (1840-1894). Cf. AUGUSTINE DEVAUX, DSp, 12, cols. 1861-1864.

[213] Prof. Corrêa de Oliveira developed this concept based on his readings of Saint Thomas and also of Father Henri Ramière, about whom we will speak later.

[214] "The Scapular, Profession, and Interior Consecration," lecture at the Third National Congress of the Third Carmelite Order (São Paulo, November 14-16, 1958), *Mensageiro do Carmelo*, special issue, São Paulo, 1959.

and grace. We then seem to witness the most exciting and heroic moves in history.

"There are also aesthetic varieties at sea. At times the sea is so limpid that you can see all the way down to the bottom, through a great liquid mass; at other times, however, it shows itself dark, impenetrable, profound and mysterious. If in certain panoramas the sea presents itself with huge and almost limitless surfaces, in other panoramas it is circumscribed by the coast's accidents and forms small closed gulfs in which, so to speak, it is takes pleasure in drawing closer to us, making itself small to be better seen and loved.

"The sea is no less varied in its rumble. Now its murmur conveys the impression of a caress that lulls one to sleep; now it becomes a mere background noise that resembles the familiar conversation of an old friend. But shortly afterward it speaks with the dominant roar of a king who wants to impose his will on all elements.

"The way it 'behaves' on the beach is also varied. Sometimes the sea arrives at the beach breathless and gasping; sometimes it moves toward it late and lazily, in waves that move languidly. At other times it seems so completely stopped that one would almost say it is contented with watching the land without touching it.

"Now then, all these diversities of the sea would seem incongruous and charmless were they not presented against the grand background of a fixed, invariable and grandiose unity. This is the beauty of unity in variety."[215]

This intimate harmony between unity and variety can be applied to everything that exists in the created universe so we can rise up to God, source of all beauty and all perfection. In this scale of perfections the place of prominence is given to the Blessed Virgin Mary.

The Beauties of the Most Holy Virgin

Mary is the apex of the beauties of the universe. Of her Saint Alphonsus Liguori writes, "Nothing is higher in the universe."[216] According to Saint Thomas, the reason for that is obvious: the more a thing approaches its principle, the more it receives from its perfection; and therefore, being the creature closest to God, Mary has participated in His perfection more than any other.[217]

Plinio says:

---

[215] "The Scapular, Profession, and Interior Consecration," op. cit.
[216] ST. ALPHONSE MARIA LIGUORI, *The Glories of Mary*, Redentoristi, Rome, 1937, vol. II, p. 92.
[217] *Summa Theologica*, III, q. 27, a. 5.

"We know from Catholic doctrine that the beauty of all things is an image of God, pure and infinitely perfect Spirit. Thus, just as man was made in the image and likeness of God, things are also images of man. The sky and sea, in their various states, are reminiscent of the human soul in its various dispositions: the complex play of human passions, the virtues of the human soul when it really reflects the holiness of God Our Lord."

"Accordingly, these aesthetic rules are means for us to consider the true beauty of holiness in man. And mainly in Our Lady, highest of all mere creatures, who has been and should be compared to the sky and the sea with such splendid appropriateness; a soul of ineffable immensity, in which all forms of virtue and beauty exist with supereminent perfection, of which none of us can have an exact idea. Our Lady is precisely that sea, that sky of virtues before which man should be awed and enraptured, and which he should seek to love and imitate with all his strength.

"Also found in Our Lady are the same unity in variety of God's gifts. This is noted very much in the fact that, being one, She presents herself to us in the admirable variety of her invocations. She is Our Lady of Peace, Our Lady of Sorrows, Our Lady of Good Death. In her all contrasts harmonize. She is at the same time Help of Christians and Refuge of Sinners; she is glorified by her incomparable humility, but all the seers who had the happiness of contemplating her comment on her sovereign majesty; she presents herself to us *"ut castrorum acies ordinata"* but is at the same time *"Mater clementiæ et misericordiæ."* We could do a study of Our Lady with the help of the same principles applied in the analysis of the sky and the sea. For example, who could contemplate seemingly irreconcilable contrasts in perfect harmony better than the Virgin Mother? Called the Virgin of Virgins, she could also very legitimately and validly be called the Mother of Mothers."[218]

From these philosophical and theological considerations, one can already have a glimpse of the profoundly Marian core of Plinian spirituality.

The Sacrality of the Temporal Order

Plinio Corrêa de Oliveira devoted most of his public action to political and social problems. Yet few of his opponents or supporters realized that for him every economic, social and political issue had a theological root. He recognizes the Church as the Mystical Body of Christ, established for the salvation of men, mother and teacher of the truth, center of sacramental and spiritual life; in short, alpha and omega of all that relates to man on this earth. The Church carries out her mission

---

[218] "The Scapular, Profession, and Interior Consecration," op. cit.

by shaping not only individuals but also temporal society according to the law of Christ. In a sacral conception of the universe, the temporal order is not totally separated from the spiritual order but, like it, is also oriented to God.

The primacy of the spiritual in no way implies a denial of the sacral dimension of the temporal sphere. In order to fully devote himself to his mission, Plinio chose a life of perfection, remaining celibate without embracing the ecclesiastical state, though recognizing its absolute prominence:

> "We should have greater attraction to that for which Providence calls us. Curiously, it is not a love, for I love the priesthood more than my vocation; if I had to fight to keep on earth either my vocation or the priesthood, I would obviously fight for the priesthood. But I feel no attraction for the priesthood, and attraction is a form of vocation. For this God gives me a special grace, but I must recognize that the grace a priest has is worth much more than mine."[219]

Plinio's whole life unfolded in the civil order: from his militancy in the Marian Congregations and in Catholic Action through his career as a politician, professor and journalist, until the founding of the Brazilian Society for the Defense of Tradition, Family and Property and other kindred associations around the world, which are civil rather than canonical entities.[220]

Man lives in temporal society, belongs to temporal society, and everything related to temporal society was the usual topic of Plinio's thoughts. It is in society that man opens himself to life, first within the family, then in social, cultural and political ambiences and so on. It is up to the laity to create a political order, society, culture, art and civil *habitat* that provides a favorable environment for souls to receive the action of the Church well. Otherwise, all the good that the Church can do in her domain will be more or less radically thwarted by a hostile civil *habitat*.

This is the reason why our author devoted the best of his intellectual effort to explicitate the features of such a *habitat*, that is, a sacral Christian civilization at the service of the Church.[221] For Plinio, the loss of sacrality in the temporal order has disastrous consequences in the spiritual order. If it is true that the Church influences and shapes society,

---

[219] AMC, 5 June 1991.

[220] JOSÉ ANTONIO URETA, "Restorer of the Temporal Order," *Catolicismo*, no. 562 (October 1997), pp. 37-41; Plinio Corrêa de Oliveira, "A Vocation in the Temporal Order," ATFP, March 2011.

[221] Cf. MARIO NAVARRO DA COSTA, "Plinio Corrêa de Oliveira: The Sacrality of the Temporal Order and the Certainty of Victory," in *Ten Years Later*, pp. 171-182.

the opposite is also true: for good or bad, a temporal society can affect the life of the Church in its earthly aspect.

From his programmatic manifesto, "The Twentieth-Century Crusade" (1951), through his essay *Notes on the Concept of Christendom* (1953), all the way to his latest book, *Nobility and Analogous Traditional Elites* (1993), we can consider this to be the true leitmotif of Plinio Corrêa de Oliveira's thought and action.

Among his notes is a book draft devoted to Christendom. The text is important, also for us to know the sources of his reflection. Many authors are frequently cited, from Joseph de Maistre to Father Luigi Taparelli d'Azeglio, but the name that appears on almost every page, with references and precise and detailed quotes, is that of Saint Thomas Aquinas. Plinio profoundly studied and knew the *Summa Theologica*, especially in relation to those passages referring to Christendom. He shows the political and social consequences of the Thomist conception of the universe:

> "In Saint Thomas, a Catholic learns that inequality is a necessary condition for the perfection of the created order. And consequently, inequalities of power, knowledge, social class and fortune are intrinsically legitimate and indispensable to the good order just as long as they are not accentuated to the point of denying the dignity, sufficiency and life stability to which all persons are entitled for their condition as men, for their work and so on."[222]

In his book *Nobility and Analogous Traditional Elites*, Plinio develops traits of an organic society in which the individual is part of a set of social bodies and orders that protect and help him to improve himself and to develop his own individuality.[223] The family, whose structure offers a real social model, is the foundation of organic society. In it "the father was a true miniature king"[224] just as the king was a true "father" to his people.

The opposite of organic society, which reached its zenith in the Middle Ages, is the "mechanical" society characteristic of totalitarianism, in which all social functions are absorbed by a centralizing revolutionary power. "Organic society is a social order oriented toward the common good that naturally and spontaneously develops, allowing man to pursue the perfection of his essentially social nature.[225]

---

[222] *Philosophical Self-Portrait.*
[223] CID ALENCASTRO, "Organic Society and Revolutionary Society," *Catolicismo*, No. 733 (January 2012), pp. 12-17.
[224] *Catolicismo*, November 1951.
[225] JOHN HORVAT II, *Return to Order. From a Frenzied Economy to an Organic Christian Society*, American TFP, Hanover (Penn.), 2013, p. 142.

Medieval Christian civilization conveyed the image of a hierarchical and diversified society, a reflection of the metaphysical order of the universe.[226] The whole medieval society harmoniously conformed to the natural order placed by God in creating the universe and to the supernatural order inaugurated with the Redemption and inspired by the Church. This was the great civilization that slowly but vigorously emerged from the disintegration of the barbarian age, under the influence of the natural and supernatural energies of baptized peoples oriented to Christ.

A sharp historian of institutions describes it thus: "In the ecclesiastical order, patriarchs, primates, archbishops and bishops, arch-priests, pastors and vicars, superiors of Orders, congregations and religious communities, university rectors, deans of faculties and colleges presidents exercise the power entrusted to them, by their respective constituencies or social bodies, without trespassing beyond their limits. The same is done in the civil order by kings, princes, every lord great and small, all the way to the least populated community and to the last guild of craftsmen. Finally, in the order of the family, in which the civil and religious come together as in the time of patriarchs, the *pater familias* is vested in a threefold authority: marital, paternal, and corporate. Every power of governance comes from above, not from below. It springs from a heavenly source and spreads in waterfalls not only among men but also among the angelic choirs and legions of the elect: *per ordines et gradus.*"[227]

The states and nations in the Middle Ages and the *Ancien Régime* were "organic societies" formed not by a set of individuals but by families and intermediate groups, placed between the simple individual and the state. The term "organic" derives from a comparison with living beings endowed with organs and functional parts which, while subjected to the influence of a single principle, enjoy nevertheless a distinctive character and relative autonomy. At least until the outbreak of the French Revolution, Christian Europe can be defined as a society formed by multiple intermediate groups or "orders," every one of which is

---

[226] On medieval Christendom, cf. among others EMILE LOUSSE, *Le Moyen Age,* Desclée de Brouwer, Paris, 1944; GONZAGUE DE REYNOLD, *La formation de l'Europe,* vol. VI, *Le toit chrétien,* Plon, Paris, 1957; RAFFAELLO MORGHEN, *Medioevo cristiano,* Laterza, Bari, 1962; GIORGIO FALCO, *La santa romana repubblica. Profilo storico del Medioevo,* Ricciardi, Milano-Napoli, 1968; RÉGINE PERNOUD, *Lumières du Moyen Age,* Grasset, Paris, 1981; FRANCESCO ELÍAS TEJADA, *Europa, tradizione, libertà. Saggi di filosofia della politica,* translation, introduction and preparation by G. Turco, Edizioni Scientifiche Italiane, Napoli, 2005; ALFRED SAENZ, S.J., *La Cristiandad y su cosmovisión,* Gladius, Buenos Aires, 2007; JOSÉ PEDRO GALVÃO DE SOUSA, *La rappresentanza politica,* translation, introduction and preparation by G. Turco, Edizioni Scientifiche Italiane, Napoli, 2009.

[227] E. LOUSSE, *Le Moyen Age,* pp. 15-16.

characterized by exemptions, different rights and privileges, but always within the framework of a unified and organic conception of the world.

The organization of pre-revolutionary society was based on matching functions and rights, services and privileges. The status of every person was adapted to the role he played in society. Society, writes Emile Lousse, "rises like a harmony of unequal relationships established between the various levels, and in each level, between leaders and subordinates."[228]

According to Roland Mousnier,

> "the monarchical state crowns the state of orders and bodies or 'states' such as the clergy, nobility, cities, free peasants; bodies, that is to say, trade guilds, chambers of commerce, officer corps, judges and ministerial officers, universities, colleges of various kinds; territorial communities forming bodies such as fiefdoms, privileged cities, provinces, parishes. The monarch reigns over these subjects and uses but does not destroy them. On the contrary, he protects and develops them, procuring them wealth and prosperity."[229]

> Plinio observes, "Since the social fabric is an extensive network of individuals, families, and intermediate bodies, we may conclude that, from a certain viewpoint, it is also an ensemble of diverse hierarchies that coexist, collaborate, and intertwine. Above them hovers, in the temporal sphere, the majesty of the perfect society, the State; and in the spiritual sphere (the highest), the majesty of the other perfect society, the Church."[230]

The structure of this society presents itself as non-egalitarian but broadly participatory: "In it, class, influence, prestige, wealth and power are participated, from top to bottom in different ways according to each degree, by bodies with their own peculiarities. In this way, at one time you could say that even in the most modest home, the father was the king of his children; and at the summit, the king was the father of fathers."[231]

Church and Christendom as the *unum* of the Created Universe

The reflection on Christendom is not limited to relations between Church and State but extends to the issue of relations between the Church and society in all their aspects; and it requires delving deeper into the relationships between nature and grace, and between the natural order and

---

[228] Idem, pp. 26-27.
[229] ROLAND MOUSNIER, *Monarchies et royautés*, Librairie Académique Perrin, Paris, 1989, p. 202.
[230] *Nobility and Analogous Traditional Elites, http://www.tfp.org/tfp-home/books/nobility.html.*
[231] Idem, p. 103.

the supernatural order. One cannot conceive Christendom outside its supernatural life, nor can one conceive a supernatural order deprived of its natural base.

Christendom is born from the action of the Church in the temporal order. The Church inspires not only the realization of an order internal to man but also of an external order in the temporal sphere. In this sense, the Church is the Mystical Body of Christ, and Christendom is the mirror of Christ's physiognomy just as a creature is a mirror of the Creator and a work of art is the mirror of the artist.[232] Plinio points out how

> "There is an analogy between Christendom and the soul: a single mortal sin kills a soul; a single serious defect strips Christendom from its title of Christendom."[233] "We have seen the Church require from the Mystical Body the realization of: a) an internal order in man; b) an order external to man, in the temporal sphere."[234]

Relations between temporal order and religious order, between Church and State, and more broadly between the Church and Christendom are to be understood within God's grand design upon the created universe. In what sense, although distinct, do they form an *unum*?

> "They form an *unum* simply in this: God created the whole universe and did not intend for it to become useless when the Church was founded. Rather, He created the whole universe to serve as a pedestal for the Church. He destined human society to be a beautiful stone, a beautiful wall on which the Church's torch could cast its lights. Neither did He intend to render human society useless when He created the Church. Obviously, when creating human society He did not want men to say, "it is so beautiful that I don't need the Church."[235]

> "Since man is a being of the natural order and it is through God's concession that he is penetrated by His grace – a created participation in supernatural life – he is an *unum* containing both natural and supernatural. He has his natural life and also something created which participates in the divine life. By his own *unum,* man essentially has, therefore, the need to consider supernatural things in order to see their manifestations and reflections in natural things; and to see how natural things are manifested and reflected in supernatural things. He needs to see both things in order to see a whole.

> "For this reason, the Church can only be seen in all her beauty within Christendom. In a family of Roman Catholic and Apostolic nations where everything is Catholic, from the shape of a key to the city's gates to

---

[232] General outline of the book *Christendom*, p. 6.
[233] Meeting, 21 January 1989.
[234] Idem.
[235] RRR, 22 November 1980.

the design of a rooster atop a steeple's tower with a poise that shows its Catholicism, man places that Catholic note in everything. The Church is in the midst of Christendom like a housewife in the middle of her family and belongings. She is a queen full of suavity, sweetness, majesty, which explains all the rest and shines in the eyes of her children.

"So, too, the Church in a secular nation gives somewhat of an impression of a soul without a body. Conversely, a very well organized secular nation gives the impression of a body without a soul."[236] "When holiness encompasses the lay state and penetrates the secular order it manifests itself as more powerful, vigorous, ampler and more complete because it is able to assimilate unto itself an order which, after original sin, has something adverse to the sacred order."[237]

The loss of sacrality, which corresponds to a separation between the spiritual and the temporal order, liquidates the Catholic spirit:

"Either the Catholic spirit is made of this ineffable *unum* or it is not Catholic, and overall we doubt it is a spirit. Deep down, every relationship has something ineffable that forms something unique in its own way. That happens all the more so with these two related pyramids, the Church and the State."[238]

"The temporal society is not supreme. The Church has a sacrality that the State does not. But considered as a 'State of Christians,' whose members are all Christian (and by that I understand Catholics and therefore members of the Mystical Body of Christ), that State is made up by people for whom it is normal to live the life of grace. And the whole mechanism of human society and of the Christian State is to the pagan State as holy water is to regular water.

"As such, a kind of blessing hovers upon Christendom, that is, over the temporal order conceived as consisting of Catholics and living the Catholic way. It is not the Mystical Body of Christ but somehow touches on the Mystical Body of Christ, not from the outside in, but is a penetration by the Mystical Body of Christ in that society, in that State, which makes the ensemble of nations called Christendom have something sacral about it.

"And when one says that Christendom gathered as a whole, for example, to crush Communism, it is the States that gathered. They did so in a secular coalition steeped in the supernatural, which makes this temporal society, which is Christendom, touch on the sacral. And as such it completely transcends the common State.

---

[236] RRR, 22 November 1980.
[237] *Sacrality* (MNF 1985-1995).
[238] Idem.

"Now, one can say that since temporal society is sovereign in its own sphere and has the supreme power, everything that is supreme in a natural way tangentially relates to God. And that which is supreme in a society steeped in grace, not only tangentially relates but actually touches on God, becomes blessed like holy water.

"Whence the blessed character of monarchs in Christendom, more so of the Holy Roman Emperor than any other, as he is the head of that ensemble and the *unum* is worth more than the parts. But then also kings and others vested in authority, among whom I would not hesitate to place the Doge of Venice or the heads of the bourgeois republics – the free cities – just as long as they had a truly supreme power and did not live under a kind of suzerainty of other powers. Consequently, one would not understand for them in the Reign of Mary not being installed with a certain anointing. The coronation of the King of France really was a consecration. But this consecration gave the fullness of sacrality to something which, from other standpoints, already had that sacrality, which is the king of the Most Christian Kingdom of the Franks."[239]

The Monarchic Principle in the Universe

Love of the monarchic and hierarchical principle that governs the universe is the decisive trait of Plinian apologetics.

"More than fidelity to a dynasty or a longing for the past (which is also a good thing, as a longing for the past can be very respectable), monarchy is a doctrine that calls into view a principle. And this principle, which is a corollary of the aristocratic principle, is not merely a political principle but a principle of the universal order. It is a metaphysical and religious principle."[240]

"It is the principle that the ideal order for the universe is the monarchical and aristocratic order. This is a metaphysical principle and should not be seen as a merely political principle. It has political repercussions in the sense that whenever possible one should have a monarchy, but it does not mean that one should be necessarily a monarchist. This, in concrete, is another matter."[241]

"The monarchical principle states: whenever there are beings in any order such as in the mineral, botanical, animal, human, angelic order gathered together by natural affinity (i.e., because they are of the same type, the same genus, etc.) or by conventional affinity (men who always gather for certain things), or by an occasional affinity (i.e., something fortuitous), the tendency of those gathered beings is to fit in around a

---

[239] MNF, 26 April 1989.
[240] NOR, 31 January 1969.
[241] EVP, 4 March 1974.

principal being that places them in order, vitalizes their characteristics, and directs them to their end.

"Take, for example, an artistic ensemble or a choir. The choir is made up of people of unequal musical qualities; those with greater musical qualities support the mediocrity of others participating in the musicality of the choir.

"In every collection of anything there are greater and smaller. In this aggregation of greater and smaller, they all support one another, but the greater provide more support to the smaller than the smallest to the greater; and the same principle ends up by establishing the monarch.

"There is a principle of Saint Thomas that says: 'Similis simili gaudet,' the similar rejoices in its counterpart. This is to say that a similar being thrives in contact with its similar, is toned in contact with its similar.... The whole tendency of ultramontanes to meet one another and of revolutionaries to gather comes from this phenomenon. It is a search for support; it is the monarchical principle operating among them.

"This monarchical principle then combines with the aristocratic principle. Why? Because for the most part this monarchical 'distillation' or refinement is done in two degrees or more: a group 'distills' a monarch who is monarch only of that group but does not cover the whole genre. And those monarchs, in that they are like small spheres... encompassed by a larger sphere, distill another monarch, who distills another monarch, etc. Anyway, this process goes all the way to distill the monarch of the most comprehensive sphere. And the natural pinnacle of aristocracy is the monarchy. On the other hand, the natural base of the monarchy is the aristocracy; these are the small monarchs on whom the great monarchy rests."[242]

Plinio Corrêa de Oliveira loved monarchy as an expression of the unitary principle of the universe; and the point where he could more clearly see the analogy between Christendom and the Church was precisely the reversibility between the Church and monarchy. This gave rise to his expression, "Catholic, hence monarchist, monarchist, hence Catholic."[243]

"It is a matter of form of government and religion. In other words, it is a reversibility of values whereby once something is stated in the temporal sphere it has its counterpart in the spiritual sphere and vice versa. This presupposes that the two spheres be parallel and, in a sense – not in every sense, but in general – contain reversibility, a reversible complementarity." [244]

---

[242] BCM, 11 June 1966.
[243] EVP, 5 December 1994.
[244] ALM, 9 January 1994.

The temporal and spiritual orders are distinct, but not separate. The relationship between the two spheres is not only one of generic cooperation, but analogy. Each of the spheres influences the other in its own way, perfecting or deforming it. It is the principle that you cannot understand the spiritual order without considering the temporal order and vice versa.

"The temporal order can only be built and well understood when it is fully imbibed with the sacrality of the spiritual order. Hence both have sacrality; sacrality is the same in both but in different degrees and ways of being.

"The fact that this sacred order exists in the spiritual and temporal spheres with this reversibility explains the 'Catholic hence monarchist, monarchist, hence Catholic.' In other words, the Church attains her perfection while shaping a temporal society."[245]

"There is in the Church the hierarchical organization that you know. To this hierarchical organization corresponds a certain state of mind, which is the hierarchical spirit proper to the Church, and which today is hidden, denied, trampled under foot. And that made the Church have all that pomp, majesty, seriousness, that ability to teach, condemn, punish, canonize, corresponding to a number of other attributes belonging to the one that has the key to the kingdom of heaven. He who opens it on earth opens it in heaven; he who closes it on earth closes it in heaven. This is the spirit of the Church."

"This nourishes and thrills the person with a Catholic mentality, he who accentuates these features in a balanced fashion and as much as he can, leading other Catholics to observe and love this.

"Now monarchy, which has an organization analogous to this one, produces precisely an order which, applied to the temporal sphere, is similar to that of the Church and generates a state of mind similar to the Church's. In the final analysis it reflects in the temporal order everything that is proper, but not exclusive, to the spiritual order.

"There is therefore a very great analogy and similarity between the Church and the State. Being a monarchist, hence a Catholic, and a Catholic, hence monarchist, means possessing that common trait or that whole gamut of spiritual traits common to a Catholic and a monarchist, and that make a Catholic individual to tend to be a monarchist, and a monarchist to tend to be a Catholic. The Church is symbolized by the Catholic State, and to a lesser degree one can also say that the Catholic State symbolizes the Church."[246]

---

[245] EVP, 5 December 1993.
[246] EVP, 28 November 1993.

CHAPTER III

EGALITARIAN ANTI-METAPHYSICS

The Premises of Chaos

Denial of the Christian concept of the universe inexorably leads to chaos. Chaos is the moral and social disintegration of a world that rejects the metaphysical order of the created universe:

> "If there is a common denominator unfolding today in the private and public life of many nations, one can say that it is chaos. Chaotic prospects seem to repeat themselves and we increasingly tread the paths of chaos, no one knows how far."[247]

Since the 1930's, Plinio saw chaos as the logical outcome of an anti-Christian society.[248] Philosophically, the Plinian concept of chaos is no different from that of Saint Thomas Aquinas, although he expounds on all its social and political consequences.

Chaos is not a positive but a negative reality; and it always presupposes an order in which it can spread, like an illness that needs the human body to grow but ceases with the patient's death. Like evil, disorder "is not a part of the universe," says Saint Thomas Aquinas, precisely because "its nature is neither substance nor accident but only deprivation."[249] Therefore, chaos does not exist by itself but only as deprivation in the being that it invaded. "In fact," Saint Thomas explains, "that which is completely devoid of good is not a being, nor is it among beings."[250]

Plinio expounds this topic thus:

---

[247] TFP Press Service, 12 April 1993.
[248] Cf. for example "Adveniat Regnum tuum," *Legionário,* no. 328, December 25, 1938: "If the contemporary world is to leave the chaos in which it finds itself it must first of all turn to the Church."
[249] ST. THOMAS AQUINAS, *In II Sent.*, d. 46, q. 1, a. 3.
[250] ID., *In II Sent.*, d. 46, q. 1, a. 3.

"Everything that exists has a being; and it is proper for the being with its predicates to develop and react in a certain way. So there is a basic rule for everything that exists, even to chaos. One could ask whether this is not a play on words, for the existence of chaos is not the existence of what exists; chaos is rather non-existence; it is disorder and hence a relationship that is a non-relationship; it is an order that is a lack of order and therefore one cannot speak of rules for chaos. On the other hand, it is true that once a state of chaos is verified to exist in a place, procedures specific to the state of non-chaos do not apply to the state of chaos. In one way or another, this is something like a rule. Hence it follows that in the manner of a rule or ordering principle, even chaos has its ordering principle: disorder and all that is deduced from disorder."[251]

So what are the "rules," or rather premises of chaos? They are all the consequences that derive from two active factors: from non-being (deprivation), and from negation of being.

"Chaos is non-being. Now, this non-being is incapable of peaceful coexistence with being; it has incompatibilities with that which *is*. It is a kind of *inimicitias ponam* whereby *being* cannot exist where chaos is installed. It thus has certain destructive properties that cannot fail to destroy. It is like a corrosive agent that is not a non-being but turns a being into a non-being, or like a drug that produces inertia and inaction. In this sense they are a bit like chaos.

"So from this you could draw something similar to a rule. The fundamental rule of non-being – of which it is proper to have no rule, and we need to see clearly the contradiction within it – is that it acts in the sense that nothing might be. And it acts intolerantly. It is totally destructive." [252]

Despite its destructive nature, chaos is not the same as nothingness:

"It is wholly negative, but it is not nothingness. What is the difference between chaos and nothingness? Nothingness somehow exists. Let us say there are bodies that make up the outer universe. The space they occupy is not infinite, nor are they infinite. They exist, so to speak, wrapped in nothingness. What is that nothingness in which they are wrapped? It is not a substance, for otherwise it would not be nothingness. What is it, then? It is non-being. Non-being is non-being. But there is some point in the world of being in which the boundary between being and non-being is felt. On that point, being meets non-being, and then the non-being is not. At a certain point the order of being, which is not infinite, ceases."[253]

---

[251] MNF, 18 March 1992.
[252] Idem.
[253] Idem.

The act of being of created things is limited by nothingness, which is the privation of being of all that is created. In an absolute way, God alone *is*.

Gnosis: Quintessence of All Heresies

Chaos is not spontaneous but the application to reality of an unnatural conception of the world. To the metaphysical view of Catholic Tradition is opposed a counter-metaphysics that our author identifies with Gnosis.[254]

Gnosis is a form of initiatory knowledge antithetical to Catholic knowledge, which, with changing versions, has gone through two thousand years of history, from antiquity to the present day.[255] In his *Ecclesiastical History*, Eusebius of Caesarea, the first Church historian, like the Fathers of the Church that preceded him, attributes the origin of Gnosticism to Simon the Magician, of whom the Acts of the Apostles says, "Simon was a magician in that city and seduced the people of Samaria by saying he was someone great. And everyone, from the least to the greatest, lent him an ear, saying: This man is the power of God, which is called great" (8:9-25).

He was succeeded by Menander, who "gave rise to a new force like a forked snake with two heads from which sprang the leaders of two different heresies: Saturnine of Antioch and Basilides of Alexandria, who founded heretical schools inimical to God, the former in Syria, the latter

---

[254] For an introduction to the topic starting from the sources, cf. KURT RUDOLPH, *Die Gnosis - Wesen und Geschichte einer spätantiken Religion*, Vandenhoeck & Ruprecht, Göttingen data; SIMONE PÉTREMENT, *Le Dualisme chez Platon. Les gnostiques et les manichéens*, Presses Universitaires de France, Paris, 1947; ID., *Le dieu separé. Les origines du Gnosticisme*, Cerf, Paris, 1984; GILLES QUISPEL, *Gnosis als Weltreligion*, Origo, Zürich, 1951; ROBERT M. GRANT, *La gnose et les origines chrétiennes*, Fr. tr., Editions du Seuil, Paris, 1964 (1959); HANS JONAS, *The Gnostic Religion: the Message of the Alien God and the Beginning of Christianity*, Beacon Press, Boston, 1958; BORIS MOURAVIEFF, *Gnosis*, 3 vols., La Colombe, Paris, 1961-1985; KARLMANN BEYSCHLAG, *Simon Magus und die christliche Gnosis*, Mohr, Tuebingen, 1974; HENRI-CHARLES PUECH, *Sulle tracce della Gnosi*, Adelphi, Milano, 1985; ANTONIO ORBE, S.J., *Introducción a la teología de los siglos II y III*, 2 vols., Università Gregoriana, Roma, 1987; JACQUES LACARRIÈRE, *Les gnostiques*. (nouvelle edition révue et modifiée), Editions Metailie, Paris, 1991; GIOVANNI FILORAMO, *L'attesa della fine. Storia della gnosi*, Laterza, Roma-Bari, 1987; JULIEN RIES, *Gnostici e manicheismo. Gli gnostici. Storia e dottrina*, It. tr., Jaca Book, Milano, 2010; Id., *Gnosticisme*, in DHGE, XXI (1986), cols. 264-281.

[255] The most important testimonies on Gnosis are found in ecclesiastical writers that often quote textual excerpts: Irenaeus (*Adversus haereses*); Hippolytus (*Refutatio omnium haeresium*); Tertullian (*Adversus Valentianes*); Clemens Alexandrinus (*Stromata*); Pseudo-Tertullian (*Adversus omnes haereses*); Philastrius (*De haeresibus*); Epiphanius (*Panarion*); Theodoretus (*Haeretic. Fabularum compendium*). The 1946 discovery near Nag Hammadi in Egypt of a Gnostic library in the Coptic language increased our knowledge of Gnosis.

in Egypt."[256] Basilides was particularly active in Alexandria during the years 117-161 and was master of Valentinus, who continued his work in the third century.

The fundamental principle common to all Gnostic sects is esotericism, the idea of a teaching reserved only for the initiated, said to have been preserved from antiquity and to have been betrayed by the Catholic Church.

Gnosis strongly influenced modern thought, especially through German romanticism and idealism, from Schelling to Hegel;[257] it is claimed by theosophy[258] and by the "traditionalism" of René Guénon;[259] it influences psychoanalysis, especially Carl Gustav Jung's "profound psychology,"[260] surrealism,[261] the "New Age" culture;[262] and it permeates Catholic modernism and progressivism in the twentieth century.[263] The relationships of modernism with Gnosticism and occultism are identified, among others, by Father Emmanuel Barbier and Father Gioachino Ambrosini, of the Society of Jesus.[264]

For some authors, like Eric Voegelin, Gnosticism is precisely the characteristic of modernity.[265] In his book interview, *Crossing the Threshold of Hope*, John Paul II mentions the danger of Gnosticism stating that this heresy "has never withdrawn from the camp of

---

[256] EUSEBIUS, *Ecclesiastical History*, IV, 7.

[257] AUGUSTE VIATTE *Les Sources occultes du romantisme*, Honoré Champion, Paris, 1979 (1927-1928), 2 vols.; ERNST BENZ, *Les sources mystiques de la philosophie romantique allemande*, Vrin, Paris, 1968; JACQUES D'HONDT, *Hegel secret; recherches sur les sources cachées de la pensée de Hegel*, PUF, Paris, 1968.

[258] Among modern neo-Gnostics we recall Helena Petrovna Blavatsky (1831-1891), foundress of the Theosophical Society, and Rudolph Steiner (1861-1925), founder of anthroposophy.

[259] On René Guénon (1886-1951), cf. DARIO SACCHI, "I fondamenti metafisici del neo-gnosticismo: René Guénon," in *Studi cattolici*, 445 (1998), pp. 181-185; Marie-Françoise James, *Esotérisme et Christianisme*, cit. passim.

[260] ROBERT SEGAL (prepared by), *The Gnostic Jung*, Princeton University Press, Princeton, 1982. G. ANTONELLI, *La profonda misura dell'anima. Relazioni di Jung con lo gnosticismo*, Liguori, Napoli, 1990.

[261] JACOB TAUBES, *Messianismo e cultura: saggi di politica, teologia e storia*, It. tr., Garzanti, Milano, 2001.

[262] On the New Age as a form of neo-Gnosis, cf. G. FILORAMO, *Antica e nuova gnosi: proposte per un confronto*, in Various Authors, *Ritorno della gnosi?* prepared by ILARIO TOLOMIO, Gregoriana Libreria Editrice, Padova, 2002, pp. 22-29.

[263] EMANUELE SAMEK LODOVICI, in *Metamorfosi della gnosi. Quadri della dissoluzione contemporanea*, Ares, Milano, 1979, brought out Gnostic aspects of the though of Hans Küng and Karl Rahner (pp. 56-102).

[264] Cf. ADELE CERRETA, *Le origini esoteriche del modernismo. Padre Gioacchino Ambrosini e la teologia modernista*, Solfanelli, Chieti, 2012. Father Ambrosini (1857-1923) illustrates well the analogies between the theses of the book *Il Santo* by Antonio Fogazzaro (1842-1911) and those expounded in works such as *The Key to Theosophy* by Blavatsky and *Christianity from the Theosophical Standpoint*, by Annie Besant.

[265] ERIC VOEGELIN, *La nuova scienza politica*, It. tr., Borla, Torino, 1999, pp. 141-167.

Christianity....in clear if not declared conflict with what is essentially Christian."[266]

A Gnostic, as the word itself says, does not "believe," he "knows." Gnosis is thus presented as "knowledge" or "science" of divine things. But Gnosis is also claimed to have intuitive or experimental knowledge of the divine. It is presented as a "knowledge technique" thanks to which man comes into possession of the key to the cosmic mystery and "recognizes" his own divine nature, canceling his individuality in the unconscious *All*.[267] In this respect, he is a "mystic" opposed to Christianity.

Kabbalah, theosophy, hermeticism, occultism are part of the same Gnostic counter-metaphysics studied by many authors, from Gershom Scholem[268] to Father Meinvielle.[269] Plinio Corrêa de Oliveira and his school have devoted years to studying Gnosis, especially in MNF meetings, finding it to be the heart of the anti-Christian Revolution and quintessence of all heresies.[270]

From the Egyptians to Plato

Discussions on the origins of Gnosis are reflected by disagreement on the use of the term Gnosis or Gnosticism, preferred by those who ignore Gnosis' pre-Christian roots and seek to reduce it to a mere "variant" of Christianity. Gnosis certainly was not contemporary or subsequent to Christianity, but preceded it and inspired a great number of pagan religions.

One should keep in mind that according to Catholic tradition God communicated an early Revelation to our forefathers, although we are unable to know the content of those first truths or how that communication took place.[271] That early revelation was adulterated and corrupted by the infidelity of peoples. Next to the red thread of Divine Revelation there developed a pseudo-revelation that distorted the early metaphysical truths, beginning with the notion of being. The Egyptians,

---

[266] GIOVANNI PAOLO II, *Varcare le soglie della speranza*, Mondadori, Milano, 1994, p. 99.

[267] For Gnostics, G. FILORAMO notes, "to know" means "to become that same reality that is known," "transforming oneself, through illumination, into the very object of knowledge, thus overcoming and canceling out the dichotomy between subject and object" (*L'attesa della fine. Storia della gnosi*, p. 67).

[268] GERSHOM SCHOLEM, *La cabala,* It. tr., Edizioni Mediterranee, Roma, 1982.

[269] JULIO MEINVIELLE, *De la Cabala al progressismo*, Edivi, Segni, 2013.

[270] RRR, 7 October 1973.

[271] "Common theological teaching accepts as certain the existence of an early Revelation in the beginning of mankind. And this teaching appears to be confirmed by findings of the comparative history of religions" (CARLO COLOMBO, EC, X [1953], col. 1021).

who had a memory of that revelation, altered its contents.[272] According to Prof. Plinio, Gnosis appears in history like a parasite that devours all remnants of the primordial truth.

> "When the Catholic Church spread throughout the Mediterranean basin, including North Africa, and became the world's greatest spiritual empire, Gnosis emerged incubated in the Church as a hidden heresy of people that held that Catholic doctrine had two interpretations: one of the enlightened, the perfect, etc., and another for fools, individuals who do not understand the arcane secret of things; and those are we ourselves, who believe in the Catholic Faith and in the Creed according to the terms the Catholic Church teaches."[273]

According to the interpretation of the Church Fathers, Greek philosophy was born and developed through the influence of divine grace, which paved the way for Christianity.[274] However, from a certain standpoint Plato can be considered the father of Gnosis because he made explicit some aspects of its thought. He sought to transform the Gnosis transmitted by the Egyptians into a new metaphysical system by stating that visible things are not the primary reality but refer to a perfect and absolute reality, a first being founded on itself. This is an aspect that philosophers such as Cornelia de Vogel[275] have brought to light and which Prof. Plinio also emphasizes.

> "Led by the grace proper to the Greeks, Plato sought to make a metaphysics from that wisdom that he received – but metaphysics understood in the obscure sense of the word adopted by the Egyptians, meaning something different from metaphysics. The word metaphysics has two meanings. One is metaphysics considered as a function of the notion of being, starting from the physical being as it presents itself. And the other is monistic, finding that there is nothing but physical reality (and a pseudo-spiritual reality which is nothing but the physical reality of spirits and which is the same matter in another dimension or state).

---

[272] Egyptologist EMIL AM LINEAU (1850-1915) emphasized the influence of Egyptian doctrines such as divine emanation and solar theology on the early Gnostics (cf. *Essai sur le gnosticisme, ses développements et son origine égyptienne*, Leroux, Paris, 1887; cf. also Jean Doresse, *Les livres secrets des gnostiques d'Egypte*, Plon, Paris, 1958).

[273] RRR, 11 April 1987.

[274] In his speech in Regensburg on September 12, 2006, Benedict XVI denounced the process of de-Hellenization of contemporary culture, described its historical origins, and stated that "the encounter between the Bible's message and Greek thought" was not by chance but turned out to be a decisive encounter between faith and reason." *Insegnamenti*, II (2006), pp. 257-267.

[275] Cf. CORNELIA DE VOGEL, *Platonismo e Cristianesimo. Antagonismo o commi fondamentali?* prepared by Giovanni Reale and Enrico Peroli, It. tr., Vita e Pensiero, Milano, 1993, p. 103.

Something else altogether is the true metaphysics, which goes beyond the physical and affirms the absolutely spiritual being."[276]

Thus, in Plato there are two aspects: a tendency towards authentic metaphysics, which Aristotle and Saint Thomas later developed, but also a Gnostic dimension that spoils his thought. According to Plinio, in Plato one finds the contradiction of a personality that contributed to overcoming Gnosis but remained its prisoner.

> "It is no longer the contradiction inherent to Gnosis but the contradiction of an individual that at the same time is no longer Gnostic but still is, and who does not realize the phenomenon happening within him. Add to this his need to cheat, as he confessed, in order not to be persecuted as Socrates was, which led him to cloak his thinking even further, and it becomes hard to figure out what he saw in all this."[277]

> "But that does preclude our saying that he felt a need to expose it as a system, and this indicates a phobia of incoherence, a need to build a series of coherent truths around him, and a thought-out system of the universe. There is in this a root of grace and a desire to know the total being, to have an explanation that excludes error, and a notion of the struggle of coherence against incoherence, a kind of fundamental notion of error and truth implicit within the system. As such, at the same time that he tried to explain Gnosis and systematize it, he revealed a state of mind that deep down was anti-Gnostic, in which underlies Aristotle and all that followed him."[278]

Pantheism and Emanationism

Emanationism is a doctrine common to all Gnostic sects.[279] The Catholic Faith teaches us that God is pure spirit, pure act. Gnostics introduce into the notion of God concepts of potency and act which, according to the Aristotelian-Thomistic philosophy, do not characterize God but rather every being that He created. Potency in fact is a limit, and God is unlimited and eternal. But according to Gnostics, in the divine whole which would only be a god in potency, defined by them as "pleroma,"[280] there was a tearing up which by emanation caused all the realities that compose the universe. The dilacerations of the pleroma gave

---

[276] MNF, 4 March 1965.

[277] MNF, 4 March 1965.

[278] Idem.

[279] Cf. GIUSEPPE FAGGIN, *Emanatismo,* EF (1979), cols. 49-52.

[280] According to Valentinian Gnosis, the term "pleroma," from the Greek "fullness," indicates the inclusion in the divine fullness of the totality of its emanations (cf. CLEMENTE ALESSANDRINO, *Stromata*, IV, 13; I, *Refutatio omnium haeresium*, VI, 29).

rise to a kind of hemorrhage of divine particles that are to it like drops of water to the ocean.[281]

This emanation is a universal process, a perpetual "becoming" of God in the world and in man. The first principle, the Abyss, is an indeterminate essence that is specified in a multiplicity of beings and things. In this process, the tearing up of the primordial monism leads to a dualist system in which two deities, one good and one bad, relentlessly fight each other.

Prof. Plinio explains that according to Catholic doctrine, creatures are not divine particles, for God is absolutely transcendent and entirely distinct from creatures:

> "God is transcendent, that is, entirely distinct from creatures, in relation to which He has infinite, absolute and eternal superiority. He created the angels and later the entire visible universe, drawing each creature from nothing. Nothing existed before, each creature began to exist because He willed it."

> "This conception of the origin of the universe involves a conception of the nature of the universe, which is not divine. It is created and therefore transient, owing all its life to God, Who created it for His own glory so that its existence should be reputed as a good because it gives glory to God; and therefore the creation of a universe distinct from God, different from the transcendent God, it is a good as such and should make us rejoice."[282]

The central idea of Gnosis is that every man contains a divine spark or membrane that he should free from the darkness of matter. Plinio amply explains it, showing all its fantasies and contradictions:

> "Every man has within himself a divine membrane that needs to be activated through mental exercise. This activated membrane gives man the possibility of being a little 'god,' with dominion over nature. When he dies, that membrane remains alive and reincorporates itself into the universe. He resurrects in the form of another being, incorporated into another being. His body dissolves, but that is a kind of eternal life. In this way man stays away from all religions and all moral laws."[283]

> "These Gnostic precepts affirm that two things are true: the first is that God does not exist, that is, he identifies with nature and is therefore impersonal and in a confused manner immanent not only in people but in all existing beings. The second is that this 'god' is sparse and scattered in all existing beings, and he is not a being distinct from others; nor are human beings distinct from each other as they imagine, they have no

---

[281] RRR, 6 August 1988.
[282] Ibid.
[283] RRR, 5 August 1974.

individuality completely defined and distinct from the individuality of others.

"According to Gnostics, since the great individuality par excellence that is God does not exist, small individualities likewise do not exist, they have no reason for being. We deceive ourselves thinking that we have our own individuality. We are nothing but an achievement, a drop of this immense substance, this immense divine fluid present in all things. We have the illusion that we are detached persons made in the image and likeness of a personal God we assume to be personal, detached, different from us and transcendent in relation to us.

"According to gnosis, we have the illusion of being different persons, but this illusion is a lie which is the great evil of humanity. The whole of mankind forms nothing but one whole, only one immense person that, in relation to the lower layers of humanity, inferior to nature, is only an overdeveloped part of the universe in which intelligence was condensed. We are able to think and to want; in us intelligence condensed and our will was defined.

"For Gnostics, other beings have neither intelligence nor will but are moving in that direction. So much so that animals have attained this to a certain point, plants to a lesser degree, while inanimate objects have nothing. But things will get there through the course of evolution, and there will be a time when men will understand they are but only one being. Perhaps animals might then ascend to the condition of men, that is, begin to think and to imagine they are distinct beings and so on. But deep down these are illusions. The great reality is that there is only one 'god,' immanent and scattered through all things, and not a personal God. Therefore, as a person, God does not exist. We are the underdeveloped part of that impersonal 'god,' and behind us is a wake of other underdeveloped parts.

"This 'god' unaware of itself because he is present in all things is the tip of this whole ensemble that is the cosmos, of which we are a more developed part while others are successively less developed. This would be the Gnostic doctrine."[284]

Gnostic Egalitarianism

Plinio Corrêa de Oliveira then goes on to develop a point that no scholar has highlighted: the egalitarianism that Gnosis opposes to the articulated and hierarchical vision of Catholic metaphysics.

There is a clear reversibility between pantheism and egalitarianism. On the metaphysical plane, the negation of all inequality leads to the primacy of non-diversity and therefore to a rejection of the principles of

---

[284] RR 5 October 1974.

identity and non-contradiction. The end result is "egalitarian" pantheism, for if the real does not have specific inequalities and identities, the difference between men and God also crumbles and everything is confusingly deified. On the other hand, pantheism denies divine transcendence and thus necessarily denies any form of superiority and hierarchy even among creatures, blending everything in a nebulous and indistinct magma. Plinio says:

> "The world of pantheism is fundamentally egalitarian, while Catholic Civilization is fundamentally anti-egalitarian. The reason for this discrepancy is found in the very essence and conception of God that both civilizations uphold as their foundation."[285]

In this pantheism is found the Gnostic aspect of the Revolution.

> "Saint Thomas teaches that the diversity of creatures and their hierarchical arrangement is a good in itself for in this way creation reflects better the perfections of the Creator.[286] He also says that Providence established inequality both among angels and men,[287] in the earthly paradise, and in this land of exile.[288] Hence a universe with equal creatures would be a world in which the resemblance between creatures and Creator would have been canceled to the greatest possible extent. Therefore, to hate any and all inequality in principle is tantamount to metaphysically placing oneself against the best elements or resemblance between the Creator and creation; it is to hate God."[289]

God had no need of creatures and was not obligated to create. He created the world out of love, generosity, goodness. But on creating the world He could only create multiple and unequal creatures.

> "This is founded on His nature. His nature is such that a single creature could not sufficiently represent Him. He can only create beings to His likeness and not otherwise. But no creature as such is able to sufficiently resemble God. God creates multiple creatures so that, in conjunction with one another, He forms a mosaic which reflects an image that each little pebble would be unable to form of itself."[290]

Hatred of Determination

The hatred of all things specific, particular, defined, is characteristic of Gnosis. Gnosis affirms the indetermination of all things:

---

[285] RRR, 17 October 1981.
[286] Cf. *Summa Contra Gentiles*, II, 45; *Summa Theologica*, I, q. 47, a. 2.
[287] *Summa Theologica*, I, q. 50, a. 4.
[288] Idem, I, q. 96, a. 3 and 4.
[289] *Revolution and Counter-Revolution*, op. cit., pp. 101-102.
[290] RRR, 17 October 1981.

"Selfishness is not the '*summum*' of determination, but an affirmation of indeterminacy out of hatred for determination." [291]

Gnostics therefore reject all forms of ontological identity and essential individualization:

"They hate otherness, multiplicity, and the less perfect. One of the most characteristic traits of Gnosis is to hate the least perfect, and in the perfect, to hate the degrees of perfection. Gnostics deny that a perfection that has degrees is perfection, and are contented with nothing but absolute perfection." [292]

"Because of a seeming incompatibility between unity and variety, Gnostics deny that a being can have variety and still be one. The difference between the two doctrines derives from these two positions. Indeed, according to Catholic teaching, since variety in unity is possible, by definition a being is nothing but a variety that is united or a unity that is varied, and no beings exist otherwise. From this comes our formulation that a being is something that is; it is such and such a thing, it is a *unum* that is necessarily varied." [293]

Negation of unity in variety results in the deconstruction of the individual ontological identity as an objective datum. Gnostics abhor all that is finite, individualized, determined. For a Gnostic, the finite is evil, and the infinite is undetermined:

"Only by denying his own 'I' can [a person] return to the perfect unity of the pleroma, to cease being a part to become totality." [294]

Gnostic anthropology requires the destruction of the human body so that the soul can be absorbed and merged into the divine pneuma.

Gnosis denies analogy because analogy presupposes diversity, and the Gnostics want to nullify all that is multiple, diversified, and hierarchical:

"From the fact that Gnosis denies analogy and we affirm it, one understands all the rest: Gnosis abhors plurality, diversity, and the hierarchical. Gnosis abhors the nuanced and even logic, which, being a sequence of thought, continually works with the concept of analogy. It is impossible to think without the concept of analogy. For a Gnostic, logic already is an acceptance of analogy." [295]

---

[291] MNF, 19 May 1967.

[292] MNF, 12 December 1964.

[293] MNF, 11 April 1967.

[294] E. SAMEK LODOVICI, *Metamorfosi della gnosi*, p. 155.

[295] MNF, 13 April 1967.

While for traditional metaphysics God is pure act, a being by essence, distinct from creatures composed of act and potency, for Gnostics the primordial universe is potency in an abysmal state, devoid of act. Being determined, the act is an evil as such. Thus evil enters the universe through determination.

> "For Gnostics, the true universe, the initial abyss, is potency incapable of act; and the act or determination is an evil. At this point we need to know how a Gnostic composes his universe in a positive way. The answer would be this: For a Gnostic, rejecting the act is the same as rejecting absolute truth, for act is definition; it is what specifies and determines. That which is precise and determined has a fixed and absolute character, whereas what is imprecise and indeterminate has a relative character. In this dichotomy between act and potency, the act represents the absolute and potency represents the relative. A universe without act is a universe without the absolute, one that as relative can admit all kinds of relatives, in a world of appearances and of fickle and mutable things that become one another, none having real consistency, which is potency. It could even admit a relative that claimed that the absolute exists but only as long as that statement was seen as having a merely relative value. This is very important so one does not to fall into the folly of excluding any formulation from the absolute of the Gnostic universe, for this formulation also exists."[296]

The Gnostic system is apparently monistic, but at the base of Gnosticism there is dualism, that is, opposition between God and matter, between a good God and an evil anti-god.

> "Despite monistically affirming that there is only one universe, Gnosis is essentially dualistic. It is monistic in its own universe. Its universe is supposedly upright, straight, and relative; the universe of potency is monistic. But outside its universe there is an unexplained anti-factor that is evil. Curiously, this factor is absolutely evil. The only absolute that fits in with Gnosis is an evil absolute. And here there is no relative. This absolute evil is God Our Lord; and we know well that the 'relative' has two horns, a tail and a trident. This is obvious. But if you are asked whether Gnosticism is dualistic or monistic you should not answer either question in the affirmative. The answer depends on the standpoint from which you look at it: it is dualistic if you consider the total being (but for them, even being hardly means being); if you consider only the world of potency, it is monistic, it has that simplicity and seeming harmony."[297]

---

[296] MNF, 19 April 1967.
[297] MNF, 25 April 1967.

Furthermore, the Gnostics deny the principle of non-contradiction both as an ontological principle and as a logical principle. Their reasoning is therefore based on a contradictory postulate, but once this initial contradiction is admitted their cosmology develops evenly. From incoherent premises they develop a coherent doctrine. Gnosis could be called a "logical" system based on illogical premises.[298]

> "The Gnostic system is entirely illogical; it takes incongruous premises and from these incongruous premises it concludes with logic all the way to the end. This incongruity in the premises of Gnosis lies in the fact that every individual initially has an upright idea of being from which he cannot escape, and which comes from a certain sense he has. A Gnostic admits this idea concomitantly with a proposition contrary to this idea. From something originally incongruous he logically deduces a fully coherent system." [299]

Objective evidence is the ultimate criterion of all natural truth and certainty in the human mind.[300] But there are those who, affected by a sort of mental "inversion," seek to transform the absolute nature of evidence into a personal and relative option. Now, if we admit the possibility of denying evidence, the end result is what Prof. Plinio defines as "criteriological sin."

> "There is a flawed, erroneous movement of soul by which, placed before this evidence, man has a temperamental incompatibility that leads him to commit a sin of criteriological nature. This sin is always the affirmation that since these evidences are not structured and do not start from a syllogism they are essentially arbitrary. They are mere postulates that we can accept or reject as any other postulates."[301]

The "criteriological sin" consists in demanding proof of the evidence. But since by definition evidence needs no proof, the relativist rejects it saying that one can accept both what the evidence shows and its opposite.

> "This position, which deep down is the substance of rationalism – making everything result from proofs, including proof itself – results in a horrible lack of principles. From it the Gnostic deforms in himself something of a psychological character, which is the certainty of evidence. It is reality knocking on the soul and drawing from it that primeval reaction which is the 'is.' And it is a kind of feeling of certainty

---

[298] MNF, 1 & 3 May 1967.
[299] MNF, 3 May 1967.
[300] J.GREDT, OSB, *Elementa philosophiae aristotelico-thomisticae*, pp. 96-103.
[301] MNF, 7 July 1967.

independent from demonstration. But it is not gratuitous because it is in accordance with the first and natural functioning of the human soul. This is precisely what the Gnostic deforms by saying that it is arbitrary. And it is arbitrary because it is not based on a syllogism."[302]

In the final analysis, the criteriological sin is a radical and original distortion of metaphysics that arises from a likewise distorted way of seeing reality.

"The innermost secret of Gnosis is the affirmation of an order of being, or if you will, of a being in which all things contradictory meet and coexist. And coexist peacefully in such a way that there are no internal frictions or explosions even though it is contradictory. The human mind is unable to fathom how this might be."[303]

The "Mystical Experience" of a Universe in Perpetual Conflict

In Gnosis, logical contradiction is overcome by what could be called a (pseudo) "mystical experience." This experience supposedly shows us that the things that exist or "live" are in perpetual conflict. Gnosis accepts all the elements that constitute the order of the universe according to the perennial philosophy but claims they are in contradiction with one another.

"And this conflict is one between the logical order and the ontological order; the conflict of true causes among themselves, the conflict between cause and effect, substance and accident, act and potency. All these things that constitute the order of the universe are conflicting with one another. And these various conflicts result from contradictions, for the act is not a complementary element of potency, but an enemy of potency; for causes do not combine to produce cooperation, but to produce hatred. Effects hate their cause, as the cause hates its effects, because there is contradiction. Hate is the experience of contradiction. And all these contradictions together produce disgust, nausea. And this nausea and disgust make you try to escape from contradiction to a highest and most refined contradiction in which the same problem is posed in more 'refined' terms. This is true both in the logical order and in the ontological order. And just as in a discussion a problem can be posed in an increasingly refined way, so also the conflict of ontological contradiction gradually refines beings. This tragic state of weeping and conflict is what makes the universe advance. This conflict exists in the specifically metaphysical plane." [304]

---

[302] Idem.
[303] MNF, 19 May 1967.
[304] MNF, 25 August 1967.

This conflict is repeated on the plane of actually existing beings that, as such, are bearers of contradiction. For Gnostics the cosmos is an immense conflict and incessantly evolves through this conflict.

> "If everything is relative and continuously evolving, there is a relative order which opposes an absolute order out of dialectical necessity. And since they claim there is an order of non-transcendent beings, a non-transcendent order, there has to be *aliunde* something that is transcendent and conflicts with that non-transcendent order....They admit that there is an absolute which, without ceasing to be absolute in the proper sense of the word, is coupled to a relative more categorically relative, in such a way that the absolute invades the relative and vice-versa. And there is a struggle between the absolute and the relative, which is not the struggle of various relatives among themselves but a bigger struggle between the whole relative order against what they would call the absolute order. Analyzed by a Thomist philosopher this position would be nothing but the shallowest relativism. For an absolute that consents to be coupled to a relative does not deserve to be called absolute. It is not an absolute but a contradictory statement by a relative absolute that would ultimately turn out to be something relative."[305]

Gnostic Evolutionism, from Darwin to Teilhard de Chardin and Others

Strictly speaking, the term evolutionism indicates a scientific-philosophical theory attributed to Charles Darwin who in his most famous work, *The Origin of Species*,[306] saw natural selection as the main driver of the evolution of life on Earth. In a broader sense, evolutionism is a cosmological vision that applies the theory of evolution not only to man and all living species but also to the entire universe. The scientific theory presents as a "fact" the birth and transformation of the universe from primordial matter to increasingly complex structures all the way to human life. This philosophical theory purports to explain the reality of the universe as matter in perpetual transformation. It is actually a cosmogony, or basically a theogony: a fanciful narration of an imagined past to justify a radical aversion to the metaphysical principles of transcendence, causality, and order.

Indeed, evolutionism dissolves the hierarchical nature of reality, the distinction between living species, and finally the very idea of Creation,

---

[305] MNF, 25 August 1967.
[306] CHARLES DARWIN, *The Origin of the Species*, London, 1859; *L'origine delle specie o la preservazione delle razze prilegiate nella lotta per la vita*, It. tr., Newton Compton, Milan, 2008.

leading to a confused and egalitarian pantheism.[307] Matter is said to be imbued with the divine, nay, to be divinity's way of being. Man is said to be the self-consciousness of the universe and scientists are regarded as the wizards that can awaken it. In evolutionist mythology the passage from Darwin to Father Teilhard de Chardin[308] is significant. In his cosmic evolutionism, Teilhard reverses the Gnostic theory of descent from spirit to matter by emanation, imagining instead an ascent through evolution from matter to spirit, which he defines as "the superior state of matter."[309] The dogma of the existence of a transcendent, personal and creator God is sacrificed on the altar of this cosmic evolution of which Christ would be the "omega point."

Plinio Corrêa de Oliveira delves deeply into the relationship between the Gnostic philosophy and Teilhard's evolutionary theogony, distinguishing three different gamuts of evolutionism.

"In the first gamut, the Darwinian one, it is nothing but a kind of naturalistic theogony without God, a theogony of nature that could be expressed thus: in the beginning was the minuscule, and the minuscule contained within itself all possibilities of differentiation. With that it gradually became differentiated from the simplest to the more complex and specialized [state]. And this is evolution. The only merit of this Darwinian fable is to draw attention to the fact that the universal process starts from a certain point and reaches an X point.

"In reality, this is inserted into another evolutionism which is a denial of the Darwinian one and pretends not to realize that the Darwinian one exists: At first there was a series of determined beings, and evolution is the march of all those beings toward indetermination and homogenization. And the end of evolution is to reach an omega point where all things, so to speak, are transformed into man and deified. This is the evolutionism of Teilhard de Chardin. We see that it is a march opposed to Darwin's.

---

[307] For a critical analysis, cf. *Evoluzionismo: il tramonto di una ipotesi*, prepared by R. DE MATTEI, Cantagalli, Siena, 2009. Cf. also Msgr. PIER CARLO LANDUCCI, *La verità sull'evoluzione e l'origine dell'uomo*, La Roccia, Roma,1984, 3rd ed.; DANIEL RAFFARD DE BRIENNE, *Pour en finir avec l'évolution*, Perrin & Perrin, Paris, 1999; DOMINIQUE TASSOT, *L'évolution. Une difficulté pour la science, un danger pour la foi*, Téqui, Paris, 2009.

[308] Pierre Teilhard de Chardin (1881-1955), French Jesuit ordained in 1911, was repeatedly censured by the Holy See for his heterodox theses. Cf. ROSINO GIBELLINI, *Teilhard de Chardin. L'opera e le interpretazioni*, Queriniana, Brescia, 1981, with a bibliography. On Teilhardian Gnosticism, cf. ALAIN TILLOY, *Le Père Teilhard de Chardin, Père de l'Eglise ou pseudo-prophète?* Ed. Saint-Michel, Paris, 1968; J. MEINVIELLE, *De la Cabala al progressismo*, pp. 433-442; MGR A. COMBES, *Teilhardogénèse, Epemerides carmeliticae*, 14 (1964), pp. 155-194.

[309] PIERRE TEILHARD DE CHARDIN, *Le Coeur de la Matière*, Ed. du Seuil, Paris, 1976, p. 45.

"A third gamut is this: When studying the second type of evolutionism we realize that deep down it fights against an opposing factor that it gradually overcomes, which is the individualization factor. So we should ask how that pluralization started. Here enters the theogonic fact, the claim that an unknowable opposing principle intervened at a certain point and initiated this march toward homogenization. Perhaps these principles could be joined in the same conception. Darwin would narrate the action of the 'bad act' element act as having hurt that initial simplicity and moved toward differentiation. And Teilhard de Chardin would explain redemption thus: how to return from the plural element to the lost initial unity.

"Darwin would be the first step and Teilhard de Chardin would actually be the second. And unbridled occultism would be a third gamut, beyond Teilhard de Chardin. God, whom the devil described as an 'evil act' element, is the one that made that mistake. Otherwise, how can a follower of Teilhard's, who marches toward unity, consider Darwin's views, seeing that Darwin's explanation goes from unity to plurality? He cannot help but feel that Darwin has described decadence. And things are perfectly enmeshed; it is a perfectly intelligible whole. This is why the followers of the Teilhardian way say they consider Darwin superseded. They do not polemicize with Darwin because it is the first degree of initiation, overcome by the second. These are not contradictory initiations but explain successive layers of reality." [310]

Teilhard opposes to the historical Christ of the Gospel a cosmic Christ that identifies with the evolution of the universe.[311] He speaks of an "elevation of the historical Christ to a universal physical function" and of a "final identification of cosmogenesis with Christogenesis."[312] Christogenesis is the development of the total Christ until its epilogue in the pleroma.[313] "Pleroma is that mysterious synthesis of the uncreated and the created, the great completion (both quantitatively and qualitatively) of the Universe in God."[314] That universe to which Teilhard addressed the litany, found on his desk after his death: "Heart of Jesus, Heart of Evolution, unite me to You."[315] God is "coextensive" with the universe, grows with the universe, and co-evolves with the world. In a

---

[310] MNF, 25 April 1967.

[311] Cf. ATTILA SZEKERES, *La pensée religieuse de Teilhard de Chardin et la signification théologique de son Christ cosmique*, in *Le Christ cosmique de Teilhard de Chardin*, prepared by A. SZEKERES, Ed. du Seuil, Paris, 1969, pp. 333-402.

[312] CLAUDE CUENOT, *Teilhard de Chardin*, Ed. du Seuil, Paris, 1963, p. 142.

[313] PIERRE TEILHARD DE CHARDIN, "Le Christique," in *Le cœur de la matière*, p. 109.

[314] ID., *La Parole attendue*, 1940, Cahier 4, op. cit. in JEAN MARIE MORTIER, *Avec Teilhard de Chardin*, "Vues ardentes," Ed. du Seuil, Paris, 1967, p. 135.

[315] Idem, p. 139.

sense, God ends up being the mind or mental pole of the universe, just as the universe becomes the body or physical pole of God.

The last horizon is occult Gnosticism: a return to the "fathers" of the counter-church, Menander, Basilides, Valentine.[316] In this new religion, to employ the language of former Canon Roca,[317] who joined top secret societies, Christ becomes the totalization of humanity.[318]

If the metaphysics of Gnosis opens the abyss of nothingness, the "mystical experience" of this nihilism in turn opens the way to the demon, prince of the abysses where one can only hate the truth and the dazzling beauty of Being. An initiatory chain connects those who hand down these occult theses from the beginning of mankind to the present time. In its lodges, Freemasonry keeps the secrets of a subverted view of the universe that drags its adherents to the abyss of perdition. And this is the innermost core of the Revolution's *mysterium iniquitatis,* the tip of whose veil Plinio Corrêa de Oliveira began to lift.

---

[316] Cf. JEAN VAQUIÉ, "Le retour offensif de la Gnose," *Lecture et Tradition,* no. 110 (Nov.-Dec. 1984), pp. 1-49; JEAN-CLAUDE LOZAC'HMEUR, *Fils de la Veuve. Recherches sur l'ésoterisme maçonnique,* Editions de Chiré, Chiré-en-Montreuil, 2002, passim.

[317] Paul Roca (1830-1893), ordained a priest in 1858, was a disciple of Alexandre Saint-Yves d'Alveydre (1842-1909) and preached a scientific Christianity in a series of works condemned by the Holy Office and placed on the Index in 1888. Cf. *James,* pp. 229-230.

[318] Cf. PIERRE VIRION, *Il governo mondiale e la contro chiesa,* with notes by Bruno Tarquini, It. tr., Controcorrente, Napoli, 2004, pp. 351-401.

PART TWO

THE SPIRITUAL SCHOOL

CHAPTER I

CONTEMPLATION OF THE SACRAL ORDER
OF THE UNIVERSE

Variety and Characteristics of Spiritual Schools

Plinio Corrêa de Oliveira was not only an intellectual master but above all the founder of a spiritual school, which is the set of doctrines and practices founders leave as a legacy to those who follow their examples and works. The existence of different spiritual schools within the Church expresses the multiplicity of divine perfections, each differently reflected in the souls of men.[319] This plurality of spiritual schools, which taken as a whole "form a more perfect image of the unique message of the Gospel,"[320] can be linked to religious families (Benedictines, Carmelites, Dominicans, Franciscans, Jesuits, etc.) or to the personality of a spiritual master and the influence of his work. Recognition of a founder's charism is not tied to his canonization. In fact, many saints were canonized centuries after the founding of their work, while others have never been canonized by the Church, like Cardinal de Berulle,[321] who cannot be denied the title of founder of a spiritual school.

In order to be serious and authentic a spiritual school must be founded on a metaphysical and moral doctrine rooted in the tradition of the Church, but it cannot be reduced to a theoretical formulation. Its fecundity is also measured through the personal testimony of those called

---

[319] Cf. JOSEPH DE GUIBERT, S.J. (1877-1942), *Ecoles spirituelles et unité de la spiritualité catholique,* in *Leçons de théologie spirituelle,* Apostolat de la Prière, Toulouse, 1943, pp. 108-122; P. SATURNINO PANI, O.F.M., *I princìpi fondamentali della spiritualità cattolica secondo le varie scuole di spiritualità,* Edizioni Francescane, Roma, 1954; LUCIEN-MARIE DE SAINT-JOSEPH, O.C.D., *Ecole de spiritualité,* DSp, IV (1960), cols. 116-128.

[320] L. M. DE SAINT-JOSEPH, *Ecole de spiritualité,* col. 127.

[321] Pierre de Berulle (1575-1629), French theologian and cardinal, was one of the protagonists in France's religious life at the time of the Counter-Reformation; inspired by Philip Neri, he founded in Paris the Oratory of Jesus and Mary Immaculate. Cf. RAYMOND DEVILLE, *L'école française de spiritualité,* Desclée de Brouwer, Paris, 1987.

to belong to that school. While we must reject the principle that experience precedes doctrine, those who follow a doctrine should practice it consistently, as the Gospel teaches. In this sense, as Plinio Corrêa de Oliveira notes, "the history of a soul is the history of its enthusiasms." [322]

The master of a spiritual school is not only its founder but also includes those who live its charism with greater perfection. In this sense, a school of spirituality can be defined as a particular way of conceiving and living religion in common by a certain number of individuals who resort to a founder regarded as their master.[323]   If there is no school without a teacher, there is also no school without disciples; and the testimony of disciples through their life and example is precisely what helps to focus on the core of a spiritual school. Thus, Saint Bonaventure helps us understand Saint Francis; Saint Thomas Aquinas develops the charism of Saint Dominic; and the grandeur of Saint Ignatius shines in Saint Francis Xavier and Saint Francis Borgia.

However, it would be a mistake to imagine that the founder of a spiritual school introduces a style of prayer and action on his own human initiative. We have to remember that, in every age, it is not the founder but Divine Providence that bestows the graces most suitable for the purpose that It wants to achieve. These graces are not given only to the founder but to all who are called to correspond to the same providential plan. The Holy Ghost knows the needs of the Church and prepares men to carry out their intended mission. A spiritual school is thus formed organically around the figure of a master, thanks to the decisive influence of divine grace.

Excellent works on the spiritual life and Christian perfection were published in the twentieth century. It suffices to think of the studies of Father Garrigou-Lagrange[324] and spiritual manuals by Fathers Tanquerey[325] and Royo Marin.[326] These treatises are certainly useful for understanding the theological foundations of any spirituality, and to answer questions that may arise among those wishing to delve deeper into

---

[322] BCM, 20 May 1967.

[323] L. PANI, *I principi della spiritualità*, p. 21.

[324] R. GARRIGOU-LAGRANGE, *Perfection chrétienne et contemplation, selon saint Thomas d'Aquin et saint Jean de la Croix*, Édition de la vie spirituelle, Saint-Maximin (Var) 1923; *Traité de théologie ascétique et mystique. Les Trois âges de la vie intérieure, prélude de celle du ciel*, Les Éditions du Cerf, Paris, 1938-1939.

[325] ADOLPHE TANQUEREY, *Compendio di Teologia Ascetica e Mistica*, It. tr., Desclée, Rome-Tournai, 1928. On Adolphe Tanquerey (1854-1932), Sulpician theologian, cf. DTC, XV, 27-48, Tables, cols. 41-46; Irénée Noyen DSP, XV, cols. 25-27.

[326] ANTONIO ROYO MARIN, O.P., *Teologia della perfezione cristiana*, It. tr., Paoline, Roma, 1965. Antonio Royo Marin (1913-2006) joined the Dominican Order in 1939 and was ordained a priest in 1944. He was professor emeritus of Moral and Dogmatic Theology at the Saint Stephen University in Salamanca.

this matter. Rather than proposing a spiritual path, these works offer us elements of judgment to distinguish true spirituality from false, and show us what all spiritual paths have in common. St. Therese of the Child Jesus' *Story of a Soul* [327] is not a treatise on ascetics and mysticism but indicates a way of Christian perfection: the "little way of spiritual childhood" which, though part of the Carmelite school, has its own characteristics that differentiate it from the spiritual path of St. Teresa of Avila.[328]

Plinio Corrêa de Oliveira never wrote a treatise on the spiritual life but outlined the characteristics of a life of perfection for people born in the twentieth and twenty-first centuries, the era, as we shall see, of the decisive battle between the Revolution and the Counter-Revolution. Anyone wishing to reduce his teaching to a detailed list of spiritual practices or to a simple rule of life to attain Christian perfection would be mistaken. Rules are necessary, and especially in a world deprived of them, but they are not the most profound aspect of the spiritual life. Plinio practiced and recommended daily Holy Communion and the entire rosary, consecration to Our Lady according to the method of Saint Louis Marie Grignion de Montfort, wearing the miraculous medal and the Carmelite scapular,[329] venerating angels and saints, relics, and going on pilgrimages. All this, however, is nothing but the expression of a profound, God-centered and Mary-centered spiritual life, some aspects of which we intend to analyze.

Interior Life, Life of Grace

Plinio Corrêa de Oliveira's spiritual life greatly benefited from reading *The Soul of the Apostolate* [330] by the famous Trappist Abbot Dom

---

[327] Saint Therese of the Child Jesus (1873-1897), a Carmelite nun at the convent of Lisieux, which she joined in 1878, was beatified (1923) and canonized (1925) by Pius XI. John Paul II proclaimed her Doctor of the Church. Cf. her *Œuvres complètes*, Cerf-Desclée de Brouwer, Paris, 1992. A list of writings about her is updated by *Archivium Bibliographicum Carmelitanum.*

[328] Saint Teresa of Avila (1515-1582), Doctor of the Church and great reformer of the Carmelite Order. It is worth recalling the relations of this Carmelite saint with the spirituality of the Society of Jesus (JUAN ANTONIO ZUGASTI, *S. T. y la Compañia de Jésus. Estudio historico-critico,* Razón y Fe, Madrid, 1914) and more broadly with the Catholic Counter-Reformation (RICARDO GARCÍA VILLOSLADA, *S. T. de J. y la Controreforma Católica,* Carmelus, 10 (1963), pp. 231-262. On her very vast bibliography, *cf.* H. PARENT DE CURZON, *Bibliographie thérésienne. Ouvrages français et étrangers sur S.T. et sur ses oeuvres. Bibliographie critique,* Paris, 1902 and, successively, collections of the journals *Carmelus* and *Archivium Bibliographicum Carmelitanum.*

[329] F. ANTUNES ALDUNATE, "Plinio Corrêa de Oliveira, a Contemplative," in *Ten Years Later,* pp. 183-188.

[330] Jean-Baptiste Chautard (1858-1935) heard his calling to become a Trappist monk and at age nineteen entered the Cistercian monastery of strict observance (Trappists) at Aiguebelle, which

Chautard, the work he studied the most[331] after Saint Louis Grignion de Montfort's *Treatise on True the Devotion*.

Dom Chautard's work is dominated by a single idea: the need of interior life in order to do apostolate. "Christian life, piety, interior life, sanctity: in all these we find no essential difference. They are only different degrees of one and the same love. They are the half-light, the dawning, the rising, and the zenith of the same sun."[332]

For Dom Chautard, the substance of the apostolate is for the apostle to superabundantly develop the grace of God in his soul and transmit it to others. Indeed, man's true life is not the superficial and external bodily existence, destined to decay and die, but the immortal life of the soul. What shall it profit a man to gain the whole world and forfeit his soul, the Gospel asks? (Mk. 8:36-37). The supernatural life begins with baptism, which, with its sacramental grace, plants the germ of a new life. This new life springs and is fed by Jesus Christ, Who is the only Way, Truth, and Life (Jn. 14:1-6).

Dom Chautard defines the interior life as "the state of activity of a soul which strives against its natural inclinations in order to regulate them, and endeavors to acquire the habit of judging and directing its movements in all things according to the light of the Gospel and the example of Our Lord."[333] This definition is important because it sets the spiritual life on an objective foundation, the Divine Law, and not on a purely individual experience. Also for Plinio the interior life means not only constant prayer and assiduous frequency of the Sacraments, but an effort to always conform, in thought and action, to the doctrine, practice and examples of Jesus Christ and of the Catholic Church.

In an article in *Legionário* of April 30, 1939, he wrote:

---

he later saved from ruin. In 1897 he was elected Abbot of Chambaraud and in 1899 Abbot of Sept-Fons. He energetically defended his order from the secularist policy and stood up to Georges Clemenceau, the famous anticlerical minister who became known as the "Tiger" but bowed to the personality of the French monk. "The man's strength is seen in his powerful personality, imbued with all the calm of a contemplative, all the resoluteness of an iron will, and all the majesty of a strong, profound mind, fully penetrated by the things of God. His gaze, as it were, synthesizes all these qualities; a noble and dominating gaze with which Dom Chautard worked wonders. During a trip to the East, he found a caged lion, looked at him intently, and hypnotized the beast..." ("Delicate Souls without Weakness, and Strong without Brutality," *Catolicismo*, no. 52 (April 1955). *Cf.* FR. MARIE GODEFROY, *Chautard,* DSp, II (1953), cols. 818-8120; BERNARD MARTELET, *Dom Chautard, abbé de Sept-Fons*, Médiaspaul, Paris-Montréal, 1994. Pope Benedict XVI recommended his work to all "fervent Christians" (*Homily in Lourdes* on September 15, 2008, *Insegnamenti*, IV, 2 [2008], pp. 335-336 [333-338]).

[331] *Cf.* Meetings of October 7, 1971 and May 21, 1990.

[332] DOM JEAN-BAPTISTE CHAUTARD, *The Soul of the Apostolate* (Trappist, Kentucky, 1946), p. 13. http://www.olmc-mission.org/soul_of_the_apostolate.pdf.

[333] Idem.

"In the will, this interior life must generate intense love for all that the Church commands, a zeal of obedience manifested not only in deeds but in feelings, not only in general lines but in the minutiae, not just in advice but especially in example. To think like the Church thinks, to feel like the Church feels, to act as the Church commands, and then to recognize in all this the work of God in us: behold the ideal of interior life."[334]

We must not think that the interior life means giving up one's own abilities and attitudes to live in a manner at variance with our nature. Instead, the interior life immensely enhances our natural qualities.

"These natural qualities, elevated by zeal to an apex, and crowned by the virtues that come only from supernatural life, are the achievement of the work of interior life. The interior life is not only or mainly an enhancement of one's natural qualities, but it is also that. If we want to be energetic, zealous, prudent, active, intelligent, skilled apostles, we must want to be really and sincerely pious. The apostle's ideal is to have all his natural and supernatural qualities placed at the service of the sanctification of souls."[335]

In an article of March 14, 1943 in the same journal, dedicated to Pope Pius XII, Plinio explained how the interior life presupposes an ascetic effort to fight the inclinations to evil and error coming from our nature corrupted by original sin. In order to live the interior life man needs to examine himself and his defects with the firm resolution to correct and amend himself.

"Hence the expression, 'interior life.' Man must be engaged in constant self-analysis. He needs to know how his soul is at all times; why he is acting in this or that way; if it is licit for him to proceed in this or that way; whether feeling in this or that way regarding a certain event conforms to Catholic morals. This effort is called 'life' not only because it governs every man's life but because it is so intense and should be so continuous that it is for man like a parallel existence that unfolds on a higher and deeper plane than his outer existence. And it is called 'interior life' precisely because it requires man to have the uninterrupted habit of analyzing and governing himself, acting and living 'within himself' incessantly."[336]

The Virtue of Recollection and Calm

Recollection is a key element of the interior life. It is the soul's ability to value things according to their hierarchical and architectonic

---

[334] *Legionário*, 30 April 1939.
[335] Idem.
[336] *Legionário*, 14 March 1943.

order. Recollection is a selection of one's attention: it means paying more attention to one thing than to another. The virtue of recollection collects and orders the powers of the soul in the right direction.

"A recollected spirit is not one that pays attention only to one thing but rather watches all things and places them in their proper hierarchy."[337]

In this sense, recollection is an effort of the intellect to order the reality that surrounds us. Another aspect of recollection is, "when dealing with lower things, to seek to relate them to superior things; to try to see the higher things in the lower."[338] In this respect, recollection is an "architectonic" virtue, capable of building the edifice of the soul according to the right priorities.

The vice opposed to recollection is dissipation. By paying attention to what is not worthy of it, the dissipated person destroys instead of building. His is a vagrant thought that roams about uncontrolled by his intellect and will.

The recollected soul is necessarily stable:

"Stability is but the transposition of recollection to the order of action. Dispersion, dissipation, is the opposite of recollection in the order of thought. In the order of action, dissipation is to do things contradictorily, stupidly, without continuity or depth: it is the progress of progressives. A man recollected in thought is consistent in action. Stability is only one aspect of recollection; it is recollection in action just as recollection would be the stability of thought."[339]

Stability is first of all productive and fecund. It is fecund because it is animated by a continuous movement even inside a routine, and because its fruits are lasting. A man recollected in thought is stable and steady in action.

Complementary to recollection is calm, a state of mind whereby a person's temperament, instincts and sensibility react in a way entirely proportionate to what the person has before him.[340] Calm is not slackness of soul: rather it presupposes recollection, spiritual tranquility, a pensive mind. The loss of this spirit characterizes the history of Europe after World War II with the arrival on the scene of the Hollywood myth, of which Plinio was an implacable critic.[341]

---

[337] BCM, 29 April 1967.
[338] Idem.
[339] Idem.
[340] *Calm*, p. 13.
[341] *The Crusader of the Twentieth Century*, pp. 46-49.

Seriousness as a Premise of Sacrality

Recollection prepares the soul for seriousness, a virtue seldom dealt with by moralists and spiritual writers but which for Plinio is a prerequisite for having a sacral vision of the universe.

> "Seriousness is one of the elements of sacrality, a prerequisite of sacrality. One who is entirely serious manages to be sacral; and one who is sacral is necessarily serious. If a person loses seriousness while still sacral, he in fact retains a varnish of sacrality, but it is not the true sacrality."[342]

It is worth dwelling a bit on seriousness because the lack of seriousness is precisely one of the most serious defects in the way of life of today's Catholics.

Seriousness harmoniously opposes joviality, a virtue that Aristotle called "eutrapelia," which is the ability to be pleasant and likable to others. Today, in a certain type of "open" Catholicism prevalent especially among young people, "eutrapelia" seems to have been unilaterally raised to the highest rank of Christian virtues. Yet, if we look at the lives of the saints we see they wisely alternated moments of seriousness with others of jest and sharp wit. And this – as the Dominican theologian Giovanni Cavalcoli observes – is true Christian seriousness, true wisdom. It is not a grim, haughty and gloomy stiffness of self-righteousness, but seriousness full of sweetness, simplicity and humility, so attractive in Saint Philip Neri, and which we so direly need. Nowadays, exaggerated esteem for joy and laughter hide a substratum of hedonism, pride, emptiness and ultimately despair, so common among frustrated people who "drink to forget."[343]

To renounce seriousness is to forget the eternal end of man, his supernatural destiny that places him at tragic crossroads: eternal happiness or eternal damnation. Losing this awareness leads to lack of seriousness.

For Plinio, seriousness is "the disposition of mind to see the truth head-on, entirely as it is and in its hierarchy; and thus to attribute greater value to higher things and less value to those that are not."[344]

The first element of seriousness is entire objectivity:

> "Seeing reality entirely as it is, without veils, prejudice, distortions or inadequacies;[345] "without any weakness (e.g. failing to see things as

---

[342] BCM, 17 June 1967

[343] GIOVANNI CAVALCOLI, O.P., "La serietà cristiana," in *Libertà e persona*, March 20, 2013.

[344] *Idealism*, p. 119.

[345] BCM, 22 April 1967.

they are) and respecting the hierarchy of truths."[346] "It is a seriousness that comes from above and returns on high. This seriousness is not primarily to refrain from laughing. It is fundamentally the attitude of a contemplative, admiring, enraptured and calm mind, capable of roaring or singing like an angel according to the circumstances it encounters."[347]

Seriousness was the virtue typical of the Middle Ages, but Plinio also identifies it as a distinctive feature of modern saints such as St. Therese the Little Flower, a model of seriousness in the way she lived and died. In her last few weeks she faced terrible temptations against the faith with inalterable seriousness. Yet,

> "She did not consent to any doubt against the faith, made no concession to the devil, not even a half-concession. And she drank the cup until the last but one drop. She was spared from the last because at the last moment, which was to have been the cruelest, she had such an ecstasy that she got up and seemed flooded with heavenly light – she departed, she had died.

> "Afterward, a rain of roses that began falling on the earth, bought by a deluge of spiritual blood. The thousand smiles that her devotion opened on earth resulted from a thousand groans from her soul and body. And she wanted it because she was serious to the end. So serious that she realized that to be a heroine she had no need of a military apparatus or the externals of heroism. She died conscious of her own heroism.

> "Saint Thérèse was so certain she would be canonized that in the last period of the disease, when they cut her nails or removed her pillow and some hair fell from her eyebrows, she would say, 'Keep these things carefully, because they will make a lot of people happy.' She already perceived that she was like a tree impregnated with precious resin of which every falling drop had extraordinary value in the eyes of God and men, and would bring graces. St. Therese was so serious, and her examination of conscience was so serious, that she had confidence in the limpidity of her own soul. And still in this life she sang her own holiness on account of the confidence she had in her own seriousness....I am certain no warrior in history marched toward death in a more resolute and heroic way than St. Therese of the Child Jesus."[348]

How does the seriousness of saints translate into a person's behavior?

> "Seriousness in acting is a consequence of seriousness in thinking. You do what you have to do entirely and soon, that is, without wasting

---

[346] BCM, 29 April 1967.
[347] BCM, 12 August 1990.
[348] SD, 1 January 1973.

time with useless interruptions. A useless interruption is lack of seriousness in all its abomination."

Let us see a perfect example of this in Our Lord Jesus Christ:

"He did what He had to do entirely: in a superabundant Passion He suffered continually to the end in one fell swoop. He did not stop or ask to rest even once. He had to suffer, and so He suffered until the end, without useless interruptions."[349]

Seriousness is linked to the sadness that never leaves a Christian even in moments of greatest joy, as he lives in a valley of tears and not in Paradise.

"The soul of the truly sacral man is steeped in nostalgia. Nostalgia for things that did not happen on earth but should have; things he never got to know but understood they had to be in a certain way. It is also a position of sadness for what should have been achieved but he was unable to achieve through his own fault or that of others. Thus, he has a kind of resigned sadness over a plan of God that was not fully realized. The beauty of sadness is found less in sadness than in resignation. And because this is so, a truly superior person with sacral spirit is very pensive. These things make him think about what he sees around him, in others, etc."[350]

Love of God and Sublimity

What unites all spiritual schools is their purpose: the glory of God. In this sense they are all theocentric. An "anthropocentric" spiritual school would be a contradiction in terms. "Like it or not, to say that a spirituality is anthropocentric is to say that it is not truly Catholic," Father de Guibert observes.[351]

For this reason it makes little sense to speak of "Christian humanism" or "anthropological spirituality." Overcoming humanism and anthropocentrism is a precondition of the spiritual life. The glory of God is the ultimate and absolute end of Christian life and the essence of perfection. All Christian life is summed up in this compendium: "You shall love the Lord your God with all your heart, with all your soul, with all your strength, with all your mind." Charity, which unites us to God, our ultimate goal, is the most excellent of all virtues. "*Caritas autem est quae unit nos Deo, qui est ultimus finis humanae mentis.*"[352]

---

[349] BCM, 22 April 1967.

[350] MNF, 28 December 1985.

[351] J. DE GUIBERT, S.J., *Ecoles spirituelles*, p. 112. The criticism is directed to Henri Brémond. Cf. DE GUIBERT, art. *Brémond,* in Dsp, I, col. 1934; and the reference to *Histoire littéraire* by Father CAVALLERA, in *Revue d'Ascéthique et de Mystique*, 3 (1922), cols. 301-311.

[352] *Summa Theologica,* II-IIae, q. 184.

The essence of Christian perfection, for Plinio, is also the supernatural love of God and neighbor.[353] This is not a sensible love but a firm resolution to sacrifice oneself entirely for God and for His glory, and to love creatures only for His sake.

In this sense, staunch theocentrism is the first characteristic of Plinian spirituality. It is a spirituality in which God's glory comes before the salvation of the soul. It is to render glory to God, to love and serve Him, and as a result of this generous choice, to save one's soul. The ultimate end of man, as the Catechism recalls, is to know, love and serve God on this earth in order to enjoy Him in Paradise.

> "At the essence of this conception of life is the idea that the only form of true happiness in life is for a person to attain the purpose for which he exists; and by achieving his end he becomes happy. No matter what it costs, however much it hurts and how difficult it may be, having attained his end the person is happy."[354]

Seeking the glory of God means to search in all things what is higher, more elevated and sublime.

> "In our soul, the love of the sublime should be dominant rather than merely a trait, so as to become the continuous orientation of our soul. It is our specific way of loving God. Others traits also exist but are not as salient. One has a desire to see, even in the smallest of things, its highest aspect."[355]

> "When a person takes a position before the sublime, he places himself in an attitude of self-denial. When he loves the sublime entirely and perfectly, he has an admiration that leads him to renounce himself and to sacrifice. When he does not take that position before the sublime, his ideas of abnegation and self-sacrifice are entirely impractical; they do not cross his mind."[356]

There are, recalls Plinio, two ways to holiness, two ways to sanctify one's life by making it perfectly conform to God's will.

> "One is a vocation to give up all things earthly, including what is legitimate. To renounce completely, to the limit of the conceivable, in order to serve God entirely. Another vocation is to use what God has given in such a legitimate and holy way that the person is thereby sanctified to a high degree.

> "Two typical examples would be Saint Louis the King and Saint Francis of Assisi. Saint Francis of Assisi took dispossession and poverty

---

[353] A. TANQUEREY, *Compendio di teologia ascetica e mistica*, no. 310.
[354] RST, 23 April 1964.
[355] AMC, 5 June 1991.
[356] COM, Sublimity.

to an extreme; Saint Louis was a saint on the pinnacle of the temporal order, which was the royalty and Kingdom of France. They are different vocations.

"Which is the most perfect state? That of the person who renounces everything, or that of one who has everything but dominates it all in this way? Note that to give themselves entirely, Saint Francis and all religious renounce the disposition of themselves and of their freedom and assume a condition similar to that of a slave. Those who act like Saint Louis have everything in abundance, but show extraordinary self-control while commanding everything." [357]

"My spirituality consists in a way of seeing the order of the universe. In everything I see it appears very clear that the order of the universe is sublime: all creatures, not only of the visible but also of the invisible universe, the angels, and above them, God Our Lord. Each element that composes the order of the universe somehow participates in this sublimity. In the visible universe, this happens above all with men." [358]

A Sacral Spirituality

The sacral is the apex of sublimity. Plinio Corrêa de Oliveira introduces an important distinction between the terms sacred and sacral. He notes that the adjective sacred pertains to things of the ecclesiastical order, while sacral most aptly indicates objects pertaining to the temporal order. The papal tiara is an example of a sacred object; the crown of Charlemagne is a sacral element. [359] While the spiritual is distinguished from the temporal, the latter, though different from the former, can be sacralized, that is, ordained according to God.

"The sacred belongs to the Church, and sacral is temporal society's way of being sacred. Sacrality is fitting to temporal society." [360]

Pope Pius XII often employed the expression *consecratio mundi,* consecration of the world, to the lay apostolate to define freedom of action in the temporal sphere. [361] Paul VI defines it as "re-establishing a relationship with God in something according to its own order and the requirements of its nature in the plan intended by God." [362]

In the final analysis, sacred is all that refers to God. And among all things that can be referred to God, nothing is more sacred than the Holy Sacrifice of the Mass, in which the God-Man Himself, Jesus Christ,

---

[357] MNF, 14 November 1986.

[358] AMC, 5 June 1991.

[359] *Primeval Innocence,* p. 82.

[360] SNC, 15 February 1992.

[361] Cf. PIUS XII, *Discorsi e radiomessaggi,* III, p. 460; XIII, 295; XV, 590, XIX, p. 459.

[362] PAUL VI, Audience of April 23, 1969, *Insegnamenti,* VII (1969), p. 929 (928-931).

renews in a bloodless way the sacrifice "which is the paramount event in history, the one with supreme sacrality and next to which the most extraordinary historical events are nothing."[363]

While the Holy Sacrifice of the Mass can be celebrated only by a priest's sacred hands, any man can develop the sacral spirit needed to order all things to God according to the purpose and the degree of hierarchy proper to them.

> "The sense of the sacral makes us see that all things that exist on earth essentially are mere appearances of the things that exist in heaven. The latter exist in an order of reality that is not the earthly order of reality but much stronger and more substantial than it is; in an eternal, perennial, immutable and perfect order of reality that is reflected in this transitional, imperfect, precarious order full of defects that we have here on this earth."[364]

The sacral sense of life is expressed in this

> "...gravitas of spirit: this elevation of soul, this seriousness, this sweetness, this unction, this strength, this dynamism and at the same time this static character of the soul that sees and knows that all things are nothing but a mirror of a more profound reality that actually exists in God Our Lord."[365]

Temperance as a Source of Sacrality

Ascesis is above all self-control, control over the disordered motions of one's soul and passions. Of all moral virtues, temperance is the one that introduces man to sacrality by regulating his ascetic effort. Plinio had a vision of temperance higher than that typically expounded by writers of treatises, who placed greater emphasis on its negative aspect. Instead, he emphasized its positive aspect and the harmony that temperance establishes among the powers of the soul. For him, the apex of this equilibrium is expressed in the sense of sacrality of one's interior life:

> "Sacrality is an ordering junction of all tendencies so that in a sacral man they find their point of equilibrium, of temperance. If you take away sacrality, all tendencies lose their temper and balance. Sacrality is the magnetic pole and point of equilibrium of man's tendencies; all tendencies find their fullness in the sacral spirit."[366]

Temperance can be considered in three aspects:

---

[363] MNF, 26 April 1989.
[364] BCM, 7 May 1966.
[365] Idem.
[366] BCM, 22 April 1967.

"First, in the relations of this tendencial area with the intellect and the will; for example, temperance in Our Lady was perfect. She had no inner movement that was not entirely in accordance with her intellect and will.

"A second aspect of temperance is a corollary of the first: There is a proportion among these various instincts whereby none preponderates so much as to weaken the others. For example, the instinct of combativeness is a noble and beautiful instinct; but imagine a person in which this impulse or state of mind has so developed as to make him incapable of compassion. Here a certain balance has already been lost and his soul has been deformed. He has an intemperate combativeness, which has somewhat gone astray.

"A third aspect of the question is for a person's sense, impulse or instinct considered as such not to grow so much as to wear itself out. For example, a person that likes painting so much that he overdoes it to the point of getting sick of painting. Obviously there was an erroneous hypertrophy whereby the person liked painting too much and the thing wore itself out....

"Seen as a whole or in each of its parts, temperance makes this whole mechanism subject to the intellect and the will; and in such a way according to nature that the impulse never extinguishes anything that opposes it within that tendential zone, nor does it extinguish itself." [367]

When man's profound tendencies are ordered, they group around the *princeps* tendency, which is sacrality:

"After original sin, man of himself is incapable of entirely ordering his tendencies, but grace enables him to do so. To the degree that grace acts, to the degree that his tendencies are in order they group around the master tendency, which is sacrality.

"In every ordered man there a fundamental tendency of his whole being toward that which is sacral. When it exists, this tendency has a dynamism by which it places the other tendencies in order, and the individual tends toward that temperance in everything else. The true foundation of temperance is the tendency toward the sacral. Conversely, when the tendency toward the sacral is in disarray, all other tendencies as a whole are not placed in order. In the order of tendencies, the sacral draws everything behind it." [368]

---

[367] BCM, 28 January 1967.
[368] BCM, 15 August 1967.

Ascetic Life and Contemplative Life of the Soul

The apex of sacrality, the highest good man's soul can obtain, is the contemplation of God and His perfections.

Saint Thomas defined contemplation as "a simple view of the truth."[369] The highest among all the truths that human intelligence can know is God, source of all truth, supreme Truth that enlightens all others. Hence, Father Cornelio Fabro observes, "knowledge of God is the supreme task of the human intellect."[370]

While it is an essentially intellectual act, contemplative life begins with a loving movement of the will toward God and fulfills its purpose in God's love. Thus, the love of God is the deepest and most effective root of contemplative life.[371]

After death the just will be able to contemplate God face to face and inebriate themselves with His perfections: infinite beauty, truth, goodness, justice and mercy, which they will know in a single Divine Substance. This loving and unitive knowledge, eternally indissoluble, which satisfies the natural longing of the human soul, will be the joy of the blessed in Heaven.[372] But only in Heaven, after death, will our contemplation – called beatific – be perfect. On earth it is only initial and imperfect.[373]

Habitual grace is already preparation and almost anticipation of the beatific vision: Father Tanquerey writes, "it is the germ that already contains the flower, though it will only blossom later; it is therefore of the same kind as the beatific vision, and participates in its nature."[374]

Some theologians have sought to separate ascetics from mystics, reserving the gift of contemplation for the latter. In fact, as Father Garrigou-Lagrange explained, it would be a mistake to imagine them separate, just as it would be wrong to think that the first stage is wholly human and the second fully divine. That would risk creating a division, or even worse a contrast between a phase of the spiritual life that forgets the role of grace, and a phase that sets aside the role of the human will. The former would risk falling into Pelagianism, which conceives the spiritual life in purely stoic and moralistic terms. The latter would tend toward quietism, which ignores the contribution of human virtues and

---

[369] *Summa Theologica*, II-IIae, q. 180, a. 3 ad 1. On contemplation, cf. the entries of P. LEJEUNE, DTC, III, cols. 1616-1631 and UMILE BONZI DA GENOVA, in EC, IV, cols. 438-450.

[370] C. FABRO, *L'uomo e il rischio di Dio,* Edivi, Segni, 2014, p. 149.

[371] ST. THOMAS AQUINAS, 3 S., D. 30, a. 4, a. 2.

[372] *Summa Theologica* I, q. 12, a. 1.

[373] St. Thomas speaks of an *"inchoatio beatitudinis, que hic incipit et in futuro terminatur"*(*Summa Theologia*, II-IIae, q. 180, a. 4; *De Verit.,* q. 11, a. 8).

[374] A. TANQUEREY, *Compendio di teologia ascetica e mistica*, no. 109.

attributes everything to grace. Instead, there is continuity between the various stages on the path to perfection.

Therefore, in the spiritual life there is no distinction between asceticism as an ordinary way reserved for many, and mysticism as an extraordinary way reserved for a few: both are eminently one and tend to the height of perfection. The spiritual life is asceticism, but all its phases are concatenated.[375] Indeed, holiness is not reserved for a few but is the normal goal of every Christian life, of every baptized person, as Jesus himself commanded every Christian by saying, "Be ye therefore perfect, even as your Father in heaven is perfect" (Mt. 5:48).

Every Christian, rather than only a few souls, is called to the heights of contemplation, the apex of Christin perfection and anticipation of the beatific vision.[376] "It was not closed in the Cenacle among chosen disciples that Saint Paul spoke of the indwelling of the Holy Ghost among the just. He preached it in public letters read on Sundays at the assemblies of Christians in Corinth, Rome or Ephesus." [377]

The way of Christian perfection, Plinio Corrêa de Oliveira indicated, is found in this line of continuity from a phase in which man's ascetical effort is preponderant, to another in which Our Lord Himself comes to meet him and take him to the heights of contemplation. It is an organic development of the interior life under the hidden but irresistible action of grace in the soul.

Admiration

The leading thread of our interior life consists in constantly giving primacy to the divine over the human in our way of thinking and acting.

> "The interior life consists in continually analyzing and relating all that we see to God, to the Catholic Church, to Our Lady."[378]

This spiritual practice presupposes an ascetical effort but is open to contemplation. This is done through admiration, which is a form of elevating oneself to God through created things.[379]

---

[375] On the unity of the spiritual life, cf. Fr. GARRIGOU-LAGRANGE, O.P., *Perfezione cristiana e contemplazione secondo S. Tommaso d'Aquino e S. Giovanni della Croce,* It. tr., Viverein, Monopoli, 2011, 2 vols., vol. I, pp. 21-58; Fr. AMATO DAGNINO, of the Saverian Missionaries, *La vita interiore secondo la Rivelazione, studiata dalla teologia e insegnata dalla Chiesa,* Edizioni Paoline, Milano, 1960, pp. 28-41.

[376] *Summa Theologica,* I-IIae, q. 69, a. 2 c. and ad 3; II-IIae, q. 182, a. 4, ad 3. Cf. also F. JORET, O.P., *La contemplation mystique d'après saint Thomas d'Aquin,* Societé Saint-Augustin, Desclée De Brouwer, Lille-Bruges, 1927, pp. 62-67.

[377] F. JORET, O.P., *La contemplation mystique,* p. 63.

[378] EXT, 7 July 1989.

[379] Cf. *Primeval Innocence,* pp. 95-194.

A man with interior life

"sees all things according to God. And by seeing them according to God he discerns what is good and what is evil, what is truth and what is error. And he must have a profoundly admiring soul. A soul incapable of admiration is incapable of having a true life of piety. He takes and gradually analyzes those various aspects of Catholic doctrine about God, sin, Redemption, the Incarnate Word, the Divine Maternity, the sacraments, the Church, the Law of God, and becomes more and more enthused, delving ever more profoundly, and admiring more and more.

"The things of the Church are susceptible of such a profound understanding, so rich and even inexhaustible, that if one spent a whole life thinking about one of them there would still be something more to draw from it. An interior man, according to the cravings of his soul, thinks about this or that, relates it with the other, and the more he relates, the more he knows. This is to 'see.' The more he knows, the more he admires: this is to 'judge.' Admiration is a judgment, is a conclusion that something is admirable and therefore he admires it. Only after that does he 'act,' by doing apostolate; but what an apostolate it is that is done by a soul so imbued with meditation and admiration!

"Now, this meditation and admiration are called prayer. Praying is not only saying prayers, though it is largely that; but to a venerable degree, to pray is to elevate one's mind to God, that is, not to think only of things palpable but to transcend the tangible and think of God. Then you have the elevation of the mind to God. Praying is relating all things in this way, with one's mind set in God, to imbue oneself with the Catholic spirit to spread it around oneself."[380]

God not only can be known, but also contemplated and loved through the created universe. Man "must habitually have a contemplative and meditative gaze about the things he sees in order to be, in this sense, a contemplative of earthly life, a person able to contemplate by observing earthly life."[381]

According to theologians, to contemplate means "to look at an object with admiration."[382] Admiration is the feeling that more easily makes us rise to God starting from sensible things. According to Giovanni Cardinal Bona, "contemplation is a prolonged elevation of the mind to God, the sure intuition and joyous admiration of existing truths, enjoying the taste of eternal sweetness."[383] The *Dictionnaire de Spiritualité* defines admiration as "the sentiment that results from a lively perception of

---

[380] SD, 22 May 1976.
[381] RRR, 28 August 1973.
[382] A. TANQUEREY, *Compendio di teologia ascetica e mistica*, no. 1297.
[383] GIOVANNI CARDINAL BONA, *Cursus vitæ spiritualis*, t. II, Paoline, Alba, 1941, pp. 182-183. R.

physical or moral beauty, grandeur, goodness, achieved to a superior degree."[384] Admiration is also an amazement that arises in face of the unexplained, says Saint Augustine,[385] who in his *Confessions,* like Saint Francis of Assisi in his *Canticle of the Creatures*, gives us an eloquent example of this spiritual attitude.

All the great spiritual masters, from Saint Bernard of Clairvaux in *De consideratione*[386] to Saint Robert Bellarmine in *Scala creaturarum,*[387] link contemplation with admiration. Indeed, in everything He made, God placed a distinctive note that arouses our admiration. Plinio Corrêa de Oliveira belongs to this school; for him admiration is the first stage in the sacral contemplation of the universe. The love of God is the end of man and the highest act of a creature, but God can be loved in the things He created as one rises from them to Him.

So one can understand the words of Saint John, often repeated by Plinio: "For he that loveth not his brother, whom he seeth, how can he love God, whom he seeth not?" (1 Jn. 4:20).

> "Here one might say, if you do not love the order of creation that you see, how can you love God, whom you do not see? To see the order of creation with excellent precision and purity is the most excellent way one has, in this order of things, to love God."[388]

The whole reality that surrounds man is admirable, and God wants us to live in constant admiration of the created universe so we can admire Him as reflected in it. The most important effect of admiration is that it is exercised on the will, exciting love. "Love easily makes you admire, and admiration makes you love," says Saint Francis de Sales.[389] For his part, Plinio says that the Commandment to "love God above all things" includes "admiring God above all things and recognizing His sublimity and excellence above all excellence." [390]

Admiration, the first stage of sacral contemplation, is "the ability to marvel humbly and disinterestedly."[391] "Admiration has two degrees. One is for the person to admire what he has before him, and the other is to relate that to God Our Lord so as to place Him as the final object of

---

[384] R. DAESCHLER, *Admiration*, DSp, I (1937), cols. 202-203.

[385] ST. AUGUSTINE, *De Genesi contra Manichaeos*, PL, 34, col. 180.

[386] ST. BERNARD OF CLAIRVAUX, *De considerazione*, PL 182, col. 806.

[387] ST. ROBERT BELLARMINE, *De ascensione mentis in Deum per scalas creaturarum*, Apud Jacobum Mascardum, Romae, 1616.

[388] MNF, 22 March 1991.

[389] ST. FRANCIS DE SALES, *Traité de l'Amour de Dieu*, 1, VII, chap. 4.

[390] NOR, 15 May 1968.

[391] SDS, 19 June 1971.

admiration.   God is the author of what I admire, and has those qualities in an infinite way.   Rather than possessing them, He *is* those qualities." [392]

We should therefore admire that which is admirable in everything, without envy or egalitarian spirit, but with love and profound humility. To admire means to recognize the other's superiority.   The act of admiration is typical of the humble, not the proud, who is focused on himself, or the envious, who hates the superiority of others.   We should admire "disinterestedly, for we have no role to play…and in the joy of feeling small." [393]   That admiration, which is the starting point of sacral contemplation, is also its point of arrival.   In it we find "God's sublimity and excellence above all excellence, and the end of the path of all sublimity and all excellencies that can be considered." [394]

Plinio employs the term "transsphere" [395] to indicate that superior sphere of the spirit in which contemplation opens to a hypothetical world that transcends the ephemeral aspects of reality, and transfigures reality by placing it in a mythical but real dimension.   Indeed, God contains all reality, existing and possible, and all that exists is admired and contemplated not only as it is but as it could be, according to the plans of God.

Contemplation of the Temporal Order

A child's innocence is a paradigm of this type of contemplation.   The child has an immediate intuition of first certainties, of the first principles. Innocence is not only to not commit faults but above all to preserve an internal order of the spirit: harmonious, calm, full of idealism.   In this sense, innocence is not a privilege of childhood but an ideal model of interior life.

Innocence characterized the Middle Ages, a time when this state of soul permeated all social classes.   A man who lost his innocence should meditate on the ancient Breton legend of the *cathédrale engloutie*, [396] the cathedral submerged for centuries in the sea but whose bells rung by angels were heard by fishermen from time to time.

"No one can fail to perceive the extraordinary beauty and poetry of this legend.   Primeval innocence is not something the devil is able to

---

[392] SD, 11 February 1977.

[393] SD, 19 June 1971.

[394] NOR, 15 May 1968.

[395] MNF, 2 July 1977.

[396] An ancient maritime legend tells the story of the "cathédrale engloutie," the cathedral of a coastal village in Brittany submerged by sea waters after a mysterious cataclysm. Fishermen say that on some moonlit nights, between the lapping of the waves they can hear the sound of the cathedral bells rung by angels, a prelude to its future triumph emerging from the waters. French composer Claude Debussy (1862-1918) dedicated a famous prelude to this legend.

completely eradicate from our soul. It remains there like a cathedral submerged by the waters of sin but which still exists in us. From time to time the bells of this innocence chime and make us feel, as it were, an inner melody, nostalgia, hope....The way to restore a child's innocence in adulthood – to use the image of the submerged cathedral – is to ensure that the submerged cathedral which is our innocence, kept within us submerged in the waters of sin, stop being submerged and resurface once again."[397]

So we should try to win back our lost innocence. Innocence is not a childhood privilege but can be recovered and attain its fullness in mature life. Thus one should try to grow in innocence until the hour of death. We must regain innocence to discover the pleasure of being small, feeling greatly exceeded, admiring those that are superior, rising by the whole scale of beings all the way to God, source of all admiration.

Our sacral admiration should embrace everything: from nature to persons, peoples and history.

"Sacral contemplation is the contemplation of the image, likeness and vestiges of God in the universe, that is, in the world around us, in cities, families, institutions, art, animals, plants, and details of each object."[398] "All that is beautiful, good and true is the object of a contemplative mind."[399]

The religious sphere is certainly superior to the temporal one. However, since nothing can be taken away from God and everything must be brought back to Him, the temporal order also can be the object of contemplation. Society and the State have a sacral end, and to the extent that they attain that end they deserve to be admired and contemplated.

"Sacral contemplation, therefore, is to look at the temporal world with religious admiration." [400]

"What does a man do when he stops along the way to watch a military parade or a religious procession, to look carefully at a building or landscape, to observe a particularly important or picturesque scene of everyday life, or to see a theater play? He contemplates, that is, he focuses his attention on a certain object, ascertains what is true or false, good or bad about it, accepts it, consents to it and as it were assimilates its truth and goodness in his own soul; and when the thing has something bad about it, he experiences dissonance with it, refuses it and purges from himself something bad which that thing might have communicated to him.

---

[397] SDS, 27 December 1975.
[398] *Primeval Innocence*, p. 69.
[399] Idem, p. 71.
[400] Idem, p. 75.

"Man, having before his eyes relative and contingent beings that reflect the absolute Being, considers in those beings something that exists in God in an absolute way, through the channels of his senses he somehow appropriates that good in the very act of considering it and configures himself accordingly. In short, though marked by the conditions inseparable from this earthly life, he makes a characteristically contemplative act. Unfortunately, when making such acts of contemplation, many people fail to rise to God in any way but stop at the selfish and limited enjoyment of the relative being before them. Their knowledge is often flawed and welcomes error rather than truth; contemplation leads them to assimilate the bad rather than the good.

"Obviously, just as there are good contemplations, there are also bad contemplations. There are triumphs of the world, the flesh and the devil. Nonetheless, although it may be purely natural, and the action they realize is essentially contemplative and affirms that man has a tendency to contemplation that cannot be dulled.... Contemplation is neither pure knowledge nor pure love: it is also assimilation. In fact, it is proper to love to produce assimilation between two beings. Hence one of the most essential traits in man's nature is his susceptibility to be profoundly influenced by other men, but especially by those he admires.

"Imitating is a tendency inherent to all, and it is far from being something degrading or ridiculous as such. Unworthy persons can be the object of imitation; there can also be imitations in which, although having worthy persons as their object, someone errs by trying to assimilate his ways in an excessively exact way, in something which is unique to a person and non-transferable to another. There are errors in imitation as in any other human operation. But as such, to imitate and assimilate are legitimate and constant functions of the human mind, fulfilling most profound needs of our being. If we assimilate as we should, if we imitate those we should, we perfect ourselves and increase our likeness to God, reflected in the mirror of His creatures.

"To imitate, to serve as an example, are obligations of every man, essential operations to perfect his soul, profoundly inherent in the social life of souls. They are modes established by Providence and endowed with great efficacy for the exercise of the powers of the soul, development of the mind and conquest of that perfection which is the wedding garment with which we prepare for the perfect banquet of the soul: the perpetual contemplation of God."[401]

Language, gestures and rituals are elements that have great cultural and educational importance for the common good of peoples.[402] In the

---

[401] "Christendom, Sacrality in the Temporal Order," *Catolicismo*, no. 574 (1988), pp. 16-32.

[402] "Do Symbols, Pomp and Riches Have a Function in Human Life?" *Catolicismo*, no. 82 (October 1957). Also on the topic of the ceremonial surrounding papal power, see the two studies, "The Ceremonies of Eisenhower's Swearing-in in Light of Catholic Doctrine," and

firmament of the Church are harmoniously reconciled seemingly contradictory extremes, such as a monk's solitary vocation, inspired by a total renunciation of the world, and the splendor of pontifical ceremonies, that at one time expressed the greatest pomp of which the world was capable. There is no contradiction between these two orders of values. Plinio explains:

> "The doctrinal basis upon which these two holy extremes meet and harmonize is very clear. God Our Lord gave us creatures so that they help us get to Him. Thus, culture and art, inspired by faith, should put in evidence all the beauties of irrational creation and all the splendors of talent and virtue in the human soul. That is called Christian culture and civilization. In this way, men are formed in truth and beauty, in love for the sublime, for hierarchy and order that reflect the perfections of the Creator in the universe. And so the creatures actually contribute to our salvation and to divine glory.

> "On the other hand, they are contingent, transitory beings; God alone is absolute and eternal. We need to keep that in mind and stay away from creatures, despising them, to think only about the Lord. In the first way one rises to God considering all that the creatures are; and in the second, one rises to Him considering what they are not. The Church invites her children to tread both paths with the sublime spectacle of her pomp and the consideration of the admirable sacrifices that She alone knows how to inspire and effectively accomplish." [403]

Loving God through the *Pulchrum*

According to the *philosophia perennis,* beauty is a transcendental property of being, that is, a perfection which befits each thing that exists, without exception. As a property of being, the *pulchrum* is connected with the transcendental attributes of the *verum,* because what is known by the intellect is pleasing, and to the *bonum,* because the object of beauty satisfies the sensible appetite. Beauty is the splendor of the true and good,[404] indeed it is a synthesis of truth and goodness.[405]

"Why Was Our Poor and Egalitarian World Awed at the Pomp and Majesty of Coronation?" *Catolicismo*, no. 27 (March 1953) and no. 31 (July 1953).

[403] "Poverty and Pageantry, Harmonious Extremes in the Firmament of the Church," *Catolicismo* no. 96, December 1958.

[404] Cf. ELDERS, *La metafisica dell'essere*, op. cit., I, p. 167. On *"pulchrum"* in Saint Thomas, cf. *Summa Theologica*, I, q. 5, a. 4; I, q. 39, a. 8; I-IIae, q. 27, a. 1 ad 3.

[405] "Beauty in the created order is the splendor of all the transcendentals reunited: of being, of the one, of the true and of the good, or, more particularly, it is the radiance of a harmonious unity of proportions in the integrity of the components (splendor, proportio, integritas, cf. I, q. 39, a. 8)" (R. GARRIGOU-LAGRANGE, O.P., *Divine Perfezioni*, It. tr., F. Ferrari, Rome, 1923, p. 337).

The whole Christian tradition is dominated by the principle that attachment to creatures, and especially to their sensible beauty, is bad; conversely, enjoying them as tools to elevate oneself to God is good. Scotus of Erigena gives this example: Consider an elegant golden vase decorated with precious stones. Two men contemplate it, one wise and the other vicious. Both enjoy the delight of beauty. But the vicious is moved at the same time by a desire to possess it; he thinks of the object in relation to himself. The virtuous man is not moved by greed or selfishness but celebrates, in the beauty of the vase, the infinite beauty of God.[406]

Similar is the doctrine of Alexander of Hales. Facing the beauty of creatures one can have a twofold attitude: to rise to their efficient cause, the supreme Beauty, or to dwell in them, relating them to us. "If we use the world only in terms of our own interests, we act badly; if we use it to accomplish what God wants, we do well."[407]

For Plinio also, the glory of God, the ultimate goal of man and of history, is the contemplation of His beauty and constitutes man's happiness. Indeed, if in knowing the truth the soul is moved towards its end, which is the Divine Good, it does so with even greater impetus when it sees God through the beauty of created things.

> "God's beauty is reflected throughout the hierarchical and harmonious totality of all beings so that, in a sense, there is no better way for us to know the infinite and uncreated beauty of God than by analyzing the finite and created beauty of the universe, considered not so much in each being but as a whole. God is also reflected in a higher and even more perfect masterpiece than the cosmos: the Mystical Body of Christ, the supernatural society we venerate as the Holy Roman Catholic and Apostolic Church. She constitutes a whole universe of harmonic and varied aspects that chant and reflect, each in its own way, the ineffable and holy beauty of God and of the Word Incarnate. Contemplating the universe, on the one hand, and Holy Church, on the other, we can rise to the consideration of the holy, infinite and uncreated beauty of God."[408]

It could be said, by analogy, that the human soul has the possibility of knowing and loving the Church through her works, and, *in primis,* through the perfections of Christian civilization, of which the Church is the mother. Contemplating a cathedral, listening to a Gregorian or a polyphonic melody, reading a masterpiece such as the *Divine Comedy* or *The Lusiads,* infuses in our soul the possibility of understanding that the

---

[406] E. DE BRUYNE, *Etudes d'esthétique médiévale*, II, p. 513.
[407] Idem, pp. 523-524.
[408] "The Scapular, Profession, and Interior Consecration," lecture at the Third National Conference of the Third Carmelite Order (São Paulo, November 14-16, 1958), *Mensageiro do Carmelo*, special issue, São Paulo, 1959.

Church, which Pius XII defined as "the vital principle of human society,"[409] is the supernatural source of all that is beautiful, good and true which man has produced in history.

Light of Christ, Light of the Church

It is proper of beauty to shine. One cannot study a Gothic cathedral without thoroughly analyzing the role that light plays in it. Art historian Erwin Panofsky has shown that, just as scholastic philosophy is dominated by the principle of *manifestatio*, Gothic architecture is dominated by the "principle of transparency." In both cases, light plays a decisive role.[410] In the footsteps of De Bruyne, Hans Sedlmayr expounds the medieval model of the hierarchy of light: "pure light 'gives shape' to matter. The more light penetrates it, the more matter becomes luminous and expansive, the more the bodies become fine, subtle, pure, simple, bright. Conversely, the more matter refuses light, the more the capacity of light to move and expand is diminished; bodies then become more opaque, dense, dark, heavy, defined and compact."[411]

Divine light is both present and differently reflected in the various creatures as in a mirror. One could say that, when the meaning of a thing is manifested, this divine presence is what gives it its light. A soul in the state of grace has a wonderful beauty because it reflects God. Every soul in the state of grace is illuminated by the divine light like a cathedral's stain glass window by sunlight. The Fathers compare it to those transparent bodies, which, receiving the sunlight, are penetrated by it and acquire incomparable splendor that they spread all around.[412] "So also our soul, like a crystal globe illuminated by the sun, receives the divine light, shines brightly, and its splendor is reflected on the objects that surround it."[413]

In the twentieth century, Plinio Corrêa de Oliveira once again proposes this metaphysics of light and sees the light par excellence in Jesus Christ, perfect specimen and ultimate perfection of all images. *Lux in tenebris lucet* (Jn. 1:5) are the words with which the beloved disciple announced to his time and to coming centuries the great event that dissipated darkness.

---

[409] PIUS XII, Speech to New Cardinals on 20 February 1946, *Discorsi e radiomessaggi*, VII (1945-1946), p. 395 (pp. 384-398).

[410] E. PANOFSKI, *Architecture gothique*, p. 102.

[411] HANS SEDLMAYR, *La luce nelle sue manifestazioni artistiche,* It. tr., Centro Internazionale Studi di Estetica, Palermo, 1985, p. 64.

[412] SAINT BASIL, *De Spiritu Sancto*, IX, 23, PG, XXXII, col. 109.

[413] A.TANQUEREY, *Compendio di teologia ascetica e mistica*, No. 112.

Two great lights illuminate the firmament of history: the birth of Jesus Christ and His Resurrection. When the world was plunged in darkness, the star guiding the Magi Kings came to rest on the grotto in Bethlehem. Plinio recalls the words of Scripture:

> "Today the Light will shine upon us, because the Lord has been born unto us. His Name is Admirable, God, Prince of Peace, Father of the future age, and His kingdom will have no end" (Is. 9:2-6, Introit to the second Christmas Mass).

He comments:

> "The darkness that covered the earth when the Savior was born was the idolatry of the Gentiles, the skepticism of the philosophers, the blindness of the Jews, the hardness of the rich, the rebellion and idleness of the poor, the cruelty of rulers, the covetousness of businessmen, the injustice of laws, the defective constitution of the State and of society, the subjection of the whole world to the tyranny of Rome. It was in that thickest of the darkness that Jesus appeared as a light. What is the mission of light? Obviously, to dispel darkness. In fact, little by little the darkness gave way. And in the order of visible realities the victory of light consisted in the establishment of a Christian civilization which, at the time of its integrity, and despite imperfections inherent to human things, was an authentic reign of Christ on earth."[414]

If darkness preceded the birth of the Savior, thick darkness followed His death until the hour of the Resurrection. From the Holy Saturday ceremony, Plinio drew the expression *Lumen Christi.*

> "At night, at dusk, still in the dark, a light is lit: Our Lord Jesus Christ resurrects, the paschal candle is lighted, and the priest enters the church with a lighted candle and sings three times: "Lumen Christi." Soon the whole church is illuminated by the paschal candle. To me this expression, *Lumen Christi,* is immensely beautiful, immensely noble, meaning a thousand things."[415]

Lumen Christi is the irresistible divine splendor. It is

> "a certain shine, a certain light found in Our Lord Jesus Christ, the light of His whole Person and thus the light of His divine nature shining through His human nature which has another light for its supreme perfection and righteousness as human nature. And all that He said and did, having been said and done by Him, shines in different degrees but always intensely and with great splendor. This is why one cannot read the Gospel without emotion. All of it has *Lumen Christi.*"[416]

---

[414] "Lux fulgebit hodie super nos," *Catolicismo,* no. 36, December 1953.
[415] RRR, 1 October 1973.
[416] Idem.

But the *Lumen Christi* is also the light of grace that floods the soul with its gifts, a light that guides every man who has

> "that notion, the discernment of that light he sees shine on things, in souls, in institutions, which is the very *Lumen Christi*, the opposite of the devil's darkness. And it floods him when, by dint of exercising this discernment in what I have just said, and having this supernatural vision, the person wants the dominion of Our Lord Jesus Christ through Our Lady and the Church to be recognized, acclaimed and fully practiced by all men in both the ecclesiastical and civil spheres."[417]

Finally, the term *Lumen Christi* can also be applied to the Church and to Christian civilization to the extent that they reflect Jesus Christ:

> "In her teaching, governance, way of being, liturgical, artistic and cultural manifestations, the Church has a form of brilliance that comes from Our Lord Jesus Christ and thus can be called *Lumen Christi*."[418]

> "*Lumen Christi* is a certain notion of totality that one has while considering the hierarchical order, the metaphysically unitarian order that reigns in the universe and also in the spiritual society (the Holy Roman Catholic and Apostolic Church) and in temporal society, that is, Christendom, this huge family of nations now reduced to ashes mixed with mud and a few sticks, still lit on their tips, floating amid the disaster."[419]

The "Primordial Light" of the Soul

The *Lumen Christi* shines in all of creation not only as a whole but also in every single creature. And among all creatures, this light shines preeminently in a man who responds to grace. The love of God is inseparable from love of neighbor because every man should be loved as having been created by God in his image and likeness.

> "Every person has his meaning. From the dullest, smallest and last of men to the greatest of men, all have their meaning. To such a point that sometimes one looks at a person and clearly sees, 'he means such a thing.'...Every human creature – indeed also non-humans, creatures from lower kingdoms – has an *unum*, and this *unum* has something symbolic. Every man symbolizes something."[420]

Interpreting and commenting on physiognomies of exceptional men, saints or revolutionaries, was a constant note in the intellectual activity of Plinio Corrêa de Oliveira. A man's way of being is in fact expressed in

---

[417] RRR, 22 June 1973.
[418] RRR, 22 November 1980.
[419] RRR, 15 November 1980.
[420] EVP, 28 July 1985

his physiognomy, deportment, manners and also attire, of which their alteration in history is linked to changes in human types and personalities.[421]

> "Since God wanted to create each man, and since every man is unrepeatable, this unrepeatability in man is founded on a perfection of God.... So by loving in that person the perfection that exists in God, I love God who is that perfection."[422]

All the great spiritual writers have expounded on the existence of a capital vice or defect in every man. Knowing one's own capital defect is an indispensable means of making progress in the spiritual life. Plinio Corrêa de Oliveira enriches the study of spiritual theology with an extraordinarily important notion: the existence alongside the capital defect of a capital virtue, queen and custodian of all other virtues. The *primordial light*, as he defines it, is not a virtue properly speaking but "a complex of virtues ordered and coordinated among them."[423] This light shines in the depths of every human soul.

The primordial light includes all powers of the soul: intellect, will, and sensibility. Subjectively understood, it is an attribute of the soul; objectively, it is the particular form of divine perfection to which the soul tends.

> "Man has variable dispositions of soul according to events in his life: he can have joy, sadness, anguish, hope, etc. But there is an underlying attitude of soul that gives rise to those ups or downs. That state of mind has a kind of rulership over the other states of soul because these last for as long as they are influenced by an external circumstance, which now gives them more impetus, now less. However, this disposition of soul occupies most of the life of an ordinary man. This is the state of mind he is normally in. Knowing well that state of mind is very important for all the rest of the spiritual life.

> "This state of soul corresponds to man's temperamental, emotional, volitional reaction facing the universe as a whole. For the whole universe usually has something that does not change; and if it does, it changes in the accidents. It is in the face of it that man's underlying attitude of soul takes a stand. It is a normalcy within man that corresponds to normalcy within the universe. This common attitude of man before the whole universe must be very harmonically varied, for the universe usually and stably presents very different aspects from its intrinsic standpoint and also from man's standpoint.

---

[421] "Dress, Hierarchy, and Egalitarianism," *Catolicismo*, no. 133, January 1962; cf. also "The Habit and the Monk," *Catolicismo*, no. 62, February 1956.
[422] EVP, 11 June 1989.
[423] MNF, October 1957.

"A day which is neither brilliant nor extremely ugly, a normal day, moderately contains elements of beauty as well as ugliness, deficiency, and, therefore, on a small scale, also elements of all the changes the weather goes through throughout the year. Accordingly, on a normal day, radiant sunshine, awful depressions, etc. occur on a moderate, small scale. The variety of all things is more or less contained within this normal range, as if it were its own seed.

"It is normal for man, placed before this, to have a corresponding state of soul which is properly what is called equilibrium. It is the starting point of everything else. This state of mind is somewhat different in each person, but not much, because the universe is not optically different to each man. The universe thus gives us a lesson in equilibrium."[424]

"In the final analysis, our primordial light is the knowledge we have of what we should be."[425]

Deep in our soul there always remains an idea of how we should be or should have been:

"And life's great frustration occurs when man looks at himself and realizes that he is not as he should be. The great joy that man can have in this life is when he looks at himself and says, 'despite such and such setbacks, defeats, drawbacks and missteps, I ended up being what I should be!' Then he feels truly realized.

"To realize oneself therefore is not to have great fortune, great situation or great social representation, power or any such thing. To realize oneself is to achieve that of which we are the draft, the definitive type we should be when we die, when we surrender our souls to God. It corresponds to Our Lord's marvelous expression when dying, 'Father, unto thy hands I commend my spirit'; this is the expression we all should have when we die. In one way or another we feel that we are as it were taking our soul and delivering it to God. More or less as an artist who has just finished touching up a work of art and delivers it to him who ordered it to see if the artwork fits the order placed. We are a masterpiece of grace and of our cooperation with grace within us. God has commissioned this work of art. Upon expiring, we should offer to God this work of art.

"Our primordial light ultimately is the knowledge we have of what we should be. The fact that all the powers of our soul, stimulated by grace, deep down have this knowledge and a tendency for this: this is the primordial light. It is beyond doubt that, considered from a personal point of view, our primordial light is the means we have to realize the glory of God in relation to our persons."[426]

---

[424] MNF, 17 May 1990.
[425] SD, 22 January 1971.
[426] SD, 22 January 1971.

Every man is composed of the being that he receives and the essence that specifies him. But there is also an actualization of being (potency becomes act) that expresses what it actually is. The primordial light and the capital vice are linked to this actualized form of being. They can be considered as the ultimate principle of individuation of all created beings "in such a way that the capital vice and the capital virtue are born of the act of being but for different reasons and in different ways; for the capital virtue and the primordial light are correlated to the act, whereas the capital vice is an abuse, a distortion of the act of being."[427]

The life of men and peoples is suspended between the light of Christ and the abyss of sin, and man must understand that in his life

"these individual battles, from light to light and from darkness to darkness, are small aspects of an immense war which is the war of history around this fundamental point: will the world's peoples and nations of the entire world – officially, authentically and seriously in their laws and customs and in the personal life of each individual – recognize Our Lord Jesus Christ as the light that shines in the darkness and reject the darkness? Yes or no? This is the great question."[428]

---

[427] MNF, 9 May 1967.
[428] RRR, 14 July 1973.

CHAPTER II

COMBATIVE AND CHIVALROUS SPIRITUALITY

The Virtue of Grandeur

Among the many names we can give Plinian spirituality, chivalrous spirituality is certainly one of the most appropriate.

The word chivalry immediately evokes an era between the eleventh and thirteenth centuries that reached its apex with the epic Crusades.[429] However, the chivalrous attitude of soul is not limited to any specific historical time. The best work on chivalry is the one by Léon Gautier.[430] Based on medieval sources, he studied the origins of chivalry and its code of honor, and minutely described the knight's private and military life, always connected to his "militancy" in defense of the Church and of Christian civilization.

Here is a significant image: "When our knights attended Mass, just before the Gospel reading we saw them draw their swords in silence and hold them in their hands until the end of the sacred reading. That gallant attitude meant: If the Gospel needs to be defended, here we are! This is the spirit of Chivalry."[431]

---

[429] Cf. FRANCO CARDINI, *Alle radici della cavalleria medioevale*, La Nuova Italia, Firenze, 1982; GEORGES DUBY, *La société chevaleresque,* Flammarion, Paris, 1988; KARL FERDINAND WERNER, *Naissance de la noblesse. L'essor des élites politiques en Europe*, Arthème Fayard, Paris, 1998; JEAN FLORI, *La chevalerie*, Edition Jean-Paul Gisserot, 1998; It. tr., *La cavalleria medievale*, Il Mulino, Bologna, 2002; ALFREDO SAENZ, *La Cavalleria. La forza delle armi al servizio della verità inerme,* It. tr., Il Cerchio. Rimini, 2000.

[430] LÉON GAUTIER, *La Chevalerie*, Pardès, Puiseaux, 1989 (1884). Léon Gautier (1832-1897), born in Le Havre, Normandie, was professor of paleography at Ecole des Chartes from 1871 and coupled his activity as a scholar with a fervent apostolate (he prepared twenty-fve editions of the Song of Roland). He authored about one hundred historical, liturgical, apologetic and literary studies. When he died, they said of him: "More than a professor, sage or scholar he was a great soul" (A. D'ESNEVAL, DBF, vol. XV, col. 837 (835-837). His masterpiece is the book *La chevalerie* (1884) in which he recalls the spirit and life of medieval chivalry. Cf. also CHARLES BAUSSAN, *Léon Gautier*, P. Lethielleux, Paris, 1944.

[431] L. GAUTIER, *La Chevalerie*, p. 30.

This spirit of service was symbolically expressed by the ceremony of investiture and delivery of the weapons. The oldest known ritual of chivalrous induction, reported by historian Jean Flori, contains this significant formula: "As for you, about to be knighted, remember these words of the Holy Ghost: 'Gird thy sword upon thy thigh' (Ps. 44:4). This is indeed the sword of the Holy Ghost, Who is the Word of God. Accordingly, uphold the truth; defend the Church, orphans, widows, those who pray and those who work; rise promptly against those who attack Holy Church so that you may appear in the presence of Christ, crowned and adorned with the sword of Truth and Justice."[432]

A typical trait of the knight is grandeur of soul, also known as the virtue of magnanimity. Magnanimity has nothing to do with ambition, which is essentially self-centered. Magnanimity, instead, is distinguished by generosity and selflessness. Father Tanquerey calls it a "noble and generous disposition to undertake great things for God and neighbor."[433] It is opposed to cowardice and incompatible with mediocrity. "In this sense," Father Royo Marin says, "it is the crown, ornament and splendor of all other virtues."[434]

A "great" man is "superior," not because he is proud but rather because he is oblivious to himself on behalf of the higher principles that guide him. Plinio explains it with words that deserve to be read attentively.

> "True grandeur exists, it is superiority; superiority in the order of grace, of nature, and of mission. But man does not have this true grandeur mainly for his own advantage or benefit, but for the glory of God. He is great to serve, to fight for something that is not him. And he turns away from his mission to the degree that he seeks to appropriate the fruits of his struggle to aggrandize himself.

> "He has to be disinterested, selfless, and not even look at his own grandeur to contemplate it vainly, because he loses it at the moment he thus looks at it. And if he has to contemplate it, he should simply say: 'what God has given me belongs to God, and I return it to Him. For God I will employ even the last breath of my life; that is what I will do.'

> "Everything in him that might be higher than in others thus takes a grandeur that is no longer human but which participates in the very grandeur of God. God Himself enters this relationship as the final end for which that grandeur is destined. And thus that great man whom God created to serve Him, that great man acts like Our Lord Jesus Christ, Man-God, Who came to earth to accomplish a mission.

---

[432] J. FLORI, *La cavalleria medievale*, p. 36.
[433] A. TANQUEREY, *Compendio di teologia ascetica e mistica*, no. 1083.
[434] A. ROYO MARIN, O.P., *Teologia della perfezione cristiana*, no. 324.

"Was that mission ennobling? It was. But it was a mission that consisted in being denied, reviled, mistreated, crucified. He accepted this mission. Though greater than everyone else, He accepted not to reign but to die on the Cross as a criminal, for that was the purpose. He was not given grandeur to dominate the earth but to establish the Kingdom of the Eternal Father on earth. And for Him it was indifferent to die on the Cross or anything else; for Him the capital element was that the Eternal Father be served. Here you have the first note of true Catholic grandeur. It is a selfless grandeur that does not look for ostentation, self-advantage, to oppress others, be praised by them or use them for its own advantage, but looks only to those who are higher than it is."[435]

The Sacral Sense of Honor

There are words that have an indefinable charisma; among them is the word *honor*.[436] While it might appear empty to some, superior men immediately grasp its meaning. The notion of honor is at the heart of chivalrous spirituality. Gautier writes, "All chivalry is contained in these four words: "Rather death than dishonor."[437] Plinio Corrêa de Oliveira would have signed that statement. He says:

> "Honor is the distinctive note of my spiritual life. It is to see God, Our Lady, all life and the whole universe in the light of honor. Hence my true happiness consists in honor, to be continually considering things from the standpoint of honor."[438]

Plinian philosophy is a real metaphysics of honor, derived from his metaphysics of essences, which rises all the way to the sacral contemplation of the universe. If everything that exists must indeed be watched and admired, it also deserves to be praised and honored. But honor should be rendered to persons and not things, and given above all to God, the most perfect, personal and subsisting Being. "To God alone be honor and glory for ever," says Saint Paul (1 Tim. 1:17). Saint Peter adds: "Honor all men. Love the brotherhood. Fear God, honor the king" (1 Pt. 2:17). To God alone should all honor be rendered, an absolute that theologians define as worship of *latria*. Honor rendered to men is called *dulia*.[439] This honor is not absolute but rendered unequally, according to the dignity of the persons honored.

Honor is an asset of the spiritual order that has God, source of all honor, as its point of reference. Indeed, all goods are gifts of God; and

[435] EXT, 15 August 1976.

[436] EVP, 15 August 1976.

[437] L. GAUTIER, *La Chevalerie*, p. 29.

[438] EVP, 19 December 1976. Cf. also ADOLPHO LINDENBERG, *Aspects of Dr. Plinio's Spirituality–Avenging God's Honor*, manuscript.

[439] *Summa Theologica*, II-IIae, q. 25, a. 1, ad 2.

Saint Thomas explains that honor is rendered to a person in recognition of the good that exists in him.[440] Honor has to do with the good intrinsic to the one being honored: it is recognition of his value and is thus diversified according to the specific gifts of each individual.[441] "Therefore," the Angelic Doctor writes, "we love all our neighbors with the same love of charity because it refers to a single common good which is God, while we render various honors to different people according to their individual virtue." [442]

This Thomistic perspective is at the foundation of the Plinian metaphysics of honor. For Plinio, honor is first of all the feeling of respect we owe our dignity and that of our neighbor.

> "Respect is the feeling one devotes to a person who is more than us in the order of honor."[443] "Hence respect is always an attitude of recognizing superiority, happy to see that superiority exists, and even nourishing oneself by contemplating the other person's superiority disinterestedly, with enthusiasm, elevating oneself."[444]

Honor is first of all respect for one's dignity, and then for the dignity of others. Hence it is related to the awareness of one's own role and mission.

> "A person aware of his own dignity day and night lives in the presence of God; and when he takes a vacation from dignity, he takes a vacation from God."[445] "This kind of total dignity is the integrity of dignity. It is the dignity in all of man's ways of being. And this total dignity is the sole gift of true Roman and Apostolic Catholics. It is so much a gift that we get to know a person's catholicity by his dignity."[446]

The respect we owe ourselves and others comes from the dignity of our vocation, of our status, which is first of all that of baptized persons.

> "Every human creature, however modest, has his own, natural and inalienable dignity. Even greater, immeasurably greater, is the dignity of the last and most obscure son of the Church as a Christian, that is, a baptized person, as a member of the Mystical Body of Our Lord Jesus Christ."[447]

---

[440] Idem, q. 27, a. 1 ad 2.

[441] Honor, Saint Thomas explains, is found in the one who honors, not in the one that is honored *(Summa Theologica*, II-IIae, q. 99, a. 2.).

[442] *Summa Theologica*, II-IIae, q. 25, a. 1 ad 2.

[443] EVP, 23 May 1976.

[444] EVP, 3 January 1988.

[445] EVP, 17 September 1978.

[446] EVP 24 September 1978.

[447] "Dignity and Distinction for Great and Small," *Catolicismo*, no. 33, September 1953.

What renders a person excellent is the dignity of his status or mission. Saint Thomas says: "Indeed, honor is due to God and to more excellent persons as a sign and testimony of a pre-existing excellence, but honor is not what renders them excellent."[448]

Developing this concept, Plinio states that dignity is the intrinsic value of a mission; honor is dignity while manifesting itself or being recognized by others.[449]

> "Honor is a kind of projection or reverberation of dignity. Dignity is reflected through honor. Therefore, behind the notion of honor is the notion of dignity, which is linked to a scale of values found in the order of being: that particular mission exists and in its being it is more than another; this one has greater dignity, which is expressed by a different honor."[450]

Honor is part of the virtue of Religion. It is the virtue by which one renders the homage due to anyone who is intrinsically superior. [451] The sacral shines in temporal society through honor:

> "Honor is the transparency of the sacred in secular society."[452] "The notion of honor is one of the most intrinsic notions of the concept of sacrality. No one will have any idea of what a sacral thing is if has no notion of the intrinsic honor of what is sacral as compared to other forms and degrees of honor. I say more: it is impossible for an individual to be Catholic without having the notion of honor in the highest esteem and as a normative value of his life."[453]

Honor is also, and above all, a participation in what is high and sublime:

> "There is no true honor where no grain of the sublime is found. And honor is hierarchical by definition. Honor is not like this: God, sublime, in the highest heaven, and beneath, everyone equally participating in Him. Saint Thomas shows that this is metaphysically impossible. True honor is to love degrees of honor to the degree they participate in the sublime. Honor is participation in the sublime. The degrees of honor are the order within the sublime."[454] "We could say that created honor is a participation in the uncreated Honor."[455]

---

[448] *Summa Theologica*, I-II, q. 2, a. 2.
[449] EVP, 30 May 1990.
[450] Idem.
[451] EVP, 15 July 1973.
[452] EVP, 22 July 1976.
[453] EVP 23 May 1976.
[454] EVP, 29 August 1976.
[455] EVP, 29 August 1976.

Honor can be considered in relation to oneself, in relation to others, and in relation to God.

> "In relation to oneself, honor is the state in which an individual reaches a level of perfection proportional to his nature and possibilities."[456]

> "Honor in relation to God is for the individual to attain a superior degree of perfection through which he gives God that special form of glory of resembling Him in a superior way, overcoming himself and his own nature, and resembling the greater and inserting himself in Him. This is to fully honor God."[457]

As far as honor in relation to neighbor is concerned,

> "...if in the eyes of God, every human creature is excellent and an image of Him, I owe to that human creature, even if it is lesser than me, that tribute due to all that is excellent according to God. So I should deal with every human person with the respect that God treats his creatures, in which He consented to see His own likeness however tiny that thing may be. And to honor an individual who is more, equal or less than me is to give him the whole consideration that God placed in him, whereby he resembles God. This is to honor him."[458]

All civilizations have recognized honor.[459] It is a central aspect of manliness, just as modesty is the central aspect of female identity. The Middle Ages was the era in which the sense of honor developed the most:

> "The idea of honor is fundamentally medieval. The civilization of the Middle Ages is the civilization of honor. One does not understand the Middle Ages except as fully imbibed with the criteria of religious honor, sacral honor."[460]

The sense of honor survived in aristocratic classes even after the end of the Middle Ages. The noble was the one who served the true religion and the legitimate sovereign with generosity and selflessness. What distinguished a noble from a commoner was his attitude in the face of death. The bourgeois were afraid of death and tried to avoid it at all costs.

---

[456] EVP, 19 September 1976.

[457] Idem.

[458] Idem.

[459] Cf. FRANK HENDERSON STEWART, *Honor,* Chicago University Press, Chicago, 1994; JAMES BOWMAN, *Honor. A History,* Encounter, New York, 2006. See also VICTOR G. KIERNAN, *Il duello: onore e aristocrazia nella storia europea,* It. tr., Marsilio, Venezia, 1991.

[460] EVP, 22 July 1973.

The nobles were trained to deal with a raised visor. Waging war was their occupation.[461]

Honor and Human Dignity

There is a radical difference between the anthropocentric conception of human dignity and Plinio Corrêa de Oliveira's God-centered conception. For modern anthropocentrists, man is the supreme value and therefore no other value can be placed above human life. According to the traditional view, there are values that transcend man and for which he must be ready to sacrifice his life. The honor of God, country, family, one's own honor, expressed mainly by the given word, makes up the sense of honor in Christian civilization. In this regard, there is a connection between honor and sacrifice. Sacrifice is the way in which one honors a loved one. For this reason, the Holy Sacrifice of the Mass is the supreme form of honor.

Plinio sustains that honor, like glory, is legitimate only when an individual does not defend it as something of his own but as higher than himself. Honor has nothing to do with pride, because it is a virtue. As Saint Thomas says, honor is the prize of all virtues. And he explains that if it is sinful to desire honor in a disorderly fashion, they are worthy of reproach who neglect it, not avoiding dishonor.[462]

Honor can be lost, and defending it is all the more important as the loss is irreparable. Betrayal is the most dishonorable act that a man can commit; fidelity is the most honorable attitude.[463]

Ernest Hello, a great writer, says that honor is above all respect for one's given word. A man's signature is his name, his name is his word, and his word is his honor. This is why in current language one says "he dishonored his own name." He who is not faithful to his word dishonors his name. "Name is honor, and rising a bit, name is glory. Glory is augmented honor, crowned honor, honor dressed in purple."[464]

Loss of honor is typical to a relativist society. Fidelity to one's word is indeed an element of psychological and social stability. When this element is lacking, no one can rely on anyone and everything becomes changeable and fleeting. Fidelity to the given word is an expression of

---

[461] Cf. JEAN-PIERRE LABATAUT, *Les noblesses européennes de la fin du XV à la fin du XVIII siècle*, Presses Universitaires de France, Paris, 1978, It. tr., *Le nobiltà europee,* Il Mulino, Bologna, 1982, pp. 99-111.

[462] *Summa Theologica*, II-IIae, q. 131, a. 1, ad 1.

[463] ERNEST HELLO, *L'homme-La vie-La science-L'art*, Perrin, Paris, 1911, pp. 42-56. Ernest Hello (1828-1885), a Catholic writer and journalist closely linked to Louis Veuillot, is the author of philosophical and theological writings characterized by a profound *sensus fidei*. Cf. among others, *Physionomie des saints*, Ed. du Sandre, Paris, 2005 (1875).

[464] E. HELLO, *L'homme*, p. 52.

consistency; and consistency, just as the sense of honor, sometimes requires heroism.

The sense of honor, which someone might imagine to be as bygone as the centuries of chivalry, is instead especially alive in ages of decadence, fed by the spiritual energy of a human nature that does not change over the ages. While the future of the twenty-first century is fraught with puzzles, it is hard to imagine a future without individuals ready to make as their own a motto that belongs to man's very being: *for the sake of honor*.[465]

Addressing TFP volunteers, Plinio says:

> "Honor is our primordial light."[466] "Honor is for the TFP as poverty for Franciscans and obedience for Jesuits. We are of the school of honor. And therefore, in the light of honor all virtues for us have light, and virtues without honor have no light for us. Honor must be present in all schools of holiness but may not set as dominant a note as did chastity, for example, in Saint Louis Gonzaga. We are the Saint Louis Gonzaga of honor. And thus we see the struggle of the Counter-Revolution against the Revolution in terms of the fight of honor against dishonor."[467]

> "We should strive to discern honor in everything that exists on earth. We should try to see honor as the dominant note.... I would say more: the goal and compass of our spiritual life is not only the search for true honor but the hallmark of the civilization we want to establish. It will either be the civilization of honor or it will be nothing. Either the Reign of Mary is the reign of honor or it is nothing. The state in which man feels his own honor for the love of God, and feels honored, is a heavenly state on earth."[468]

Courtesy as Social Asceticism

Léon Gautier identifies courtesy as an eminently chivalrous virtue right next to honor: Courtesy, he writes, "is one of the finest words of our language and renders the same sound as chivalry and honor."[469]

Courtesy is the visible and symbolic expression of the dignity with which men should treat one another. Man's dignity is indeed expressed in words and gestures that keep him away from all baseness and vulgarity

---

[465] Everything revolves around the notion of honor in the book of memories in which Countess Marion Dönhoff (1909-2002) evokes the conspiracy of July 20, 1944 and the resistance of German aristocrats against Hitler. Cf. *Um der Ehre Willem. Erinnerungen an die Freude von 20 Juli*, 1994, It. tr., *Per l'onore. Aristocratic tedeschi contro Hitler*, preface by R. DE MATTEI, Il Minotauro, Rome, 2002.

[466] EVP, 2 January 1977.

[467] EVP, 13 June 1976.

[468] EVP, 19 December 1976.

[469] L. GAUTIER, *La chevalerie*, p. 132.

and elevate him to what is high and sublime. Courtesy is the code of ceremonies and rites that has ruled these gestures and words over the ages. For this reason, in the history of Europe, the ordination of a priest, the dressing of a knight, the graduation of a doctor or the reception of an ambassador were regulated by specific rituals.

Every society founded on strong principles has its symbols, rituals and etiquette, which convey the meaning of an event or mission. Courtesy decays when the principles of a society decay.[470] While the system of rules that goes under the name of courtesy is certainly conventional, Plinio emphasizes:

> "Conventions are necessary. The natural order requires conventions."[471]

Prof. Plinio dedicates profound reflections to the topic of courtesy, but he expressed it above all in his whole style and way of being, so affable and courteous that someone might even see it as ceremonious.[472] In fact, Plinio's amiable ways were not artificial but natural and spontaneous and resulted not only from his upbringing but from his spiritual formation.

Courtesy was one of the things he admired the most in the *Ancien Régime*, that system of beautiful manners that had been refined over centuries and represented a real social asceticism. In this regard, Plinio comments:

> "In Christendom, politeness was the liturgy of charity, which disappeared when gravitas, temperance and humility fled that body of principles. There was still a frivolous, iron-clad etiquette with a proud conception of man but without genuine content, for charity was dying. But it was admirable."[473] "Courtesy in the *Ancien Régime* appeared very much in the way people dealt with one another. But except for very rare cases I am not aware that courtesy in the *Ancien Regime* disseminated a truly noble way of referring to more serious, holier, deeper and more tiresome issues to the point of making them objects of salon conversation.

---

[470] Cf. for example, NORBERT ELIAS, *La civilltà delle buone maniere*, It. tr., Il Mulino, Bologna, 1982; *Rituale, cerimoniale, etichetta* (prepared by SERGIO BERTELLI and GIULIANO CRIFÒ), Bompiani, Milano, 1985; ALAIN MOUTADIER, *Dictionnaire raisonné de la politesse et du savoir-vivre. Du Moyen Age à nos jours*, Seuil, Paris, 1997; MAURICE H. KEEN, *Origins of the English Gentleman: Heraldry, Chivalry and Gentility in Medieval England, c. 1300-c. 1599*, Tempus, Stroud, 2000; FRÉDÉRIC ROUVILLOIS, *Histoire de la politesse de 1789 à nos jours*, Flammarion, Paris, 2008.

[471] *Patriarchal Society, Organic Society* (CSN).

[472] Cf. LUIZ NAZARENO DE ASSUMPÇAO FILHO, "Small Episodes, Great Lessons," *Catolicismo*, no. 658 (October 2005), pp. 14-19; A. LINDENBERG, "Plinio Corrêa de Oliveira – Mentality, Tastes, Conversation, Social Relationships," in *Ten Years Later*, pp. 54-88.

[473] Meeting, 21 January 1999.

They certainly spoke about such things in the salons, but in a certain superficial frou frou, without delving deeply into them."[474]

As an effort to control one's instincts, courtesy is a form of asceticism. A typical example is offered by Queen Marie Antoinette of France when, on the scaffold, she apologized to the executioner for having involuntarily bumped him.[475]

> "But the habit of practicing asceticism, the habit of acting against one's lower impulses, causes the person to win it all with ease, naturally, elegantly, with distinction. At the bitterest time, it was a victory over the wrong impulse."[476]

Plinio does not limit this social ascesis to a code of good manners. A soul with faith should rise from practice to theory and know how to move from "savoir faire" to "savoir penser":

> "This know-how has indefinite extensions of asceticism eager to extend to all fields of life and to attain a truly unimaginable splendor. No one can have an idea of what the splendor of the world would have been had the *Ancien Régime* continued on a straightforward path from the Middle Ages. No one can have an idea of what that progressive march of asceticism based on the supernatural – not the asceticism of a pure fakir – would have been like had the world not experienced the decline from the three Revolutions."[477]

Our Lord Jesus Christ embodies the perfection of that courtesy which, when dealing with others, expresses an extremely high view of the world and an infinite love of neighbor.

> "I am not saying that no form of courtesy existed before Our Lord Jesus Christ. But even when such forms of courtesy were sumptuous they were such a far cry from true courtesy that we could say that courtesy was born with Him and historically emanates from His Person. He is the arch-perfect model of courtesy; from Him emanated a certain love calling for reciprocity, and this reciprocity was courteous treatment. By loving people the way He did He lifted them up to a moral level where

---

[474] CSN, 23 August 1986.

[475] Marie Antoinette Josepha Johanna of Hapsburg Lorraine (1755-1793), archduchesse of Austria and imperial princess, known simply as Marie Antoinette, was Queen of France and Navarre from May 10, 1774 to September 21, 1792 as wife of King Louis XVI. Her last words before being guillotined on October 16, 1793 were an extreme act of courtesy to the executioner, Henri Sanson, on whose foot she inadvertently stepped: "Monsieur, I beg your pardon, it was involuntary." About her last days, which she bore with extraordinary dignity, cf. G. LENOTRE, *La captivité et la mort de Marie-Antoinette: les Feuillants, le Temple, la Conciergerie, d'après des relations de témoins oculaires et des documents inédits*, Archeos, Paris, 2012 (1897); Paul et Pierrette Girault de Coursac, *La Dernière Année de Marie-Antoinette,* F.X. de Guibert, Paris, 1993.

[476] RRR, 3 November 1974.

[477] Idem.

they learned how to deal with others on that level. So He gave individuals the gift to respond to Him the way He had treated them. That came from Our Lord and was an effect of grace.

"I have the impression that it took many centuries for this Christian type of virtue to deeply penetrate customs and blossom in the form of courtesy. For example, the early Catholics in the catacombs still practiced forms of Roman courtesy, therefore sub-courtesy. Those Roman greetings such as 'Hail,' 'Vale,' were much less nuanced than they later became; they were much less rich in feeling, more formal, almost legal. They did not have the warmth of courtesy that blossomed when the love of Our Lord Jesus Christ began to gradually permeate customs. Then, the perfect courtesy was born.

"But His love was a social habit transmitted from generation to generation through education, participation in the same Faith, participation in His love, etc. That was in continuous ascent until the Middle Ages and only began to decline when the Revolution began. But it decayed slowly, like a dead leaf. Among men there remained a substratum of the love of Our Lord Jesus Christ and therefore something similar to Christian courtesy; and that substratum remained even when they had already become atheists. As Saint Pius X put it, that substratum was the perfume of a flower still in the vase even though it had already died.

"Christian courtesy survived for a while just as some light still lingers on the horizon when the sun goes down. For some time it even survived the very virtue of Christian charity – God's love. And at one point it ended up by dissipating. When people lost that last reflex, the revolutionary way of treating one another began. That courtesy is a fruit of religion to such an extent that it is so from every standpoint. And it alone fully deserves the name courtesy. When religion decays, courtesy decays. And when religion disappears, courtesy takes a while but eventually disappears as well."[478]

The Moral Profile of the Medieval Noble

Plinio's moral standard is embodied in the profile of the medieval noble he describes in his last book, *Nobility and Analogous Traditional Elites*.

In the Middle Ages and the Ancien Régime, being a noble could not be reduced to a profession. The title of nobility, accompanied by a coat of arms and a motto, summed up a set of values to which the medieval noble subjected himself.

"Two essential principles defined the physiognomy of the noble:

---

[478] CSN, 23 August 1986.

"1. In order to be the exemplary man placed at the summit of the fief as the light atop a chandelier, the noble had to be, by definition, a Christian hero disposed to endure any sacrifice on behalf of the good of his king and his people. He had to be the armed defender of the Faith and Christendom in the frequent wars against pagans and heretics.

"2. In every field, he and his family had to give a good example – or better, an excellent example – to their subordinates and peers. In virtue as in culture, manners, taste, the decoration of the home, and celebrations, their example had to motivate the whole social body so that everyone would improve in every field."[479]

These two principles had an admirable practical scope.

"During the Middle Ages, they were lived with authenticity of conviction and religious sentiment. In this manner the physiognomy of the Christian gentleman and the Christian lady appeared in European and later in Western culture. Gentleman and lady: two concepts that, throughout the ages and despite the successive dilutions inflicted by the gradual secularization in the *Ancien Régime*, always designated the excellence of a human standard. Even in our time, in which both titles have lamentably become obsolete, they nevertheless continue to designate this excellence.[480]

Plinio does not hesitate to apply the term "sacrifice" to the life of protocol and good manners.

"Sacrifice. The word deserves to be emphasized, for it had a central importance in the life of the noble. It was present even in his social life in the form of an ascesis that deeply marked it. Indeed, good manners, etiquette, and protocol were developed according to standards that demanded from the noble a continual repression of what is vulgar, rough, and even offensive in so many of man's impulses. Social life was, in some aspects, a perpetual sacrifice that became more demanding as civilization progressed and refined itself.

"This statement may elicit a skeptical smile from some readers. However, if they wish to see how true it is, let them consider the mitigations, simplifications, and mutilations that the bourgeois world, born of the French Revolution, has gradually imposed upon the etiquette and ceremony that have survived to our days. Without exception, all these changes were introduced to offer ease, insouciance, and bourgeois comfort to the *nouveaux riches* bent on conserving as much as possible, in the midst of their recently-acquired opulence, the vulgarity of their previous lifestyle. Thus, the erosion of good taste, etiquette, and good

---

[479] *Nobility and Analogous Traditional Elites in the Allocutions of Pius XII to the Roman Patriciate and Nobility,* at http://www.tfp.org/tfp-home/books/nobility.html.
[480] Idem.

manners resulted from a spirit of laissez-faire, a desire to "unwind," and the prevalence of the spontaneous and extravagant whims of "hippieism," which reached an apex in the unbridled rebellion of the Sorbonne in 1968 and in subsequent youth movements such as 'punkism.'"[481]

At this point Plinio dwells on the moral profile that stands out so remarkably in many nobles and shows the harmonious diversity of the evangelical virtues.

"Many saints of noble birth renounced their social condition to practice the perfection of virtue in the earthly self-denial of the religious state. How splendid were the examples they gave to Christendom and the world!

"Other noble saints, however, remained amid the splendors of temporal life. With the prestige of their station, they stressed in the eyes of the other social classes the magnificence of the Christian virtues, and set a good moral example to the collectivity they headed. They did this to the advantage not only of the salvation of souls, but of temporal society too. In this sense, nothing is more beneficial to the State and society than having in its highest ranks persons shining with the sublime respectability that emanates from the saints of the Catholic Church.

"Moreover, these saints – so worthy of reverence and admiration because of their elevated station – were especially loved by the multitudes due to their constant and exemplary practice of Christian charity. Indeed, there are innumerable beatified and canonized nobles who, without renouncing the earthly honors of their rank, stood out for their particular love for the needy. They earnestly practiced a *preferential option for the poor*.

"Many nobles who chose the admirable self-denial of religious life also shone in this solicitous service to the needy. They became poor with the poor to lighten the earthly crosses of the destitute and prepare their souls for heaven."[482]

Combative and Militant Spirituality

In Plinian spirituality, kindness and courtesy in manners are inseparable from an attitude of relentless struggle against evil. Christian life is a struggle: a painful and unceasing war, the goal of which is eternal life and which ends only with death. The success of this struggle is due above all to the action of grace. Father Tanquerey writes, "We must not forget that the grace given us is the grace for struggle and not the grace for peace; that we are warriors, athletes, ascetics; that like St. Paul we

---

[481] *Nobility and Analogous Traditional Elites,* p. 111.
[482] Idem, pp. 111-112.

must fight on to the end if we would merit the crown. 'I have fought the good fight: I have finished my course: I have kept the faith. As to the rest, there is laid up for me a crown of justice, which the Lord the just judge will render to me in that day'" (2 Tim. 4:7-8).[483]

The idea of spiritual combat and militancy runs through the Old and New Testaments.[484] If warlike Israel prefigures the *Ecclesia militans* in struggle and storms, Job's lament expresses above all the life of man conceived as a struggle:[485] *"Militia est vita hominis super terram"* (Job 14:24).

Jesus Christ proclaims the peacemakers blessed and preaches love for enemies (Mt. 5:10; Lk. 6:27-35). However, He affirms that He came not to bring peace but the sword (Mt. 10:34-35; Lk. 12:51-53). Saint Paul clearly designates the enemies that must be fought and describes the weapons one needs to don: sword, breastplate, etc. (Eph. 6:14-17; 1 Thess. 5:8; Rom. 13:12). A Christian is an "athlete" and a "soldier" who fights to the death (Eph. 6:10). "For he also that strives for the mastery is not crowned, except he strive lawfully" (2 Tim. 2:5). The final prize is a "crown of glory" (2 Tim. 4: 6-8). The end of the fight is not human glory but the glorification of Jesus Christ (I Cor. 1:28-31).

Christians have followed this model from the earliest centuries. Thus Saint Clement of Rome, in his *Letter to the Corinthians* (c. 97), gives the example of the military life, insisting on the necessary hierarchy between superiors and inferiors.[486] Christian officers and soldiers who were martyred at that time were not put to death for refusing to serve in the army as Christians, but for refusing to participate in pagan ceremonies imposed by the persecutors or for refusing to perform acts of idolatry and apostasy. Such is the example of Saint Eustace, Saint Sebastian, Saint Maurice, the *Legio XII Fulminata* (the "Thunderbolt Twelfth Legion") destroyed under Marcus Aurelius, and the Theban Legion decimated under Diocletian and Maximian.

Before Charlemagne, Constantine the Great was the pre-figure of a model sovereign and Christian warrior. On the eve of the Battle of Milvian Bridge, at Saxa Rubra, on October 28, 312 he had a vision of a radiant cross in the sky with the inscription *in hoc signo vinces*. During the night, Christ appeared to him in a dream and ordered him to adopt that

---

[483] A. Tanquerey, *The Spiritual Life-A Treatise on Ascetical and Mystical Theology,* no. 227.

[484] Cf. among others JOHANN AUER, *Militia Christi,* DSp, X (1980), cols. 1210-1223; CHRISTINE THOUZELLIER, "Ecclesia militans," in *Etudes du droit canonique dediées à G. Le Bras,* t. 2, Sirey, Paris, 1965, pp. 1407-1423.

[485] CHRISTINE THOUZELLIER, *Ecclesia militans,* p. 1407.

[486] ST. CLEMENT OF ROME, *Lettera ai Corinzi,* 37. 1, tr. Edizioni Studio Domenicano, Bologna, 2010, p. 171; A. JAUBERT, "Les sources de la conception militaire en 1 Clément 37," *Vigiliae christianae,* 18 (1964), pp. 74-85.

symbol for the next day's battle. Constantine's victory closed the era of persecution, opening a new era in the history of the Church.[487] The very term *sacramentum* is taken from military language, according to the model of allegiance to the flag.

Next to the model of the martyr typical of the first three centuries of the Church, a new prototype appears in the figure of Charlemagne, the "new Constantine," the Christian warrior tasked with defending Christendom from the attacks of its enemies and to ensure by armed force the triumph of the Catholic Faith and the Church. Dante will later place in the fifth heaven of paradise, that of Mars, the shining souls of Charlemagne and Roland, among the fighters for the Faith right next to Joshua, Judas Maccabaeus, and the main protagonists of the Crusades.[488] For her part, by approving veneration of "Blessed Charlemagne" in the diocese of Aachen, the Church indicated the "just" and "warrior" king as a model for the faithful.[489]

The Spiritual Exercises of Saint Ignatius

Contemplating the ruins of Christendom, Plinio Corrêa de Oliveira knew and deeply loved the Church and decided to serve her. From his love for the Church was born the decision to defend Christian civilization by openly confronting its enemies.

> "Christian combativity exclusively means legitimate self-defense. It has no other form of legitimacy. And a Christian is always led to fight out of love for something offended. Every fight is all the more vigorous the higher the love with which one fights. For that reason there is in the Catholic no greater combativeness than that with which he fights in defense of the Church, outraged, denied, trampled upon."[490]

Plinio Corrêa de Oliveira's combative spirituality was formed at the school of the *Spiritual Exercises* of Saint Ignatius of Loyola,[491] an inspiring book that, according to Saint Francis de Sales, produced more saints than the letters of the alphabet it contained. In the Apostolic Constitution *Summorum Pontificum* of July 25, 1922,[492] Pius XI

---

[487] Cf. R. DE MATTEI, *Just War, Holy War: An Essay on the Crusades, Islamic Jihad, and Modern Tolerance,* Livraria Civilização Editora, Porto, 2002; Ricardo da Costa-Armando Alexandre dos Santos, "The Thought of St. Thomas Aquinas (1225-1274) on Military Life, Just War, and the Military Orders of Chivalry," in Almudena Blasco Valles and Ricardo da Costa (coord.), "The Middle Ages and the Crusades," *Mirabilia* (January-June 2010), pp. 196-218.

[488] DANTE ALIGHIERI, *Divina Commedia,* III, 8, 43-45.

[489] ROBERT FOLZ, *Etude sur le culte liturgique de Charlemagne dans les églises de l'Empire,* Slatkine rpt., Genève, 1973.

[490] *Legionário,* no. 637, October 22, 1944.

[491] Cf. "Fight Manfully and to the End," *Catolicismo,* no. 67 (July 1956).

[492] PIUS XI, Const. Ap. *Summorum Pontificum* of July 25, 1922, AAS 14 (1922), pp. 420-422.

designated Saint Ignatius the heavenly patron of all spiritual exercises with terms similar to those used by Pope Leo XIII when he declared Saint Thomas Aquinas patron of Catholic schools.

And in his Encyclical *Mens Nostra* of December 20, 1929, Pius XI states that "the excellence of spiritual doctrine altogether free from the perils and errors of false mysticism, the admirable facility of adapting the exercises to any order or state of man, whether they devote themselves to contemplation in the cloisters, or lead an active life in the affairs of the world, the apt coordination of the various parts, the wonderful and lucid order in the meditation of truths that seem to follow naturally one from another; and lastly the spiritual lessons which after casting off the yoke of sin and washing away the diseases inherent in his morals lead a man through the safe paths of abnegation and the removal of evil habits up to the supreme heights of prayer and divine love; without doubt all these are things which sufficiently show the efficacious nature of the Ignatian method and abundantly commend the Ignatian meditations."[493]

From Saint Ignatius, Plinio learned that "the soul of every man is a battlefield in which good and evil confront each other."[494] Furthermore, the *Spiritual Exercises*[495] are fully focused on a relentless logic from which a Christian's militant attitude is derived; he is called to choose between two standards, "that of Christ, our supreme Captain and Lord, and that of Lucifer, the mortal enemy of our human nature."[496]

"Saint Ignatius had good reason to expect great results from his meditation on the two standards. His worldview was so crystal clear that it was worth an apologetic page."[497] "I only learned about the Exercises when I was young, about nineteen or twenty. When I quit, so to speak,

---

[493] PIUS XI, Enc. *Mens nostra* of December 20, 1929, EE, *Pio XI, 1922-1929*, pp. 405-407 (pp. 374-409).

[494] "Fight Manfully and to the End," *Catolicismo*, no. 67 (July 1956).

[495] The book on the *Spiritual Exercises* resulted from a "clear illumination" through which the Lord deigned "open the eyes of the intellect....and make things known in such an excellent way that they seemed new" (SAINT IGNATIUS OF LOYOLA, *Autobiografia*, no. 30). It was written at Manresa in 1522 and solemnly approved by Paul III on July 31, 1548 with the brief *Pastoralis officii*, the first of countless documents by almost forty Popes in over four centuries. The first texts of the exercises (called *archetypal*) with their variants were published with critical notes by JOSE CALVERAS and CANDIDO DE DALMASES, *Monumenta Ignatiana. Institutionum Historica Societatis Jesu*, Rome, 1969. On the genesis and influence of the *Exercises*, cf. HENRI WATIGRANT, *La génèse des Exercices de San Ignacio*, Yvert et Tellier, Amiens, 1897; IGNACIO IPARRAGUIRE, *Historia de la práctica de los ejercicios*, Institutum Historicum Societatis Jesu, Bilbao-Roma, 1946. Cf. also HUGO RAHNER, S.J., *Ignatius von Loyola und das geschichtliche Werden seiner Frömmigkeit*, Pustet, Graz-Salzburg-Wien, 1947; JUAN PLAZAOLA, S.J. (prepared by), *Las fuentes de los ejercicios espirituales de San Ignacio, Actas del Simposio Internacional* (Loyola, Sep. 15-19, 1947), Ediciones Mensajero, Bilbao, 1998.

[496] ST. IGNATIUS OF LOYOLA, *Esercizi Spirituali*, nos. 136-138, It. tr., prepared by Fr. GIOVANNI FILIPPO ROOTHAN, S.J., Editrice Ancora, Milan, 1967, pp. 166-169.

[497] "3rd Act?" *Legionário*, no. 419, September 22, 1940.

worldly life to become a fervent Catholic, one of the things I bought was the *Exercises of Saint Ignatius of Loyola*. When I first read the Exercises of Saint Ignatius, I thought: this is the perfect and complete expression of logic. That logic came into me – just as my gaze can land on a wall perpendicular to me – and touched me to the depth of my being; and I thought: 'my spirit rejoices in finding here the perfect logic I always looked for but had never found in any book at all!' That was the logic of Saint Ignatius.

"Deep down Saint Ignatius' *Spiritual Exercises* are my whole way of thinking about the spiritual life. They are ultra reasonable because they were revealed by Our Lady at Manresa; I am a devotee to Our Lady, her slave, and so this forms a perfect circle."[498]

"In Saint Ignatius' biography, grandeur, nobility, purity and intransigence are the four major points we should be frequently enthused about."[499]

"We are children of the fight because we are children of the Mother who fights and continually crushes the head of the serpent. We are fighters by vocation and lose our physiognomy and spirit when we do not feel like fighters. We are in the fight, we live in the fight, we live for the fight, and we hope to die in the fight." [500]

"White Heresy" and the End of Christian Heroism

Combativeness requires a heroic spirit. Heroism is the primary characteristic not only of chivalry, but of holiness. That includes not only the great number of fighter saints canonized by the Church[501] but also other saints, as holiness requires the heroic exercise of all virtues. In this respect, Plinio says,

"Every knight would be a saint in the true sense of the word, for if his life's conditions changed, for example, if a knight of Baldwin the Leper[502] were transported through time and named Cardinal Secretary of

---

[498] EVP, 8 April 1973.

[499] EVP, 24 June 1973.

[500] RRR, 17 January 1976.

[501] Cf. RINO CAMILLERI, *I santi militari*, Piemme, Casale Monferrato, 1992; GERALDINA BONI, *La canonizzazione dei santi combattenti nella storia della Chiesa,* Libreria Editrice Vaticana, Città del Vaticano, 2012.

[502] Baldwin IV, King of Jerusalem, called "the leper" for the serious illness that struck him since childhood, showed his courage fighting against Saladin and was one of the few Christian commanders to defeat the Moor, chasing him all the way to the Syrian city of Aleppo (1176). Although undermined by the increasingly terrible illness he personally led his troops into battle on horseback for as long as his health allowed; later he would have himself carried to the battlefield on a stretcher. In the last years of his young life the disease made him blind and partially paralyzed. He died in Jerusalem in 1185 at the age of twenty-four.

Saint Pius X, he would have done for Saint Pius X as a cardinal of the Roman Curia the same as Cardinal Merry del Val did.[503]

"It is the essence of the knight to face enormous obstacles; to show dedication, love of God, of Our Lady and of Holy Church, in order to overcome those obstacles; and to generously give of himself in such a way as to go through two forms of martyrdom: The first is to lead a life that would not be worth living were it not out a desire for the supernatural – because he has faith, for otherwise he would not accept that life. Secondly it is to go all the way to martyrdom if need be with the special grace God gives the martyr at the hour "H," which is not the same grace he has up until that moment. This is the definition of a saint."[504]

Saint Aloysius Gonzaga, Saint Stanislaus Kostka and Saint John Berchmans[505] were three saints whose chastity shone in a preeminent way. They exercised this virtue to a heroic degree, to the point of making us forget their heroism.

"But God established knights as a family of souls which is for heroism as the three Jesuit saints are for purity. They are, as it were, personifications of purity. They are knights, and in them we see heroism as we saw purity in Saint John Berchmans. Providence created Chivalry to glorify heroism in a super-excellent way; for the other virtues, when practiced to a heroic degree, are of such value that they almost do not make us think of heroism."[506]

For Plinio, this militant conception of life is an expression of love of neighbor. In Heaven we shall love without having to sacrifice ourselves, but charity on earth presupposes sacrifice.[507]

"Combativity has this special form of beauty which is immolation. If we take the word 'immolation' – not in the sense of allowing oneself to be trounced but rather leaving all one has to entirely engage in the struggle out of love for something that is beyond what is one's own – we realize why an individual who is a warrior down to the hilt is a knight."[508]

---

[503] Rafael Merry del Val y Zulueta (1865-1930), born in London to an aristocratic Spanish family, he was ordained in 1888; made secretary of the Conclave of 1903; St. Pius X appointed him Cardinal Secretary of State. He closely collaborated with the Pope until the latter died, in 1914. Cf. P. G. DAL GAL, *Il servo di Dio card. Raffaele Merry del Val*, Paoline, Roma, 1956; JOSÉ M. JAVIERRE, *Merry del Val*, Juan Flors, Barcellona, 1965.

[504] EVP, 22 July 1979.

[505] Saint John Berchmans (1599-1621), with Saints Stanislaus Kostka (1550-1568) and Aloysius Gonzaga (1568-1591), is the patron of student youth.

[506] EVP, 22 July 1979.

[507] A. TANQUEREY, *The Spiritual Life: A Treatise on Ascetical and Mystical Theology*, no. 321.

[508] EVP, 23 July 1978.

"Militant faith is the faith capable of inspiring heroism. And for us it is synonymous with love of the cross, for our cross is carried as a knight would carry it; our cross is to be chivalrous."[509]

The nineteenth century was an age of great spiritual revival, especially in France. The nation that had been more deeply affected by the hurricane of the Revolution saw the development, as a reaction, of a new atmosphere of devotion and piety and a strong movement called ultramontane, affirming the rights of the Church.[510]

Ultramontanes opposed liberal Catholics who rejected the attitude of categorical opposition to the Revolution and tried to establish forms of accommodation with the modern world. They were willing to give up publicly affirming the Church's rights in order to maintain freedom of worship and religion.

This attitude reflected a tendency to an intimate and sentimental religiosity dominated by the *subjective* reason of saving one's soul over the objective motive of God's glory, and above all by a renunciation of heroism. This intimate spiritual attitude was the result of liberal separation between the religious order and the temporal order. Catholics were pushed to abandon the political and social camp and take refuge in devotional practices. Prof. Plinio attributes to Msgr. Emery,[511] rector of the Saint-Sulpice Seminary in Paris, a large part of responsibility for that change and analyzes his ambiguous role in the French Revolution.[512] In 1792, many Christians faced martyrdom and are now canonized for refusing to take the "liberté-égalité" oath as Emery advised them to.[513] He was not a follower of the French Revolution but the father of a "third party" that sought to find a halfway point, more practical than ideological, between the Church and the Revolution.

---

[509] EVP, 3 September 1989.

[510] The term "ultramontanism" was created and used in the 1800's in a derogatory sense to describe the attitude of Catholics "beyond the Alps" loyal to the doctrine and institutions of the Papacy, regarding the question of relations between the spiritual and temporal orders. In France, the fight between liberal and "ultramontane" Catholics developed especially after the rise of Napoleon III to power.

[511] Jacques-André Emery (1732-1811), elected superior general of the seminary of Saint Sulpice in 1782, after having been twice arrested and freed during the French Revolution, became one of the main promoters of reconciliation between the Church and Napoleon. Cf. J. LEFLON, DHGE, XV, 394-397, ID., *M. Emery*, 2 vols., Paris, 1944-1947; EUGÈNE LEVESQUE, DTC, IV (1911), cols. 2416-2418; IRENÉE NAVY, DSp, IV (1960), cols. 609-610; Id., *Saint-Sulpice* in DSp, XIV (1990), cols. 170-181.

[512] Cf. SD, 4 November & 25 January 1980.

[513] Cf. JEAN DE VIGUERIE, *Christianisme et Révolution. Cinq leçons d'Histoire de la Révolution française,* Nouvelles Editions Latines, Paris, 1986, pp.122-124. Cf. also CLEMENT TOURNIER, "L'Aa toulousaine contre le serment de liberté-égalité," *Revue d'histoire de l'Eglise de France,* 119 (1945), pp. 311-317.

Msgr. Emery spread the mentality of conciliation and concessions that tend to subordinate the Church to the world in the belief that the Church cannot fully convert the world. But while there was a vigorous reaction against Catholic liberalism, a reaction whose program was the Syllabus[514] of Pius IX, no analogous counter-offensive took place against this spiritual attitude. Plinio called this tendency to compromise the "white heresy mindset" just as Dom Chautard speaks of the "heresy of works," understood not as a doctrinal heresy but "a form of religiosity or action in which virtue is conceived as something alien to heroism or is heroic only on one track."[515]

White heresy is diametrically opposed to the spirit of Saint Ignatius and the Crusades:

> "The medieval crusader pretty much believed that war was waged on the battlefield. Saint Ignatius of Loyola extended the concept of war to one's whole life: everything became the fight. Then white heresy came and said: everything is non-fight except for war. But this is a distortion, for Saint Ignatius expanded the concept and we should expand it further as follows: everything in life is mainly struggle. We do not say that 'everything is struggle' but 'everything is primarily struggle; struggle is the main sense of all things.'"[516]

One risks replacing heroism with a spirit of accommodation with the world, exchanging the primacy of the glory of God with the salvation of one's soul. In fact, as Dom Pollien aptly emphasizes, the most elevated thing we should see in Religion is not our salvation but the glory of God. Indeed, Religion consists "more in respecting the rights of God than in saving one's own hopes; more in glorifying God than becoming a blessed. The essence of religion is God's honor; its accessory is man's happiness, which necessarily follows the honor of God." [517]

It is characteristic of white heresy to extinguish the noblest passions that could guide a Christian: love of justice as such, hatred of sin, and the will to exterminate evil. It thus gives rise to a new kind of Catholic deprived of great ideas and doctrinal horizons but also of great passions, beginning with the ability to have hate, indignation and wrath.

> "The new man of the new century is a man without anger. The twentieth century should be the century without anger in which only the

---

[514] Cf. Pius IX, *Syllabus*, ASS, 3 (1866-67), pp. 168-176, It. tr., EE, *Pio IX*, II, pp. 520-545.

[515] EVP, 22 July 1979.

[516] EVP, 8 April 1973.

[517] D. Francesco di Sales Pollien, *Cristianesimo vissuto*, It. tr., Marietti, Casale Monferrato, 1964, p. 56.

non-angry have the right to survive and in which there is no room for anyone who is choleric and affirms the absolute."[518]

Dissociation between virtue and heroism is the beginning of a spiritual decadence, which Plinio summarizes thus:

"From the moment the ideal of Chivalry went into decline, subconscious sophistries about heroism were born in the piety of the faithful. They are:

1. Heroism and holiness are distinct; you can be a hero without being a saint, and when we venerate a saint we venerate virtues distinct from heroism. For example, the purity of Saint Aloysius Gonzaga or the wisdom of Saint Thomas Aquinas. Therefore, a saint does not need to be heroic.

2. By its nature, heroism is something better suited to the secular sphere than the religious one. A priest is not a hero in the ordinary sense of the word. There was a priest, who later became bishop, who told me that a priest is an intermediary being between man and woman. Priests are not familiar with the idea of heroism as inculcated by Chivalry, that is, heroism that can attain all forms of the virtue of fortitude.

3. Well analyzed, a hero is an unbalanced man just as, well analyzed, a poet is a madman. He is singled-minded, gutless or heartless, but unbalanced.

4. Human life finds all its meaning and fulfillment without fighting. Therefore it is better not to have combat than to have it. And every misfortune or difficulty that forces us to fight is a failure. Taking it easy is the essence of life."[519]

The Courage and Grandeur of Chastity

Of all the various forms of heroic courage a man should have, "the greatest, or one of the greatest is to have the courage to decide to be pure."[520]

"Of voluntary celibacy, there is never enough praise that one can give to it. Celibacy is dedication par excellence because a truly chaste man renounces a lot of things in order to live for his ideal. Celibacy only has meaning when man decides to live for an ideal higher than the family ideal. Otherwise, chastity has no meaning. Therefore, it is par excellence a virtue by which we renounce the amenities and attractions of family life to serve a higher ideal, an ideal with this specific characteristic: it gives no rewards on earth but in Heaven, and is therefore the height of

---

[518] EVP, 3 November 1985.
[519] EVP, 22 July 1979.
[520] *Chivalry Dies Not,* p. 182.

dedication. It is dedication properly focused on God, for the ideal is the purest and closest reflection of God."[521]

The practice of chastity bestows grandeur for two reasons:

"Chastity is the virtue that most emphasizes man's spiritual aspect and places his carnal and material aspect under the proper yoke. Now since man is spirit and matter and his greatness is found in his spirit (for by his matter he would be waste), the purer he is the more the spirit factor dominates and elevates him with true and pure grandeur. Chastity is therefore grandeur. Even more: no grandeur is true grandeur without chastity."[522]

"We will have purity only when we understand how impurity fundamentally nauseates and displeases man as he realizes that his body solicits impurity in an attractive way that dominates his soul in a ravishing way. And the dominated soul then perceives its own disorder and degradation for having become a slave of matter.

"The pure soul is not an enemy of matter; it is a friend of matter but to the extent that matter subjects itself to it. When the soul appeals to higher things, to the marvelous, the 'transsphere,' the metaphysical and notably the supernatural – to Faith – it manages to dominate the body. The result is that a man is entirely chaste only when he loves this hierarchy of which the more immediate manifestation in him is the dominance of his soul over his body. But it is also the dominance of the metaphysical over the physical, the supernatural over the natural, the Church over temporal society, the governing Church over the governed Church, of the Pope over the hierarchy, all in a cascade of inequalities.

"When man's soul is well formed in this way, he either becomes forcefully combative, or fails to carry this out. Hence purity in the Catholic sense is like a palace with a central building and two wings. One wing is anti-egalitarianism, the sense of hierarchy, and the other is the fighting spirit."[523]

Plinio resolutely states that a chaste man has much greater strength and courage than those devoid of the virtue of purity. He explains:

"What is courage, in the final analysis? Courage is the firmness of principles and ardor for ideals by which we hold back fear, sacrifice our physical integrity and our lives or risk any intellectual or moral danger for the benefit of our ideals.

"In simpler terms: if a man has an 'x' ideal with principles firm enough to be really convinced of it and hold it as true, he has an ardent

---

[521] SDS, 3 February 1973.
[522] COM on *Chivalry*, p. 29.
[523] EVP, 25 January 1981.

desire whereby he loves that ideal more than his own life. If that happens, at the moment when he feels fear of being killed, hurt, slandered, despised, persecuted, whatever, he is able to hold back that fear and sacrifice for his ideals.

"Therefore, courage is defined essentially as firmness in thinking, wanting and holding back; this is courage.

"Chastity is firmness par excellence. It is precisely that high degree of firmness and courage by which, when man is convinced that he should be pure, he understands the incomparable beauty and nobility of the ideal of purity. When he understands that this is the will of God and it is the way it should be, when he loves this purity he loves God's will, refuses the suggestions of temptation and remains pure.

"The act of fidelity to purity, substantially and by definition, is an act of courage. The pure person is courageous; the courageous person is pure. Both things are as reversible as a part of a whole and a whole in the part."[524]

Saint Joan of Arc, the Virgin Warrior

Saint Joan of Arc[525] is the antithesis of "white heresy," the model of virgin warrior in which two virtues, chastity and heroism, come together admirably.[526] She was a virgin to the point of being able to assume a man's fighting function while keeping all her femininity.[527]

"I have the impression that Saint Joan of Arc radiated virginity and that it was easier to keep chastity being around her than by reading a whole treatise. That virginity glittered in a special way at the time of combat. Pugnacious, courageous, bold and self-assured virginity reduces impurity to a state of cowardice; before a person like Saint Joan of Arc, impurity's possibility of resisting is like a tumor's to a doctor's scalpel: zero! He cuts, the boil bursts, and it is over.

---

[524] COM on *Chivalry*.

[525] Saint Joan of Arc (1412-1431), a young peasant from Domrémy, was favored with heavenly voices that encouraged her to help Charles VII, King of France, in his work to liberate the country from the English. Arrested by the English and judged for witchcraft, she was burned at the stake on May 30, 1431. She was declared blessed by Pope Pius X on April 18, 1909 and declared a saint by Benedict XV on July 10, 1920. The conclusion of St. Joan of Arc's work can be known thanks to two exceptionally valuable historical sources: the documents of the two lawsuits against her. The first contains the transcription of Joan's long and numerous questionings during the last few months of her life (February-May 1431). The second, of her rehabilitation, contains the testimonies of about 120 eyewitnesses to all the periods of her life. This latter trail, opened under the authority of Pope Callixtus III, concluded with a solemn ruling declaring her condemnation null and void (July 7, 1456; II, pp. 604-610). (Cf. *Procès de Condamnation de Jeanne d'Arc*, 3 vols., and *Procès en Nullité de la Condamnation de Jeanne d'Arc*, 5 vols., ed. Klincksieck, Paris 1960-1989).

[526] SDS, 5 March 1977.

[527] COM on *Chivalry*, pp. 99-100.

"Virginity is a beautiful virtue and Saint Louis Gonzaga personified it in a splendid way. But except for Our Lady, who is naturally beyond comparison, at least in my eyes there is something in the virginity of Saint Joan of Arc that draws one's imagination and senses over any other form of virginity because it is connected to the heroism of fire and blood. Why? Because it is contradictory for a virgin in her fragility to be a warrior, let alone a general; that contradiction with femininity appears, and purity coupled with femininity and strength produces a special beauty."[528]

The *Lumen Christi* shone eminently in Saint Joan of Arc:

"The pulchrum of an ideal is reflected in the soul of those who fight for it. For example, Saint Joan of Arc radiated light at every moment of her life. Even at the tragic moment when the flames began to lick the wood to which she was tied, Saint Joan of Arc shone more than the actual flames. It was a reflection of the great love of God that drove her."[529]

"The entire warlike ideal of the Middle Ages lives on in Saint Joan of Arc....and opens for women the possibility of becoming saints in a way molded par excellence after the strong woman praised by the Gospel." [530]

Life and Death of a Knight

A man's life is summed up in the hour of death, the time when we will be infallibly judged by God according to our love. But if it is important to die well, living well is the best way to prepare for the last encounter.

The spirit of sacrifice is what distinguished a nobleman from the bourgeois and commoner and made him resemble a priest:

"For a nobleman, waging war was an act of holocaust for the glorification of the Church, the free dissemination of the Faith, and legitimate common good in the temporal sphere."[531]

"For the medieval knight, war was the pinnacle of life.... And a knight's death was the most important act in his life. The typical death of a perfect knight was not caused by sickness while lying in bed but took place in combat, facing the adversary and risking his life to defeat him. War, therefore. Death is conceived while confronting an earthly foe...who is an agent of the prince of death who lies eternally in the sepulcher of hell. And the pinnacle of life is to know how to offer it.

"Keeping all due proportions, as this example is so much higher, just as the apex of the Mass is the Consecration, in which Our Lord offers Himself, so also the knight offers himself at the hour of death. He knows

---

[528] MNF, 1 June 1989.
[529] SD, 16 February 1990.
[530] CSN, 14 September 1991.
[531] *Chivalry Dies Not,* p. 144.

that he renounces everything for the sake of a cause that is worth everything, and with this his life works out right.

"The beauty of a knight's death is to be daring, to expose himself to danger, eventually to die or win in a joyful and jubilant way because in battle he loves the pulchrum of battle, he practices the holy *pulchrum* of complete self-offering and lives the beauty of that supreme act. He gives himself up and is glad to do so because he manages to do what he wanted. He dies a saint!" [532]

"Under these conditions, the medieval knight understood the beauty of his life and his death, the beauty of war, but above all the beauty of death, of that supreme moment he had to sacrifice his life and experienced the joy of sacrifice by considering the beauty of giving his life to wound the adversary and thus rise to heaven."[533] "Even more beautiful than to live, is to die; death is the apex. And this is at the height of the notion of Chivalry." [534]

The Spirit of Chivalry as the Antithesis of the "Ecumenical" Spirit

The essence of chivalry is a fighting spirit that frontally opposes the pacifist and ecumenical mentality of our times. Plinio Corrêa de Oliveira describes it thus:

"What I defined as spirit of chivalry is not only the spirit of fighting on a battlefield because compelled by duty, but a taste for the fight as such and for risk as such on account of the intrinsic beauty of combat and risk, of force opposing force, good opposing evil, reason opposing error, reasoning overcoming sophistry. All kinds of fencing and clashes have their own beauty when it comes to the clash of truth against error and good versus evil. In this militant conflict the truth shines with a special light and error appears with special blackness.

A man earnestly committed to this fight on the side of good feels especially linked to the absolute, which is God Our Lord. When fighting for a principle, he exposes his life, reputation, assets or anything else and does it forcefully, trying to destroy the adversary. In so doing he implicitly affirms the principle that his cause is an absolute, eternal and true, a reflection of God. Our Lord deserves for both him and his adversary to disappear, as contingent things must disappear before the Eternal and Absolute. So the essence of Chivalry is a taste for risk and combat as a religious way of giving glory to God."[535]

---

[532] EXT, 11 October 1990.
[533] Idem.
[534] SDS, 3 August 1974.
[535] RRR, 23 September 1974.

From this spiritual perspective, the "mission" of the Plinian school is to "mark all Christendom with the spirit of chivalry by:

1. emphasizing the militant character of the Church and of Christendom to its ultimate limits;

2. taking to its furthermost limits the understanding that the spirit of Chivalry involves the combat of ideas and counter-revolutionary psychological warfare, symbolic warfare, etc. in everyday life and in everyday manners." [536]

"We should ask Our Lady to really grant this rotten and decaying century the supreme mercy of having the ideal of Chivalry reborn. Against it, revolutionaries object: 'The ideal of Chivalry is not an ecumenical ideal, and we want to make ecumenism win.' We answer: 'Precisely for this reason we want its rebirth, for ours is the anti-ecumenical ideal. We are the opposite of ecumenism.'"[537]

To me, runaway pacifism and secularism have always seemed related, not on the surface, but in their foundation. And it always seemed to me that pacifists of all kinds did not want to consider that, since the world is a vale of tears, fights and conflicts would necessarily and occasionally arise. It was a deplorable necessity but the result of original sin and other sins of men; but that deplorable reality was such that it would be even more deplorable if there were no fight. For man conceived in original sin would be amputated and deformed if he had no possibility at all of taking up at times the fight for the sacral to the ultimate of all forms of dedication.

"Legitimate war takes on a note of sacrality. It is a holocaust even with no religious reason. When there is a border dispute a man goes to war to defend his country's rights and does so for a moral reason: one of God's Commandments obliges him to go to war. And for a knight the war is holy, not in its immediate but ultimate goal: to fulfill his duty to his country.

"Hence the existence in every war of a sense of sublime holocaust that gives life a beauty that is indispensable for composing some of its aspects in this world, as a consequence of original sin and actual sins."[538]

---

[536] EVP, 9 April 1978.

[537] RRR, 16 February 1991. As such, the term ecumenism, whose meaning is clearly explained by Pius XI in the Encyclical *Mortalium animos* of January 6, 1928 (AAS, 20 (1928), pp. 5-16), is neutral, but today it has taken on a relativist meaning contrary to the principle that, by natural law and Divine Law, the sole true Religion is the Roman Catholic and Apostolic Religion founded by Jesus Christ as a visible and sovereign society destined to gather all men into her bosom.

[538] MNF, 14 April 1989.

CHAPTER III

MARIAN SPIRITUALITY

If a man's testament offers us the key to understand his life, this is especially true of Plinio Corrêa de Oliveira, whose simple and moving will reveals the core of his spirituality. In the document, dated January 10, 1978, the year of his seventieth birthday, Plinio writes, among other things:

"In the name of the Most Holy and undivided Trinity, Father, Son and Holy Ghost. And of the Blessed Virgin Mary, my Mother and Lady. Amen. I, Plinio Corrêa de Oliveira...declare that I have lived and hope to die in the Holy Roman Catholic and Apostolic Faith, which I hold with all the strength of my soul. I cannot find sufficient words to thank Our Lady for the privilege of having lived since my very first days and of dying, as I hope, in the Holy Church. To it I have always devoted, currently devote, and hope to devote until my last breath absolutely all my love. All the persons, institutions, and doctrines I have loved in the course of my life and currently love, I have loved and love solely because they were or are in accord with the Holy Church, and in the measure to which they were or are in accord with the Holy Church. Likewise, I never opposed institutions, persons, or doctrines except insofar as they were opposed to the Holy Catholic Church.

"I likewise thank Our Lady – without being able to find adequate words – for the grace of having read and disseminated the Treatise of True Devotion to the Most Holy Virgin, of St. Louis Marie Grignion of Montfort, and of having consecrated myself to Her as Her perpetual slave. Our Lady was always the Light of my life and from Her clemency I hope She will continue to be my Light and my Help until the last moment of my existence.

"Again I thank Our Lady – and with what emotion – for having granted me to be born of Dona Lucília. I revered and loved her to the utmost of my capacity and, after her death, not a single day passed without my remembering her with unspeakable longings. Of her soul I also ask that she assist me until my last moment with her ineffable goodness. I hope to meet her in Heaven amidst the luminous cohort of souls who most specially loved Our Lady."[539]

In Plinio's will, devotion to Our Lady and love of the Church form a single whole and are both the basis and culmination of his counter-revolutionary militancy. He also points out the immense affection and gratitude he had towards his mother, Lucilia Ribeiro dos Santos,[540] who spiritually formed him and who was always close to him with extraordinary kindness, an earthly image of the heavenly Mother's boundless goodness. It was Dona Lucilia who opened the soul of her son to understand the mystery of the Cross and to have a tender, passionate, but manly and combative devotion to the Blessed Virgin Mary.

Our Lord not only offered His life for us but left His most holy Mother to protect, support and guide us through the difficult times of our lives. Mary is not only the Mother of God but also the Mother of all men, of all the living: Most Holy, Immaculate, Mediatrix, co-Redemptrix, Queen of heaven and earth. "Mother, spiritually indeed, but truly Mother of the members of Christ, who we are," says Saint Pius X, quoting from Saint Augustine (*L. de S. Virginitate,* c.6).[541] This spiritual motherhood results from her *fiat* in Nazareth, for she knew that by conceiving Jesus, the Head of the Mystical Body, she consented at the same time to our supernatural birth as members of that Body. That maternity was later ratified on Calvary, as the Gospel recounts: On the cross, when He "had seen his mother and the disciple standing whom he loved, he saith to his mother: Woman, behold thy son. After that, he saith to the disciple: Behold thy mother" (Jn. 19: 26-27).

Were we to sum up the cardinal points of Plinian spirituality, we should say that it was sacral and anti-egalitarian, combative and chivalrous, and in its apex, profoundly Marian.

Crusade and Love of the Cross

The first great truth that Plinio learned from childhood and through which he overcame his nature is that what gives sense and meaning to man's life: sacrifice and suffering. Man is not made for pleasure but for heroism, and the redeeming Cross of Christ traces the path of our existence.

---

[539] Cf. *http://www.pliniocorreadeoliveira.info/UK_19780110_SealedTestament.htm#.Vw1YE1TyuUk.*
[540] Cf. the pages dedicated to her in *The Crusader of the 20th Century,* pp. 35-41, and J. S. CLA DIAZ, *Dona Lucilia,* Artpress, São Paulo, 1995.
[541] ST. PIUS X, Encyclical *Ad diem illum laetissimum,* February 2, 1904, *Pii X P. M. Acta,* I, pp. 147-166; EE, *Pius X,* pp. 40-69.

"In the old days, when someone wanted to show that something had a supreme dignity he would place a cross on it. Men were baptized in the shadow of the cross, were married in the shadow of the cross, put crosses on their shields, in their homes, and died looking at the cross. In other words, the cross marked man's entire life. This is due to the fundamental idea that life was made for suffering and heroism. And he that speaks of heroism speaks of the cross."[542]

Our Lord addressed this invitation to all his disciples: "If any man will come after me, let him deny himself, and take up his cross, and follow me" (Mt. 16:24). The essential condition to follow Jesus and love Him is to renounce oneself, that is, the evil tendencies of one's nature, and to carry one's cross by accepting suffering, deprivation, humiliation and in general all the hardships God sends us to perfect ourselves. Saint Louis de Montfort's *Letter to the Friends of the Cross* was among Plinio Corrêa de Oliveira's favorite readings.[543] From it he drew a spiritual combativeness born from the Cross and turned toward a radical consistency.

Based on various authors, Plinio explains that one of life's greatest deceptions is to think that you can be happy by avoiding suffering.[544] In fact, man suffers more when he does not suffer than when he does suffer, because after the fall of Adam the human soul is made to suffer. The real problem is the meaning and purpose of human suffering, for "the only true form of happiness in life is for the person to achieve the end for which he exists."[545]

In the twentieth century, under the influence of the theological and spiritual errors of Americanism and modernism, there arose a superficial conception of the spiritual life that tends to reduce or even eliminate the role of suffering. In Catholic circles, a blind optimism spread that implied ignoring the presence of evil and error in history. Plinio identifies the causes of this spiritual distortion in a defection of the noblest faculties of the soul: the will and the intellect. Escaping from suffering derives not only from a refusal of the person's will to suffer but also of his intellect to

---

[542] SD, 14 September 1964.

[543] *Lettre circulaire aux amis de la Croix*, in *Œuvres complètes de saint Louis-Marie Grignion de Montfort*, Ed. du Seuil, Paris, 1966, pp. 217-262.

[544] A. TANQUEREY, *La santificazione e divinizzazione del dolore,* It. tr., Desclée, Roma, 1932; GABRIELE M. ROSCHINI, *Il problema del male,* Jonica, Roma, 1959; CHARLES JOURNET, *Il male. Saggio teologico*, It. tr., Borla, Torino, 1963; ENRICO ZOFFOLI, *Il male itinerario della speranza*, edizioni Segno, Udine, 1994; ALBERTO CATURELLI, *El abismo del mal*, Gladius, Buenos Aires, 2007.

[545] RST, 23 April 1964.

think, as thinking is arduous: "To think seriously requires a enormous effort."[546]

"Saint Thomas says in the *Summa Contra Gentiles:* 'Now, if no evils were present in things, much of man's good would be diminished, both in regard to knowledge and in regard to the desire or love of the good. In fact, the good is better known from its comparison with evil, and while we continue to suffer certain evils our desire for goods grows more ardent. For instance, how great good health is, is best known by the sick; and they also crave it more than do the healthy.'[547] The human mind, by strictly analyzing good without comparing it with evil, easily fails to acquire a thorough knowledge of that good. And the result is that without that comparison the person's very vision of the good is diminished and fails to attain the fullness it should."[548]

Theology identifies in original sin the remote cause of all the physical and moral evils of the universe, reminding us that "Wherefore as by one man sin entered into this world, and by sin death; and so death passed upon all men, in whom all have sinned" (Rom. 5:12). All the world's disorder and evils have their source in the original sin Adam transmitted to humanity.[549] The original sin was a separation between man and God that weakened at the same time man's soul and body, producing a moral disorder culminating with sin and a physical disorder culminating in death. God created man immortal, but after sin, as Saint Augustine says, human life became "a race towards death."[550]

Suffering has meaning, Plinio says,

"Because if there is a reason for evil to exist in the universe, then there is a reason for suffering. Both things are combined. If there is a reason for pain and even sin to exist, since pain and sin are either evil as such or causes of evil, each in its own way is evil or a cause of evil and so they have a reason for being."[551]

Original sin created the need for constant struggle within the human soul, which entails effort and suffering.[552] For man conceived in original sin, opposition, adversity and pain are necessary conditions to attain true happiness in heaven and partial happiness on earth. A life completely without suffering would not be one of delights but of hell. Either man

---

[546] Idem.

[547] http://genius.com/St-thomas-aquinas-summa-contra-gentiles-book-iii-q-1-83-annotated.

[548] RST, 30 May 1964.

[549] "In the dynamysm of original sin," Saint Thomas Aquinas comments, "this is the order: first Adam corrupted nature with his sinful act; then the corruption of nature spread to persons; and finally, from a sinful person, this nature was transmitted to others" (*In II Sent.*, d. 31, q. 1, a. 1).

[550] St. AUGUSTINE, *De Civitate Dei*, 12:10.

[551] RST, 16 June 1964.

[552] RST, 15 May 1964.

suffers and gives meaning to his suffering or he falls into that depressive suffering that paradoxically arises from the absence of suffering. Plinio finds the most profound reason for this in the famous phrase that opens the *Confessions* of Saint Augustine: "Thou hast made us for Thee, Lord, and our heart is restless until it rests in Thee." [553]

> "So this is what I maintain: nothing is more appropriate than suffering to confer nobility to the soul, and there cannot be nobility without suffering. We can imagine people with all kinds of temperaments and types of personality: if we take away their appreciation for pain (and pain actually suffered), these souls become absolutely worthless." [554]

Without suffering, man is unable to fully develop the perfections that enrich his soul:

> "Original sin created in the human mind circumstances such that without suffering man is unable to acquire any degree of spiritual perfection, however modest and most elementary. And suffering is a kind of oxygen in which all virtues develop. If this oxygen is lacking, they wither and die." [555]

The Cross defeated evil in the world:

> "The cross is the symbol of the Passion of Our Lord Jesus Christ, of all the suffering a Catholic carries in this life, with which, in union with Our Lord Jesus Christ, he opens for himself the doors of Heaven. Placing the Cross of Our Lord Jesus Christ higher than all things was a concern of the entire Christian civilization. In cities, the highest buildings used to be church towers, topped by a cross. The cross also topped the crowns of kings. When they wanted to make a very important document, on the top of the document they inscribed the cross. In short, all the highest things that man could conceive had the Cross of Our Lord Jesus Christ, bringing the idea that while His mission was not exhausted on the cross, that was its central point. And that the most admirable and the most adorable of all that Our Lord had done was to have suffered and died on the cross." [556]

In a world that abhors suffering, Plinio always tried to infuse both love of the fight and of the redeeming Cross of Christ; a love repugnant to human nature but attainable with the supernatural help of grace.

> "Everyone abhors suffering, any form of suffering. Love of the cross is a grace that cannot be obtained without a special favor. It is a grace from Heaven to be obtained through Our Lady in view of her merits and

---

[553] ST. AUGUSTINE, *Confessions,* 1, 1.

[554] RST, 23 April 1964.

[555] RST, 16 May 1964.

[556] SD, 14 September 1964.

sorrows, and above all of the infinite merits of Our Lord Jesus Christ and His Passion. This is the grace we should ask for, and that is how the soul becomes vigorous."[557]

Love for the Cross is not love of suffering for its own sake but is the highest expression of love for the One who took upon Himself all the physical and moral pains of the universe, except for sin, to obtain our eternal happiness.

"Of course its immediate object is love of pain, but it ultimately is love of Our Lord Jesus Christ while crucified, love of His Passion and death. It is love for the Cross, the material object of His torment; but behind it is the acceptance of the principle that after original sin it is necessary for man to suffer, and that a man who is not resolved in his soul to face sufferings, indeed to feel their weight upon himself and to do his duty, is worth nothing. However, if he is willing to accept suffering, to accept the cross, then he changes completely.

"There will be large crosses or small crosses according to each person's spiritual school. But what is needed is to renounce the myth that life should unfold without the cross. It is by forming a strong soul in this sense of the word, in union with Our Lord Jesus Christ and through the tears of Mary, to obtain the energy to suffer what Providence asks: Great suffering if Providence so asks, little suffering if Providence so asks, but always saying 'yes' to the crosses requested by Providence. This is the love of the cross we are dealing with."[558]

The Passion of Christ must be the model for every Christian:

"It turns out that to see the real picture we need not look at Our Lord's fight with the men who haunted Him but rather at the struggle of the Man-God against the devil to wrest mankind from his claws. In this sense, Our Lord's Incarnation was an assault, His preaching was a challenge, and His death was the crushing of Satan. In the logic of the struggle He came to wage, victory would come from His oblation, since he had to win as a victim. It is a very special situation: a victim was needed in order to win. He won as a victim."[559]

The Crusades as a Spiritual Movement

The spiritual movement of the Crusades was the highest expression of men's love of the Cross in history.

Calling Plinio Corrêa de Oliveira the "Crusader of the twentieth century" expressed the dominant note in his life, a continuous appeal to others to join him in the crusade for the restoration of the Kingship of

---

[557] SD, 3 May 1966.
[558] Idem.
[559] EVP, 15 July 1979.

Christ over souls and societies. He always had a supreme admiration for the epic crusades, which had the same brightness, translucent beauty, upward momentum and creative power as the works of Saint Thomas Aquinas and the cathedrals.

Strictly speaking, the term *Crusades*[560] refers to the military expeditions the Papacy undertook between the eleventh and thirteenth centuries to liberate the Holy Sepulchre. Historically they may be placed between the Council of Piacenza of 1095, in which Pope Urban II launched the first appeal to the Crusades, and the fall of Saint John of Acre, the last Christian stronghold in the Holy Land, in 1291.

In a broader sense, the Crusades can be understood as armed expeditions in defense of the Faith and of Christian civilization. This is the case of the Spanish Reconquista and the expulsion of the Moors from the nascent Kingdom of Portugal.[561] The Spanish Reconquista lasted almost eight centuries, from the battle of Covadonga in 722 to the fall of Granada in 1492. In later centuries, the Muslims attacked Europe again and were defeated in the battles of Lepanto (1571), Vienna (1683), and Budapest (1686).[562]

In the strict sense, however, the Crusades were something more, and also different. At Lepanto and in Vienna, Christian knights fought to defend their faith but also their own land, threatened by Islam. The war in the Holy Land instead was conducted for eminently spiritual purposes.

---

[560] Bibliography on the Crusades is most extensive. Cf. among others, René Grousset, *Histoire des croisades et du royaume franc de Jérusalem*, Perrin, Paris, 1999 (1934-1936); Paul Rousset, *Histoire des croisades*, Payot, Paris, 1957; Kenneth M. Setto, ed., et al., *A History of the Crusades,* University of the Pennsylvania Press, Philadelphia, 1955-1989, 4 v.; Hans E. Mayer, *Geschichte der Kreuzzüge*, W. Kohlhammer, Stuttgart, 1965; Michel Balard, *Les Croisades et l'Orient latin*, Colin, Paris, 2001. On the idea of the crusading spirit, cf. Carl Erdmann, *Alle origini dell'idea di crociata* (1935), It. tr., Centro Italiano di Studi sull'Alto Medioevo, Spoleto, 1996; Michel Villey, *La Croisade. Essai sur la fondation d'une théorie juridique*, Vrin, Paris, 1942; Paul Alphandery-Alphonse Dupront, *La Cristianità e l'idea di Crociata* (1954), It. tr., Il Mulino, Bologna, 1983 (new edition with a postface by Michel Balard, Albin Michel, Paris, 1995); Jean Richard, *L'Esprit de la croisade*, Cerf, Paris, 1977; Etienne Delaruelle, *L'idée de croisade au Moyen Age*, La Bottega d'Erasmo, Turin, 1980; Jonathan Riley-Smith, *The Crusades: Idea and Reality*, 1095-1274, E. Arnold, London, 1981; idem, *The First Crusade and the Idea of Crusading,* Athlone, London, 1993; K. Elm and C. D. Fonseca, ed., et al., *Militia Sancti Sepulcri, Idea e Istituzioni: Atti del Colloquio internazionale tenuto presso la Pontificia. Università del Laterano,* April 10-12, 1996, Vatican City, 1998; P. Rousset, *Histoire d'une ideologie. La Croisade*, L'Age d'Homme, Lausanne, 1999; Jean Flori, *La guerre sainte. La formation de l'idée de croisade dans l'Occident chrétien*, Aubier, Paris, 2001.

[561] Dom Afonso Henriques, the first king of Portugal, started the expulsion of the Moors from the country, crushing them at Ourique (1139). His descendants finished that task two centuries before the Spaniards.

[562] Cf. Massimo Viglione, *"Deus vult?". Cambiamento e persistenza dell'idea di Crociata nella Chiesa. Dal II Concilio di Lione alla morte di Pio II (1274-1464),* Edizioni Nuova Cultura, Rome, 2014.

It is important to emphasize that the main purpose of the Crusades was never political or economic but always eminently religious: reconquering the Holy Land and, depending on the historical moment, preserving the Christian kingdom of Jerusalem, established during the First Crusade. Along with the Holy Shroud, the empty tomb of the Holy Sepulchre was a living testimony of the Resurrection and the most precious relic of Christendom. The Crusades were veritable armed pilgrimages to resume proper veneration for these relics, but also great movements of the soul whose profound meaning Plinio Corrêa de Oliveira grasped better than many historians.

> "Urban II went to Clermont to convoke the Crusade because the earlier calls previous to his appeals encountered a certain inertia among the nobility. In that sleepy state the nobility did not correspond to the dream it should have of itself. But speaking to knights at Clermont, Blessed Pope Urban II had the grace of reviving in them a dream that they received in a semi-deteriorated state. And placed before the purity of that dream they became enthused: *Deus Vult!* They were sensitive to something they had been less responsive to earlier, because the ideal they had in mind was somewhat deteriorated.

> "Then the Crusade arises, and subsequently there is a continuous flow of Crusaders as a result of the impulse given by Urban II. But they were mixed with other Crusaders who had a deteriorated ideal of nobility, and so some crusades worked out while others did not. The story of the Crusades is much less beautiful than the story of the crusading spirit."[563]

> "Except for something extremely exceptional that needs to be very well demonstrated, the Crusade's normal purpose was to fulfill the hope that grace instilled in the soul of Blessed Urban II and the Crusaders when they set themselves in motion. This is the purpose.

> "Now, a collateral, clearly secondary but indispensable purpose is to form those who will fight in the Crusade, so that they win the prize of heroes not just externally with the sword, but inside their own souls through renunciation, self-denial and things inherent to the soul.

> "And the third purpose is to be a world history saga that shows contemporary and successive generations the splendor of the Church, the beauty of sanctity, and the depravity and infamy of evil: that which the ancients called the chastening of peoples."[564]

The Crusades were one of the most beautiful movements of soul in the history of the Church. That movement of soul corresponded to a great

---

[563] AMC, 5 September 1989.
[564] MNF, 9 January 1979.

grace that has not been extinguished. Even today the word "Crusader" is laden with fascination and reverberates in many hearts. Indeed, the idea of crusade is not only an historical event limited to the Middle Ages, but a constant in the Christian soul, a state of mind, a category of the spirit that goes through moments of eclipse but is destined to resurface in various forms. To try to suppress the idea of crusade means to expunge the very idea of Christian combativeness.

> "The spirit of Crusade is a form of love of the Cross given to those with a special vocation to admire and understand the beauty and sublimity of the Crusade with a super enthusing, enthralling and marvelous vision of the fight. The crusader is a fighter who finds his cross in the fight and whose life of struggle is a cross he carries with joy, because he loves to fight, he is an enthusiast of the fight, and because to him the fight metaphysically represents something very great." [565]

> "However, this is no ordinary heroism but a special heroism illuminated by Religion, by faith and by certainties of all kinds, with extraordinary disposition and courage to support any form of pain, suffering or risk; with a warlike impetus and a capacity to strike unprecedented and perhaps unparalleled in history. When you talk about the Crusades, all these concepts come together and shine in one's eyes with a light of Faith and Religion." [566]

There is a close link between the Crusades and martyrdom. But in some respects, the epic saga of the Crusades is even superior to that of martyrs, for martyrdom is a supreme test that comes suddenly. A martyr's dramatic alternative is between fidelity to Christ, which opens the gates of heaven, or the cowardice of apostasy, which unlocks those of hell. Also those without a heroic vocation have the duty to bear witness even to the shedding of their blood.

Unlike martyrdom, waging a Crusade is a choice that supposes the heroic vocation of devoting one's whole life to fight for the Church and for Christian civilization. This means to be willing not only to lose one's life in battle but to "die" in all the tough trials of daily life. The number of those who fell decimated by fatigue, hunger and disease in expeditions to free the Holy Sepulchre was higher than those killed in battle, not counting the terrible spiritual and moral trials they sustained, being distant from family, uncertain about the future, misunderstood and sometimes even betrayed by their Christian brethren.

Plinio notes:

---

[565] MNF, 1 September 1989.
[566] SD, 21 October 1972.

"The crusading warrior is placed with the idea before him that he may die; and facing the idea of death he is reminded of the Judgment, Hell and Heaven, and he wants death, Judgment and Paradise, but not Hell; and this idea illuminates the crusader from head to toe. Even more, he knows he will suffer much, will be separated from family, can be imprisoned and become a slave of infidels without the help of religion; but he does not want the Sepulcher, where the Perfect par excellence was laid to rest, to remain in Muslim hands. He sees all that head on, and with joy. This joy in pain, in difficulty – and the impetus with which he departs toward this joy – is the definition of Christian, Catholic courage; it is the highest aspect of knighthood."[567]

"By seeing in Him the Redeemer, Who led the coherence of His mission to the ultimate sacrifice, and did not flinch before any suffering to fulfill His mission, the crusader obtained a sacrificial idea of life that broke the idea of a life of pleasure, and made one understand that life becomes beautiful and is successful if man entirely fulfils his sacrifice as Jesus Christ took His cross to the top of Golgotha."[568]

Military Orders in the Middle Ages and the Hatred of Sin

In the Crusades, the Church exercises *potestas gladii ecclesiastica*, the power of coercion not only spiritual, but also material, which derives from her legal nature as *societas perfecta*, independent of any human authority. From her character as a perfect society, the Church has, *pleno jure*, the power of coercion both on the spiritual and material planes. The Crusades are a historic expression of this right of the Church to employ material force to attain her supernatural end.

The clearest expression of the ecclesiastical *vis armata,* derived from the Church's *potestas coactiva,* is that of the religious-chivalric orders which became the main military instruments of the Holy See between the twelfth and eighteenth centuries. As men religious, the members of military orders professed the three traditional vows according to a Rule approved by the Holy See. As soldiers, they formed a standing army devoted to waging war in defense of the Faith.

"The military orders," Cardinal Castillo Lara writes, "are a faithful expression of what could be considered an ecclesiastical *vis armata.* Indeed, its members were at the same time soldiers and monks. As men religious they professed the three traditional vows under a Rule approved by the Holy See. As soldiers, they formed a standing army ready to wage battle wherever the enemies were to threaten the Christian religion. Their

---

[567] AMC, 8 November 1989.
[568] AMC, 2 January 1990.

exclusively ecclesiastical end and their dependence on the Holy See under the vow of obedience made them soldiers of the Church."[569]

The main military orders were the Hospitalers of Saint John, later called "Knights of Rhodes" and then "of Malta," the Knights Templar, and the Teutonic Knights, which were born and developed at the time of the Crusades. The latter added a fourth vow to the three traditional vows of chastity, poverty and obedience: that of never retreating in battle. The Templars represented the ideal of warrior monks *par excellence*.[570] They joined "the cordial manners of the monk and the courage of the warrior,"[571] as Saint Bernard of Clairvaux described them in *De laude novae militiae*, written between 1132 and 1135.

Plinio certainly thought of the Rule that Saint Bernard gave the Templars when he identified the principles of purity and anti-egalitarianism as "the profound driving forces of the courage of the Knights Templar. In their golden age, those knights were extraordinary and served as a rampart to Christian civilization. They defined the perfect type of the Catholic knight."[572]

Saint Bernard devoted a memorable page to the spirit of the Templars and more generally of the religious and military Orders of his time:

> "The Knights of Christ[573] may fight the battles of the Lord with peace of mind, without fear of sinning if they smite the enemy or are in danger of death; for inflicting death or dying for Christ is no crime but often merits glory. Indeed, in the former case one renders glory to Christ, and in the latter one obtains Christ Himself. The Lord undoubtedly accepts the death of his foe as punishment, and gives himself as consolation to his knight even more gladly. The Knight of Christ kills

---

[569] ROSARIO CASTILLO CARDINAL LARA, *Coacción eclesiastica y Sacro Romano Imperio*, Pontificio Ateneo Salesiano, Turin, 1956, p. 109.

[570] On the Templars, cf. among others, GEORGES BORDONOVE, *Les Templiers*, Fayard, Paris, 1963 (second edition 1977); J. FLORI, *La guerre sainte. La formation de l'idée de croisade dans l'Occident chrétien,* Aubier, Paris, 2001; BARBARA FRALE, *I Templari*, Il Mulino, Bologna, 2004; ALAIN DEMURGER, *Les Templiers. Une chevalerie chrétienne au Moyen Âge*, Le Seuil, Paris, 2005.

[571] St. Bernard of Clairvaux, *Liber ad milites Templi. De laude novae militiae*, introduction, translation and notes by C. D. Fonseca, in F. Gastaldelli et al, eds., *Trattati, Opere di S. Bernardo*, I, Scriptorium Claravallense-Fondazione di Studi Cisterciense, Milan, 1984, I, pp. 425-484.

[572] SDS, 3 February 1973.

[573] The "Knights of Christ" of whom St. Bernard speaks in this passage are the Templars of the golden age of that Order. In Portugal the Order of the Temple was replaced by the Order of the Knights of Our Lord Jesus Christ, or simply Order of Christ, under whose patronage the discovery of Brazil took place. The Order was established on March 14, 1319 by the Bull *Ad ea ex quibus* of Pope John XXII at the request of King Dom Dinis, to inherit the properties and Portuguese privileges of the Order of the Temple, which had been extinguished by the Holy See and by the King of France, Philip the Fair (translator's note).

with his conscience at peace and dies with even greater assurance. By dying, he favors himself; by killing, he favors Christ. A soldier bears a sword for a reason. He is a minister of God to punish evildoers and to exalt the good. When he kills an evildoer he is not a murderer but an 'evilcide,' if I may so put it, a killer of evil. He should be seen as both an avenger at the service of Christ and a defender of the Christian people. Thus, when he dies one should not think that he is dead but rather in eternal glory." [574]

As evidenced by this page of Saint Bernard, the vocation of the Military Orders expresses the notion of *vindicatio* mentioned by Saint Thomas in the *Summa Theologica*. The Angelic Doctor considers vengeance a specific virtue annexed to justice.[575] Fr. Royo Marin notes how it is a virtue difficult to understand nowadays, as it can be easily confused with a sin against charity; however, revenge is a divine perfection "that consists in maintaining due moderation in all circumstances while punishing."[576] Saint Thomas explains that one needs to take into account the state of mind of the one who inflicts punishment: "If his intention is directed chiefly to hurt the punished person and stops there, then his vengeance is altogether unlawful because it is proper of hatred to take pleasure in the evil of others"; but "if the avenger's intention is directed chiefly at some good" such as "to save God's justice and honor, then vengeance may be lawful provided that the due circumstances are observed."[577]

The saints rightly ask for revenge on enemies and rejoice in it, according to the Psalm: "The just shall rejoice when he shall see the revenge" (Ps. 57:11).[578] Indeed, the good bear with the wicked by enduring patiently and in due manner the personal insults they receive from them: but they "do not tolerate the wrongs they inflict on God and their neighbor."[579] When the insults are addressed to God and the Church "one is bound to avenge them as is evident in the case of Elias (2 Kings 1:9 ff.), who had fire come down on those who had come to capture him."[580] Moses was moved with holy wrath against the golden calf (Ex. 32), and so was Mathathias (I Mac. II), since "it is impious to endure with too much patience insults made to God."[581]

---

[574] St. Bernard of Clairvaux, *De Laude novae Militiae*, cit., col. 924.

[575] *Summa Theologica*, II-IIae, q. 80.

[576] A. Royo Marin, O.P., *Theology of Christian Perfection*, no. 315; *Summa Theologica*, IIa-IIae, q. 108, a. 2, ad 3.

[577] *Summa Theologica*, II-IIae, q. 108, a. 1; http://www.newadvent.org/summa/3108.htm .

[578] Idem, II-IIae, q. 83, 8, ad 2.

[579] Idem, II-IIae, q. 108, a. 1, ad 2.

[580] Idem, q. 108, a. 1, ad 4.

[581] *Summa Theologica*, I-II, q. 136, a. 4, ad 3.

Revenge expresses the hatred for evil, which every Christian is bound to have. The love of God presupposes a radical hatred of evil.[582] The Gospel often speaks of the world's hatred for the disciples of Christ (Mt. 24:9; Mk. 13:13; Lk. 21:17; Jn. 17:14): "If the world hate you, know ye, that it hath hated me before you" (Jn. 15:18), and warns us not to hate our own brothers (1 Jn. 3:15) but rather to love our enemies and do good to those who hate us (Lk. 6:27). However, Jesus invites us to hate our family and our very lives (Lk. 14:26; Jn. 12:25; Mt. 10:37 and 8:21; Lk. 9:60) if they separate us from him. As Saint Augustine says, the hatred of sin is virtuous because it is opposed precisely to evil's hatred against the light.[583]

Hate can be a passion as noble as love if directed at the enemies of God and at sin. Our Lady gives us an example of this perfect hatred of sin. She loved God and hated evil more than the devil hated God and loved evil.

Plinio asks:

"Will She perhaps not find a love greater than this satanic hatred? Would there not be greater hatred than the devil's at the service of the sacral hatred of the most Pure and Immaculate Heart of Mary? Can a man not hate the devil with greater hatred than the one with which the devil hates God? Is it not part of the Secret of Mary to have a hatred of angelic dimensions? To gauge this well, we should not think only about the angels of heaven, usually not presented to us as hating, but about Satan's minions who were condemned, and say: our hatred for them must be greater than their hatred for us."[584]

From this perspective, a wise Dominican theologian, Father Roger-Thomas Calmel, speaks of the need for "Christian wrath" that at times imposes itself: "whatever its excesses or deviations may be, it suffices to read the Gospel to understand that it may become holy."[585]

The spirit of the Crusades was not only an act of legitimate self-defense against Islam's aggression, but also the expression of a spirit of holy wrath and profound indignation for the sins committed against the Holy Sepulchre and against Our Lord. Indignation led to a desire to make reparation for the insults, exterminate evil, carry out a holy vengeance. The Crusaders manifested God's justice falling upon His enemies. The main reason the Crusades failed was the weakening of this feeling of indignation and holy anger, which was necessary to annihilate the enemies of the Catholic faith and of Christian civilization.

---

[582] Cf. ANDRÉ DE BOVIS, *Haine*, DSp, VII (1969), cols. 29-50.

[583] ST. AUGUSTINE, *In Joannis Evang.* 12, 13, PL, 35, 1491 b.

[584] RRR, 26 January 1980.

[585] R.TH. CALMEL, O.P., *Si ton oeil est simple*, Impr. du Viguier, Toulouse, 1955, pp. 45-46.

The decadence of the Crusades was a consequence of the loss of this spirit of *vindicatio* and hatred of evil.

> "God's perfection must lead man to such a pinnacle of love that he reaches the summit of indignation and fury and becomes a true warrior. The Crusaders were such extraordinary warriors because they loved God. And to fight for God you need to love Him much; but to love Him much you need to hate His adversaries much. Without love there is no hatred, and without hatred there is no love. They are the two sides of the same coin."[586]

> The last crusaders "had an insufficient furor that did not fully express God's wrath – as it had in the First Crusade – and without this furor God did not deem them as apt instruments to win for Him." [587]

Salve Regina, Mater Misericordiae

The magnanimity, fortitude and heroism of Chivalry have nothing to do with proudly boasting of one's own strength. The awareness of his own finiteness pushes man to humility. From humility is born mercy, and from mercy, confidence. Consistent with his militant spirit, Plinio Corrêa de Oliveira was always categorical in his affirmations and negations, manifesting his indomitable fighting spirit in all his public activities. However, those who knew him personally remember another unmistakable feature of his personality, seemingly contrasting with the former: Plinio's attitude in his words, gestures and gaze was always one of profound goodness and mercy towards others. The goodness he manifested to everyone was assuredly a reflection of his continuous abandonment to God's mercy.

As the Passionist theologian Father Enrico Zoffoli observed, awareness of the radical insufficiency of the human creature, essentially relative and contingent, is expressed in feeling our own misery. And the answer to this feeling of misery is the mercy of God, Who, having created us from nothing out of love, keeps us alive and helps us by supplementing our limitations.[588]

The whole spiritual life – Plinio repeated – is a daughter of mercy:

> "A spiritual life that ignores this becomes unbearably heavy, unbearably hard, unbearably cold. It is impossible for us to love God if we only have the idea of a God who is just towards us and nothing else. We need this idea of a merciful God who is condescending with us, who has

---

[586] SDS, 21 October 1989.
[587] MNF, 19 October 1989.
[588] E. ZOFFOLI, "Misericordia e giustizia di Dio," *Teologica,* no. 4 (July-August 1996).

mercy on us and forgives our faults; without it we are unable to love God."[589]

Were it not for a continuous intervention of God's mercy, no one could be saved: "Salvation is a work of God's mercy."[590] God, infinite mercy, gave Our Lady the mission of helping the miserable who lift up their eyes to her in this vale of tears. Devotion to Mary is therefore necessary to obtain divine mercy, which alone can assure salvation. The word mercy is linked to "misery." The first thing necessary in order to nourish a serious devotion to Our Lady is to have a profound, lively and continuing awareness of one's own misery. This certainty of being powerless and helpless is what pushes us to confide in the Virgin's mercy:

> "Recognizing one's own misery is therefore a kind of opening of the soul to Our Lady's mercy and goodness, a kind of convivial relationship with her in which the person sees well that She is the highest created personification, representation and holder of mercy and goodness in the order of creation, and that we can continually obtain them if we continually have recourse to her, but like beggars, kneeling with hat in hand, beating our chest and understanding that we have no right to claim it. Then Our Lady turns to us with all sweetness, kindness and patience, even for outlandish requests.

> "If we do not place ourselves in this perspective, the *Salve Regina* and *Memorare* have no meaning, nor do certain invocations such as *Refugium peccatorum*. We need to have this idea of goodness, this idea of forgiveness, and this continuing appeal to forgiveness and to goodness without which nothing makes sense."[591]

> "Personally, what attracts me the most in Our Lady is to consider her as Queen and Mother of Mercy, who has every kind of compassion and all kinds and degrees of forgiveness, guardianship, protection, and even privileges. Our Lady has privileges for all those who know how to ask her for them. And we should ask Her for all kinds of privileges. We should present ourselves in Heaven adorned and illuminated with privileges as if they were jewelry....

> "And when I look at some defect of mine I feel sad about it but enchanted considering that...from the depths of his misery, a man raises his eyes and addresses the highest of merely created beings; his gaze enters the eyes of that being, his voice enters the ears of that being, his heart enters the heart of that being, and he is heard and heeded. What a

---

[589] RST, 26 August 1967.
[590] Idem.
[591] RRR, 18 June 1968.

magnificent hierarchy in which the smaller can so surely reach the greatest!

"This is also why I like very much the Penitential Psalms: *De profundis clamavi ad te Domine: Domine exaudi vocem meam.* From the depths of the abyss in which I am I cried out to Thee. Lord, hear my prayer! I am enchanted to see the abyss, and on the other side of it, Our Lady, compassionate, smiling, ready to help. Then the whole distance turns into a delightful closeness, a caress, a certainty of receiving marvelous protection. This, which is a celestial paradox but not a contradiction, is the point of repose of my soul in all afflictions. This is how my spiritual children should be."[592]

Even more than Mary's holiness, what always struck Plinio the most was the compassion with which Her immaculate holiness turned toward those who are not saints.

"In addition to her virginal, royal holiness and everything else you might want (you can never say enough about her), what impresses us is the compassion with which Our Lady looks at those who are not holy, having pity on them and heeding them. Her mercy is the size of her other qualities: inexhaustible, most patient, most clement, ready to help at any time in an unimaginable way, never with a sigh of weariness or exhaustion or impatience. Always willing not only to repeat but even to outdo herself. Accordingly, after a great act of mercy that was poorly responded to, there comes even greater mercy. And, so to speak, our abysses keep on attracting her light to the depths. And the more we flee from her, the more her graces are prolonged and shine in our direction."[593]

A prayer particularly dear to Plinio, after the Hail Mary and *Salve Regina,* was the *Memorare,* attributed to Saint Bernard of Clairvaux. In this prayer we turn to Our Lady with the full and absolute confidence, that never were any of those left unaided who had recourse to her protection, implored her assistance and asked for her help. How could Our Lady, who abandons no one, not even those who turn away from her, fail to heed those who cast themselves at her feet?

So Plinio invites us to ask Mary to restore our hearts:

"Come therefore, O thou, the best of all mothers, and for the sake of that which was blossoming in me, restore me; recompose in me that love for thee and make of me the complete realization of that son without stain that I would have been, had I not been so miserable. Give me, O my Mother, a repentant and humbled heart, and make shine once again before my eyes that which, through the splendor of thy grace, I had once

---

[592] EXT, June 1974.
[593] CSN, 9 January 1982.

begun to love so very much! Remember, O Lady, this David and all the sweetness that thou hadst placed in him. So be it!" [594]

Saint Therese of the Child Jesus

If the aspect of the Blessed Virgin that touched Plinio's heart the most was her boundless mercy, one can understand the devotion he had for the saint of mercy par excellence, Saint Therese of the Child Jesus. *The Story of a Soul,* which Plinio read before he turned twenty, touched him so deeply that he confided to a close friend:

> "Before reading this book I thought my goal was to be a very good Catholic; but from then on I understood sanctity, that I should be a saint, and made the decision to be one." [595]

Plinio asked Saint Therese to let him know the best way to achieve perfection. And after a novena to the saint of Lisieux he discovered the treatise on *True Devotion to the Blessed Virgin Mary,* by Saint Louis Grignion de Montfort, a work that was the foundation of his Marian-centered life. From then on, Plinio prayed to Saint Therese every day, feeding on the spirituality of a nun whose desire to fight in the Crusades combined with that of immolating herself to God's merciful love.

Saint Therese had a burning desire to "do everything" for the love of God and of the Church, a desire Plinio fully shared in his soul. In this famous page of the *Story of a Soul,* Saint Therese describes the multiplicity of vocations she would like to embrace.

> "To be Thy Spouse, O my Jesus, to be a daughter of Carmel, and by my union with Thee to be the mother of souls, should not all this content me? And yet other vocations make themselves felt – I feel called to the Priesthood and to the Apostolate – I would be a Martyr, a Doctor of the Church. I should like to accomplish the most heroic deeds – the spirit of the Crusader burns within me, and I long to die on the field of battle in defense of Holy Church....

> "O Jesus, my Love, my life!... How to reconcile such contrasts? How to fulfill the desires of my poor little soul?... Charity provided me with the key to my vocation.

> "I understood that since the Church is a body composed of different members, the noblest and most important of all the organs would not be wanting. I knew that the Church has a heart, that this heart burns with love and that it is love alone which gives life to its members. I knew that if this love were extinguished, the Apostles would no longer preach the

---

[594] *Preces,* p. 397.

[595] Caio Vidigal Xavier da Silveira, "The Unknown St. Therese the Little Flower: The Centennial of a 'Hurricane of Glory,'" *Catolicismo,* no. 561, September 1997.

Gospel, and the Martyrs would refuse to shed their blood... I understood that *love embraces all vocations, that it is all things, and that it reaches out through all the ages, and to the uttermost limits of the earth, because it is eternal.* Then, beside myself with joy, I cried out: "O Jesus, my Love, at last I have found my vocation. *My vocation is love!* Yes, I have found my place in the bosom of the Church, and this place, O my God, Thou hast Thyself given to me: in the heart of the Church, my Mother, I will be love! ...Thus I shall be all things: thus will my dream be realized!!!"[596]

This page by Saint Therese is a manifesto of Catholic faith that Plinio makes his own:

"She understood that working, existing, praying and acting to augment love in everyone and increase the degree of charity in the Catholic Church would be like a prodigious life spring emerging within the Church: Prophets would be faithful, doctors would be lucid, apostles would be indefatigable, warriors would be indomitable, and everything in the Church would begin to move with renewed intensity. And she understood that she should die as a victim of love. A victim of merciful love so that others also would love, and through this strengthening of love within the Church all vocations would be fulfilled.

"Had she known the vocation of those called to love the Catholic Church, and represent fidelity during the period of the worst infidelity, and therefore somehow to do all apostolates at all times and everywhere, how gladdened would she have been, and how desirous she would have been to have that vocation if only she had known it! So one understands well how useful her merits were and how much she is praying for us from heaven....So let us ask Saint Thérèse that love be increased deep in our souls; and that she may also increase our love, enthusiasm, veneration and tenderness for the Holy Roman Catholic and Apostolic Church."[597]

Plinio venerated Our Lady under different titles and images: Aparecida, Patroness of Brazil, the Virgin of Guadalupe, Patroness of the Americas, Our Lady of Good Success of Quito,[598] Our Lady of the Miracle[599] in Rome, the Mother of Good Counsel of Genazzano,[600] Our

---

[596] ST. THERESE OF THE CHILD JESUS, *Opere Complete*, Libreria Editrice Vaticana, Città del Vaticano, 1997, p. 221.

[597] SD, 3 October 1967.

[598] In her apparitions (1582-1634) to the abbess of the convent of the Immaculate Conception in the city of Quito, Mother Mariana Torres y Berriochoa (1563-1635), today a venerable, Our Lady of Good Success guaranteed her protection on the monastery and prophesied the fate of the Ecuadorian nation and also of Western Christendom and the universal Church. Cf. SD, 2 February 1985.

[599] On January 20, 1842, with the same features with which she had appeared at Rue du Bac, the Virgin Mary appeared to the Jew Alphonse Ratisbonne, instantly converting him to Christianity. The Cardinal Vicar of Rome authenticated the apparition, and in 1942 Pope Pius XII elevated the Church to the rank of Basilica.

Lady Help of Christians, whom he venerated in the Salesian Church of the Sacred Heart of Jesus in São Paulo. He was also a devotee of the three great apparitions at Fatima, La Salette[601] and Lourdes, whose close links he clearly understood.[602]

The Virtue of Confidence

At a chapel of the Roman Seminary in Rome there is an image of Our Lady of Confidence that is venerated, which seminarians who later become priests remember with affection throughout their lives. That image was also dear to Plinio, whose lips often repeated the invocation, *Mater mea fiducia mea.* Nothing is denied to those who confide in Our Lady. This devotion, so necessary in the troubled era in which we live, is a "little way" leading to the Blessed Virgin like the one indicated by the Saint of Lisieux: a spiritual way of abandonment to Divine Providence and of immense confidence in Mary's mercy.

Plinio loved and suggested reading a booklet inspired by grace: the *Book of Confidence* by Fr. Thomas de Saint-Laurent.[603] The work begins with memorable words: "O Voice of Christ, mysterious voice of grace that resoundeth in the silence of our souls, Thou murmurest in the depths of our hearts words of sweetness and of peace. In response to our miseries, Thou repeatest the counsel so often given by the Divine Master during His mortal life: 'Confidence, confidence!' These divine words, so full of tender compassion, as they fell from His adorable lips, effected a

---

[600] In 1468, as Turkish armies invaded Albania, a fresco of Our Lady disappeared from the town of Shkoder in Albania and miraculously reappeared in Genazzano (province of Rome) on a wall of the church of the Augustinian friars, where Our Lady of Good Counsel was already venerated. After many miracles the fresco and devotion to the Mother of Good Counsel were promoted by the Augustinian Fathers, and the sanctuary became an important spiritual center.

[601] The message of La Salette takes its name from a hamlet in the diocese of Grenoble where, on September 19, 1846 two young shepherds, Maximin Giraud and Mélanie Calvat, had an apparition of Our Lady who revealed to them a secret destined to raise numerous controversies. The full text of the message, transmitted to Pius IX on July 18, 1851 but considered lost, was rediscovered in the archives of the Congregation for the Doctrine of the Faith (the former Holy Office) by Fr. Michel Corteville. Cf. René Laurentin and Michel Corteville, *Découverte du secret de La Salette. Au-déla des polémiques, la vérité sur l'apparition et ses voyants*, Fayard, Paris, 2002. The authenticity of the apparition was officially recognized by the Bishop of Grenoble, and a shrine was built at the place.

[602] RRR, 25 November 1974.

[603] RAYMOND DE THOMAS DE SAINT LAURENT, *The Book of Confidence*, Irish Society for Christian Civilization, 2009 at http://isfcc.org/2009/07/18/the-book-of-confidence/. Father Thomas de Saint Laurent was born in Lyons in 1879 and died at Uzès in 1949. Ordained a priest in 1909, he was pastor and later canon at the Cathedral of Nimes, chaplain of Catholic Youth, chaplain of the Carmel of Uzès, and Apostolic missionary, working intensely as a preacher, writer, and spiritual director.

marvelous transformation in the souls of those to whom they were addressed."[604]

Plinio comments:

> "This interior word is neither a light nor something that appears bright and luminous. It does not result from something we saw outside ourselves but is said to us gratuitously within our souls. It is a confidence that penetrates us and produces in our souls the act of confiding. And we go confidently forward, convinced that it is something rational. It is the most rational thing there is, as we are heeding the voice of God within us. We are the blessed to whom God speaks not only through our ears but also internally, within the soul. We follow this word and forge ahead with it. This is confidence amid confusion."[605]

Confidence is not a sentimental attitude but the culmination of the two theological virtues, faith and hope. Quoting Saint Thomas Aquinas, Father de Saint-Laurent defines confidence as *spes roborata*, "a hope fortified by solid conviction."[606] The difference between hope and confidence, says the author, is not in nature but only in degree and intensity. "The faint glimmer of the dawn and the dazzling splendor of the sun at its zenith are part of the same day. So hope and confidence pertain to the same virtue; one is only the complete blossoming of the other."[607]

This attitude of filial and unlimited abandonment, which according to theologians represents the pinnacle of spiritual life, is necessary not only to those wishing to achieve perfection in everyday life, but especially to those who selflessly want to dedicate themselves to the service of the Counter-Revolution amid the thousand difficulties of the present age.

---

[604] R. DE THOMAS DE SAINT LAURENT, *The Book of Confidence*.
[605] *Calm*, pp. 117-125.
[606] *Summa Theologica*, II-IIae, q. 129, art. 6, ad 3.
[607] R. DE THOMAS DE SAINT LAURENT, *The Book of Confidence*.

PART THREE

THE THEOLOGY OF HISTORY

CHAPTER I

THE CATHOLIC THEOLOGY OF HISTORY

Philosophy or Theology of History?

A prisoner of the history in which he is immersed, contemporary man is unable to transcend it and judge it. Christianity, instead, teaches us to be in the world without belonging to the world, to live in history while raising our eyes beyond it.

In a single glance the early Christians embraced all history, from Creation to the end of the world, and recognized Jesus Christ, the Son of God, King of the universe, as the center and dividing line of history. God is indeed the Creator of time, and the Second Person of the Holy Trinity, the Son of God, became man in a historical time and place on earth. The whole truth of Christianity is contained in a historical event: the Incarnation, Passion, Death and Resurrection of Jesus Christ, true God and true Man.

In history, the work of God is fulfilled and the human saga is inserted in the plan of Divine Providence, which governs history. The theology of history is nothing but a reflection of the mode of operation of Divine Providence in history.

In this sense, the theology of history is not an intellectual occupation for theologians but a vital need of the Catholic soul; it is the meaning we must give our existence. The theology of history should enlighten not only our private life but that of families, nations, the Church, and humanity as a whole, from the beginning to the end of the created world.

A great theologian of history of the nineteenth century, Father Henri Ramière, S.J., wondered whether it is more appropriate to speak of philosophy of history or theology of history. If by philosophy of history one understands a philosophical science intended to fully explain historical facts based on purely rational principles, we must reject this hypothesis. Indeed, to state that it is possible to explain historical events without resorting to Divine Revelation is to deny Revelation. Father Ramière states, "There is nothing more absurd than to say that the Son of

God became man and then deny His influence on mankind. There is no middle ground: either we deny the Incarnation of the Word of God or we recognize that it is the very fulcrum of history and the true solution to all social enigmas."[608]

But in order to interpret historical events, a theologian needs data provided by reason and historical science. By raising man to the supernatural order the Incarnation did not destroy the natural order but rather ennobled and completed it. Precisely for this reason, as of that moment the natural order as such ceased to be complete and self-sufficient, so to speak. Dom Prosper Guéranger writes, "Man was divinely called to the supernatural state; this state is the end of man, and the annals of humanity must offer traces of that."[609]

This means that historical investigation cannot be separated from philosophy, which for its part cannot do without theology. Dom Guéranger explains that "there is not and there cannot be true knowledge in man outside of Revelation. The supernatural Revelation as such was not required: man had no right to it; but God gave and promulgated it, and since that time nature alone is no longer sufficient to explain man. The presence or absence of grace, grace itself, occupies the first place in the study of anthropology."[610]

Therefore, understood as a purely natural historical science, the philosophy of history is insufficient to explain the story of mankind unless it is enriched by the data of Revelation. This is not to deny the possibility of a rational investigation of history, but to integrate it with supernatural considerations.

Historical science cannot do without philosophy because it is its rational base, but must be completed by the data offered by theology. Father Ramière continues: "Only the theology of history can give history its soul, life and unity, ultimately making it a science."[611] That is why we concur with his definition that "properly understood, historical science

---

[608] HENRI RAMIÈRE, S.J., *O Reino de Jesus Cristo na História. Introdução ao estudo da teologia da História*, Civilização, Porto, 2001, p. 182.

[609] REV. FR. DOM PROSPER GUÉRANGER, *Le sens chrétien de l'histoire*, in *Essai sur le naturalisme*, Delacroix, s.l. 2006, p. 365 and *Jésus-Christ roi de l'histoire*, Association Saint-Jérôme, Saint-Macaire, 2005. Dom Prosper Guéranger (1805-1875), Benedictine, ordained in 1827, abbot of the Benedictine Priory of Solesmes and founder of France's Congregation of the Order of St. Benedict, was the restorer of monastic life in France. For his writings see *Institutions liturgiques*, 4 vols., Société Générale de Librairie Catholique, Paris, 1878-1885. About him, see L. SOLTNER, *Solesmes et dom Guéranger (1805-1875)*, Solesmes, Sable-sur-Sarthe, 1974; PAUL DELATTE, O.S.B., *Dom Guéranger. Abbé de Solesmes*, Abbaye de Solesmes, Sablé-sur-Sarthe, 1984 (1909) and CUTHBERT JOHNSON, O.S.B., *Prosper Guéranger (1805-1875): A Liturgical Theologian*, Pontificio Ateneo S. Anselmo, Rome, 1984.

[610] DOM GUÉRANGER, *Le sens chrétien de l'histoire*, pp. 365-366.

[611] H. RAMIÈRE, *The Kingdom of Jesus Christ on Earth*, p. 217.

must be defined as the exposition of events in which human freedom is unerringly guided by Divine Providence in order to establish the Kingdom of Jesus Christ on earth despite the resistance of the rebellious spirits."[612]

Saint Augustine's *De Civitate Dei*

In this respect, Saint Augustine was the first major author who was both a philosopher and a theologian of history. In the letter *Saepenumero considerantes,* of 1883, Pope Leo XIII writes:

> "Augustine himself, the great Doctor of the Church, first of all outlined and developed the philosophy of history. Among those who have come afterward, those who have referred to the same Augustine as teacher and guide and were carefully trained on his writings and meditations have obtained noteworthy results in this area. On the other hand, error again and again diverted from the truth those who strayed from the footsteps of that great man, for in analyzing the paths and the events of States they failed to understand the real causes that govern human events." [613]

Saint Augustine composed his masterpiece, the *City of God,*[614] meditating on the historical events of his time. In 410 he was Bishop of Hippo, in Africa, elderly and in poor health, when he heard the terrible news of the sack of Rome by Alaric's Goths. His reflection on those dramatic events is at the origin of a work to which he devoted thirteen years of his life and which he called the *City of God,* but which, as he himself acknowledged, could have been called *The Two Cities.*[615]

Saint Augustine sees the Church founded by Christ, the City of God, rise in its splendor on the ruins of the Roman Empire. Against it stands an enemy city, which he calls the City of the devil. These two cities are destined to relentlessly fight each other in history, which is the battlefield of human freedom. He studies their origin, development, and the end to which they tend.

The two opposing societies coincide with the two allegorical biblical cities: Babylon, symbol of perverse humanity, bound to perdition, and Jerusalem, symbol of the Church in her twofold aspect, militant and

---

[612] IDEM, p. 13.

[613] LEO XIII, Letter *Saepenumero considerantes,* August 18, 1883, BELLOCCHI, *Leone XIII (1878-1903)*, I, *1878-1891*, p. 163 (pp. 158-165).

[614] *De Civitate Dei* by Saint Augustine (354-430), comprised of twenty-two books written between 413 and 425, is his most influential work over the ages. "It is a tedious, almost daunting, task to make a review of all the copies that have been preserved of the Latin text of *The City of God....* Except for the Scriptures, no book has been more read and copied than this, with the possible exception of St. Gregory's *Morals"* (ANDRÉ WILMART, *La tradition des grands ouvrages de saint Augustin,* Miscellanea Augustiniana, II [1931], pp. 279, 261).

[615] ST. AUGUSTINE, *Retractiones,* 2, 43, PL, 32, col. 468.

triumphant. The two cities have intermingled on earth always and everywhere, and hence their clash is constant and universal. Love is the force of attraction and cohesion that gives rise to them and sustains them. For Saint Augustine, all human activity is reduced to love: "The two cities, Babylon and Jerusalem, were therefore created by two loves: the former is the love of self to the point of despising God; the latter, the love of God even to the point of contempt for self."[616] The radical choice is between God, to Whom the humble of heart are intimately united, and the devil, to whom the proud and selfless are irrevocably bound. The essence of this combat is moral: we have to choose according to the direction that love gives our life.[617]

Humanity lives on earth between these two cities, the infernal and the heavenly, going through its testing period. It is the object of contention between the two enemies. But no compromise is possible between the two cities. Saint Augustine's theology of history merely clarifies the evangelical maxim that "no man can serve two masters; for either he will hate the one and love the other, or else he will stand by the one and despise the other" (Mt. 6:24; Lk. 16:13).

The Doctor of Hippo faced the historical problem of the fall of the Roman Empire, but also the problem of evil: the terrible mystery of iniquity rooted in every man's soul. The Augustinian notion of the two opposing cities is diametrically opposed to Gnosticism and Manichaeism, which oppose light and darkness, spirit and matter, good and evil as two antagonistic creations by a good God and a bad God. The foundation of the two cities' antagonism is not a metaphysical dualism but a moral dualism. This enigma is solved by another mystery, that of divine grace. *"Omnes peccaverunt et egent gloria Dei, justificati gratis per gratiam ipsius"* (Rom. 3:23-24).

The influence of Augustine's theology of history over the ages is profound:[618] Historians find it in the sermons of Saint Caesarius, Bishop of Arles (c. 470/471-c. 542),[619] in Pope Saint Gregory's *Morales* (540-c. 604),[620] in *De Salutaribus documentis*[621] by Saint Paulinus, Patriarch of Aquilea (first half of the eighth century to 795); in the polemics by Benedictine Abbot Beatus of Liebana (730-c.798), in the *Disciplina*

---

[616] St. AUGUSTINE, *The City of God,* book XIV, chap. 28.

[617] MSGR. ANTONINO ROMEO, *Il presente e il futuro nella Rivelazione biblica*, Descléee, Roma, 1964, pp. 1-32.

[618] Cf. FERDINAND TOURNIER, S.J. (1854-1926), "Les 'Deux cités' dans la littérature chrétienne," in *Études*, 123 (5-6 1910), pp. 644-665.

[619] PL, 39, col. 1877.

[620] PL, 76, col. 750.

[621] PL, 40, col. 1053.

ecclesiastica[622] of Rabanus Maurus (784 - c. 856), Abbot of Fulda and Archbishop of Mainz. Also inspired directly by the *City of God* are: the Belgian theologian and Benedictine Abbot Rupert of Deutz (c. 1075/1080-c. 1130), the philosopher and mystic Hugh of Saint Victor (1096-c. 1141), the Scottish theologian Richard of Saint Victor (1123 - c. 1173). To these names should be added those of Paul Orosius (375 - c. 420), Saint Leo the Great (390-461), Salvian of Marseilles (400-490), and the Anglo-Saxon monk Saint Bede (672-735).[623]

Saint Augustine's theology of history influenced not only pastors, theologians and mystics but oriented the action of kings and emperors. Historian Giorgio Falco recalls that Charlemagne, eager for knowledge, had them read for him *De Civitate Dei* during meals and kept pencils and tablets under his pillow at night to learn to write and do longhand writing exercises during his frequent vigils.[624] The Middle Ages represent an effort to achieve Augustine's *City of God* on earth: an ever present dream, although never fully realized.

People in the Middle Ages read and meditated on the *City of God*, but most importantly they lived its underlying teaching. The modern world rejected the *City of God*, not because it has not read Saint Augustine's work but because it turned its back on his conception of history.

From the City of God to the City of Man

Over the subsequent centuries, Catholic theology has one of highest expressions in Bossuet's *Discours sur l'histoire universelle,* published in 1681.[625] In the same century we watched the "metamorphoses of the City of God," that is, the birth of a philosophy of history that secularizes the Augustinian vision, transforming the notion of Providence into one of immanent progress in history.[626] From humanism to the Enlightenment,

---

[622] PL, 112, col. 1203.

[623] PAOLO SINISCALCO, *Il senso della storia. Studi sulla storiografia cristiana antica*, Rubbettino, Soveria Mannelli, 2003.

[624] GIUSEPPE FORNASERI (GIORGIO FALCO), *La Santa Romana Repubblica. Profilo storico del Medioevo*, Riccardo Ricciardi Editore, Napoli, 1942, p. 127.

[625] JACQUES-BÉNIGNE BOSSUET (1627-1704), *Discours sur l'histoire universelle, depuis le commencement du monde jusqu'à l'empire de Charlemagne,* S. Mabre-Cramoisy, Paris, 1681, *Continuation de l'histoire universelle depuis l'an 800.... jusqu'à l'an 1700,* A. Chevalier, Luxembourg, 1704, later compiled in the *Discours sur l'histoire universelle....,* M. David, Paris, 1707-1708. Bossuet was Bishop of Meaux, a great orator, polemicist and spiritual author, but his work was affected by Gallicanism. About him, see A. LARGENT, DTC, II (1926), 1049-1089; E. LEVESQUE, DHGE, IX (1937), 1339-1391.

[626] Cf. E. GILSON, *Les métamorphoses de la cité de Dieu*, Librairie Philosophique J. Vrin, Paris, 2005.

history is presented as a continuous and unlimited improvement toward a future deemed inevitably better than the past and the present.

In the *Esquisse d'un tableau historique des Progrès de l'esprit humain* (1793), the Marquis of Condorcet predicts a continuous and endless improvement of mankind, "marching with a firm and sure step on the road of truth, virtue and happiness,"[627] through ten stages that have their watershed in the Revolution of 1789. With the French Revolution, the "Word of Progress" supposedly became incarnate in history; that is what Kant states in the second part of *The Conflict of the Faculties*.[628] The interpretations of history by Hegel, Marx and Comte are based on a rethinking of the French Revolution, seen as a decisive stage in the progress of humanity.

The idea of Progress[629] reached its apogee in the nineteenth century. The romantic philosophy of absolute freedom replaced that of the Enlightenment with a conception of history as self-creation and self-redemption. Hegel thus defined history as *Weltgeist*,[630] "the rational, necessary path of the spirit of the world."[631] Faith in the progress of history replaced faith in Divine Providence, and history takes on the role of "redemptrix" of humanity on a journey in which the immanent horizon replaces the supernatural one, and the "historic future" replaces heavenly Paradise. The idea of progress dominates the main currents of European thought in the nineteenth century, from liberalism to socialism, and penetrates the Church with modernism.

The socialist-communist revolutions of the twentieth century set out to achieve in history Marx's philosophy of praxis, which claims that the task of philosophers is not to know the world but to transform it. The end

---

[627] Marie-Jean-Antoine Caritat, Marquis of CONDORCET (1741-1784), *Esquisse d'un tableau historique des progrès de l'esprit humain* (1795); It. tr., *Quadro storico dei progressi dello spirito umano* (1793-1794), Rizzoli, Milano, 1989, p. 330. The work was placed on the Index (Decree of September 10, 1827).

[628] IMMANUEL KANT, *Il conflitto delle facoltà* (1798), It. tr., Morcelliana, Brescia, 1994, pp. 164-165.

[629] On the idea of progress, see among others, JULES DELVAILLE, *Essai sur l'histoire de l'idée de progrès jusqu'à la fin du XVIII siècle*, Alcan, Paris, 1910 and more recently, REINHART KOSELLECK, *Progresso*; It. tr., Marsilio, Venezia, 1991; ROBERT A. NISBET, *History of the Idea of Progress,* II ed., Transaction Publishers, New Brunswick, NJ, 1994; FRÉDÉRIC ROUVILLOIS, *L'Invention du progrès. Aux origines de la pensée totalitaire, 1680-1730*, Kimé, Paris, 1996; PIERRE-ANDRE TAGUIEFF, *Du Progrès. Biographie d'une utopie moderne*, Librio, Paris, 2001; It. tr., *Il progresso. Biografia di una utopia moderna*, Città Aperta, Troina (En), 2003.

[630] Literally, in German, "spirit of the world" (translator's note).

[631] G. W. F. HEGEL, *Lezioni sulla filosofia della storia*, It. tr., Laterza, Bari, 2003, pp. 10-11.

result was a huge bloodbath, a sacrifice paid as tribute to the fetish of history.[632]

The fall of the Berlin Wall (1989) and the collapse of the Twin Towers (2001) brought down with them that atmosphere of boundless confidence in the upward march of history. The nihilism announced by Nietzsche[633] seems to come true at a time when history appears to lose its meaning and objective purpose. If for modern philosophy the world is ruled by reason, for postmodern thought history does not contain in itself the reason for its own existence.

The Counter-Revolutionary Theology of History

During the nineteenth and twentieth centuries only a few Catholic authors had the courage to propose a theology of history founded on the primary role of Divine Providence. Exponents of this ultramontane or counter-revolutionary[634] school are Count Joseph de Maistre,[635] Juan Donoso Cortés[636] and a few others.[637] This line of thinking is

---

[632] Cf. for example, *Le Livre noir du communisme; crimes, terreur, répression*, STÉPHANE COURTOIS, NICOLAS WERTH, JEAN-LOUIS PANNÉ, ANDRZEJ PACZOWSKI, KAREL BARTOSEK, JEAN-LOUIS MARGOLIN, Robert Laffont, Paris, 1997.

[633] Cf. F. NIETZSCHE, *Frammenti postumi 1885-1887*; It. tr. in *Opere,* Adelphi, Milano, 1975, vol. VIII, fr. 11 (411), pp. 392-393.

[634] Missing is an organic and profound exposition of the thought of the Catholic Counter-Revolution. This subject is dealt with, heterogeneously and with strong chronological limits, by DOMINIQUE BAGGE, *Les idées politiques en France sous la Restauration*, PUF, Paris, 1952; JEAN-JACQUES OECHSLIN, *Le mouvement ultra-royaliste sous la Restauration: son idéologie et son action politique (1814-1830)*, Librairie générale de droit et de jurisprudence, Paris, 1960; JACQUES GODECHOT, *La Contre-Révolution: doctrine et action, 1789-1804*, Presses Universitaires de France, Paris, 1984; RENE REMOND, *Les Droites en France*, Aubier, Paris, 1982, reprinted; STEPHANE RIALS, *Révolution et Contre-Révolution au XIX siècle*, Albatros, Paris, 1987; JEAN TULARD (prepared by), *La Contre-Révolution. Origines, histoire, posterité*, Perrin, Paris, 1990 (limited to 1815). Also highly useful is a series of articles by Prof. FERNANDO FURQUIM DE ALMEIDA on "French Catholics in the Nineteenth Century" in *Catolicismo*, from no. 1 (January 1951) to no. 80 (August 1957).

[635] Count Joseph de Maistre (1753-1821), along with Viscount Louis de Bonald, was the most important French-language representative of counter-revolutionary thought in the nineteenth century. His reference edition is *Œuvres complètes* (Vitte et Perrussel, Lyons, 1884-1887, 14 vols., reprint by Slatkine, Geneva, 1979-1980). Cf. also the *Œuvres,* prepared by PIERRE GLAUDES, Robert Laffont, Paris, 2007, followed by a *Dictionnaire* and an ample bibliography. Cf. also MARC FROIDEFONT, *Théologie de Joseph de Maistre*, Garnier, Paris, 2010; CAROLINA ARMENTEROS, *L'idée française de l'histoire: Joseph de Maistre et sa posterité, 1794-1854*, Classiques Garnier, Paris, 2013.

[636] Juan Donoso Cortés, Marquis of Valdegamas (1809-1853), deputy at the Cortes and follower of Queen Maria Cristina, gave up the liberalism of his youth to embrace integral Catholicism. The work that summarizes his thought is *Ensayo sobre el Catolicismo, el liberalismo y el socialismo* (Madrid, 1851) (English translation, *Essay on Catholicism, Liberalism and Socialism,* Preserving Christian Publications, Boonville, New York, 2014). See the introductory study with which CARLOS VALVERDE prefaced the edition of his *Obras completas*, BAC, Madrid, 1970, vol., I, pp. 1-166 (with ample bibliography). Cf. BERNARDO

characterized by a full adhesion to the Pontifical Magisterium in all its statements and by a profound meditation on the historical process initiated by the French Revolution. All the Popes of the twentieth century echoed this theology of history in their teachings.

Pope Leo XIII promulgated the Apostolic Letter *Annum Ingressi*, also known as *Parvenus à la vingt-cinquième année*, [638] shortly before his death on March 19, 1902, on the twenty-fifth anniversary of his pontificate. In this key document he summarizes the history of the struggles and triumphs of the Church, seeking "to weigh attentively in its origin, causes and various forms the implacable war that is waged against the Church, and denounce its pernicious consequences to indicate a remedy."[639]

The Pontiff identifies among the stages of the anti-Christian Revolution the rebellion of "the pseudo-Reformation of the sixteenth century" and "the contemptuous and mocking philosophism of the eighteenth century."[640] "From this source have flowed the poisonous and destructive systems of rationalism, pantheism, naturalism and materialism, which renew under different appearances the ancient errors victoriously refuted by the Fathers and apologists of early Christian times."[641] For Leo XIII, practical atheism necessarily gives rise to an upheaval in the moral and social order that logically and consistently results in anarchy. A return to Christianity, identified with and achieved by the Catholic Church, is the only solution to the ills that afflict society and which are destined to worsen.

The apostolic letter ends with words of confidence in the ultimate victory of the persecuted Church: "Nineteen centuries of a life passed in the midst of the ebb and flow of all human vicissitudes teach us that the storms pass by without ever affecting the foundations of the Church."[642] As for her final triumph, it depends upon Him who watches with wisdom and love over His immaculate spouse, and of whom it is written, "Jesus Christ, yesterday, today and forever" (Heb. 13:8.).[643]

In the twentieth century, Plinio Corrêa de Oliveira is the one who gathered the legacy of those authors, while a majority of Catholic

---

MONSEGU, C.P., *Clave teologica de la Historia segun Donoso Cortes*, Ediciones "El Pasionario," Madrid, 1988.

[637] Among them, Fr. ROGER TH. CALMEL, O.P., in his *Théologie de l'histoire*, 2nd ed., Dominique Martin Morin, Bouère, 1984.

[638] *Leo XIII*, Apostolic Letter *Annum Ingressi* of March 19, 1902 @ http://www.tfp.org/tfp-home/catholic-perspective/annum-ingressi-apostolic-letter-of-pope-leo-xiii.html.

[639] Idem.

[640] Idem.

[641] Idem.

[642] Idem.

[643] Idem.

thinkers, even when keeping philosophical and moral orthodoxy, tend to accept the idea of a historic irreversibility of progress. Catholic thinkers entrenched themselves behind the ramparts of the Magisterium but abandoned the field of the theology and philosophy of history to the enemies of the Church.

Plinio Corrêa de Oliveira and the Theology of History

The whole thought and action of Plinio Corrêa de Oliveira developed around a grand theoretical and practical vision of the theology and philosophy of history. *Revolution and Counter-Revolution*, published in April 1959, on the occasion of the one hundredth issue of the journal *Catolicismo*,[644] is the essay in which he condenses the essence of his thought and explains the meaning of his action in the field of ideas.[645]

Just as the *City of God* is a meditation on the sunset of the Roman Empire, *Revolution and Counter Revolution* can be seen as a meditation on the decline of Christian civilization. Plinio Corrêa de Oliveira asks what the essence of the contemporary crisis is, and gives the same answer as Saint Augustine, finding its profound reasons in the human heart.

The love of God can have infinite manifestations. It can push some men to spread the Faith around the world by establishing the Church, her rites and institutions; it can lead others to leave their families and possessions to devote themselves to a life of prayer and penance, to dedicate their lives to the poor and the sick, or to produce masterpieces in the field of beauty such as cathedrals or theological and moral *summae* in the field of truth; finally, it can lead some to take up arms and shed their blood to defend the conquests of the Gospel by raising the flag of the Cross against infidels.

Like the love of God, so also self-love have can have countless manifestations, produced by a moral climate dominated by disordered passions. Self-love can blind a man's life, drive him away from his one

---

[644] *Revolution and Counter-Revolution*, Commemorative edition of the fiftieth anniversary of its publication, Artpress, São Paulo, 2009. The work went through four editions in Portuguese, five in Spanish, three in Italian, two in English, two in French, and one in German, Polish, Romenian, Russian, Belarussian, Lithuanian and Estonian. It was published in full in magazines of Chile and Spain for a total of 94,000 copies and was partially transcribed in magazines in Europe, the Americas, and Africa. It received letters of support by Archbishop Romolo Carboni, Apostolic Nuncio in Peru (July 24, 1961) and Father Anastasio Gutierrez, CMF (September 8, 1993), Dean Emeritus of the College of Canon Law of the Lateran University and member of the Commission for the Revision of the Code of Canon Law, regarded as one of the greatest canonists of the twentieth century. On the genesis of this work, cf. CAIO VIDIGAL XAVIER DA SILVEIRA, "How the Providential Work *Revolution and Counter-Revolution* Was Born," *Catolicismo*, no. 706, October 2009, pp. 26-34.

[645] *Philosophical Self-Portrait*.

true good and lead an entire society to rebel against God by triggering a process of disintegration capable of developing in history.

Corrêa de Oliveira describes with great acuity the dynamism of disordered passions, which springs from *amor sui,* self-love, and he shows how a victorious reaction against the Revolution can only be born from an opposite passion that is equally total and dominant. That passion is *amor Dei,* the love of God, which becomes love for the Church and for Christian civilization:

> "In other words, either the world converts and faithfully fulfils the Augustinian vision of the 'City of God,' in which each nation takes the love of God to the point of giving up everything detrimental to other peoples, or the world will be that city of the devil in which everyone takes self-love to the point of forgetting God."[646]

Plinio summarizes the main doctrinal elements of *Revolution and Counter-Revolution*[647] in the following points:

> "a) the mission of the Church as the sole Master, Guide, and Fountain of Life of peoples toward the perfect civilization;
>
> b) the continuous opposition of the disordered passions, especially pride and sensuality, to the influence of the Church;
>
> c) the existence of two opposing poles in the human spirit towards one of which it necessarily heads: on one side, the Catholic Faith, which instills love for order, austerity, and hierarchy; on the other, the disordered passions, which provoke immodesty and revolt against law, hierarchy and any form of inequality, and which finally lead to doubt and to a complete denial of the Faith;
>
> d) the notion of a process – understood without prejudice to free will – by which individuals or peoples, feeling the attraction of the two opposing poles, gradually draw closer to one and away from the other.
>
> e) the influence of this moral process over the development of doctrines. Bad tendencies incline toward error, good tendencies toward truth. Great modifications in the mentality of peoples are not mere results of doctrines elaborated by small groups of intellectuals serenely lucubrating at the margins of society. For a doctrine to find resonance in a people it is usually necessary for that people to have affinity with that doctrine. And the very lucubrations by the learned in their studies are

---

[646] "A Medicine that Aggravates the Illness," *Legionário,* no. 491 (February 8, 1942).

[647] LUIS M. SANDOVAL PINILLOS writes: *"Possibly, the most complete and systematic presentation of the Counter-Revolution...is the one contained in the book by Plinio Corrêa de Oliveira, Revolution and Counter-Revolution,* an inescapable reference" (*Consideraciones sobre la Contrarrevolución,* Speiro, Madrid, 1990, p. 3).

often influenced more than one thinks by the appetites of the ambience in which they live."[648]

[648]   *Philosophical   Self Portrait*,   http://www.tfp.org/tfp-home/plinio-correa-de-oliveira/ philosophical-self-portrait-plinio-correa-de-oliveira.html.

CHAPTER II

REVOLUTION AND COUNTER-REVOLUTION

What the Revolution Is

It is no coincidence that the book *Revolution and Counter-Revolution* does not open with a description of Christendom but with a denunciation of the revolutionary process that attacks Christian Civilization. This is a fundamental point of the intellectual method of Plinio Corrêa de Oliveira, who states "the vision of evil prepares the mind for fully understanding good."[649]

"Revolution" is the term with which the Brazilian thinker defines the contemporary crisis, or rather the historical and philosophical cause of this crisis, whose gravity is much greater today than in the years he diagnosed it. This crisis is universal because all peoples have been affected by it to a greater or lesser extent; it is unique in its essence; it is total inasmuch as it encompasses all domains of human activity. In fact, in its impulse, it dominates a whole series of minor crises, and above all "it constitutes a critical process already five centuries old. It is a long chain of causes and effects that, having originated at a certain moment with great intensity in the deepest recesses of the soul and the culture of Western man, has been producing successive convulsions since the fifteenth century." [650]

The word "Revolution," which originally indicated the celestial motion of the stars, took on a new meaning in the eighteenth century and especially after the French Revolution, which became the archetype of all revolutions, including those that historically preceded it.[651] Voltaire even speaks of a "revolution of the spirits," a revolution of minds whose seeds were being sown by the Enlightenment's philosophers. In 1769 he writes: "It has already been going on for fifteen years, and after such a beautiful

---

[649] RST, 30 May 1964.

[650] *Revolution and Counter-Revolution* (Spring Grove, Pennsylvania: The American Society for the Defense of Tradition, Family and Property, 2003), p. 13 (https://www.tfp.org/books/rcr.pdf).

[651] Cf. among others KARL GRIEWANK, *Il concetto di rivoluzione nell'età moderna. Origini e sviluppo*, It. tr., La Nuova Italia, Firenze, 1979.

dawn it will see its full day in another fifteen."[652]   This concept of a true regeneration or *palingenesis* of society assumed its modern meaning precisely because of developments in France between 1789 and 1795.[653] However, it should be understood in its profound meaning, which is not socio-political but metaphysical.

> "The Revolution is truly Revolution when fully carried out according to an erroneous metaphysics, in its most completely erroneous aspect, and seeks to completely transform the sensible world. To the degree that it is only some participation in the wrong metaphysics or only seeks to partially or incompletely adapt reality, but not on a radical scale, to that extent the Revolution's initial R gradually wanes.

> "A simple disorder carried out merely with a remote, almost imponderable, imperceptible, local, episodic, circumstantially erroneous metaphysical substratum cannot be properly called a Revolution. It is an event of revolutionary character, substratum, but not the Revolution properly so-called."[654]

The Historical Stages of the Revolution

The idea of a revolutionary process is present in Plinio's writings well before the publication of *Revolution and Counter-Revolution*. In an article published in *Catolicismo* in 1951, he writes:

> "What characterizes this Revolution, which has lasted for four hundred years, is the eminently gradual process of its development. In the sixteenth, seventeenth and eighteenth centuries it was primarily religious, as political institutions remained more or less intact. From 1789 to the end of the nineteenth century it was essentially political. From that point on it invaded the economy, the only one area of social life left to subvert. In parallel, from the sixteenth to the eighteenth century it passed from Christianity to deism. The nineteenth century marked the apogee of atheism. The twentieth century is the century of pantheism properly speaking. Finally, the sixteenth to the nineteenth century was the era when

---

[652] FRANÇOIS AROUET DE VOLTAIRE, letter of March 2, 1769 in *Oeuvres*, prepared by the Marquis of CONDORCET, Société Litteraire Typographique, Kehl 1785-1789, vol. XLVI, p. 274.

[653] On the French Revolution, in addition to the classic work by PIERRE GAXOTTE, *La Révolution française*, Fayard, Paris, 1928, new ed. prepared by JEAN TULARD, Complexe, Paris, 1988, cf. *Le Livre noir de la Révolution française*, prepared by RENAUD ESCANDE, O.P., Cerf, Paris, 2008, and the recent synthesis by PHILIPPE PICHOT-BRAVARD, *La Révolution française*, preface by PHILIPPE DE VILLIERS, Via Romana, Paris, 2014. On the cultural origins of the French Revolution, see the classic works by PAUL HAZARD, *La crise de la conscience européenne 1680-1715*, Fayard, Paris, 1968 (1935) and DANIEL MORNET, *Les Origines intellectuelles de la Révolution française*, Armand Colin, Paris, 1933. The best summary on its religious aspects is the one by JEAN DE VIGUERIE, *Christianisme et Révolution*, op. cit.

[654] MNF, 16 March 1965.

the pro-divorce ideal expanded. The twentieth century is the great century of the expansion of free love.

"This great Revolution does not advance by leaps. It took four hundred years to reach the point it has. And one must recognize that today it seems very close to its goal." [655]

The historical stages of this centuries-old process are the three great revolutions of Western history: Protestantism, the French Revolution, and Communism. Plinio Corrêa de Oliveira thus sums up this process:

"1) The Pseudo-Reformation was a first revolution. It implanted, in varying degrees, the spirit of doubt, religious liberalism, and ecclesiastical egalitarianism in the different sects it produced.

2) The French Revolution came next. It was the triumph of egalitarianism in two fields: the religious field in the form of atheism speciously labeled as secularism; and the political field through the false maxim that all inequality is an injustice, all authority a danger, and freedom the supreme good.

3) Communism is the transposition of these maxims to the socio-economic field. These three revolutions are episodes of one single Revolution, within which socialism, liturgism, the *politique de la main tendue* (policy of the extended hand), and the like are only transitional stages or attenuated manifestations."[656]

The Origins of the Revolutionary Process

Counter-revolutionary thinking in the nineteenth century developed stinging criticism of the French Revolution, but did not always grasp all its roots and consequences. In 1970, French scholar Louis Daménie[657] dedicated a book to synthesizing works by critics of the French Revolution, showing the complementarity of the theses of two counter-revolutionary authors: Jesuit priest Augustin Barruel,[658] one of the first analysts of the anti-Christian conspiracy, and historian Augustin Cochin,[659] who enriched the study of the Revolution by explaining its

---

[655] "The Century of War, Death and Sin," *Catolicismo*, no. 2 (February 1951).

[656] *Revolution and Counter-Revolution*, pp. 3-4.

[657] LOUIS DAMENIE, *La Révolution. Phénomène divin, mécanisme social ou complot diabolique*, DMM, Bouère, 1988. On the author, see "Louis Damenie (1911-1972)," *L'Ordre français*, 161 (May 1972).

[658] AUGUSTIN BARRUEL, S.J. (1741-1820), *Mémoires pour servir à l'histoire du jacobinisme*, Fauche, London, 1797-1798 (4 vols.) – Hamburg 1798-1799 (5 vols.). The French Jesuit's *Mémoires* have been published by Diffusion de la Pensée Française, Chiré-en-Montreuil, 1974, with an introduction by Christian Lagrave. About him, see P. DUCLOS, DHCJ, vol. I, pp. 158-159, with bibl.

[659] AUGUSTIN COCHIN (1876-1916), Catholic historian from an Orleanist family, author of *Les sociétés de pensée et la démocratie moderne: Études d'histoire révolutionnaire*, Plon-Nourrit et

dynamics. Many other names could be added to these two. However, Daménie was unaware of the work of Plinio Corrêa de Oliveira. On the one hand, Plinio reworked and systematized the preceding counter-revolutionary thought with extraordinary capacity for synthesis, and on the other hand he enriched it with new and unexplored dimensions.

For Plinio Corrêa de Oliveira, the origins of the revolutionary process date back to the fourteenth century, when Christian Europe began to see a change of mentality that became increasingly clearer during the fifteenth century. During this period there was a profound change of mentality that led to a desire for an order different than the medieval one. The man of the fourteenth and fifteenth centuries replaced the then dominant love of God with self-love, a smug self-sufficiency which Saint Augustine calls as "*Amor excellentiae propriae*" (love of one's own excellence) to define pride.[660] Just a few lines sufficed for the Brazilian thinker to describe that new mentality:

> "The desire of earthly pleasures is being transformed into craving. The amusements are becoming more frequent and more sumptuous, increasingly engrossing men. In clothes, manners, language, literature and art, the growing yearning for a life full of pleasures of the imagination and the senses is producing progressive manifestations of sensuality and softness. It experiences a slow decay of the seriousness and austerity of ancient times. Everything tends to gaity, affability, the frivolous. Hearts are detached gradually from the love of sacrifice, from true devotion to the Cross, and aspirations to holiness and eternal life. Chivalry, in other times one of the highest expressions of Christian austerity, became amorous and sentimental. The literature of love invaded all countries. The excesses of luxury and the consequent eagerness for gain extend to all social classes."[661]

A humanism which was born and developed between the fourteenth and fifteenth centuries in the shadow of the Italian courts is the first revolution, the most successful because, unlike the subsequent ones, it did not encounter a genuine and vigorous reaction. The Popes of the fifteenth century, with few exceptions, welcomed and protected humanism, renouncing the great ideal of the Crusades. Humanism, through figures

---

Cie, Paris, 1921; *La Révolution et la libre-pensée. La Socialisation de la pensée (1750-1789). La Socialisation de la personne (1789-1792). La Socialisation des biens (1793-1794)*, Plon-Nourrit et Cie, Paris, 1924. His studies influenced the historic "revision" of FRANÇOIS FURET (*Penser la Révolution française,* Gallimard, Paris, 1978). About him, see FREDERIC E. SCHRADER, *Augustin Cochin et la Revolution Française*, Le Seuil, Paris, 1992.

[660] ST. AUGUSTINE, *De Genesi ad litteram*, 11, 14.

[661] *Revolution and Counter-Revolution*, p. 14.

such as Erasmus of Rotterdam,[662] the father of the Protestant Revolution, beyond seeming differences, forms a single coherent block with that of the Renaissance. It recalls the famous statement by Erasmus that "Ego peperi ovum Lutherus exclusit" ("I laid the egg that Luther hatched")[663] is confirmed by the most recent historical discoveries.[664]

Three Revolutions, the Same Spirit

The French Revolution was a new and more energetic aspect of the same spirit. It assumed the anarchic and egalitarian daydreams of humanism and Protestantism and transposed them to the political and social level.

Just as, according to Ronald H. Knox, "there is an underground world of heresy that secretly undermined the structure of medieval Europe,"[665] there is also an underground world of Anabaptists and religious groups or sects that sought to "renew early Christianity by giving it a radical and programmatic interpretation."[666] This underground world of radical sects was not a marginal phenomenon but was the driving force of the religious Revolution of the sixteenth century, prefiguring the theses and arguments of the second great Revolution, the French Revolution, which was the transposition of the Protestant Reformation to the political and social level.

> "The French Revolution was marked by the spirit of Protestantism to such an extent that the constitutional church it organized was nothing save a poorly veiled instrument for the implantation of actual Protestantism in France. The egalitarian, anti-monarchical, and anti-aristocratic orientation of the French Revolution is the projection in the civic sphere of the egalitarian tendency that led Protestantism to reject the aristocratic and monarchical elements of the ecclesiastical hierarchy. The communist ferment that worked the extreme left of the Revolution, and eventually made itself explicit in such movements as that of Babeuf, was nothing save the secular analogy of the communist movements, like the Moravian

---

[662] On the Dutch humanist Erasmus of Rotterdam (1466/1469-1536), cf. JOHAN HUIZINGA, *Erasmo* (1924), It. tr., Einaudi, Torino, 1975 and the pages dedicated to him by RAMON GARCIA DE HARO, in *Historia teologica del modernismo*, Universidad de Navarra, Pamplona, 1972.

[663] ERASMUS, Lettera 1528 to John Caesarius of December 16, 1524 in *Opus Epistolarum*, Oxford University Press, vol. V, London, 1924, p. 609.

[664] *Revolution and Counter-Revolution,* op. cit. See, for example, GEORGE WILLIAMS. *Radical Reformation,* Westminster Press, Philadelphia, 1962; SILVANA SEIDEL MENCHI, *Erasmo in Italia, 1520-1580,* Bollati Boringhieri, Torino, 1987. Silvana Seidel Menchi quotes some sentences by the Roman Holy Office that underline the subversive religious charge found in Erasmus' works (pp. 310-313).

[665] RONALD A. KNOX, *Illuminati e carismatici,* It. tr., Il Mulino, Bologna, 1970, p. 531.

[666] DELIO CANTIMORI, *Eretici italiani del '500,* Sansoni, Firenze, 1939, p. 152.

Brotherhood, which produced what could be called the Protestant extreme left. The effects of Humanism, the Renaissance, and Encyclopedism in the French Revolution were evident in the complete secularization of the State, the Greco-Roman masquerade, and the continual evoking of the republics of classical paganism."[667]

From the Jacobins, the most radical wing of the French Revolution, socialist sects were born and developed within a few years that sought to bring to completion the work of the Protestant Revolution, by suppressing all forms of authority and social inequality.[668] The Communist theorist Friedrich Engels includes among the direct precursors of socialism the Anabaptists of Thomas Müntzer, the "Levellers" of the English Revolution, the Enlightenment philosophers of the eighteenth century from Morelly and Mably[669] to Rousseau, whose *Social Contract* "found its realization in the Terror."[670] For his part, the anarchist Kropotkin cites among the forerunners of socialism the names of the Bohemian heretic Jan Hus[671] and the Anabaptists, and stresses that the French Revolution "was the source of all the communist, anarchist and socialist ideas of our era."[672]

In his second thesis on Feuerbach (1845), Karl Marx says that man must find the truth of his thinking in practice; and in his eleventh thesis he argues that the task of philosophers is not to interpret the world but to transform it.[673] The philosopher is replaced by the revolutionary, and the revolutionary must show in practice the power and effectiveness of his thought. Communist theoretician Antonio Gramsci sums up the historical

---

[667] *Philosophical Self-Portrait,* p. 377.

[668] R. DE MATTEI, *A sinistra di Lutero. Sette e movimenti religiosi nell'Europa del '500,* Città Nuova, Roma, 1999.

[669] The *Code of Nature* (1755) by Étienne-Gabriel Morelly (1717 - c. 1782), was a 'sacred' text of leftist thought adopted by Babeuf and Marx. In it the author describes the utopia of a primitive socialist society founded on the common ownership of goods and the abolition of private property (cf. JACOB TALMON, *The Origins of Totalitarian Democracy,* Secker & Warburg, London, 1952; It. tr.: *Le origini della democrazia totalitaria,* Il Mulino, Bologna, 1967, pp. 76-79).

[670] FRIEDRICH ENGELS, *L'evoluzione del socialismo dall'utopia alla scienza,* It. tr., Editori Riuniti, Roma, 1958, pp. 15-17.

[671] Jan Hus (1370-1415) was a Bohemian religious agitator who founded the Czech national Church. Condemned for heresy, he was executed in Costance, Switzerland, on July 6, 1415. Cf. ARNALDO M. LANZ, EC (1951), cols. 1513-1516.

[672] PIETR KROPOTKIN, *La Grande Révolution 1789-1793,* Stock, Paris, 1909, It. tr., *La Grande Rivoluzione 1789-1793,* Edizioni "Anarchismo," Catania, 1987, p. 378. The same genealogical tree, from Müntzer to Babeuf, is outlined by MIKAIL BAKUNIN in *La Comune e lo Stato,* Samonà e Savelli, Roma, 1970, pp. 34-35.

[673] KARL MARX, *Tesi su Feuerbach,* It. tr. in FEUERBACH-MARX-ENGELS, *Materialismo dialettico e materialismo storico,* prepared by CORNELIO FABRO, La Scuola, Brescia, 1962, pp. 81-86.

and dialectical materialism and its resulting revolutionary strategy with the formula "philosophy of praxis":

> "The philosophy of praxis presupposes all this cultural past: Renaissance and Reformation, German philosophy and the French Revolution, Calvinism and English classical economics, secular liberalism, and this historicism which is at the root of the whole modern conception of life. The philosophy of praxis is the crowning point of this entire movement of intellectual and moral reformation, made dialectical in the contrast between popular culture and high culture. It corresponds to the nexus, Protestant Reformation plus French Revolution." [674]

This itinerary precisely matches the one drawn by Plinio Corrêa de Oliveira in *Revolution and Counter-Revolution*.

Medieval and Christian Civilization

The goal of the revolutionary process was to destroy Christian civilization, of which medieval Christendom, as Leo XIII teaches, was the highest historical expression.

> "There was a time when the philosophy of the Gospel governed the states. In that epoch, the influence of Christian wisdom and its divine virtue permeated the laws, institutions, and customs of the peoples, all categories and all relations of civil society. Then the religion instituted by Jesus Christ, solidly established in the degree of dignity due to it, flourished everywhere thanks to the favor of princes and the legitimate protection of magistrates. Then the Priesthood and the Empire were united in a happy concord and by the friendly interchange of good offices. So organized, civil society gave fruits superior to all expectations, whose memory subsists and will subsist, registered as it is in innumerable documents that no artifice of the adversaries can destroy or obscure."[675]

In his Encyclical *Il fermo proposito* of June 11, 1905, Pius X reaffirmed: "The civilization of the world is Christian. The more completely Christian it is, the more true, more lasting and more productive it is of genuine fruit."[676] And in the Letter *Notre Charge Apostolique* of August 25, 1910, he recalled that "civilization is not something yet to be found, nor is the New City to be built on hazy notions; it has been in existence and still is: it is Christian civilization, it is the Catholic City. It has only to be set up and restored continually

---

[674] ANTONIO GRAMSCI, *Quaderni dal Carcere* [*Prison Notebooks*], critical edition by the Gramsci Institute prepared by VALENTINO GERRATANA, Einaudi, Torino, 1975, vol. III, p. 1860.

[675] LEO XIII, Encyclical *Immortale Dei*, of November 1, 1885, AAS, vol. XVIII (1885), p. 169.

[676] ST. PIUS X, Encyclical *Il fermo proposito*, *Pii X Acta*, II, pp. 112-132; It. tr., EE, Pius X, pp. 133 (pp. 131-145).

against the unremitting attacks of insane dreamers, rebels and miscreants: *Omnia instaurare in Christo* (Eph. 1:10)."[677]

The Christian civilization of which Saint Pius X and Leo XIII speak is medieval civilization, a daughter of the Catholic Church, which also took the name Christendom: "a projection, onto the natural field," Plinio says, "of the great supernatural reality that is the Mystical Body of Our Lord Jesus Christ."[678]

In the Middle Ages, the Brazilian thinker adds,

> "While man advances in the life of grace by the practice of virtue, at the same time he elaborates a culture – a political, social, and economic order – in entire consonance with the basic and perennial principles of Natural Law. This is what is called Christian civilization."[679] "This splendid reality, an order and a perfection more supernatural and heavenly than natural and earthly, has been called Christian civilization, the product of Christian culture and a daughter of the Catholic Church."[680] "Medieval Christendom was not just any order, or merely one of many possible orders. It was the realization, in the circumstances inherent to the times and places, of the only authentic order among men, namely, Christian civilization."[681]

According to our author,

> "The thesis more or less implicit or explicit in *Revolution and Counter-Revolution* is that, from the moment of Pentecost to the highest point of the Middle Ages, in its main general line the Church was continuously growing and developing. I am not saying there have not been phases of decline or crisis, but they were episodic and inconsequential to the general line. The subsequent filling of open voids was done in such a way that also in her explicitations the Church certainly grew very much in beauty. And what was implicit in a Catholic of the

---

[677] St. Pius X, Letter *Notre Charge Apostolique*, August 25, 1910; AAS 2 (1910), pp. 607-633, It. tr. EE, *Pio X*, pp. 837-838 (pp. 828-873).

[678] "Christendom," *Legionário*, no. 732 (August 18, 1946); cf. also "Christian Civilization," *Legionário*, no. 546 (January 24, 1943).

[679] *Philosophical Self-Portrait,* p. 366.

[680] "The XXI Century Crusade," @ http://www.tfp.org/who-we-are/xxi-century-crusade.html.

[681] *Revolution and Counter-Revolution*, p. 41. Plinio Corrêa de Oliveira does not deny the legitimacy of the term "Christian civilizations" in the plural to indicate the incalculable variety of aspects and nuances of a single civilization: "Nevertheless, given the identity of the fundamental principles inherent to all Christian civilizations, the great reality hovering above them all is a powerful unity which merits the name Christian civilization by antonomasia." One can likewise admit the existence of high-level aspects in non-Christian civilizations: "However, all of these civilizations were disfigured by one or another trait shockingly divergent from the very elevation they displayed in other aspects. Suffice it to remember the great extent of slavery, and the vile condition imposed on women before Jesus Christ. No civilization has ever displayed the eminent perfection inherent to Christian civilization" (*Philosophical Self-Portrait*).

early times, a Catholic of the catacombs, became enormously explicit in the Middle Ages. For example, a cathedral lay in the soul of a martyr of the catacombs like a seed lies in the ground." [682]

Over centuries of maturation and development, that which was found deep in the souls of the Catholics of the first centuries began to blossom, finding its expression in the civilization of castles and cathedrals.

"Was there a mere explicitation? Or was there also an increased blossoming of a germinal holiness that existed in the Church, transpired, and later reached higher degrees? I do not mean that the Church became necessarily holier at this time, but that the Church manifested her sanctity much more in the eyes of the faithful in general and also in the eyes of the infidels. And at one point a certain manifestation of the Church, of Christian civilization and therefore of Christendom, became a common gift of all the faithful. And through the teaching of religion and faith it was incorporated not only in the convictions, but also in the subconsciousness and traditions of countless Catholics. On the other hand, this incorporation became a tradition, a mental habit such that it was passed from one generation to the next, from progeny to progeny, over time." [683]

The Middle Ages formed a cohesive and homogeneous civilization. The civilizing work of Cluny, Saint Gregory VII, the Crusades, the Romanesque and Gothic cathedrals, the *Summa Theologica* of Saint Thomas, the Universities and corporations, Saint Dominic, Saint Francis, Saint Bernard, the Orders of Chivalry and the Holy Roman Empire, Godfrey of Bouillon, and Simon de Montfort – "all these huge sectors of human life were gradually formed but constitute a cohesive block."[684] It all formed a culture and a state of mind in which

"men lived, prayed, fought, rested, feasted, and died. Everything was done in that atmosphere. And man's common life was spent behind stained glass, at the sound of organs, in contact with granite, behind ramparts and walls ornamented with weapons. All that was the common routine. Why? Because that upward tendency, cognition – through a special grace – and I would almost say paramount discernment of the highest of the heights, penetrated deep into the soul of medieval man. He could not conceive of the possibility of making an employee's bedroom window except in a Gothic-style arch. That was the natural form of all windows, doors, communications, adornments, decorations, everything. That was the atmosphere of life." [685]

---

[682] RRR, 1 November 1980.
[683] Idem.
[684] RRR, 23 April 1988.
[685] RRR, 3 January 1981.

The Depth of the Revolution: the Disordered Tendencies

What were the causes of the decline of medieval civilization? In the Encyclical *Immortale Dei,* Leo XIII writes, "that harmful and deplorable passion for innovation which was aroused in the sixteenth century began first by throwing into confusion the Christian religion, and next, by natural sequence, invaded the precincts of philosophy, whence it spread amongst all classes of society."[686] The religious, intellectual and political and social spheres are the three fields covered by the process of dissolution the Pope calls the "new conception of law."[687]

Plinio Corrêa de Oliveira does not deny the existence of a series of intellectual errors that developed over the centuries. Those errors oppose the only truth, which is guarded and transmitted by the Church. But what is their genesis? He traces their origin to man's disordered tendencies excited by the Power of Darkness.[688] Employing current language, he includes among disordered passions all impulses to sin that exist in man as a consequence of original sin and the threefold concupiscence denounced by the Gospel: that of the flesh, of the eyes, and of the pride of life (1 Jn. 2:16).[689]

Plinio distinguishes in the Revolution three depths historically interpenetrated to some degree: tendencies, ideas, and facts. The Revolution in ideas precedes that of the facts, and is preceded in turn by the revolution in tendencies. The most profound dimension is that of tendencies.[690] Plinio deals with this issue not only in *Revolution and Counter-Revolution* but also in other writings such as the posthumous

---

[686] LEO XIII, Encyclical *Immortale Dei*, EE, *Leo XIII*, p. 351, no. 23.

[687] Idem, p. 353.

[688] H.-D. NOBLE, *Passions,* in DTC, vol. XI, 2 (1932), cols. 2211-2241; AIME SOLIGNAC, *Passions et vie spirituelle,* in DSp, vol. XII, 1 (1984), cols. 339-357; ROBERT MINER, *Thomas Aquinas on the Passions. A Study of Summa Theologica,* I-IIae, 22-48, Cambridge University Press, Cambridge, 2009. The passions can be understood in a metaphysical sense (cf. ST. THOMAS AQUINAS, *Summa Theologica,* I-IIae, q. 23, art. 2-4) and in a psychological sense. Noble defines passion as "a single act of the sensory appetite that essentially comprises an affective tendency and psychological reaction" (col. 2215). Cf. ANTONIO EYMIEU, *Il governo delle passioni (essay on practical psychology),* It. tr., Desclée & C., Roma, 1913. The author, investigating relations between ideas, feelings and acts, establishes some great psychological laws, the first of which is that an idea leads a person to the act of which it is a representation. The second principle is that an action arouses the sentiment of that which it should be the normal expression. The third is that the passion sharpens to a maximum the human psychological forces and uses them for its own purposes.

[689] *Revolution and Counter-Revolution,* op. cit., pp. 46-47.

[690] Cf. notion of *"inclinatio"* in DARIO COMPOSTA, S.D.B. (1917-2002), *Natura e ragione. Studio sulle inclinazioni naturali in rapporto al diritto naturale,* PAS-Verlag, Zurich, 1971, *passim.*

Notes on the Concept of Christendom, and *Considerations on Catholic Culture,* of 1954.[691]

He states:

> "Throughout my life as a counter-revolutionary I found a rather considerable number of people working against the Revolution in the field of ideas. I met people working in the field of political action. Yet I found no one concerned with counter-revolutionary tendencies....Tendencies influence ideas and action, and if no work is done to act upon tendencies, nothing is done. This is the reason why the counter-revolutionary action must fully take tendencies into account."[692]

While the object of the intellect is the truth, in order to love and serve the truth man needs the intervention of his will, which, according to Thomism, is the primary faculty of man.[693] Saint Thomas teaches that "a man is not said to be good by his good understanding, but by his good will."[694] As such, free will is indeed the spiritual faculty in greater conformity to the divine goodness, while the intellect is morally neutral. However, below his higher faculties – the intellect and the will – man is moved by the senses, distinguished between exterior and interior. Our five external senses are coordinated by an internal sense called common sense.

Then there is a second and more important internal cognitive faculty, the representative one (*phantasia, imaginatio*), which is the power to fix, maintain, reproduce and change the images of sensible things.[695] The *phantasia* or imagination retains, composes and reproduces acquired images from which the intellect draws abstract universal concepts to produce thoughts.[696] In addition to common sense and imagination, man has other internal senses, like animals: sensory memory and instinct or *vis aestimativa*, which is the ability to judge what is good or harmful to the animal, but which Saint Thomas defines in man as *cogitative*:[697] it is

---

[691] "Considerations on Catholic Culture," lecture of November 13, 1954 in *Catolicismo*, no. 51, March 1955.

[692] NOR, 11 July 1969.

[693] A. TANQUEREY, *Le grandi verità cristiane che generano nell'anima la pietà*, It. tr., Desclée, Roma, 1952, pp. 105 & ff.; ANDREA DALLEDONNE, *Il rischio della libertà: S. Tommaso-Spinoza*, Marchrati, Milano, 1990, pp. 54-102.

[694] *Summa Theologica*, I, q. 5, a. 4, ad 3.

[695] RÉGIS JOLIVET, *Trattato di filosofia*, III, *Psicologia*, Morcelliana, Brescia, 1958, p. 211; L. ELDERS, *La filosofia della natura in san Tommaso d'Aquino*, Libreria Editrice Vaticana, Città del Vaticano, 1996, pp. 225-226.

[696] *Summa Theologica*, I, q. 89, a. 1, c.

[697] Cf. Fr. ANGELO A CASTRONOVO, O.F.M.CAP, La *cogitativa in S. Tommaso*. Dissertatio ad lauream apud Gregorianam. Oficium Libri Catholici, Roma, 1966.

man's most noble sensory faculty because it is the place where the intellect touches the sensible order.[698]

This obscure and mysterious human sphere where sensible tendencies meet the spiritual faculties constitutes the nebulous hinterland of man's choices. Here are born and ferment the disordered passions, and especially two passions that can lead to revolt against morality and the Christian faith: pride and sensuality. It is no coincidence that Enlightenment materialists like Helvetius theorized about disordered passions defining them as "the heavenly fire that vivifies the world."[699] Born in the obscurity of the human soul, these passions are transformed into metaphysical principles that express the spirit of the Revolution: absolute equality and complete liberty.

> "It is in these sad depths that one finds the junction between these two metaphysical principles of the Revolution, namely, equality and liberty, which are mutually contradictory from so many points of view."[700]

The field of tendencies, however, is very broad and not limited only to pride and sensuality:

> "A tendency is the convergence: a) of a temperamental and biological force in a potential state which is like a still unopened reservoir; b) a movement of moral (volitional) order, also in potential state; and c) and a system of ideas in an incipient state.

> "All these related elements develop *pari passu*, fortifying one another and tending to the fullness of their satisfaction, their realization in acts, and the explicitation of their ultimate logical consequences.

> "This is not empty talk; I say 'satisfaction' because of the biological force, of 'realization' in acts because of the moral movement aiming at action; and of 'reaching the ultimate consequences' because of the intellectual system. These three things simultaneously arrive at a point where they are entirely fulfilled.

> "For example, in a family with a tendency to grow rich there is a temperamental and biological thirst for action, power and profit. There is a moral act, the decision of the will to make a fortune and to carry out the enriching acts that follow; finally, a conception of life is engendered to justify it: 'money is everything,' etc. The family takes this conception of life to its ultimate consequences over generations.

---

[698] What is certain, St. Thomas says, is that strictly speaking it is not the sense and intellect that know but rather man that knows through them: "*Non enim, proprie loquendo, sensus aut intellectus cognoscunt, sed homo per utrumque* (St. THOMAS AQUINAS, *Quaestiones disputatae de veritate*, q. 2, a. 6, ad 3).

[699] CLAUDE-ADRIEN HELVETIUS, (1715-1771), *De l'esprit* (1758), Fayard, Paris, 1988, p. 288.

[700] *Revolution and Counter-Revolution*, p. 51.

"In our conception the bio-temperamental tendency is presented as the most profound and dynamic factor. The moral tendency comes later, and then the intellectual. This is the order of dynamism for the vast majority of people. And it is especially the order for the Revolution, for a revolutionary is by definition a non-ascetic man, who acts for the sake of satisfying his impulses.

"It is proper to every disorderly human tendency to march toward a paroxysm and satisfy itself. Due to original sin, even in good tendencies man is led to reach a paroxysm and satisfy himself. The way for a tendency to last is for a person to avoid intemperance in its satisfaction. Intemperance in the fruition of the tendency is what leads it to extinction.

"For example, it is interesting to note that in families with an intemperate tendency to grow rich, after a few generations that craving is satiated and the family ceases tending toward enrichment and begins organizing the enjoyment of its acquired fortune. This tendency usually lasts for a few generations. Now if a strong temperamental reequilibrium is missing, the tendency to enjoy the acquired fortune turns into one of seeking ever greater pleasures, and thus to squander the wealth, and the family loses its money. This is an almost inevitable 'refrain.'

"This does not happen when it comes to the Counter-Revolution. The good counter-revolutionary movement may originate from a bio-temperamental movement, but the order is quickly reversed. Faith and conviction begin to drive the moral tendency, and the will directs the temperamental part. Therefore, in the Counter-Revolution the opposite takes place."[701]

"For example, naturally speaking, one of man's tendencies is to hold ceremonies to express the moral content of certain acts of human life. Hence the existence of wedding ceremonies, funerals, the enthronement of a university professor, bishop, etc. However, this tendency proper to man only manifests itself with all its equilibrium and vigor in sacral civilizations. For the sacral mind is led to conceive the intrinsic meaning of ceremony as referring to something that transcends man, to a value greater than all the men present there and around whom that ceremony unfolds. The whole internal dynamism of every ceremony revolves around a tendency akin to a conviction….Having that doctrinal conviction accompanied by this tendency, people attribute this meaning to the ceremony and it shines with all its splendor.

"To the degree that this conviction is gradually undermined, the tendency also weakens. I believe that, in general, it is the loosening of the tendency that precedes the weakening of conviction.

---

[701] BCM, 14 January 1967.

"The fifteenth century was the century of degradation par excellence, in which people switched from love of the sacral to a beginning of ostentation, no longer out of love for the sacral as such but for the sake of beauty....All that turned into a purely aesthetic theater stripped of its sacral content. When you switch from a sacral ceremony to a ostentatious ceremony, it remains for a while with its aesthetic aspect. Later it turns into a representation in which no one believes any longer; it arouses envy, hatred, and vanishes in general ridicule. So dies the sense of ceremonies.

"The nerve of the expansion of Christianity was an immense fire of sacrality in the depths of the Roman Empire.

"When man has a tendency to the sacral, an appetite and a taste for sacrality, sacrality satisfies a need of his soul and is a pleasure for him; on the other hand, when he has a doctrine that justifies the sacral and gives a logical explanation for it, all his tendencies are placed in order and temperance governs them. Conversely, when the sense of the sacral is dying, night falls upon his tendencies and they gradually begin to hallucinate and go crazy over time. The tendency to the sacral is the fundamental point for the equilibrium of a civilization."[702]

Ambiences, Customs, Civilizations

One of the most original aspects of the thought of Plinio Corrêa de Oliveira is precisely the importance he attached to the role of tendencies and ambiences in the revolutionary process.[703]

The testimony of Caio Xavier da Silveira sheds much light on this matter:

"His narrations of his early years clearly show that he was very sensitive to the imponderables of ambiences and perceived with great perspicacity the influence they exerted on people. We also know that, as a reaction to rationalism, the young Plinio became very interested in the work of French novelist Marcel Proust,[704] who shone precisely for his descriptions of ambiences. He later grew enthusiastic about the work of J. K. Huysmans, a Franco-Flemish writer who converted from Satanism to

---

[702] BCM, 15 August 1967.

[703] Cf. G. CANTONI, "The Contribution of Plinio Corrêa de Oliveira and *Revolution and Counter-Revolution* to the Development of Counter-revolutionary Thought and Action," *Cristianità,* no. 330-331, July-October 2005, pp. 33-45, now in ID., *Per una civiltà cristiana nel terzo millennio,* Sugarco, Milano, 2008, pp. 221-248.

[704] MARCEL PROUST (1871-1922). French novelist, author of the monumental *A la recherche du temps perdu* (1906-1922). Cf. version prepared by STÉPHANE HEUET, Delcourt, Paris, 6 vols., 1998-2013. Cf. among others, ALBERTO BERETTA-ANGUISSOLA, *Le Sens cachés de la Recherche,* Classiques Garnier, Paris, 2013.

Catholicism and excelled in the art of describing imponderables emanating from ambiences of the Catholic Church.[705]

With acuity, Plinio Corrêa de Oliveira drew the outline of a new apologetics centered on beauty."[706] Here is an excerpt from an article of his in 1932:

> "From a strictly religious point of view, the new kind of apologetic that Huysmans tried to establish is very attractive. He is not worried about philosophical arguments or scientific disputes in which people fence with syllogisms for or against the faith.... Huysmans makes of the Church a materially objective description in which, with unique ability, he strives to emphasize the supernatural glow that she radiates, for example, from her beautiful liturgy enriched with a moving symbolism and an enrapturing Gregorian chant, in her vehement prayers, the tumult of her contrition, her outbreaks of confidence in Divine Providence, the harmonious weeping in her offices for the deceased."[707]

In *Revolution and Counter-Revolution* he writes,

> "Given that God established mysterious and admirable relations between, on the one hand, certain forms, colors, sounds, perfumes, and flavors and, on the other, certain states of soul, it is obvious that, through the arts, mentalities can be profoundly influenced and persons, families, and peoples can be induced to form a profoundly revolutionary state of spirit."[708]

This passage is fundamental to understand his distinctive contribution to the counter-revolutionary school, also expressed in the section he wrote in *Catolicismo* for many years, "Ambiences, Customs, Civilizations." It consisted in comparative analyses of ambiences, monuments, objects of the present and the past, soaring from the observation of reality to the highest philosophical and religious principles through contrasting images. Part of this perspective was his interpretation and comments on people's faces and characteristic elements of human personality. Indeed, a man's way of being is expressed in his

---

[705] Joris-Karl Huysmans, French writer of Dutch origin (1848-1907), after the novel *À rebours* (1884) expressing a refined decadence, with the work *Là-bas* (1891) he plunged into satanism and eventually converted to Catholicism, as described in his successive novels: *En route* (1895), *La cathédrale* (1898), *L'oblat* (1903).

[706] CAIO VIDIGAL XAVIER DA SILVEIRA, "*Como nasceu a providential obra* Revolução e Contra-Revolução ["How the Providential Work *Revolution and Counter-Revolution* Was Born]," op. cit.

[707] "Huysmans II En Route," *Legionário*, February 21, 1932.

[708] *Revolution and Counter-Revolution*, p. 63.

physiognomy, deportment, manners and even attire, the changes of which in history are linked to the change in human types and personalities.[709]

An ambience is the harmony resulting from the affinity of various beings gathered in one place and exerts a profound influence on souls.

> "Men form for themselves ambiences in their own image and likeness, ambiences where their customs and civilizations are reflected. But the reverse is also true to a large extent: ambiences shape men, customs and civilizations in their own image and likeness."[710]

The wisdom with which God ordained the great ambience of creation in which we are immersed, formed by living beings that surround us such as plants and animals, and topped by man, made in God's image and likeness, is a proof of the importance of the ambience for a balanced development of people's natural and supernatural life. Social ambiences strongly influence man's tendencies and passions, which become good or bad according to the end to which they tend. These profound tendencies can exploit the weakness of the human intellect to lead man to intellectually justify his evil deeds and bad habits. In this regard, Plinio Corrêa de Oliveira liked to recall the phrase by Paul Bourget, "one must live as one thinks, under pain of sooner or later ending up thinking as one has lived."[711]

The disordered tendencies produce moral crises, erroneous doctrines, and therefore revolutions. In turn, the latter lead to new crises, new errors, new revolutions. Their crescendo is analogous to that produced in the phenomenon of acceleration by the law of gravity: tendencies feed on their own works and produce consequences that develop with proportional intensity. Like typhoons and cataclysms, the disordered passions can have an immense force, but one turned to destruction.

> "And so you understand how there can be no civilization without temperance, and how a true understanding of 'Revolution and Counter-Revolution' is seriously incomplete without studying temperance and intemperance."[712]

The Sin of the Revolution

Gnosis is the philosophical system to which disordered human passions tend. As we have seen, it is a pantheistic and egalitarian conception of the universe.

---

[709] "Dress, Hierarchy, and Egalitarianism," in *Catolicismo*, no. 133 (January 1962); cf. also "The Habit and the Monk," *Catolicismo*, no. 62 (February 1956).

[710] "Be Wise as Serpents and Simple as Doves," *Catolicismo*, no. 37 (January 1954).

[711] PAUL BOURGET, *Le démon du midi,* 2 vols., Plon-Nourrit, Paris, 1914, vol. II, p. 375.

[712] BCM, 28 January 1967.

"Individuation, which for Gnosis is evil, is a principle of inequality. Any and every hierarchy is an offspring of individuation. According to the Gnostics, the universe is rescued from individuation and inequality by a process of destruction of the 'I,' which reintegrates individuals into the great homogeneous All. The achievement of absolute equality among men and of its corollary – complete liberty in an anarchic order of things – can be seen as a preparatory stage for that total re-absorption. In this perspective it is not difficult to see the connection between Gnosis and communism.

"Thus, the doctrine of the Revolution is Gnosis, and its ultimate causes are rooted in pride and sensuality. Given the moral character of these causes, the whole problem of Revolution and Counter-Revolution is, in the final analysis, mainly a moral problem. What is said in *Revolution and Counter-Revolution* is that, without pride and sensuality, the Revolution would not exist as an organized movement in the whole world; it would not be possible." [713]

In this regard, the sin of Revolution is a "criteriological sin" because the hatred of inequalities in creation reveals a profound hatred for being: hatred for limited being of creatures and especially for the Being by essence, which is God.

"The sin of the Revolution is hatred of the order of reality, due above all to the clash of pride and sensuality with that order. It becomes a criteriological sin when an individual, out of revolutionary spirit, forges an erroneous, even metaphysical criteriology, forming a wrong idea on that specific point of metaphysics that is the issue of equality and liberty. Then the sin of Revolution is born. It combines with the criteriological sin, and both form a single block. The sin of Revolution leads to the criteriological sin and uses it as an instrument to attain its fullness. And this results in an apex of sin of Revolution and an apex of criteriological sin.

"Why is it said that Gnosis is the height of the sin of Revolution? Would it not be egalitarianism? The answer is that the problem of egalitarianism is at the very core of the problem of being. It is impossible to take a position before the problem of egalitarianism without taking at the same time a position before the problem of being as a whole. He who hates inequality, deep down hates being. Man is incited to commit a criteriological sin in order to hate being in its totality.

"In its criteriology, the sin of Revolution is Gnostic. Just like the criteriological sin, taken to its logical conclusion, it leads to the sin of Revolution. But one can say that Gnosis and egalitarianism mesh together

---

[713] Preface to the first Argentine edition of *Revolution and Counter-Revolution* (*Revolución y Contra-Revolución*, Buenos Aires, 1970, pp. 9-34); now in *Revolution and Counter-Revolution*, Italian edition, pp. 325-326.

to form a single whole. This is reasonable because a supreme error in one field must be correlated with a supreme error in another field. But in principle this does not prevent the criteriological sin and the Gnostic sin from being seen as distinct realities.

"One could ask: Since the sin of Revolution has a more powerful and dynamic starting point in pride and sensuality, does the criteriological sin have the same starting point? Of course it can be born from pride and sensuality, but it can also and very easily be born from other capital vices such as laziness. These two sins – pride and sensuality – do not have such a sharp preponderance in triggering the criteriological sin as they do in triggering the sin of Revolution." [714]

Dynamics and Speed of the Revolution

The revolutionary process had expressions that were more violent or more moderate throughout history, which Prof. Plinio calls "speeds." The first, rapid and intense, is destined to a seeming failure, at least in the short term. The second, much slower, is usually successful.

Examples of the first speed can be traced to more extreme revolutionary movements like the Anabaptists in the fifteenth century and the Jacobin and anarchist currents of the nineteenth and twentieth centuries. Examples of the second speed are moderate currents of Protestantism and liberalism which, advancing through successive stages of dynamism and inertia, favored a slide toward the same point of arrival. The goal of the two currents is the same even if the Revolution is differently manifested in each of them.

The failure of extremist currents is illusory: they create a fixed point of attraction that attracts not only moderates to absolute radicalism, but consolidates their positions. Society ends up by slowly treading along the path that the radicals wanted it to take.

"All the great Revolutions had this dynamism: they broke out and advanced to some extent but ran the risk of producing crystallizations as they overflowed from fabricated environments, such as the Sorbonne's, into peaceful and conservative ambiences. For its promoters, the Revolution had to stop it before the softies were taken over by crystallization, because for the Revolution to irritate the softies is to lose out. There is a limit as to how far a Revolution can go, a limit beyond which it cannot go. The softies are that limit, that threshold up to which it can go. When the softies crystallize, it stops.

"We notice this in all Revolutions. For example, when you study the history of the first 100 or 150 years of Protestantism you seem to be facing an anarcho-syndicalist movement of the last century. Luther,

---

[714] MNF, 18 July 1967.

Zwingli, even Wyclif and John Huss before them were men that burned, broke down, leveled, shouted, howled. One hundred years later, Protestantism seems to take on more calm, to be more judicious, more sensible, quietly conquering a terrain it would be unable to conquer with armed force. The time comes for a mask of good sense to replace that of terror. And with its seemingly good sense, the Revolution obtains what it would be unable to achieve through terror." [715]

The same happened in the French Revolution:

"After the excesses of the Terror, the Thermidorian reaction starts and the French Revolution (which was largely political, and perhaps mainly political) adopts more peaceful policies: the Directory, then the Consulate, then the lifetime Consulate, then the restoration of a brass monarchy with Bonaparte, and finally the restoration of the Bourbons.

"Now, what do the Bourbons do? The restored Bourbons play a similar role to that of King Juan Carlos in Spain: they accustom traditional France to a regime that is republican except for the fact that its head wears a crown. When the crown falls, the republic has already been established in the nation's customs. In order to do this more cautiously and with greater chances of success they did not switch directly to the republic of Charles X – a king still crowned in Reims – but placed Louis Philippe on the throne instead.

"And in Louis Philippe's monarchy the throne was completely surrounded by republican institutions. In 1848 he was sent off, retired with the abundant wealth he had inherited and accumulated during that time, and went to die in England." [716]

In this undulating movement, the republican and secularist ideal does not lose its force but adapts to people of different sensitivities, conquering ever greater layers of moderate opinion. The forces that drive the revolutionary process are keenly attentive to make sure the plan is realized without setbacks and violent shocks. In fact, in order to win, the Revolution must prevent a backlash from developing.

"The reason is that the promoters of Revolution did not want to repeat the post-revolutionary upheavals that occurred after Protestantism, the French Revolution and the Russian Revolution. Protestantism was followed by the Counter-Reformation. After the French Revolution the ultramontane movement of the nineteenth century arose, culminating still in our century with the pontificate of Saint Pius X. The universal wave of anti-Communism that followed after Communism was implanted in Russia forced them – in order to denature that wave, and in order to guide

---

[715] RRR, 23 July 1988.
[716] Idem.

events as they wanted – to fabricate a false anti-Communism themselves under the guise of Fascism and Nazism."[717]

"For seventy-eight years now I see that whenever a stone falls from the edifice of the current socio-economic order, the bourgeois in the first moment are dismayed, in the second moment they see the building has not fallen, and say, 'No, that was only a stone!' and their merry-go-round continues. And if someone tells them: 'Be careful, such and such a thing will happen,' they absolutely dismiss it as nonsense. Two or three years later, it is finished. They try to forget they had denied it, and accept it as natural.

"In other words, their first impulse before a looming danger is such a refusal of the danger that they shout: 'It's impossible!' When the danger is consummated their cry is: 'it is a fait accompli, there's nothing we can do about it, so let's continue living happily.'"[718]

The Industrial Revolution

According to Prof. Plinio, one of the points that separate counter-revolutionaries from the economic right-wing is their position before the Industrial Revolution.[719] By Industrial Revolution he understands not only the English one in the eighteenth century but in general the scientific and technological revolution that unfolded in the second half of the nineteenth century, which is identified with the scientist ideology of Progress.[720] At that time, a great dream arose on the horizon: the "construction" of modern civilization symbolized by new urban agglomerations, major steel mills, electricity, motor-driven public transportation, etc. In a few decades, technological progress made possible recording images (photography), sound (the phonograph) and movement (cinema).[721] New discoveries changed the perception of time,[722] which becomes a field of improvement for humanity. The progress of science increased man's confidence in his conquering power.[723]

---

[717] Idem.

[718] RRR, 24 October 1987.

[719] RRR, 7 April 1969.

[720] Some interesting points on this revolutionary process can be found in FRIEDRICH VON HAYEK, L'abuso della ragione, It. tr., Vallecchi, Firenze, 1967.

[721] Cf. DONALD SASSON, La cultura degli europei dal 1800 ad oggi, It. tr., BUR, Milano, 2011, pp. 691-703; PASCAL GRISET, Les révolutions de la communication XIXe-XXe siècle, Hachette, Paris, 1991.

[722] STEPHEN KERN, Il tempo e lo spazio. La percezione nel mondo tra Otto e Novecento, It. tr., Il Mulino, Bologna, 1995. In an essay on La metropoli e la vita mentale (1900), Georg Simmel commented on the influence of the universal spread of pocket watches in accelerating the pace of modern life.

[723] P. A. TAGUIEFF, Il progresso, p. 125.

The changes brought about by the Industrial Revolution modified human psychology by creating new ways of thinking and acting. Suffice it to mention the emergence of new diseases such as neurasthenia, one of the consequences of speed technology.[724]

"From the moment the train, telegraph and telephone – the Revolution's three technical T's – started to propel the world, agitation began to spread and eventually everything started to run madly; irreflection began to enter everything, frivolity of mind began to spread everywhere, and as a result people began to accept at face value all the ideas presented by advertising. No one wanted to stop to analyze, think, criticize. They would just say 'yes, yes, yes' and euphorically run after new sensations.

"While not directly ideological, all this prepares temperamental disorders and thus hamper man's ability as a being placed in the natural order, of which he is king, to operate his intellect properly. And man, who in the supernatural order needs to have recollection, pray and override the earthly with the heavenly, is reduced to a rat-race that makes it increasingly difficult for him to lift up his mind to Heaven.

"I could understand a mystic who has an ecstasy at Praça do Patriarca (downtown São Paulo), though I would be very surprised. But one cannot deny that the agitation at that square prevents someone from praying his rosary well. So, the hustle and bustle of the modern world, even in what it is not necessarily opposed to Catholic doctrine and tradition, creates a state of soul where the whole composition of the Catholic spirit becomes incompatible with the ambience thus created. It is impossible to live 'in a Catholic way' amid this whole pressure, this rat-race." [725]

"The transformations that occurred over sixty years, from 1789 to 1848, led man to accept as good and normal something that was unnatural, cacophonous, grotesque, and Dantesque. And they gradually deformed men. Large industries, excessive speed, all these things deform man's subconscious.

"Little by little the world changed. From the standpoint of ambiences and circumstances, the world became far more different between 1785 and 1885 than between 1885 and 1969. The world of 1785 had none of the inventions that arose with the great steel industry, steam, electricity, and petroleum. In its material aspects, this world is not much different from the world at the end of the Middle Ages, for example; the material picture of life is not much different from that of the late Middle

---

[724] The term neurasthenia was introduced by American physician George Miller Beard in 1869 to indicate a psychopathology due to a state of attrition and excitability of the central nervous system.
[725] RRR, 10 December 1988.

Ages. Conversely, in the next one hundred years everything changed. It was one of the greatest changes in history."[726]

The Role of Fashion

To ensure that public opinion would accept such radical changes in life style, the Revolution resorted above all to fashion.

"Fashion was the great vehicle of the Revolution. I maintain that it was more of a vehicle than the press and more than cinema and radio, both of which were nothing but slaves of fashion. Fashion broke the resistance that the Industrial Revolution might have encountered.

"Fashion inculcated the idea that a truly manly man should adjust to noise, bad odors, excessive speed, all the frantic thrills that progress imposes on nature. He should adjust not only in a resigned way but euphorically, believing that it was good and should be so. And the one who did not accept that new ambience with the proper intensity was a cretin, crazy, a fool."[727]

The mentality born of the Industrial Revolution merged with the ideology of the English and American Revolutions, presented as different from the French Revolution.

"There are two variants of the Second Revolution: the French and the English.[728] The former was expressed in the last century mainly by brazen and aggressive republicanism and an equally brazen and aggressive anticlericalism, which was the last breath of the spirit of the French Revolution properly so-called. Now the Revolution in British style was different. It was an entirely Girondin, rather than a Jacobin program: to propagandize for the Revolution in such a way as to gently and kindly but increasingly undermine, in a peaceful atmosphere, the institutions they sought to overthrow. They never took the attack to the last point; they never said they wanted to destroy what they were destroying; if that was said, it was only in books by intellectuals for their own circles, without inviting the people to participate in that banquet of revolutionary 'cannibalism.'"[729]

Julio Loredo de Izcue has written a penetrating critique of this mentality in the light of Plinian teaching.[730] In the United States, liberalism appeared more as a pragmatic and optimistic way of life than

---

[726] NOR, 16 May 1969.

[727] NOR, 23 May 1969.

[728] Plinio Corrêa de Oliveira is not referring here to the First English Revolution of Cromwell (1649) or to the Second Revolution achieved with the Bill of Rights in 1689, but more broadly to an Anglo-American revolutionary style dominated by idolatry for scientific progress.

[729] RRR, 25 November 1989.

[730] JULIO LOREDO, *Teologia della liberazione: un salvagente di piombo per i poveri*, Cantagalli, Siena, 2014, pp. 131-144.

as a coherent body of explicit doctrines. That way of life was reinforced by the Industrial Revolution and gave rise to the idea that the United States' "manifest destiny" had ushered in a new historical era, freeing the world from the oppression of past centuries.[731]   Fascinated by these theses, liberal American Catholics conceived a similar "manifest destiny" of Catholicism in the United States. Thus was born the religious "Americanism"[732] condemned by Leo XIII, which was exported to Europe and paved the way for modernism.[733]

The Agents of the Revolution: Freemasonry and the Sects

The mere dynamism of passions and human error is not sufficient to explain the victorious march of the Revolution.

> "There is a principle of Revolution and Counter-Revolution that says: all forms of evil end up being connected among themselves even when not devised by the same person or center."[734]

This connection requires the impulse and guidance of astute and experienced agents that orient a revolutionary process that is chaotic as such. This role is played by anti-Christian sects of whatever nature.

> "The production of a process as consistent and continuous as that of the Revolution amid the thousand vicissitudes of centuries fraught with surprises of every kind seems impossible to us without the action of successive generations of extraordinarily intelligent and powerful conspirators. To think that the Revolution could have reached its present state in the absence of such conspirators is like believing that hundreds of letters thrown out a window could arrange themselves on the ground to spell out a literary piece, Carducci's *Ode to Satan*, for instance."[735]

> "Generally speaking, one can classify as agents of the Revolution all the sects – whatever their nature – engendered by it, from its origin to our days, to disseminate its thought or to concatenate its plots. The master

---

[731] Translator's note: "Manifest Destiny" is an expression used by New York journalist John L. O'Sullivan in his *Democratic Review*, which explains the belief, widespread in United States in the nineteenth century, that the American people are called by God to civilize all North America, justifying an expansionist policy. Cf. Albert K. Weinberg, *Manifest Destiny: a Study of Nationalist Expansionism in American History*, Johns Hopkins, Baltimore, 1935.

[732] The word "Americanism" defines a complex of new theories attributed to Father Isaac Hecker (died 1888), a Protestant convert and founder of a new congregation of priests called the Paulists. Americanism was condemned with the Letter *Testem benevolentiae*, addressed to Cardinal Gibbons on January 22, 1899. Cf. AAS 31 (1898-99), pp. 470-479; G. DE PIERREFEU, in DSp, I, cols. 476-488.

[733] Cf. also R. DE MATTEI, *Il ralliement di Leone XIII. Il fallimento di un progetto pastorale*, Le Lettere, Firenze, 2014, pp. 212-222.

[734] Training, 17 October 1971.

[735] *Revolution and Counter-Revolution*, p. 38.

sect, however, around which all the others are organized as mere auxiliaries – sometimes consciously and other times not – is Freemasonry, as clearly follows from the pontifical documents, especially Leo XIII's encyclical *Humanum genus*, of April 20, 1884."[736]

The first papal condemnation of Freemasonry dates back to the Constitution *In eminenti* by Clement XII, of April 24, 1738. Other condemnations have followed uninterruptedly ever since.[737] Excommunication was confirmed and renewed by Benedict XIV with the Constitution *Providas,* of May 18, 1751 and by Pope Pius VII with the Constitution *Ecclesiam a Jesu Christo,* of September 13, 1821. On March 13, 1825 the Apostolic Constitution *Quo graviora* of Leo XII reiterated the previous condemnations, pointing out that they applied to every secret society, present or future, whatever its name, which had the object of conspiring to the detriment of the Church and of the powers of the State.

Along the same lines Pius VIII spoke, with the encyclical *Traditi* of May 21, 1829; Gregory XVI in the Encyclical *Mirari Vos* of August 15, 1832; Pius IX in the Encyclical *Qui pluribus* of November 9, 1846; and numerous other documents. The last major papal document on Freemasonry is the Encyclical *Humanum Genus* by Leo XIII of April 20, 1884,[738] in which the Pope denounces the diabolical plot of Freemasonry, whose ultimate purpose, the Pope says, is "the utter overthrow of that whole religious and political order of the world which the Christian teaching has produced, and the substitution of a new state of things in accordance with their ideas, of which the foundations and laws shall be drawn from mere naturalism."[739] The Popes included that condemnation in canons 684, 2335 and 2336 of the Code of Canon Law in force from 1917 to 1983.[740]

The distinction between an inherently anti-religious Latin Freemasonry and an Anglo-American Freemasonry with which one could

---

[736] Idem.

[737] Cf. JOSÉ A. FERRER BENIMELI-GIOVANNI CAPRILE, *Massoneria e Chiesa cattolica ieri, oggi e domani,* Edizioni Paoline, Roma, 1979, pp. 20-22. Cf. also J. A. FERRER BENIMELI *Bibliografia de la Masonería–Introducción Histórico-Crítica,* co-edition of Universidad Católica Andrés Bello de Caracas with Universidad de Zaragoza, Zaragoza, 1974.

[738] LEO XIII, Enc. *Humanum genus* of April 20, 1884, ASS, 16 (1883-1884), pp. 417-483; It. tr. EE, *Leone XIII,* pp. 286-321. Among the numerous documents by Leo XIII on Masonry, see the Encyclical *Dall'alto* of October 15, 1890, ASS, 23 (1890-1891), pp. 193-206; the Letter *Le insolite manifestazioni politiche dell'8 de ottobro de 1895,* Leonis XIII P. M. Acta, 15 (1886), pp. 369-375; the Apostolic Letter *Pervenuti,* of March 19, 1902, ASS, 34 (1901-1902), pp. 513-532.

[739] LEO XIII, Enc. *Humanum genus,* in EE, *Leone XIII,* p. 295 (pp. 286-321).

[740] In the new Code of Canon Law which went into force on November 29, 1983, Masonry is not expressly mentioned as it was in the previous Code.

work together is unacceptable for a Catholic and was so for Plinio Corrêa de Oliveira. The papal condemnations include all expressions of Freemasonry and not just a part of it, as is reiterated by the Sacred Congregation for the Doctrine of the Faith in its statement of November 26, 1983, in which it states that "the Church's negative judgment in regard to Masonic association remains therefore unchanged, since their principles have always been considered irreconcilable with the doctrine of the Church, and therefore membership in them remains forbidden. The faithful who enroll in Masonic associations are in a state of grave sin and may not receive Holy Communion."[741]

Masonic affiliation is sometimes difficult to prove, but Masonic culture and mentality are not hard to identify: they are expressed by a Gnostic and relativistic worldview characterized by the quest for a political and religious unification of humanity. The Gnostic affiliation of Freemasonry is established by major studies on secret societies such as those by Father Nicolas Deschamps, Msgr. Henri Delassus, Father Emmanuel Barbier, S.J. "Same organization, same secret, same pantheism, with two conflicting principles, one good, the other bad, yet both eternal: the supreme Being, author of all good, and matter, the source of all evils."[742]

According to Plinio, Gnosis

> "is the substance and religion of the driving forces of the Revolution; revolutionary sects are the churches of Gnosis, and thus Gnosis is found at the core goals of the secret forces."[743]

Msgr. Henri Delassus and the Anti-Christian Conspiracy

The topic of secret societies was dealt with between the nineteenth and twentieth centuries by many authors who documented, in a manner impossible to contest, the existence of an insidious anti-Christian conspiracy in history.[744] Father Barruel unearthed the program of the

---

[741] *Osservatore Romano*, November 27, 1983. Cf. also the study by Msgr. JOSEF STIMPFLE [1916-1996], *Die katholische Kirche und die Freimaurerei. Die Dialogkommission hat die entscheidende Frage geklärt, Deutsche Tagespost*, no. 38 (28/29-3-1986).

[742] NICOLAS DESCHAMPS, S.J., *Les Sociétés secrètes et la Société, ou Philosophie de l'histoire contemporaine*, Fr. Seguin Ainé, Avignon, 1876, pp. 582-583. Father Nicolas Deschamps, S.J. (1797-1872) studied in particular Gnostic influence on the secret society (vol. I, pp. 281-311). On this topic, see also Father PAOLO M. SIANO, FI, *Un manuale per conoscere la Massoneria*, Casa Mariana Editrice, Frigento, 2012; ID. *Massoneria tra esoterismo, ritualità e simbolo*, vol. I, *Studi vari sulla Libera Muratoria*, Casa Mariana Editrice, Frigento, 2012, above all pp. 478-529; JEAN-CLAUDE LOZAC'HMEUR, *Fils de la Veuve*, op. cit.

[743] RRR, 11 April 1987.

[744] Among these we recall Msgr. Ernest Jouin (1884-1932), Viscount Léon de Poncins (1897-1975) and Pierre Virion (1899-1908). In 1912, Msgr. Jouin founded and directed until his death the *Revue Internationale des Sociétés Secrètes*, the famous RISS (published until 1939), which

Bavarian Illuminati, founded in 1776 in Ingolstadt by Adam Weishaupt, Professor of Canon Law at that University. The goal of that sect, structured according to strict gradualism, was a communist-type social revolution. The Illuminati were discovered and their documents seized and sent to European courts by the Elector of Bavaria. But the sect survived, and remained so vigorous that in 1832 Prince von Metternich wrote that he believed it would never be destroyed.[745]

In coalition with the Illuminati were ultra-radical Jacobin exponents of the French Revolution, including François-Noël Babeuf, a disciple of Rousseau and Robespierre, and his follower Filippo Buonarroti.[746] Babeuf stirred up in France the uprising known as the "Conspiracy of Equals,"[747] with which he tried to overthrow the Directory and reintroduce the Jacobin Constitution of 1793, but he failed and was guillotined. Buonarroti picked up his legacy and organized throughout Europe a network of secret societies whose radical program to impose communism on society was revealed only to its top ranking followers. With his book *Conspiracy for Equality*, also known as *Babeuf's Conspiracy for Equality* (1828)[748] he spread the Communist project to all circles of the European left, obtaining support also from some moderate and monarchist circles. Buonarroti was the hidden mentor of a network of secret societies that gave rise to socialism and communism.

For his part, French historian Jacques Crétineau-Joly,[749] in the two-volume work *L'Eglise romaine en face de la Révolution*, published in

---

thanks to its serious documentation and the competence of its writers became a highly valuable tool to study the issue. Cf. JOSEPH SAUVÊTRE, *Un bon serviteur de l'Eglise, Mgr. Jouin (1844-1932)*, Casterman, Paris, 1936; E. POULAT, DHGE, 28, cols. 317-320; M-F JAMES, *Esoterisme et Christianisme*, op. cit., pp. 156-159.

[745] KLEMENS-LOTHAR VON METTERNICH, *Mémoires*, E. Plon, Paris, 1882, vol. V, p. 368.

[746] Filippo Buonarroti (1761-1836) actively participated in the Jacobin Society of the Pantheon and, after its closure in the "Conspiracy of Equals" of François-Noël "Gracchus" Babeuf (1760-1797), played a leading role in drafting the conspirators' program and propaganda. For his participation in the conspiracy he was sentenced by the High Court of Justice of Vendôme to deportation for life and exiled. For a summary about him, see the entry by ARMANDO SAITTA in *Dizionario Bibliografico degli Italiani*, 15 (1972), pp. 148-160, with ample bibliography.

[747] "The French Revolution," says the Manifesto of Equals, "is only the harbinger of another, much greater and far more solemn revolution which will be the last. The people have marched on the bodies of kings and of the powerful who had united against them; and the same thing will happen to the new tyrants, the new political hypocrites seated in place of the old" (cited in A. SAITTA, *Ricerche storiografiche su Buonarroti e Babeuf*, Istituto Storico Italiano per l'Età Moderna e Contemporanea, Roma, 1986, p. 308).

[748] FILIPPO BUONARROTI, *Conspiration pour l'égalité dite de Babeuf*, 2 vols., Editions Sociales, Paris, 1957 (1828).

[749] Jacques Crétineau-Joly (1803-1875), historian of the Vandée and the Society of Jesus, based on documentation received from the Holy See, explained in *L'Eglise Romaine en face de la Révolution* (Plon, Paris, 1859, 2 vols.) the whole picture of the struggle between the Catholic Church and the Revolution in the period from the pontificate of Pius VI to the beginning of that

Paris in 1859, revealed the existence of Alta Vendita, a society that represented in the sectarian world the top organizations of Mazzini and Buonarroti. That work of Crétinau-Joly was approved in a Brief of Pius IX and the authenticity of the documents reproduced therein is attested by an official note of the Secretary of Latin letters, Monsignor Fioravanti. Their veracity is confirmed, among others, by authoritative historians of the Society of Jesus, from Father Nicolas Deschamps[750] to Father Ilario Rinieri.[751] The documents by Father Barruel and Crétineau-Joly were republished by Msgr. Delassus.

Plinio read and appreciated the work of Msgr. Henri Delassus, who, as his biographer Louis Medler pointed out, can be considered "the universal heir, at the threshold of the twentieth century, of the counter-revolutionary legacy of the nineteenth century."[752]

Msgr. Henri Delassus,[753] born in 1836 in Staires, near Lille, was ordained a priest in Cambrai in 1862 and exercised his ministry in the city of Lille, where from 1875 he was director and chief editor of *Semaine religieuse de la diocèse de Lille*, a publication that was one of the bastions of Catholic resistance to liberalism, and later to modernism. In October 1914 the magazine suspended publication because of the war. It resumed publication in June 1919 and became the official organ of the diocese.

Msgr. Delassus enjoyed the confidence of Saint Pius X, who elevated him to domestic prelate in 1904, Apostolic Prothonotary in 1911, and Dean of the chapter of Lille's cathedral in 1914, recognizing on the occasion of his priestly jubilee his zeal in defending Catholic doctrine.[754]

---

of Pius IX. The work has been republished by Cercle de la Renaissance Française (Paris, 1976, 2 vols.).

[750] NICOLAS DESCHAMPS, S.J., *Les sociétés secrètes et la société,* op. cit.

[751] ILARIO RINIERI, S.J., *Della vita e delle opere di Silvio Pellico*, Roux, Torino, 1899, vol. II, pp. 5-6.

[752] LOUIS MEDLER, *Mgr Delassus (1836-1921)*, Editions Le Sel de la Terre, 2005, p. 6. This current of thought, as Msgr. Delassus' biographer emphasizes, was distinct from the nascent political school of Charles Maurras. "It is certain that [Mgr. Delassus] did not receive his political formation from Maurras or from Action Française. He neither despises nor ignores them entirely…but is heir to a much older tradition and, what is more, different from that which Maurras inherited" (L. MEDLER, *Mgr Delassus*, op. cit., p. 13).

[753] The main works by Msgr. Henri Delassus are *L'Américanisme et la conjuration antichrétienne* (Paris, 1899) and *Le problème de l'heure présente: Antagonisme de deux civilisations*, 2 vols. (Paris, 1904), later merged in *La conjuration antichrétienne: le temple maçonnique voulant s'élever sur les ruines de l'Eglise catholique* (Paris, 1910, 3 vols., with a preface letter by Rafael Cardinal Merry del Val); *La mission posthume de la Bienheureuse Jeanne d'Arc et le Règne social de Notre Signeur Jésus Christ* (Paris, 1914); *Les pourquoi de la guerre mondiale* (Paris, 1919-1922, 3 vols.)

[754] On the occasion of his priestly jubilee on June 14, 1912, Msgr. Delassus received from Saint Pius X a letter of praise which the Pope presented as an "*act of benevolence that you well deserve…be it for your devotion to Our person or for the unequivocal testimony of your zeal, both for Catholic doctrine, which you defend, for ecclesiastical discipline, which you observe,*

Msgr. Delassus' first "battle-work" appeared in 1899 under the title *L'Américanisme et la conjuration antichrétienne* [Americanism and the Anti-Christian Conspiracy]. It was followed by *Le problème de l'heure présente* [The Problem of the Present Hour], dedicated to the antagonism between Christian civilization and modern civilization, the daughter of the Revolution. A portion of this text was recast in *The Anti-Christian Conspiracy,* an admirable and systematic exposition of nineteenth century counter-revolutionary Catholic thought. He writes:

> "The Revolution essentially consists in a revolt against Christ and even a rebellion against God, nay, a denial of God…The era of Revolution is the period of most acute antagonism between Christian civilization and pagan civilization, between naturalism and the supernatural, between Christ and Satan."[755]

Prof. Plinio recalls great fighters against the secret forces with esteem and affection, including with Msgr. Delassus the name of Bishop Vital Maria Gonçalves de Oliveira, known for his famous anti-Masonic pastoral letters, murdered by Freemasonry.[756]

> "Dom Vital Maria Gonçalves de Oliveira, glorious predecessor of an unfortunate Bishop Helder Camara as bishop of Olinda and Recife, is a brother soul of ours, who fought against Freemasonry; Msgr. Delassus, who wrote *The Anti-Christian Conspiracy*….How many men spent their entire lives fighting for the love of God against Freemasonry and were persecuted or oppressed, mangled, and sometimes murdered. Heaven is full of such souls, and we should turn especially to them."[757]

The Anarchic Goal of the Revolution

The secret societies that guide the Revolution have as their goal to destroy Christian Civilization and establish a utopian "Universal Republic" in which all legitimate differences between peoples, families

---

and finally for all the Catholic works that you support and of which our times are in such a great need" (Actes de Pie X, Maison de la Bonne Presse, Paris, 1936, t. VII, p. 238).
[755] MSGR. HENRI DELASSUS, *La conjuration antichrétienne: le temple maçonnique voulant s'élever sur les ruines de l'Eglise catholique*, Saint-Rémi, 2011 (1910), vol. I, p. 68.
[756] Dom Fr. Vital Maria Gonçalves de Oliveira (1844-1878). A Capuchin, he studied at the Seminary of Saint-Sulpice in Paris; in 1868 he was ordained a priest in Toulouse, and in 1871 was consecrated bishop of the Diocese of Olinda in Brazil. He was persecuted by the Masonic government and forced to return to Paris, where he died. In his funeral eulogy, Msgr. de Ségur said he had been poisoned. He is buried in Recife and his beatification process has been opened.
[757] SD, 31 October 1970.

and social classes would be dissolved in a confused and simmering amalgamation:

> "A world in which homelands, unified in a universal republic, are merely geographic designations; a world with neither social nor economic inequalities, run by science and technology, by propaganda and psychology, in order to attain, without the supernatural, the definitive happiness of man: behold the utopia toward which the Revolution is leading us."[758]

This anarchic goal is the natural consequence of revolutionary ideological premises:

> "The effervescence of the disordered passions arouses, on the one hand, hatred for any restraint and any law, and, on the other, hatred for any inequality. This effervescence thus leads to the utopian conception of Marxist anarchism, in which an evolved humanity, living in a society without classes or government, could enjoy perfect order and the most complete liberty, from which no inequality would arise. As can be seen, this ideal is simultaneously the most liberal and the most egalitarian imaginable."[759]

In a famous page, Msgr. Jean-Joseph Gaume laid bare the nihilistic essence of the Revolution.[760]

> "If you ask it, ripping off its mask: Who are you? It will tell you: I am not what they think. Many speak of me but few know me. I am neither Carbonarism...nor riots...nor the replacement of monarchy with a republic, one dynasty with another, or a momentary disturbance of public order. I am neither the howling of Jacobins, the fury of Montagnards, the fighting on barricades, pillage, arson, agrarian law, the guillotine or drownings [of Nantes]. I am neither Marat nor Robespierre nor Babeuf nor Mazzini nor Kossuth. These men are my sons but they are not me. These things are my works, they are not me. These men and things are passing facts, while I am a permanent state.

---

[758] *Revolution and Counter-Revolution*, p. 67.

[759] *Revolution and Counter-Revolution*, p. 54. "In this society – which would live in complete order despite not having a government – economic production would be organized and highly developed, and the distinction between intellectual and manual labor would be a thing of the past. A selective process, not yet determined, would place the direction of the economy in the hands of the most capable, without resulting in the formation of classes. These would be the only and insignificant remnants of inequality. But, since this anarchic communist society is not the final term of history, it seems legitimate to suppose that these remnants would be abolished in a later evolution" (idem).

[760] Msgr. Jean-Joseph Gaume (1802-1879), particularly appreciated by Pius IX, authored many apologetic works, including *La Révolution. Recherches historiques sur l'origine et la propagation du mal en Europe, depuis la Renaissance jusqu'à nos jours*, Vitte, Lyon, 1856-1859, 12 vols.; then Secrétariat Société Saint-Paul, Lille, 1877. Cf. VITO ZOLLINO, EC, V (1950), cols. 1964-1965; R. AUBERT, DHGE, XX (1984), cols. 64-66.

"I am hatred of every order not established by man himself and in which he is not king and god at the same time. I am the proclamation of human rights without regard to the rights of God. I am the foundation of a religious and social State according to man's will rather than God's. I have dethroned God and set man in his place (man becoming his own end). That is why I am called Revolution, that is to say, overthrow."[761]

Also for Plinio, the real problem actually lies not in revealing the identity of the conspirators, but much more importantly, in showing the profound nature of the Revolution and the mechanisms by which it advances. Its agents may vary, but the revolutionary process, its mechanisms and its Gnostic and anti-Christian goal do not change:

"The doctrine of the Revolution is Gnosis, and its ultimate causes are rooted in pride and sensuality." [762]

Thus we must not imagine that such conspirators can plan everything and implement it down to its details.

"The idea that the crisis is being guided to a determined end is one of the fundamental notions in our assessment of events. But we need to know to what extent this guidance is mainly the result of a specific plot. Once you set in motion causes of moral corruption, the latter of itself is such an active and powerful agent that it develops on its own and finds powerful means to give vent to its cravings. So the piloting of immorality is done not so much by having corruption become increasingly serious, but by having it happen as quickly as possible.

"If we imagined a world as corrupt as today's but without Secret Forces, the thing would advance slower but would still keep moving where it is headed. Its impulse is born from circumstances created by the Secret Forces, rather than being led by them. They also lead it, but that is secondary; the question is the impetus proper to what they create."[763]

The Preternatural Action of the Prince of Darkness

Man is not the only actor in the great scene of human history. One cannot understand history well without referring to God, the first cause and ultimate end of everything that moves in the universe. Nor can one ignore the existence of Satan, who uses the power given him by God, the sole Lord of history, to overthrow the divine plan, if it were possible.

---

[761] MSGR. JEAN-JOSEPH GAUME, *La Révolution, Recherches historiques,* t. I, p. 18, Secrétariat Société Saint-Paul, Lille, 1877.
[762] Preface to the first Argentine edition of *Revolution and Counter-Revolution,* in "Marian Devotion, a Decisive Factor in the Clash between Revolution and Counter-Revolution," in *Catolicismo,* no. 464, August 1989, pp. 4-8.
[763] RRR, 15 May 1993.

If the Revolution is a sin, or rather, if there is a sin of Revolution, the devil cannot be alien to it.[764] Indeed, "an explosion of disorderly passions so deep and so generalized as that which gave rise to the Revolution could not have occurred without a preternatural action."[765] This sin is not individual but collective and has its essence in a violation of the First Commandment, which requires obedience to the one true God and to the One Catholic Church in every aspect of the social life of peoples. The Revolution's engine is the devil, who refused the divine order of the universe from the moment of creation.

Popes and counter-revolutionary authors highlight the satanic essence of the Revolution. The identification of this fundamental characteristic is attributed to Joseph de Maistre, according to whom "the French Revolution has a satanic character that distinguishes it from everything one has seen and perhaps will see."[766] However, the first and most profound diagnosis of the satanic nature of the Revolution was not made by the count from Savoy but by Father Pierre-Joseph Picot de Clorivière,[767] biographer of Saint Louis Marie Grignion de Montfort, a former Jesuit, and clandestine priest during the French Revolution, and later restorer of the Society of Jesus in France.

Father de Clorivière writes:

> "From the birth of Christianity, from the creation of the world, one had never actually seen a revolution that showed its wickedness so openly and took it to excesses at the same time monstrous and extravagant. However, it spread with impressive speed with the means least proportionate to success; and what should have shocked and outraged people served instead to give it new strength. A great people suddenly changed their principles, customs, laws, religion. They flaunt atheism without any pragmatic reason and against their own interests, glory and

---

[764] Cf. GUSTAVO ANTÔNIO SOLÍMEO & LUIZ SÉRGIO SOLÍMEO, *Anjos e Demonios. A Luta Contra o Poder das Trevas,* Livraria Civilização Editora, Porto, 2007 and two anthologies, ADELE MONACI CASTAGNO, *Il diavolo e i suoi angeli. Testi e tradizioni*, Nardini, Firenze, 1996; R. LAVATORI, *Antologia diabolica. Raccolta di testi sul diavolo nel primo millennio cristiano*, Utet, Torino, 2007.

[765] Preface to the first Argentine edition of *Revolution and Counter-Revolution,* op. cit.

[766] JOSEPH DE MAISTRE, *Considérations sur la France,* in *Oeuvres*, Robert Laffont, Paris, 2007, p. 226.

[767] By Father Pierre-Joseph Picot de Clorivière (1735-1820), cf. *Etudes sur la Révolution*, in *Pierre de Clorivière, contemporain et juge de la Révolution,* prepared by and with introduction by RENÉ BAZIN, J. de Gigord, Paris, 1926 (now P. DE CLORIVIÈRE, *Etudes sur la Révolution*, Fideliter, Escurolles, 1988). Cf. also *Pierre de Clorivière de la Compagnie de Jésu* (1735-1820) *d'après ses notes intimes de 1763 à 1773*, Spes, Paris, 1935, 2 vols., prepared by P. MONIER-VINARD, S.J.; also by him see entry in DSp, 2 (1953), cols. 974-979 with ample bibliography and exposition of spiritual doctrine. Father de Clorivière was the last Jesuit to make his solemn vows in France before the suppression of the Society of Jesus, and became its restorer after 1814. The cause for his beatification has been introduced.

happiness. They seem to think only of blinding and debasing themselves, eagerly seizing the means to make themselves miserable; they adopt most cruel resolutions, most senseless proposals, and welcome and applaud the most ridiculous charades.

"All this can only be explained by attributing it to the greater power allowed to the demons, to that freedom which, according to several passages of Scripture, is granted to the powers of darkness for a certain time.

"The Lord's extended permission for demons to tempt men, and to attack them with artifices of which they are capable due to their nature which is superior to our own, is a punishment from divine wrath. However, God gives them that permission regretfully and reluctantly: '*Non humiliavit ex corde filios hominum.*' He does it only for the good of His creatures: '*De suo bonus.*' He is compelled to it by our sins, pride and hardened hearts. Were it not for this, would He deliver to the fury of His enemies the children redeemed by the Blood of Jesus Christ? Thus, if the people came to their senses, humbled themselves under His omnipotent hand, recognized their folly and took a step back, God would certainly heed them, the power of demons would be halted, greater graces would be poured on those people; and fortified by this help they would triumph over the plots of hell. Such a change should be the object of our most ardent desires. But the conduct of these people warrants the fear that, for a long time, they will still not recognize their own evils. They are slaves, but call themselves free; they sink in darkness, but believe they are moving toward the light." [768]

There is a deep affinity between Father Clorivière's analysis of the French Revolution and the Plinian diagnosis of the revolutionary process. The Revolution is satanic in its essence because it is a succession of events organized in such a way as to rob God of His rights on human society and transfer them to the devil. It aims to undo the work of Creation and Redemption in order to build the social kingdom of the devil, a hell on earth that prefigures that of eternity just as the Social Kingdom of Christ, Christian civilization, prefigures the Kingdom of the heavenly Paradise. The devil remains the main architect of the Revolution but needs the cooperation of men in order to operate in history. The Revolution was born and developed thanks to this cooperation with evil, opposed to that of the righteous with God's grace; it is the realization in history of a "body" mystically opposed to that of the Redeemer, with Lucifer as its head, just as the Mystical Body of the Church has Jesus Christ as its Head and the Blessed Virgin Mary as its Mother.

---

[768] P. DE CLORIVIÈRE, *Etudes sur la Révolution*, pp. 39-40.

The action of the devil is not only the point of arrival but also the starting point of the revolutionary process, which has its origin and archetype in Satan's rebellion. Prof. Plinio states:

> "Satan was the first revolutionary. He was the chief of all angels, the most beautiful, the strongest and the most diligent of all, who so exercised his power over the angelic world as to have the most beautiful name one can imagine: Lucifer, which means *lux*, light, and then *fert*, the one who brings light before him. Lucifer had a revelation that the Second Person of the Most Holy Trinity would take on human nature and that the Word Incarnate, with a nature inferior to his own, would direct all the heavenly cohorts. And faced with this revelation, he uttered the first cry of revolution, which resonates to this day: 'Non serviam!' I will not serve!"[769]

The Counter-Revolution and the Restoration of Christian Civilization

Opposed to the Revolution is the Counter-Revolution, a "re-action," that is, an action directed against another action. It is not an abstract movement that fights ghosts; nor is it a return to the past or a generic reaction, but has to be an action "waged against the Revolution as it is in fact today, and therefore, against the revolutionary passions as they are inflamed today, revolutionary ideas as formulated today, revolutionary ambiences as seen today."[770] Its modernity and relevance are not in coming to terms with the Revolution but in knowing it in its unchanging essence and metamorphoses, and in fighting it in an intelligent and organized manner to block its way in the present juncture.

If the essence of the revolutionary spirit consists in metaphysical hatred of all inequality and any law, a counter-revolutionary finds his strength above all in a metaphysical love for truth, inequality, and the moral law. Over the last centuries the Revolution has been able to continue its course because its adversaries generally sought to counteract only some of its religious, political, social or economic expressions without grasping its profound metaphysical scope.

Prof. Plinio writes,

> "If the Revolution is disorder, the Counter-Revolution is the restoration of order. And by order we mean the peace of Christ in the Reign of Christ, that is, Christian civilization, austere and hierarchical, fundamentally sacral, antiegalitarian, and antiliberal."[771]

---

[769] SD, 11 August 1995.
[770] *Revolution and Counter-Revolution*, p. 74.
[771] Idem, p. 75.

"Order is the disposition of men and palpable things according to true metaphysics and to the true Religion. And a true counter-revolutionary movement is one that, taking notice of the Revolution, explicitates the notion of order and strives not only to defeat the Revolution, but based on the highest metaphysical reasons, to adapt the whole world of palpable things to order, and to do so in the most radical way possible."[772]

"The order born of the Counter-Revolution will have to shine even more than that of the Middle Ages in the three principal points in which the latter was wounded by the Revolution:

"A profound respect for the rights of the Church and of the Papacy, and the sacralization, to the utmost possible extent, of the values of temporal life, all of this out of opposition to secularism, interconfessionalism, atheism, and pantheism, as well as their respective consequences;

"A spirit of hierarchy marking all aspects of society and State, of culture and life, out of opposition to the egalitarian metaphysics of the Revolution;

"A diligence in detecting and combating evil in its embryonic or veiled forms, in fulminating it with execration and a note of infamy, and in punishing it with unbreakable firmness in all its manifestations, particularly in those that offend against orthodoxy and purity of customs, in opposition to the liberal metaphysics of the Revolution and its tendency to give free rein and protection to evil."[773]

The Counter-Revolution is "conservative" only to preserve, from the present, what is good and deserves to live; it is "traditionalist" but has nothing in common with the pseudo-traditionalism that preserves certain styles or costumes out of an archaeological love for ancient forms.

The actual counter-revolutionary, Prof. Plinio concludes, is one who:

"1. Knows the Revolution, order, and the Counter-Revolution in their respective spirits, doctrines, and methods;

"2. Loves the Counter-Revolution and Christian order, and hates the Revolution and 'anti-order';

"3. Makes of this love and this hatred the axis around which all his ideals, preferences, and activities revolve."[774]

---

[772] MNF, 16 March 1965.

[773] *Revolution and Counter-Revolution*, p. 76.

[774] Idem, p. 81. Plinio Corrêa de Oliveira distinguishes between "actual" counter-revolutionaries, who see the whole picture, and "potential" counter-revolutionaries, who perceive the clash only in some specific aspects. The latter should be attracted to the integral Counter-Revolution.

The Characteristic of Process in the Counter-Revolution

Like the Revolution, the Counter-Revolution is a process, characterized nevertheless by a dynamism different from the destructive process of evil. In the journey from error to truth the fraudulent metamorphoses of the Revolution do not exist. While the Revolution hides its ultimate end from its own followers, men are made to progress on the good path by knowing their own ultimate end and loving it in its entirety.

For Plinio Corrêa de Oliveira, the true counter-revolutionary apostle should make his own the norms established by St. Pius X, that Catholics should not "veil the more important precepts of the Gospel out of fear of being perhaps less heeded or even completely abandoned,"[775] to which the Holy Pontiff added, "No doubt it will not be alien to prudence, when proposing the truth, to make use of a certain temporization when it is a matter of enlightening men who are hostile to our institutions and entirely removed from God."[776]

> "Thus, in the journey from error to truth the soul does not have to contend with the crafty silences of the Revolution nor with its fraudulent metamorphoses. Nothing it ought to know is hidden from it. Truth and goodness are thoroughly taught to it by the Church. Progress in goodness is not secured by systematically hiding from men the ultimate goal of their formation, but by showing it and rendering it ever more desirable."[777]

> "We must know how to reveal amid the chaos that envelops us the whole face of the Revolution in its immense hideousness."[778]

The counter-revolutionary movement of the nineteenth century was successful because everyone clearly saw the repugnant face of the French Revolution:

> "The immensity of the maelstrom in which the old order of things had been shipwrecked had suddenly opened the eyes of many people to a host of truths silenced or denied by the Revolution down through the centuries."[779]

We must also indicate the metaphysical aspects of the Revolution and of the Counter-Revolution:

---

[775] ST. PIUS X, Enc. *Jucunda Sane* of March 12, 1904, ASS. 36 (1904). p. 524.
[776] Idem.
[777] *Revolution and Counter-Revolution,* pp. 98-99.
[778] *Revolution and Counter-Revolution,* p. 101.
[779] Idem.

"The quintessence of the revolutionary spirit consists, as we have seen, in hating, in principle and on the metaphysical plane, all inequality and all law, especially Moral Law. Moreover, pride, rebelliousness, and impurity are precisely the factors that most impel mankind along the way of the Revolution. Therefore, one of the very important parts of counter-revolutionary work is to teach a love for inequality considered on the metaphysical plane, for the principle of authority, and for Moral Law and purity."[780]

The Counter-Revolution can and must be the soul of a broad coalition that includes not only Catholics but all those who defend the natural order, summarized by the perennial principles of the Decalogue. The defense of natural law is not only a theoretical and conceptual work. One defends human nature by living according to nature, that is, according to a law common to all men, invariable and eternal. To live according to nature and according to reason means to live nobly.

The fact that Plinio Corrêa de Oliveira dedicated his last work to the nobility and traditional elites is not an extravagance, but a clear message and a precise choice.[781] He is noble who lives according to the perfection of his own nature, elevating it in his manners, courtesy, and language. When he corresponds to grace he becomes the embodiment of what most directly opposes revolutionary egalitarianism.

The Counter-Revolution and the Church

If the Revolution is a process that aims to destroy the whole Christian temporal order, its ultimate target is "the Church, the Mystical Body of Christ, the infallible teacher of the Truth, the guardian of Natural Law, and, therefore, the ultimate foundation of the temporal order itself."[782] The Revolution is an enemy that has risen against the Church to hinder the mission of saving souls that she carries out not only through her direct spiritual power, but also through her indirect temporal power.

From the Plinian perspective, the Counter-Revolution is not an end in itself but a docile instrument of the Church. For her part, the Church is neither identified with the Counter-Revolution nor needs to be saved by it. The Counter-Revolution that rises in defense of the Church "is not destined to save the Spouse of Christ. Supported as she is on the promise of her Founder, she does not need men to survive. On the contrary, it is

---

[780] Idem, p. 102.
[781] Plinio Corrêa de Oliveira, *Nobility and Analogous Traditional Elites in the Allocutions of Pius XII to the Roman Patriciate and Nobility*, The American Society for the Defense of Tradition, Family and Property , 1993 (Hamilton Press).
[782] *Revolution and Counter-Revolution*, p. 114.

the Church that gives life to the Counter-Revolution, which, without her, is neither feasible nor even conceivable."[783]

The Church is the soul of the Counter-Revolution:

> "If the Counter-Revolution is the struggle to extinguish the Revolution and to build the new Christendom, resplendent with faith, humble with hierarchical spirit, and spotless in purity, clearly this will be achieved, above all, by a profound action in the hearts of men. This action is proper to the Church, which teaches Catholic doctrine and leads men to love and practice it. Therefore, the Church is the very soul of the Counter-Revolution."[784]

The ideal of the Counter-Revolution is the exaltation of the Church.

> "If the Revolution is the opposite of the Church, it is impossible to hate the Revolution (considered in its entirety and not just in some isolated aspect) and to combat it without ipso facto having the ideal of exalting the Church."[785]

The Church is therefore a fundamentally counter-revolutionary force but is not identified with the Counter-Revolution: her real strength lies in being the Mystical Body of Our Lord Jesus Christ. Nevertheless, according to Prof. Plinio, the scope of the Counter-Revolution goes beyond the ecclesial ambit because it involves a reorganization of the whole temporal society from its foundations.[786] This social restructuring is inspired by Church doctrine but also implies countless concrete and practical aspects specifically related to the civil order.

The Driving Force of the Counter-Revolution

If the Revolution's most powerful driving force is the dynamism of human passions unleashed by a metaphysical hatred against God, the Truth and the Good, there is a symmetrical counter-revolutionary dynamics that aims at regulating the passions by subjecting them to the intellect and the will. The driving force of the Counter-Revolution is a spiritual force that stems from the fact that God governs man's intellect, the intellect dominates his will, and his will ultimately dominates his sensibility.[787] He is a servant of God but, for that very reason, he the master of himself.

> "The Counter-Revolution is a movement of souls, ideas, influences and efforts to stop the march of the great universal movement we defined

---

[783] Idem, pp. 115-116.
[784] Idem, p. 117.
[785] Idem.
[786] Idem.
[787] Idem, p. 103.

in the treatise *Revolution and Counter-Revolution.* It is an egalitarian, sensual, proud and wicked movement that began with the first whimpers of the Renaissance and the Protestant Pseudo-Reformation, continued with the French Revolution, and found its apex with Communism: this is the movement that has triumphantly advanced over centuries and which we need to stop." [788]

Such spiritual vigor cannot be conceived without taking into account the supernatural life, which elevates man above the miseries of fallen nature. For Plinio, the most profound dynamism of the Counter-Revolution is found in this spiritual force: "the struggle between Revolution and Counter-Revolution is a religious one in its essence."[789] Like every religious problem, it cannot do without the role of grace, on which every authentic moral regeneration depends.

> "One might ask, of what value is this dynamism? We respond that in thesis it is incalculable and certainly superior to that of the Revolution: *Omnia possum in eo qui me confortat* ('I can do all things in Him who strengthens me'– Phil. 4:13). When men resolve to cooperate with the grace of God, the marvels of history are worked: the conversion of the Roman Empire; the formation of the Middle Ages; the reconquest of Spain, starting from Covadonga; all the events that result from the great resurrections of soul of which nations are also capable. These resurrections are invincible, because nothing can defeat a people that is virtuous and truly loves God."[790]

---

[788] SEF, 29 January 1967.

[789] Preface to the first Argentine edition of *Revolution and Counter-Revolution,* op. cit.

[790] *Revolution and Counter-Revolution*, p. 104.

CHAPTER III

FROM THE FOURTH TO THE FIFTH REVOLUTION

The "1968 Revolution"

The revolutionary process kept advancing as editions of *Revolution and Counter-Revolution* were published around the world, and in 1968 it entered a new phase that developed from earlier stages.

The "1968 Revolution" was a political and cultural movement born in the United States that spread to Europe and peaked in France in May 1968. It was a Revolution of morals and tendencies more profound than a political revolution[791] and sought to "liberate" the instincts of individuals and masses from the yoke imposed by centuries of culture and civilization.

Workers – activists claimed – were revolutionary at the factory but reactionary in their family life. It was necessary to move the revolution from the factory to the family. May of 1968 was an attempt to bring the concept of revolution from the socio-political plane to that of human interiority, that is, from society to the individual.

In the years of student revolutions, Agnes Heller, the most famous disciple of Hungarian communist philosopher György Lukács, wrote a book significantly titled *The Sociology of Everyday Life,* in which she stated that with the 1968 Revolution, "what changed was neither the political system nor the economic structure but people's ways of

---

[791] CORRADO GNERRE, *La rivoluzione nell'uomo. Una lettura anche teologica del '68*, Fede & Cultura, Verona, 2008 and ENZO PESERICO, *Gli anni del desiderio e del piombo. Sessantotto Terrorismo e Rivoluzione*, Sugarco, Milano, 2008, offer an overview of the 1968 Revolution employing Prof. Corrêa de Oliveira's interpretative categories. Cf. also memories from protagonists: RUDI DUTSCHKE, *Ecrits politiques (1967-1968)*, Christian Bourgois, Paris, 1968; DANIEL COHN-BENDIT, *Nous l'avons tant aimée la Révolution*, Bernard Barrault, Paris, 1986; MARIO CAPANNA, *Formidabili quegli anni*, Garzanti, Milano, 2007 (1988). Among these basic texts born from the "thought of 1968," cf. GUY DEBORD (founder, with Raoul Vaneigem, of the "Situationist International"), *La Société du Spectacle*, Champ Libre, Paris, 1977 (1967).

living....and from there stem the sexual revolution and the change in educational systems."[792]

There also spread in those years works by Austrian psychoanalyst Wilhelm Reich, who presented the family as the repressive social institution par excellence and stated that "sexual happiness is the core of happiness in life."[793] According to the Marxist-Freudian philosopher Herbert Marcuse, the youth revolt is "...a rebellion at the same time moral, political, sexual. A total rebellion. It originates in the depths of individuals.... Young people are willing to sacrifice a lot of material goods to lead a life finally governed by freed vital instincts."[794]

Another leading activist, sociologist Alain Touraine, linking 1968 to the French Revolution, stated: "The citizen of 1789 had a head; to it socialists added muscle, and in the twentieth century we added sex and imagination."[795]

Immorality is inherent to all revolutions but exploded especially in that of 1968, which Plinio sees as a sexual revolution.[796] If nineteenth-century romanticism had fought reason on behalf of liberating feelings, the 1968 Revolution fought reason on behalf of sexual instincts.

The 1968 Revolution was not a failure but produced radical changes in music, art, literature, fashion, and language. Only now, fifty years later, we realize how its philosophy of life permeated, slowly but surely, the customs and mentality of Western society. This result goes beyond the fact that many of the 1968 protagonists now occupy important positions in government within the same "system" they hotly disputed. While some of them renounced their early stands, the Cultural Revolution they triggered followed its inexorable course. It suffices to think of ecology or New Age, but especially the cultural and moral relativism that characterizes contemporary society: A relativism derived directly from the 1968 Revolution.

Also for Plinio, "the Sorbonne Revolution, as a Cultural Revolution, affects minds more than institutions. Its very slow march first reached people's minds; through these, customs; and finally, institutions."[797] The Plinian thesis of the revolution in the tendencies, which precedes and prepares that of ideas, found in it a striking confirmation:

---

[792] Interview with AGNES HELLER, *L'Unità*, April 29, 1998.

[793] WILHELM REICH, *La rivoluzione sessuale*, It. tr., Feltrinelli, Milano, 1977 (1936), p. 16.

[794] *Marcuse: manifesto del nuovo Adamo*, interview prepared by MAURO CALAMANDREI, *L'Espresso*, March 12-24, 1968.

[795] Cf. "The Freedom of Post-Modern Men," interview with ALAIN TOURAINE, by Massimo Boffa, *Rinascita*, March 12, 1988, p. 20.

[796] RRR, 15 July 1990.

[797] RRR, 1 June 1991.

"Today we are living the Revolution of temperaments more than the Revolution of ideas. There is something even more profound in man, which is the deregulation of his primary instincts. The set of instincts that used to lead man to naturally tend to certain things has been thrown off balance. His very instinct of self-preservation, which touches the root of the human being the most, no longer works as before."[798]

The 1968 Revolution of instincts changed the psychological profile of young people, weakening especially their ability to reason.

"Before the Sorbonne Revolution, reasoning represented in the psychology of a young person who was 'in the wind,' at least theoretically, a primary driving element directing his life. After it there began to emerge a kind of young person who, without being a hippie properly speaking, was hippified; he lives at home but leads a more or less hippie life, a life which has something of the hippie mentality and is already fully turned to the civilization of the image.

"Accordingly, if the number of hippies is not great, their influence on society is very great. Therefore, although their victory was far from the one they wanted to achieve, they conquered some precious ground."[799]

"People are switching from a civilization based no longer on faith but at least on reason (and which even attacked faith in the name of reason), and from a morality that sought theoretical arguments to justify itself and was still founded on reason, to a sheer glorification of instinct.

"This is then a new historical era, in which man renounces reason and asceticism, and expects a future order of things to come from instinct. Just as an atomic explosion has a certain internal order and takes on the shape of a mushroom, so also man's loose instincts have a certain internal order which used to appear as disorder, due to 'obscurantism,' but which the new man claims to be the true order.

"The Sorbonne revolutionaries promise a situation that we would call chaotic disorder, but which they deem a healthy earthquake leading to some kind of order. So we have the civilization of instinct (if this can be called civilization) which opposes the dying civilization of the intellect and will.

"This civilization of instinct is obviously the glorification of original sin; for original sin dwells par excellence in the instincts revolting against reason. Original sin also dwells in an intellect weakened by the solicitation of the instincts. By saying 'the spirit is willing but the flesh is weak,' Our Lord explains that man's intellect has a certain ease to perceive his duty, but his instincts and spontaneity are weak and induce him to evil. Hence: 'watch and pray.' In other words, Our Lord's program

---

[798] EVP, 29 September 1985.
[799] RRR, 27 November 1973.

is the opposite of the weakness of the flesh. He denounces this fallible side and recommends that people employ their intellect and will with the help of grace." [800]

The Post-Modern Fourth Revolution and "Chaos Theory"

Plinio Corrêa de Oliveira deemed the 1968 "Revolution of instincts," especially in its consequences, to be a new and decisive metamorphosis of the revolutionary process.

In 1977, in his brief but prophetic pages now reproduced in the appendix to the Italian edition of *Revolution and Counter-Revolution*, Prof. Plinio added some considerations that helped clarify his thoughts, already known to those who participated in his meetings of formation and study. He explained how in evolutionist mythology the revolutionary process is not supposed to have an end. From the First Revolution another two were born: the French and the Communist Revolutions. A Fourth Revolution[801] is now arising from the dissolution of the Communist Third Revolution. Like the others, the Fourth Revolution does not negate the one preceding it but incorporates and develops it.

The Fourth Revolution is characterized by the dissolution of the political form of society, the State, along with the disintegration of reason, the sovereign faculty of the human soul. Prof. Plinio predicts that it will be a "tribal revolution":

> On the one hand, "it will be the collapse of the dictatorship of the proletariat as a result of a new crisis by which the hypertrophied State will be the victim of its own hypertrophy;"[802] on the other hand it will also be the collapse of reason, "formerly hypertrophied by free examination, Cartesianism, deified by the French Revolution, abused to no end by every communist school of thought,"[803] and now finally atrophied and replaced by the "wild thought" of structuralists.[804]

---

[800] RRR, 15 June 1968.

[801] Cf. "The Aborning Fourth Revolution," in IDEM, *Revolution and Counter-Revolution*, pp. 157f. Part III of *Revolution and Counter-Revolution* was originally published as an appendix to the work's Italian edition (1977) and later published with additional comments by the author, in *Catolicismo*, no. 500, August 1992, pp. 4-33. Updated editions of the work followed in Argentina, Chile, Colombia, Ecuador and Spain (all in 1992), the United States and Brazil (1993), Peru (1994) and in the main countries of Eastern Europe.

[802] *Revolution and Counter-Revolution*, op. cit., p. 158.

[803] Idem, p. 159.

[804] Structuralism: a current of thought in the humanities inspired by the linguistic model of Ferdinand de Saussure, which grasps social reality as a formal set of interrelations or "structures" that can only be interpreted from inside the culture that engendered it. The anthropologist and ethnographer Claude Levi Strauss was a prominent practitioner of structuralism (translator's note).

The dialectical method of Marx and Hegel could only remain valid on the condition that it replace the traditional proletarian class, already in a process of disintegration, with a new "revolutionary subject." Thus the Revolution identified a socio-cultural "new proletariat": movements of students, feminists, pacifists, ecologists, ethnic liberationists and marginalized minorities such as blacks, drug addicts, homosexuals, punks. It was necessary to give these "oppressed" minorities a revolutionary "social consciousness."

The transition from "modernity" to "post-modernity" should be considered as an element of this metamorphosis. The term *post-modernity* designates a post-Communist but by no means anti-Communist Revolution because it pursues the goal of Communism taken to its final consequences, that is, fulfilling the anarchic and egalitarian design to dissolve the State and the natural institutions of society. From this perspective, the concept of *post-modernity* includes not only the end of modern civilization but the end of the very idea of civilization and the return, if possible, to the savage society of ancient African and American Indian tribes, presented as models of "solidarity" and integration of life with nature: in a word, tribalism.

Several schools and currents of thought converge on the horizon of this Fourth Revolution: radical psychoanalysis, libertarian Marxism, structuralism, indeterministic physics, socio-biology, "profound ecology," and animalism. This galaxy of theories is disclosed under the label "complexity theory" but may be best defined as "chaos theory."[805] Indeed, it is founded on the negation of the principle of order and identity/causality in all aspects of reality, and on the affirmation of chaos as the original and dominant principle of the world, from the psychological to the physical realm, from the political to the economic realm.[806]

---

[805] A critical analysis of "Chaos Theory," in R. DE MATTEI, *1900-2000. Due sogni si succedono: la costruzione, la distruzione*, Edizioni Fiducia, Roma, 1990. Among the most significant texts on the "theory of chaos," cf. JAMES GLEICK, *Chaos: Making a New Science*, Viking, New York, 1987; GIANLUCA BOCCHI, MAURO CERUTI, EDGAR MORIN, *Turbare il futuro. Un inizio per la civiltà planetaria*, Moretti e Vitali, Bergamo, 1990; BERNICE COHEN, *The Edge of Chaos: Financial Booms, Bubbles, Crashes and Chaos*, John Wiley and Sons, London, 1996; CELSE GREBOGI, JAMES A. YORKE (ed.), *The Impact of Chaos on Science and Society*, United Nations University Press, Tokyo, 1997; CARLO FORMENTI, *Immagini del vuoto*, Liguori, Napoli, 1989; JEAN LUC MÉLANCHON, *A la conquête du chaos*, Denoël, Paris, 1991; MICHEL MAFFESOLI, *La transfiguration du politique*, Grasset, Paris, 1992. For an apologetic view on these theories, cf. FRITJOF CAPRA, *Le temps du changement*, French tr., Editions du Rocher, Monaco, 1983.

[806] ILYA PRIGOGINE-ISABELLE STENGERS, *Nuova alleanza. Metamorfosi della scienza*, It. tr., Einaudi, Torino, 1981 (1979), p. 243.

In the twentieth century, Marxism-Leninism was presented as a philosophy destined to demonstrate its truth in practice, that is, a philosophy that became history, and by becoming history, was true. Instead, for over seventy years, between 1917 and 1989, the so-called "real socialism" showed in practice the utopian character of its thinking and dragged in its collapse the major global and unifying utopias that attempted to "build" a new world during the nineteenth and twentieth centuries. From the dream of construction that inaugurated the twentieth century it went to the "dream of destruction" of "chaos theory," such as Belgian chemist Ilya Prigogine,[807] American anthropologist Gregory Bateson,[808] and French sociologist Edgar Morin. The latter announces: "From now on, disorder claims its place. Every theory must henceforth bear the mark of disorder and give a maximum of space to disorder, turned with due honors into a cosmic and immanent physical principle."[809]

The new pseudo-scientific cosmology popularized by authors such as Fritjof Capra,[810] sees the universe as a "network" of interactions in which every individual and the entire reality are intended to dissolve and merge. In this vortex-like plot, the "principle of complexity," antithetical to those of identity and non-contradiction, is elevated to a criterion inherent to reality, thereby depriving human knowledge of all objective truth or certainty. Individuals give up looking for a foundation of knowledge in order to sink into the "collective intellect" dreamed of by Pierre Lévy[811] and by the theoreticians of "mental communism." In this Gnostic and pantheistic vision, the universe is made up of a huge network of relationships so that each being lives through another and the Divinity is revealed as the "self-consciousness" of the universe, which becomes aware of its own evolution as it evolves.[812]

Tribalism and the Dissolution of the State

The subsequent decade confirmed these predictions in an extraordinary way. After a series of spectacular geopolitical convulsions

---

[807] Idem.

[808] GREGORY BATESON, *Mind and Nature. A Necessary Unity*, Dutton, New York, 1979.

[809] EDGAR MORIN, p. 97.

[810] FRITJOF CAPRA, *The Turning Point*, Simon and Schuster, New York, 1982.

[811] PIERRE LEVY, *L'intelligence collective. Pour une antropologie du cyberspace*, La Découverte, Paris, 1994, It. tr., *L'intelligenza collettiva. Per un'antropologia del cyberspazio*, Feltrinelli, Milano, 1996.

[812] LEONARDO BOFF, *Grido della terra, grido dei poveri. Per una ecologia cosmica*, It. tr., Cittadella, Assisi, 1996; Idem, *Ethos mundial. Un consenso minimo entre os humanos*, Letraviva, São Paulo, 2000.

between 1989 and 1991, the Iron Curtain crumbled and the Soviet Empire dissolved.

The *perestroika*[813] policy, announced at the plenum of the CPSU Central Committee in April 1985, was introduced only a month after Gorbachev's election as Secretary-General. It was like a return to the origins of socialism, the essence of which is not statism but a negation of the State and all forms of social inequality. According to Gorbachev, perestroika was not an abandonment of socialism or revolutionary ideals but only a "strategic variant" of Marxism-Leninism founded on the Bolshevik myth of the "dictatorship of the proletariat." The centralizing and bureaucratic Communism imposed in the USSR and its satellite countries was accused of having betrayed the "cause of human liberation," that is, the anarchic end of socialism.[814] It was necessary to find a new way to establish a "classless society" based on the principle of egalitarian self-management theorized by communists and anarchists from the beginning.[815]

On November 9, 1989 the Berlin Wall was torn down. On July 1, 1991, after Lithuania had declared its independence, the self-dissolution of the Warsaw Pact was decided. The failed coup d'etat of August 19, 1991 led to the fall of Gorbachev, replaced by Boris Yeltsin, and to a series of declarations of independence by the Baltic republics and other Soviet republics.

These spectacular events, skillfully publicized by the media, officially confirmed the collapse of the Communist regimes that had been established in Eastern Europe since the October Revolution, and the collapse of so-called "real socialism." This change, which developed from within the Soviet nomenklatura and was carried out in a seemingly incoherent fashion, almost without violent upheavals, insurrection or

---

[813] For a quick overview of *perestroika* and its effects, cf. PASCAL LAROT, *Histoire de la perestrojka. L'Urss sous Gorbatchev 1985-1991*, PUF, Paris, 1993; for an interpretation, cf. information and reflections by ANATOLIY GOLITSYN, *New Lies for Old*, Dodd, Mead and Co., New York,1984; ID., *The Perestroika Deception*, Edward Harle, London, 1995; FRANÇOIS THOM, *Le moment Gorbatchev,* Hachette, Paris, 1989; ID., *Les fins du communisme,* Critérion, Paris, 1994; ALEXANDRE ZINOVIEV, *Perestrojka et contre-perestrojka*, Olivier Orban, Paris, 1991.

[814] M. Gorbachev, *Perestroika: New Thinking for Our Country and the World*, Harper Collins, 1987, 254 pp.

[815] This typically socialist goal was laid out in the preamble of the Soviet Constitution of 1977, which read: "The supreme objective of the Soviet State is the building of a communist classless society in which communist social self-management will develop." For an analysis of the continuity of the Marxist non-State theory, cf. BOB JESSOP, *The Capitalist State: Marxist Theories and Methods*, New York University Press, New York, 1982; CLYDE W. BARROW, *Critical Theory of the State. Marxist, Neo-Marxist, Post-Marxist*, The University of Wisconsin Press, Madison (Wisconsin), 1993.

riots, Plinio interpreted as a metamorphosis of Marxism strictly consistent with the Marxist-Leninist "philosophy of praxis."

From the Fourth to the Fifth Revolution

The first three Revolutions were carried out in the name of reason. The Fourth Revolution marked the beginning of the extinction of *lumen rationis,* a constant object of Plinio's sociology and philosophy. Renunciation of the use of reason was theorized by exponents of postmodern thought, who replaced the rules of thought with magic techniques. Not surprisingly, the new religion being spread since the seventies is characterized by an attraction for magic and oriental theories on "emptiness" and "nothing." Its central core consists in merging Eastern religious tenets with spiritism, with so-called alternative medicine, mantra, yoga and Zen techniques, and with African tribal rituals based on hallucinogens.

In its statements and procedures, the Revolution often seems delusional. This is not surprising. The Revolution is properly speaking a delirium, as clearly shown by the most radical manifestations of Protestantism and the French Revolution. Those who refuse the natural order plunge into the realm of chaos, which is the dream, or better, the delirium of the devil, as Plinio explained since 1967,[816] for "there exists in the devil every form of evil that is possible or consistent with existence in creation."[817]

To the degree that Providence allows it, the goal of the Revolution is to establish the reign of the devil on earth, that is, the visible presence of the devil, known, served, and glorified as such. What is the role played by UFOs and flying saucers in this ominous scenario? Could they not be the way chosen by the devil to present himself as "redeemer" of a humanity immersed in chaos and madness? Only saints can penetrate into the abyss of revolutionary mysticism. We leave it at that, limiting ourselves to record the existence of this dark mystery.

Forty years have passed since Plinio Corrêa de Oliveira described the nascent Fourth Revolution. Today relativism, born of the 1968 Revolution, takes the form of post-humanism: a vision characterized by the overcoming of man and by transition from integral humanism to the integral destruction of the human being.[818]

How will that happen?

---

[816] MNF, 19 June 1967.
[817] Idem.
[818] Cf. JEAN-FRANÇOIS MATTEI, *L'homme dévasté*, Grasset, Paris, 2015.

"We cannot but wonder if the tribal society dreamed of by today's structuralist currents is the answer to this question. Structuralism sees in tribal life an illusory synthesis between the height of individual liberty and of consensual collectivism in which the latter ends up devouring liberty. In this collectivism, the various 'I's' or individual persons with their intelligence, will and sensibility, and consequently with their characteristic and conflicting ways of being, merge and dissolve in the collective personality of the tribe, which generates one thought, one will, and one style of being intensely common to all." [819]

The road to this tribal state of affairs "must pass through the extinction of the old standards of individual reflection, volition, and sensibility. These will be gradually replaced by increasingly collective forms of thought, deliberation and sensibility." [820]

The "savage thought" spoken about during the years of the 1968 student revolution expressed this atrophy of reason, dissolved in tribal collectivism. "We believe that the ultimate goal of human sciences is not to build man but to dissolve him,"[821] its theoretician claimed. Today, society's tribalization advances in parallel with the effacing of the *lumen rationis* and the exaltation of instincts and unruly passions.

In its itinerary from humanism to Marxism, the Revolution proudly sought to erect a self-sufficient natural order autonomous from God and His grace. The failure of the naturalistic utopia led it to a diametrically opposed design. The enemy is no longer the supernatural order but the natural order itself. The Revolution now intends to carry out a complete deconstruction of human nature and its laws. To the natural law it opposes an anti-cosmology that manifests the radical hatred of Gnostics for the divinely established order of the universe.

Radical ecology posits a cosmic egalitarianism that includes elements of nature such as mountains, plants, water, the atmosphere, and landscapes. The ecological society aims at eliminating man's rule over the nature that surrounds him, on the pretext of achieving democracy in the biosphere.[822] Gender ideology drops the distinction between man and woman, between the human world, the animal world and the plant world; and the distinction between forms of organic life and inorganic forms of existence.

The distinction between man and machine is also dropped in this "post-human" perspective. The idea of symbiosis between man and machine has gained ground especially after the development of

---

[819] *Revolution and Counter-Revolution,* p. 158.

[820] Idem.

[821] Cf. CLAUDE LÉVI-STRAUSS, *La pensée sauvage*, Plon, Paris, 1962, p. 326.

[822] Cf. BILL DEVALL, GEORGE SESSIONS, *Deep Ecology: Living as if Nature Mattered*, Gibbs M. Smith, New York, 1985.

information and digital technologies.[823] The term cyborg (contraction for cybernetic organism) is used to indicate new hybrids, that is, human beings modified by adding mechanical prostheses or components produced by technology. Hybridization with artificial devices thanks to nanotechnology is presented as "an unavoidable prospect," a horizon from which man cannot escape.[824]

On the other hand, theories on dematerialization or virtualization of human experience would liberate the "I" from its body and immerse it into cyberspace, a virtual reality created and maintained by computers through the global network.[825] Cyberspace is the "territory" and "essential medium" of "humanity's collective intelligence."[826] The real universe is overlapped by other virtual universes according to the pantheist principle that affirms a plurality of worlds and universes. Today sciences such as cybernetics, neuropharmacology, genetic engineering and nanotechnology offer new means to realize these scenarios that suppress the limits of human nature.[827]

The legalization of sins such as homosexuality and the free rein given to genetic experiments are dramatic examples of this deconstruction of human nature.

The revolutionary process attained an apex with the public promotion of homosexuality sanctioned by the European Parliament's resolution of February 8, 1994, asking member States to "open to homosexual couples all the legal instruments available to heterosexual ones." In earlier decades, Plinio Corrêa de Oliveira had called the legal recognition of homosexuality "one of the most atrocious Revolutions ever carried out in the field of morals since the Church of Our Lord Jesus Christ was founded."[828] "The practice of homosexuality is an individual sin, but when it becomes a tolerated addiction, it is a social sin in which even non-homosexuals participate when they do not react to it."[829] "Here you see how far aberration goes. It is very symptomatic that this news on

---

[823] DONNA HARAWAY, *A Cyborg Manifesto*, It. tr. of L. Borghi, introduction by R. Braidotti, Feltrinelli, Milano, 1995.

[824] *Lessico postfordista. Dizionario di idee della mutazione*, prepared by Adelino Zanini and Ubaldo Fadini, Feltrinelli, Milano, 2001.

[825] MICHAEL HEIM, *Virtual Realism,* Oxford University Press, New York-Oxford, 1998; *Electric Language: A Philosophical Study of Word Processing*, Yale University Press, New Haven, 1986; *The Metaphysics of Virtual Reality*, Oxford University Press, New York-Oxford, 1993.

[826] PIERRE LÉVY, *Cybercultura*, It. tr., Feltrinelli, Milano, 2000, p. 163. Cf. also ID., *L'intelligenza collettiva. Per un'antropologia del cyberspazio*, It. tr., Feltrinelli, Milano, 1996.

[827] Cf. FRANCIS FUKUYAMA, *L'uomo oltre l'uomo. Le conseguenze della rivoluzione biotecnologica*, It. tr., Mondadori, Milan, 2002; DAVID JAY BROWN, *Riflessioni sull'orlo dell'Apocalisse*, It. tr., Oscar Mondadori, Milano, 2006.

[828] RRR, 6 September 1964.

[829] RRR, 25 January 1975.

[proposals at the Brazilian Constituent Assembly to equate same-sex couples with a family] is released without producing the indignation it would have caused ten years ago. Today this is published and is already met with semi-tolerance, a first step toward complete tolerance. All advances of the Revolution are like that: they produce a scandal, later the scandal gradually decreases and becomes a tolerated habit; from that moment onward, the thing spreads like an oil slick."[830]

On February 22, 1994, John Paul II publicly condemned the pro-homosexual resolution of the European Parliament by saying that with it "the Parliament has wrongly awarded an institutional value to deviant behaviors not in accordance with God's plan."[831] Twenty years later, at an extraordinary Synod of Bishops convened by a Pope in the Vatican, requests were made for openness of the Church to same-sex couples.[832]

The Origins of the Crisis in the Church

The existence of a profound crisis in the Church is today a fact recognized by all. In *The Crusader of the Twentieth Century* I reported testimonies by cardinals, bishops, theologians and even Popes, from Paul VI to John Paul II.[833] Twenty years later the situation terribly worsened. This crisis comes from way back, and Plinio Corrêa de Oliveira discerned its beginnings, understood its causes, and profoundly suffered because of it, employing all his strength to fight it.

In June 1943, with a preface by Nuncio Benedetto Aloisi Masella[834] and an imprimatur of the Archdiocese of São Paulo, his book *In Defense of Catholic Action* was published.[835] Plinio's work was the first

---

[830] RRR, 15 February 1986.

[831] John Paul II, Angelus of February 20, 1994, *Insegnamenti*, XVII, 1 (1994), p. 538 (pp. 537-539). In his last book, *Memory and Identity*, John Paul II severely criticizes "the legal extermination of human beings conceived but unborn. And in this case, that extermination is decreed by democratically elected parliaments, which invoke the notion of civil progress for society and for all humanity. Nor are other grave violations of God's law lacking. I am thinking, for example, of the strong pressure from the European Parliament to recognize homosexual unions as an alternative type of family, with the right to adopt children. It is legitimate and even necessary to ask whether this is not the work of another ideology of evil, more subtle and hidden, perhaps, intent upon exploiting human rights themselves against man and against the family. Why does all this happen? What is the root of these post-Enlightenment ideologies? The answer is simple: it happens because of the rejection of God as Creator, and consequently as a source determining what is good and what is evil" (*Memory and Identity, Personal Reflections*, Rizzoli, March, 2005, 192 p. @ https://www.catholicculture.org/culture/library/view.cfm?recnum=6424.

[832] SYNOD OF BISHOPS, *Relatio post disceptationem*, October 13, 2014, no. 50.

[833] Cf. the whole Chapter VI of *The Crusader of the Twentieth Century*, devoted to "Passion of Christ, Passion of the Church."

[834] Benedetto Aloisi Masella (1879-1970), ordained in 1902, titular archbishop of Cesarea (1927) and Apostolic Nuncio to Brazil (1927-1945). Created cardinal in 1946.

[835] *In Defense of Catholic Action*, Ave Maria, São Paulo 1943. Cf. http://www.pliniocorreadeoliveira.info/UK_1943_INDEFENSEOFCATHOLICACTION.pdf. His

comprehensive refutation of errors festering within Catholic Action in Brazil and consequently around the world, especially with regard to the liturgy, spirituality, and methods of apostolate and action.[836] After a long enumeration of points concerning deviations in the doctrines and mentalities in the circles of Catholic Action, the author concluded:

> "All of them are bound, closely or remotely, to the following principles: a denial of the effects of original sin; as a consequence, a conception of grace as the exclusive factor of the spiritual life; and a tendency to do without authority in the hope that order will result from a free, living and spontaneous union of intellects and wills."[837]

The book was the first denunciation of neo-modernism that, after being condemned by Saint Pius X, resurfaced using Latin America as a "laboratory." In the subsequent years the new tendencies in the biblical, liturgical, theological and ecumenical fields merged into a single movement which Pius XII identified and condemned as the progressive "nouvelle théologie." These ideological ferments developed in the Church in a seemingly spontaneous way, without order or visible guidance, as had already happened at the time of modernism. In the encyclical *Pascendi*, Saint Pius X showed that movement's ideological unity; and three years later, in the Motu proprio *Sacrorum Antistitum* of September 1, 1910, he also suggested that it had a unified underground organization and formed a real "secret society" within the Church.[838]

In 1954, when Pius XII canonized Pius X,[839] Plinio devoted a series of articles in *Catolicismo* to honor Pope Sarto, and in 1957 celebrated the

---

analysis was shared by Rome, to the point that in 1947 the two priests who had supported Plinio Corrêa de Oliveira, Father Geraldo de Proença Sigaud (1909-1999), and Father Antonio de Castro Mayer (1904-1991), after having been "purged" from the Brazilian ecclesiastical hierarchy, were unexpectedly "promoted" by Roman authorities: Father Sigaud was designated Bishop of Jacarezinho and later Archbishop of Diamantina, and Msgr. de Castro Mayer was made auxiliary bishop with right of succession of the Bishop of Campos, whom he succeeded the following year.

[836] *The Crusader of the Twentieth Century*, op. cit., pp. 73-83.

[837] Idem, p. 88.

[838] PIUS X, Motu proprio *Sacrorum Antistitum*, op. cit., p. 655. The sentence in uppercase, which in Latin reads: "*Haud enim intermiserunt novos aucupari et in clandestinum foedus ascire socios, cum iisque in christianae reipublicae venas opinionum suarum virus inserere, editis libris commentariisque suppresso aut mentito scriptorum nomine,*" has been cut from the Italian translation, in BELLOCCHI, VII, *San Pio X (1903-1914)*, p. 425 (pp. 415-441).

[839] Saint Pius X (Giuseppe Melchiorre Sarto: 1835-1914), ordained in 1858, Bishop of Mantova in 1884, was created cardinal and promoted to the patriarchal seat of Venice by Leo XIII in 1893. He governed the Church from 1903 to August 20, 1914. About him, cf. MAURIZIO GUASCO, *Enciclopedia dei Papi*, vol. III, Istituto della Enciclopedia Italiana, Roma, 2000, pp. 593-608, with bibl.; Fr. GIROLAMO DAL GAL, *Pio X il Papa santo*, Libreria Editrice Fiorentina, Firenze, 1940; YVES CHIRON, *Saint Pie X. Reformateur de l'Eglise,* Courrier de Rome, Versailles, 2000; CRISTINA SICCARDI, *San Pio X, Vita del Papa che ha ordinato e riformato la Chiesa,* San Paolo, Roma, 1914, with a preface by Cardinal RAYMOND LEO BURKE; GIAN

fiftieth anniversary of his prophetic encyclical, *Pascendi,* calling his condemnation of modernism an historical fact as important as the Battle of Lepanto:[840]

"Had Saint Pius X not fulminated against the modernist heresy, the world would have quickly marched on to pantheism and atheism. And the whole communist action on the face of the earth would not have met the enormous obstacles it encountered. The condemnation of modernism was therefore a historical fact as important as the victory of Lepanto. And Pius XII is owed men's eternal gratitude for having presented them with such a great saint as model and protector."[841]

Plinio Corrêa de Oliveira picked up and relayed the heritage of Pius X, considering him a patron of the counter-revolutionary movement:

"The Catholic reaction that developed in the nineteenth century, the ultramontane movement that consolidated in the counter-revolutionary school of the nineteenth century, was prolonged a little into the twentieth century, and its last flower was Saint Pius X, this counter-revolutionary movement with the definition of the dogmas of the Immaculate Conception and papal infallibility, and the condemnations of the *Syllabus* and *Pascendi,* striking a blow that slowed the revolutionary process. This is something indisputable, and cannot be forgotten.

"In order to have an overall idea of the factors of deterioration in the revolutionary process, it would be necessary to bear in mind the action of grace resulting from the merits and action of several men who preceded us *in signum fidei* and are in our pre-history. We should consider ourselves sons of the Counter-Revolution. We did not inaugurate, we did not raise the early standards of the Counter-Revolution. In us the Counter-Revolution may have attained greater fullness and become more explicit. But everything that germinated in our minds to produce the Counter-Revolution as it exists in the countries where the TFP works was drawn from an ambience permeated with the influences of that counter-revolutionary process. If Saint Pius X was the golden flower that rose from that process, we can say that this golden flower dropped a seed, and from that seed was born a rose garden."[842]

PAOLO ROMANATO, *Pio X, Alle origini del cattolicesimo contemporaneo,* Lindau, Torino, 2014.

[840] Literature on modernism is abundant. Cf. among others the insightful entry by C. FABRO, EC, VIII (1952), cols. 1188-1196; RAMON GARCIA DE HARO, *Historia teologica del modernismo,* Universidad de Navarra, Pamplona, 1972; R. DE MATTEI, *Modernismo e anti-modernismo nell'epoca di Pio X. Con alcune riflessioni su don Orione,* in MICHELE BUSI, R. DE MATTEI, ANTONIO LANZA, FLAVIO PELOSO, *Don Orione negli anni del modernismo,* Jaca Book, Milano, 2002, pp. 29-88.

[841] "The Fiftieth Anniversary of *Pascendi,*" *Catolicismo,* no. 81, September 1957.

[842] RRR, 21 July 1974.

In the Appendix to *Revolution and Counter-Revolution*, the author noted how in 1959, when his work first appeared, the Church was still considered the only great spiritual force against Communist expansion around the world. In subsequent years, however, the decisive center of the struggle between the Revolution and the Counter-Revolution in temporal society gradually turned into an internal struggle in the Church between progressive and anti-progressive Catholics.

"Modernism and progressivism end up being the same thing."[843] "The two currents are very similar because what is modern represents an improvement over what is old. In one of its aspects, modernists showed enthusiasm for modern theses from the beginning of the century and a rejection of the old theses, taking sides against the old. It was therefore a front combating tradition. Progressivism is the same thing. Progressivism is nothing but modernism presented in a more vivid and dynamic way."[844]

"In fact, the very words 'progressivism' and 'modernism' are akin, at least first-degree cousins. Modern is what stands on the leading edge of progress. Progressive is that which welcomes all the impulses of modernity in order to refine itself. Progressivism and modernism are equivalent. They are slightly different labels that designate substantially the same current." [845]

"Progressivism involves a new interpretation of God, Revelation, life and man; it therefore entails a metaphysics; it is a *Weltanschauung*, a whole vision of the universe."[846] "Seen in its ultimate depths, progressivism ends in pantheism. It is a pantheistic invasion of the Catholic Church. Not only of the Catholic Church but of all churches. In its quest to unite all religions, ecumenism essentially carries a craving to make a synthesis of all gods and creeds, in a pan-religious fusion that ends up in a pan-god."[847]

The Second Vatican Council

The death of Pius XII and the election of John XXIII, in October of 1958, marked a turning point in history. The pontificate of John ushered in a new style of government "rather unusual from the standpoint of papal conduct over the last two centuries."[848] On January 25, 1959, in the Benedictine monastery of Saint Paul Outside-the-Walls, John XXIII announced to the cardinals and to the whole world his intention to convene an ecumenical Council. The announcement "had the effect of a

---

[843] RRR, 1 May 1991.
[844] RRR, 5 April 1990.
[845] RRR, 18 July 1987.
[846] RRR, 26 June 1988.
[847] RRR, 23 March 1991.
[848] DANIELE MENOZZI, *La Chiesa cattolica e la secolarizzazione*, Einaudi, Torino, 1993, p. 174.

bombshell inside the Church and perhaps even more so outside."[849] When he learned the news of the convening of Vatican II, Plinio Corrêa de Oliveira, addressing Bishop Geraldo de Proenca Sigaud, commented: "These are the Estates General of the Church! It is the beginning of the Revolution in the Church."[850]

During the first session of the Council, Plinio installed in Rome an office that actively monitored the work of the Assembly and offered efficient services to the two bishops closest to him: Most Revs. Geraldo de Proença Sigaud and Antonio de Castro Mayer. With Plinio's organizational support and strategic suggestions, the two Brazilian bishops maintained intensive contacts with Roman conservative circles. They formed a group called *"Petit Comité"* to organize anti-progressive resistance and brought together "ultramontane" Council Fathers such as Archbishop Marcel Lefebvre and the more conservative wing of Curia Fathers represented by Cardinals like Alfredo Ottaviani and Ernesto Ruffini.

After his return to São Paulo, Prof. Corrêa de Oliveira, who followed the workings of the assembly day by day, sensed, intuited the scope of the looming changes not only in the intricacies of theological language but also in significant gestures destined to have a profound impact on people. The Council was said to be pastoral and not dogmatic; but in the age of the "heresy of action," practice can have a revolutionary impact that ideas fail to attain.

In August 1963 an essay was published in *Catolicismo* titled, *The Freedom of the Church in the Communist State*.[851] In the work, devoted to whether "peaceful coexistence" between the Church and the Communist regime is licit, Plinio showed that Catholics cannot accept any *modus vivendi* with Communism that entails waiving the defense of the right of private property enshrined in the seventh and tenth Commandments. The essay was published in the Roman newspaper *Il Tempo* and distributed to the 2,200 Council Fathers and to journalists from around the world present at the Council, reverberating also beyond the Iron Curtain.[852] A petition by 450 Council Fathers calling for the condemnation of Communism was subsequently shelved.

---

[849] HUBERT JEDIN, *Chiesa della fede, Chiesa della storia*, It. tr., Morcelliana, Brescia, 1972, p. 108.

[850] RRR, 9 September 1989.

[851] Cf. *The Freedom of the Church in the Communist State*, in *Catolicismo*, no. 152 (May-August 1963); *ibid.*, no. 161 (May 1964); later titled *Agreement with the Communist Regime: For the Church, Hope or Self-Destruction?* available at http://www.tfp.org/tfp-home/statements/the-church-and-the-communist-state-the-impossible-coexistence.html.

[852] On the Polish "anomaly," that is, on the peculiar historic model of coexistence between the Catholic Church and the Communist State in Poland, cf. GIOVANNI BARBERINI, *Stato socialista e Chiesa cattolica in Polonia*, CSEO, Bologna, 1983; NORBERT A. ZMIJEWSKI, *The Catholic-*

The Second Vatican Council closed without an explicit condemnation of Communism.[853] This silence constituted an impressive omission by the historical assembly. Plinio denounced the Second Vatican Council's

"...enigmatic, disconcerting, incredible, and apocalyptically tragic silence about communism." [854] "It was the desire of this Council to be pastoral and not dogmatic. And, in fact, it did not have a dogmatic scope. But its omission regarding communism might make it go down in history as the a-pastoral Council par excellence.... Employing '*aggiornati*' tactics (about which the least that can be said is that they are contestable in theory, and are found ruinous in practice), the Second Vatican Council tried to scare away, let us say, bees, wasps, and birds of prey. But its silence about communism left full liberty to the wolves. The work of this Council cannot be inscribed as effectively pastoral either in history or in the Book of Life."[855]

"...the evidence of events singles out the Second Vatican Council as one of the greatest calamities, if not the greatest, in the history of the Church. From the Council on, the 'smoke of Satan' penetrated the Church in unbelievable proportions. And this smoke is spreading day by day, with the terrible force of gases in expansion. To the scandal of uncountable souls, the Mystical Body of Christ entered a sinister process of self-destruction, as it were."[856]

Plinio's vantage point was not that of a theologian but of a layman, philosopher, historian and man of action. His denunciation of Communism was not based on the theological merits of conciliar documents but on the concrete reality of events and their historical

---

Marxist Ideological Dialogue in Poland, 1945-1980, Darmouth Publishing Company, Aldershot (England), 1991.

[853] Today we know that in August 1962, in the French city of Metz, a secret agreement was made between the Vatican representative, Cardinal Tisserant, and Nicodemus, the new Russian Orthodox Archbishop of Yaroslav, who turned out to be a KGB agent, as has been documented after the Moscow archives were opened. With that agreement the ecclesiastical authorities committed themselves not to speak about Communism at the Council. It was the condition requested by the Kremlin to allow the participation of observers from the Patriarchate of Moscow in the Second Vatican Council (R. DE MATTEI, *The Second Vatican Council: An Unwritten Story*, Loreto Publications, Fizwilliam, NH, 2012; JEAN MADIRAN, *L'accord de Metz ou pourquoi notre Mère fut muette*, Via Romana, Versailles, 2006).

[854] *Revolution and Counter-Revolution*, p. 144.

[855] Idem, pp. 144-145. Prof. Corrêa de Oliveira reaffirmed this judgment in his 1976 *Philosophical Self-Portrait*, op. cit. He later expressed his assessment more explicitly on a theoretical plane by stating that he found in some conciliar documents a dissonance with traditional teaching (cf. SD, June 22, 1984) and even a certain systematic ambiguity, incompatible with full orthodoxy (cf. meeting of August 20, 1980).

[856] *Revolution and Counter-Revolution*, p. 145; PAUL VI, *Resoconto della conversazione con gli alunni del Pontificio Seminario Lombardo*, of December 7, 1968, in *Insegnamenti di Paolo VI*, VI (1968), pp. 1187-1189 (p. 1188).

consequences.[857] In a meeting on May 17, 1989, he said: "When I wrote in Part Four of RCR that the Second Vatican Council had been the greatest calamity in the history of the Church, I was stating something that I would affirm today [in 1989] with much greater vigor."[858]

The expression "post-conciliar period," employed to indicate the years after the conclusion of the Second Vatican Council, is historically incorrect because it assumes a non-existing rift between the historical stage opened by the Council and the one immediately following. It would be more correct to speak of a "Council era" to strictly indicate the twenty years (1958-1978) that elapsed between the beginning of the pontificate of John XXIII and the end of Paul VI's – the two Popes who respectively opened and closed Vatican II, of which, historically, they were the embodiment. In a broader sense, the conciliar era is not yet complete. As a whole, as Plinio defined it,[859] it was a "Cultural Revolution" in the Church that operated profound changes in the mentality and customs of both the hierarchy and faithful. Since then the struggle between the Revolution and the Counter-Revolution has been moving more and more from the political to the ecclesiastical field.

"For those who truly have faith and are consistent, ecclesiastical affairs are more important than temporal ones in the balance of events, and the crisis within the Church moves the State more than the State moves itself."[860] "If the Church is the center of the universe, the ecclesiastical terrain is the center of the fight."[861]

"The spiritual, religious sphere is always more important than temporal, political and earthly issues because all of man's actions regarding earthly matters stem from his religious attitudes or lack thereof. Whenever a man takes a stand facing a profound political question, it stems from a religious attitude he took earlier in life, a day ago, or ten, twenty or fifty years earlier, and which projects its effects and profoundly influences his political stand."[862]

"AIDS patients lose all their defenses[863] and are invaded by all sorts of factors of bodily degeneracy,[864] quickly marching toward death. Catholics with a progressive mentality suffer a kind of spiritual AIDS. In other words, they lose all defenses against heresy, error, sin and everything that harms the faith and affects the expansion of the Catholic

---

[857] *Revolution and Counter-Revolution*, pp. 144-145.
[858] RRR, 17 May 1989.
[859] MNF, 21 July 1989.
[860] RRR, 26 October 1974.
[861] RRR, 2 August 1975.
[862] RRR, 15 May 1985.
[863] RRR, 28 March 1992.
[864] RRR, 28 March 1992.

Church around the world; and then all sorts of errors nestle within them."[865]

The "prophetic groups" that started to emerge after the Second Vatican Council resumed the pattern of Gnostics from the early centuries and the Middle Ages: the dream of a Church without law and hierarchical authority in which everything is governed by the Holy Ghost:[866]

> "This is the ecclesiastical society that progressives hope for the future, and that corresponds to a self-managing civil society in which everyone is free to do absolutely anything he fancies, a society in which authority no longer exists and everything is decided by self-managing cliques. But in the end, not even the little group survives, but a tribal breath of 'charity' that leads hordes to group together or disband – men and women, of course – to do whatever they please. It is anarchy." [867]

Against the backdrop of negotiations for the participation of Orthodox observers in the Council, Archbishop Casaroli began his travels to Budapest and Prague (1963-1973), Belgrade (1966-1970), Warsaw (1967-1974), Moscow (1971), and Cuba (1974). On November 1, 1973, when Paul VI asked Cardinal Mindszenty to renounce the title of Archbishop of Esztergom and Primate of Hungary, the Cardinal respectfully replied with a flat refusal. Paul VI took upon himself the responsibility of declaring the primatial seat vacant, and on November 18, 1973, he informed the Cardinal of his removal from the archdiocese. On February 6, the day after the measure was published, Cardinal Mindszenty publicly declared that he had not resigned.[868] On November 13, 1975, the Pope received György Làzàr, President of the Hungarian Council, and on June 9, 1977 Jànos Kàdàr, the leading exponent of Hungarian Communism since 1956, crossed the threshold of the Vatican.

On April 10, 1974, a substantive position paper by the Brazilian TFP appeared as a paid insertion in *Folha de S. Paulo*, titled "The Vatican Policy of Détente with Communist Governments – Should the TFPs Stand Down? Or Should They Resist?" That same year, during a trip to Cuba, Archbishop Casaroli had asserted, "Catholics who live in Cuba are

---

[865] RRR, 28 March 1992.

[866] "The ideal of Gnostics and prophetic groups was to see a Church deprived of authority as much as possible and entirely without laws, in which everything is governed only by interior motions of the Holy Spirit, in the style of Pentecostalism. This hastened the destruction of the juridical aspect of the Church; it was something enormous" (RRR, 30 September 1973).

[867] RRR, 5 February 1983.

[868] By JÓZSEF CARDINAL MINDSZENTY cf. *Erinnerungen*, Ullstein, Frankfurt-Propyläen, Berlin, 1974; It. tr., *Memorie*, Rusconi, Milano, 1975. When the news of his dismissal was published on February 5, 1974, Cardinal Mindszenty issued a communique declaring he never resigned his post as archbishop nor his dignity as Primate of Hungary and emphasized that "the decision has been made solely by the Holy See" (Idem, p. 372).

happy under the socialist regime," and "Catholics and the Cuban people in general do not have the least problem with the socialist government."[869] Facing that and other no less significant episodes such as the 1971 trip to Russia by Msgr. Willebrands, President of the Secretariat for Promoting Christian Unity, to meet with "orthodox" bishop Pimen, a man of confidence of the Kremlin, and the support that Cardinal Silva Henríquez, Archbishop of Santiago in Chile, had given Marxist leader Salvador Allende, Plinio wrote on behalf of the TFP, respectfully but very firmly:

> "The Vatican policy of détente with Communist governments creates a profoundly difficult situation for anti-communist Catholics, much more as Catholics than as anti-communists.... We cannot cease the fight. A demand of our conscience as Catholics will not permit it. Since it is the duty of every Catholic to promote good and combat evil, our conscience calls us to propagate the traditional doctrine of the Church and to fight the communist doctrine.... The Church is not, the Church never was, the Church never will be such a prison for consciences. The bond of obedience to the successor of Peter, which we will never break, which we love in the most profound depths of our soul, and to which we give our highest love, this bond we kiss at the very moment in which, overwhelmed with sorrow, we affirm our position. And on our knees, gazing with veneration at the figure of His Holiness Paul VI, we express all our fidelity to him.

> "In this filial act we say to the Pastor of Pastors: Our soul is yours, our life is yours. Order us to do whatever you wish. Only do not order us to do nothing in face of the assailing red wolf. To this, our conscience is opposed." [870]

Twenty years later, the Sacred Congregation for the Doctrine of the Faith,[871] in its "Instruction on Certain Aspects of the 'Theology of Liberation,'" called Marxism "a shame of our time," apparently justifying

---

[869] Cf. *O Estado de S. Paulo*, April 7, 1974. During his trip, from March 27 and April 5, 1974 on the invitation of the Cuban episcopate, Archbishop Casaroli held talks with government figures and Fidel Castro. The following year he traveled to the German Democratic Republic, and from July 30 to August 1, 1975, on behalf of the Holy See, he participated as a special envoy of Paul VI in the final session of the Helsinki "Security" Conference.

[870] "The Vatican Policy of Detente with Communist Governments." The document was published in full in *Catolicismo* (no. 280, April 1974) and in thirty-six Brazilian newspapers and later reprinted in seventy-three newspapers and magazines in eleven countries without the least objection as to its orthodoxy and canonical correctness. Literature on *Ostpolitik* is now abundant. Cf., among others, ALESSIO ULISSE FLORIDI, *Mosca e il Vaticano*, La Casa di Matriona, Milano, 1976 and the documents compiled by GIOVANNI BARBERINI, *L'Ostpolitik della Santa Sede. Un dialogo lungo e faticoso*, Il Mulino, Bologna, 2007; ID., *La politica del dialogo. Le carte Casaroli sull'Ostpolitik vaticana*, Il Mulino, Bologna, 2008.

[871] CONGREGATION FOR THE DOCTRINE OF THE FAITH, Instruction *Libertatis nuntius*, of August 6, 1984, in DENZ-H, no. 4730-4741.

the TFP's attitude of "resistance" to the Ostpolitik. This attitude of legitimate resistance to deviations of ecclesiastical politics characterized thinking and action of Plinio over the following years.

In 1968, Paul VI spoke about the Church's "self-destruction," "attacked by those who are part of it." [872] In 1972 he said, "The smoke of Satan has entered the temple of God."[873] The "springtime of faith" that should have followed the Second Vatican Council seemed rather like a harsh winter, characterized by ominous symptoms:[874] the collapse of dogmatic certainty, relativism and a new moral permissiveness, disciplinary anarchy, abandonment of the priesthood and religious life on the part of priests and religious, the falling away from religious practice of millions of the faithful, infiltration of heresy through new catechisms and new rites, continuing desecration of the Eucharist, massacre of souls as churches were emptied of their altars, altar rails, crucifixes, statues of saints, church ornaments and paintings, all ending up in warehouses of antique dealers.

While a series of in-depth studies such as those by Romano Amerio,[875] by Mgr. Brunero Gherardini[876] and many others authors[877] marked the beginning of a serious theological and philosophical review of the Second Vatican Council, a question becomes unavoidable: Is it not possible to see a connection between what is going on and the terrible admission by Paul VI that the smoke Satan has entered into the temple of God?

Plinio Corrêa de Oliveira has no doubt: We are faced with the greatest diabolical infestation in history:

> "If the smoke of Satan has entered the Catholic Church, how could she not have arrived where she has? How could things not be as they are?"[878] "If the Church is self-destroying, obviously the psychological cause of this self-destruction is the smoke of Satan that penetrated her. So

---

[872] PAUL VI, Speech at the Lombard Seminary of December 7, 1968, op. cit.

[873] PAUL VI, Homily on the Ninth Anniversary of his Coronation of June 29, 1972, *Insegnamenti*, X (1972), p. 707.

[874] R. DE MATTEI, *Il Concilio Vaticano II. Una storia mai scritta*, Lindau, Torino, 2011, p. 575.

[875] ROMANO AMERIO, *Iota unum*, Lindau, Torino, 2009.

[876] BRUNERO GHERARDINI, *Il Concilio Vaticano II un discorso da fare*, Casa Mariana, Frigento, 2009; *Concilio ecumenico Vaticano II;. Il discorso mancato*, Lindau, Torino, 2011; *Vaticano II. Alle radici di un equivoco,L* Lindau, Torino, 2012.

[877] Cf. also STEFANO M. MANELLI, FI and SERAFINO LANZETTA, FI, eds., *Concilio ecumenico Vaticano II. Un Concilio pastorale. Analisi storico-filosofico-teorica*, Casa Mariana, Frigento, 2011; Fr. SERAFINO LANZETTA, FI, *Iuxta Modum. Il Vaticano II riletto alla luce della Tradizione della Chiesa*, Cantagalli, Siena, 2012; ID., *Il Vaticano II, un concilio pastorale. Ermeneutica delle dottrine conciliari*, Cantagalli, Siena, 2014; Abbé JEAN-MICHEL GLEIZE, "Vatican II en débat. Questions disputées autour du 21ᵉ Concile Oecuménique," *Courrier de Rome*, Versailles 2012.

[878] RRR, 23 April 1993.

how would the smoke of Satan not penetrate throughout the world and not cause this fact which should be qualified as the self-destruction of the world, an obvious reflection of the self-destruction of the Church?"[879]

The Church after the Resignation of Benedict XVI

In 2012, on the fiftieth anniversary of the opening of the Second Vatican Council, Benedict XVI promulgated a Year of Faith and stated, "As we know, in vast areas of the earth the faith risks being extinguished, like a flame that is no longer fed. We are facing a profound crisis of faith, a loss of the religious sense that constitutes the greatest challenge to the Church today."[880]

Applying a metaphor with which Saint Basil described the situation after the Council of Nicea,[881] the same Benedict XVI compared our times to a naval battle in a stormy sea in the dead of night, "in which no one recognizes the other but everyone fights everyone else."[882] And in his homily on the feast of Saints Peter and Paul on June 26, 2006, Pope Benedict described the barque of the Church as "buffeted by the winds of ideologies, filling with water, and seemingly condemned to sink."[883]

Furious winds blow from the outside, such as the massacre of Christians in the East and the secular persecution in the West. But the most terrible storms are those coming from within the Church itself. On February 11, 2013, a date now recorded in history, Benedict XVI announced to an assembly of stunned cardinals his decision to renounce the papacy. The announcement was received "like a lightning bolt out of the clear blue," in the words addressed to the Pope by Cardinal Angelo Sodano, Dean of the College of Cardinals. The picture of a lightning bolt, falling on Saint Peter's Basilica on the same day, circulated on the social networks around the world. The abdication took place on the following February 28, but earlier Benedict XVI announced his intention to remain at the Vatican as Pope Emeritus, something that had never happened and was even more surprising than his renunciation of the pontificate.

The new Pope was elected on March 13, assumed the name Francis, and introduced himself simply as "Bishop of Rome," a title proper to the Pope but only after Vicar of Christ and successor of Peter, which are its preconditions. Thirty years earlier, Plinio stated,

---

[879] Idem.

[880] BENEDICT XVI, Speech to participants in the plenary meeting of the Congregation for the Doctrine of the Faith, January 27, 2012, *Insegnamenti*, VIII, 1 (2012), pp. 128-129 (pp. 128-131).

[881] ST. BASIL, *De Spiritu Sancto,* 30, 77.

[882] BENEDICT XVI, Meeting with the clergy at Auronzo di Cadore, July 24, 2007, *Insegnamenti*, III, 2 (2007), pp. 74-75 (pp. 56-77).

[883] BENEDICT XVI, *Insegnamenti*, II, 1 (2016), p. 846 (pp. 845-849).

"The insistence on calling the Pope 'Bishop of Rome' smacks of progressivism. From the doctrinal standpoint, there is nothing wrong with it. He is the Bishop of Rome in the proper sense of the word because the condition of Pope is attached to the condition of Bishop of Rome. Saint Peter was Bishop of Rome; every Bishop of Rome succeeds Saint Peter in the general direction of the Church. That is the idea with which everyone is familiar.

"But being Pope is much more than being Bishop of Rome. The condition of Bishop of Rome is a stem for the petals of that flower, for the pistil of that flower which is the Papacy. In other words, the stem is where the petals sit, insert themselves and receive their vital sap; but the glory of flowers is in their petals. So also, the Bishop of Rome is above all Pope. This custom for a Pope to often call himself Bishop of Rome is not in the tradition of the past. The Popes of sound tradition recalled occasionally their condition as Bishops of Rome with unconcerned frankness. This designation would occasionally appear in their documents with the naturalness of health, without a desire to enhance or hide it. I find this insistence peculiar."[884]

The photograph of the two Popes praying together at Castelgandolfo on March 23, offering the image of an unprecedented pontifical "diarchy," added to the tremendous confusion of those days. While many statements by the new pope aroused misgivings among the faithful, the event, which appeared more dramatic, was the Extraordinary Synod of Bishops of 2014, which seemed to open the gates to same-sex and divorced and "remarried" couples.

In late 1994, commenting on an article by Father Jim Galluzzo of *The Wanderer*, Plinio stated:

"We are watching the beginning of a methodical work within the Church, and in all other sectors of society, not only to promote tolerance but to legitimize homosexuality, which will end up by fulfilling the wishes of the European Parliament to have same-sex unions recognized as capable of producing the same legal effects as marriage.

"If you take the most dangerous heresies, most laden with hatred and most deeply dissonant from Catholic doctrine, you will find nothing more deeply at variance with Catholic doctrine than this. It is entering, but see the way in which it penetrates. It is not through a pamphlet presented by Protestants, but by Catholics priests. The article refers to a document issued by bishops in 1976, so it is something already quite old, inviting one to a kind of mixture between homosexuals and non-homosexuals.

"It is a work carried out from the top down by ecclesiastical authorities, to make us forget the traditional doctrine and give

---

[884] RRR, 21 April 1984.

homosexuality a right of citizenship in the Holy Church of God. There will be a given moment when a manifestation of complete disagreement with this action will arise within the Catholic Church. And then we will have an official division within the Church.

"Someone might say, 'But if the vast majority of bishops are in agreement with this, there would be no division.' There is no great majority capable of changing Catholic doctrine! Now it is indisputable and clearly stated in Scripture, in all the documents of the Church's Magisterium, in all moralists, etc., that this is a sin that cries out to heaven and clamors to God for vengeance. The result: there can be no mutual understanding, period. Borders are closed off, barriers raised, etc.

"Then there will be an internal clash within the Church, and this internal shock will produce one of the greatest upheavals in history."[885]

Faced with the crisis in the Church, Plinio called for a total and categorical rejection of the process of self-demolition, while harboring feelings of extreme sadness and indignation to the fullest possible degree:

"Let　this be the topic of your conversations, the fixed-point of convergence of your thoughts, as if Our Lord Jesus Christ were being crucified." [886]

He saw in the Passion of the Church a reflection of Christ's Passion:

"How many are those who live in union with the Church at this moment as tragic as the Passion, at this crucial moment in history in which the whole of humanity is opting for Christ or against Christ?" [887]

This profound and deeply felt awareness of the Passion of the Church must not lead to loss of faith but rather drive us to intensify our acts of faith and love of God:

"In the present crisis, as in all crises that have arisen or will arise against the Church, the defeat of the Revolution is guaranteed by the promise that the gates of hell shall not prevail against her."[888] "Tomorrow, events may come up that can give the impression that the Church is crumbling and falling. Little does this impression matter, for if she fell the earth would split, but not the Church. This conviction is based first of all on Our Lord's promise: The gates of hell shall not prevail against her." [889]

"Had Our Lord not promised that the Church would not die, we would be tempted to think that she is already dead. We believe that she did not die because He said so and continues to say so. Otherwise, that

---

[885] RRR, 6 September 1994.
[886] RRR, 17 May 1987.
[887] *Via Sacra, Catolicismo*, no. 3, March 1981.
[888] RRR, 7 August 1991
[889] RRR, 10 June 1995.

would be the temptation."[890] "The Church is immortal and cannot die. I am certain that she will not die because of the promise, but I think this promise will probably be fulfilled through a miracle, for through the common ways of Providence there would be no way out for the crisis." [891]

When the storm was raging and the boat was covered by waves the disciples came to Jesus asleep, and woke Him up, saying: "Lord, save us, we perish!" He said to them: "Why are you fearful, O ye of little faith?" Then rising up, He commanded the winds, and the sea, and there came a great calm. But the men wondered, saying, "What manner of man is this, for the winds and the sea obey him?" (Mt. 8:25).

Only Jesus Christ and no one else can save the Church, for He alone is its Founder and Head. From the Vicar of Christ on earth to the last individual faithful, men can only collaborate with divine grace received through the Holy Spirit, and moving us to develop our *sensus fidei* by means of a radical fidelity to Christ and to His Law.

Predictions on the Danger of Islam

As the Church was going through an unprecedented crisis in her history, an ominous shadow rose from the East. Among Plinio's most clairvoyant forecasts are certainly those concerning the danger Islam poses to the West.[892]

The shadow of Islam has accompanied the history of Europe like a nightmare, but at Poitiers in 732, on the Crusade battlefields between the eleventh and thirteenth centuries, at Lepanto (1571), Vienna (1683) and Belgrade (1717), Christendom in arms stopped the expansion of Muhammad's religion, condemning Islam to an apparent decline. The First World War saw the collapse of the Ottoman Empire and the apparent collapse of Islam. Yet since the thirties, Plinio wrote many articles denouncing the danger of a possible rebirth of the Mohammedan

---

[890] RRR, 30 July 1994.

[891] RRR, 26 May 1984.

[892] On Islam in general, cf. HENRI LAMMENS, *L'Islam. Croyances et institutions*, Editions du Trident, Paris, 1993; BAT YE'OR, *Les Chrétientés d'Orient entre Jihad et dhimmitude*, Paris, 2007 (1991). On postmodern Islam, cf. BASSAM TIBI, *Islamische Zuwanderung. Die gescheiterte Integration*, Deutsche Verlg-Austalt GmbtH, München, 2002; ID., *Europeanizing Islam, or the Islamization of Europe*, in TIMOTHY BYRNES and PETER KATZENSTEIN, eds., *Religion in an Expanding Europe*, Cambridge University Press, New York, 2006; EFRAIM KARSCH, *Islamic Imperialism. A History*, Yale University Press, New Haven and London, 2007; ALEXANDRE DEL VALLE, *Il totalitarismo islamista all'assalto della democrazia*, Solinum, s.l., 2007; *Eurabia*, It. tr., Lindau, Torino, 2007; Id. *L'Europe et le spectre du califat*, Le Provinciales, Paris, 2010; ROBERT R: REILLY, *The Closing of the Muslim Mind*, ISI, Wilmingon, 2010.

religion.[893] In 1943, referring to the political evolution in the countries of the Middle East, he described the Islamic threat thus:

> "The Muslim danger is immense. The West seems to close its eyes to it, eyes still semi-shut to the huge yellow peril.... Today everything is done with men, weapons and money. The Muslim world has all the money and men it may want. Acquiring weapons will not be difficult...and will make it an immense power throughout the East; an active, warlike power aware of its traditions, an enemy of the West, and just as well armed; a power that within some time can be quite as influential as the Yellow race, while placed in an incomparably better geographical and economic situation."[894]

In 1944, commenting on statements by the Egyptian Prime Minister on the necessary measures to establish an Arab League, Plinio concluded an article with these words: "On this day [of the Arab Conference Meeting], at the gates of a weakened and semi-dechristianized Europe, an 'Arab danger' will arise, equal or greater than at the time of St. Pius V and the Battle of Lepanto."[895]

On June 15, 1947, Plinio published in *Legionário* an article significantly titled, "Muhammad's Rebirth," in which he predicted a "resurrection" of Islamic nations:

> "All these nations, we can say these powers, are proud of their past, traditions and culture, and are keen to keep them; and at the same time they are proud of their natural resources, political and military possibilities, and growing financial progress. They grow richer by the day, build cities endowed with an effective government apparatus, a well-trained police, strictly pagan but well developed universities, schools, hospitals, museums, in short everything that somehow means power and material progress to us. In their coffers, gold accumulates. Gold means the ability to buy weapons. And weapons mean global prestige.

> "All this transformed the Islamic world and produced in all Mohammedan peoples, from India to Morocco, a shudder that means that the millennial slumber is over. Pakistan – a Muslim Hindu state on the brink of independence – Iran, Iraq, Turkey, Egypt are the high points of

---

[893] Some of these articles have been transcribed by JUAN GONZALO LARRAIN CAMPBELL in *Catolicismo*, no. 478 (October 1990) and later published and commented on by the same author in *Plinio Corrêa de Oliveira: Previsiones y Denuncias en defensa de la Iglesia y de la civilizacion cristiana*, Petrus Editora, Sao Paulo, 2009. In an interview on the religious situation in the world, Jesuit JOÃO B. LIBÂNIO, a leading exponent of Liberation Theology, recalled: "In 1940, Plinio Corrêa de Oliveira gave the Jesuits a lecture impregnated with a whole messianic idea [sic!], saying that Islamism was the great problem of Christianity. Fifty years ago, either it was prophetic, or history gradually went that way for other reasons. The fact is that what he intuited has been confirmed" (*Jornal Indústria & Comércio,* Curitiba, August 26-27, 1996).
[894] "The Lebanese Question*," Legionário*, December 5, 1943.
[895] "7 Days in Review," *Legionário*, October 1, 1944.

the movement of Islamic resurrection. But in Algeria, Morocco, Tripolitania [now Lybia], Tunisia, unrest also grows intense. The vital nerve of Islam revives in all these peoples, rekindling in them a sense of unity, a notion of common interests, concerns of solidarity, and a taste for victory. None of that stayed in the realm of possibility. Today the Arab League, a vast confederation of Muslim peoples, unites the entire Muslim world. It is, in reverse, what Christendom used to be in the Middle Ages. The Arab League acts as a large block facing non-Arab nations and fosters insurrection throughout North Africa.... Does it take a lot of talent, insight, and exceptionally good information to realize what this danger means? [896]

In 1947, with the suggestive title, "Sons of Darkness and Sons of Light," he wrote:

"All [Mohammedan powers] are going through a truly amazing nationalist and religious revival. The breath of this revival runs the vast belt spanning from Morocco's Atlantic coast to Pakistan. And thanks to the religious revival of what we might call 'Islamdom,' the whole Mohammedan world has taken an interest in the Palestinian problem.... In turn, the fight is helping to further stimulate the pan-Arab and pan-Mohammedan revival. Events are thus giving Muslims around the world an ever stronger awareness of their unity, power, and common religious and political interests." [897]

Today Islam is becoming the twenty-first century Communism, proposing to the West in new terms the messianic and pseudo-religious dimension of twentieth century totalitarianism.[898] The "secular religions" of the twentieth century appealed to the need for the sacred inherent to the human soul. At a time when, with the fall of the Soviet Union, the Communist Revolution seems to have dissolved in the pragmatism of technological society, its stage as a "secular religion" is replaced by Islamic radicalism in the name of fighting against a corrupt and oppressive West. As Roger Garaudy announced when he switched from the Communist faith to the Muslim one, Islam recovers the prophetic dimension of the Revolution that characterized the great subversive movements of Western history from the Anabaptists to Communism.[899] The Gnostic and nihilistic inspiration of modern Jihad, underlined by

---

[896] "Muhammad's Rebirth," *Legionário*, June 15, 1947.

[897] "Sons of Darkness and Sons of Light," *Legionário*, October 19, 1947.

[898] The definition of Communism as the "20th century Islam" was made by JULES MONNEROT, in *Sociologie du communisme*, Gallimard, Paris, 1993 (later Haller, Paris 2004-2005, 3 vols; the first volume is titled *L'Islam du XX siècle*).

[899] ROGER GARAUDY, *Promesses de l'Islam*, Editions du Seuil, Paris, 1998, p. 176.

some scholars,[900] is placed in direct continuity with the revolutionary process described by Plinio Corrêa de Oliveira.

Venerable Bartholomew Holzhauser and Islam

Venerable Bartholomew Holzhauser[901] was born in 1613 in Longnau, near Augsburg, in Bavaria. He was a parish priest in Bingen and founded a congregation of secular clerics who lived as a community, known as the Bartholomites. He died in the odor of sanctity on May 20, 1658, in the diocese of Mainz, where he rests in the Church of the Holy Cross.

Venerable Holzhauser, individually endowed with the gift of prophecy, is known for his *Visions* and *Interpretatio in Apocalypsin*, an unfinished work first published in Bamberg in 1784. The sixth and final book, *Interpretatio,* is devoted to an exegesis of chapters 12 to 15 of the Apocalypse, in which the author interprets relationships between the Church of Christ and Islam as a continuing and relentless war that will never end except in the way history concludes: "...the most cruel, most terrible, and very long war with which the Prince of darkness, Lucifer, would destroy the Church if it were possible." [902]

The devil, *simia Dei*, "God's monkey," imitates God's works to do evil, with a perverse end. Just as he opposes the Antichrist to the true Christ, the devil also opposes the kingdom of Christ with a counterfeit temporal kingdom, which in the Latter Times, according to Venerable Holzhauser, will be the Muslim religion. Islam has therefore a providential although negative mission to accomplish, which runs throughout the history of the Church as the embodiment of the devil's anti-social kingdom. Islam is indeed the "implacable and hereditary enemy" of Christianity, "and although for the consolation of the Church its strength will be at times almost eliminated, some of its reign will nevertheless remain until the coming of the son of perdition. The latter will make Islam rise again, heal its wounds, enter it, subdue many kingdoms; it will ultimately rule, and with it Lucifer will unleash his fury."[903]

---

[900] LAURENT MURAWIEC, *The Mind of Jihad*, Cambridge University Press, Cambridge, 2008.
[901] Bartholomäus Holzhauser (1613-1658), priest (1639), canon regular at Tittmoning in Bavaria, later dean at St. Johann in Tirol and pastor of Bingen, he founded the Order of the Bartholomites. Author of numerous works, all posthumous, including *Explicatio in Apocalypsim* (1684). Cf. MICHAEL ARNETH, DSp, VII (1969), cols. 590-597.
[902] *Venerabilis Servi Dei Bartholomaei Holzhauser, Instituti clericorum juxta Ss. Canones in Germania restauratoris, Interpretatio in Apocalypsin*, Typis Congregationis Mechitharisticae, Vindobonae, 1850 (1684), p. 216.
[903] Idem.

In its historical manifestation, the red dragon of the Apocalypse, the blood-thirsty beast that threatens the Woman-Church, "is the Mohammedan, that is, Turkish, empire, which as a very strong beast, with diabolical instinct, unceasingly persecutes" Christians with "the sole purpose of exterminating Christendom and the Roman Empire." [904]

Reading the commentary on the Apocalypse by Ven. Bartholomew Holzhauser, Plinio Corrêa de Oliveira was struck by what he said about Islam, presenting it almost as a fulfillment of the revolutionary process. Recalling the fact some years later, he commented,

> "In the book, Ven. Holzhauser did not mention the three Revolutions in that order, but they were there. Later he comes to a final period in which, to my surprise, the Islamic danger appeared as the great danger for Christendom. And he spoke of the evil of Islam, although in such a summarized way that I did not understand it well.

> "For someone accustomed to the logic of the three Revolutions, the rise of Islam would seem completely secondary. Islam would be a dead, dismembered adversary that no longer has vigor or a future and therefore one could not imagine it with the dynamism of a movement that would become a major danger, capable of riding atop the three Revolutions of the tri-revolutionary process.

> "Many years earlier, articles of mine had mentioned the possibility that Islam would have some kind of resurrection and play a very great role in the world, etc. But I considered that role only from the political point of view: that Islam could become a great power and the Revolution might ride the horse of Islam to finish its work. I never thought that Islam would ride the Revolution.

> "However, out of respect for the Venerable, who was obviously making a prophecy in those pages…I suspended my judgment about this point: that Islam could become a force that would add to the tri-revolutionary process, increasing the severity of the danger, and that Islam would ride atop the three Revolutions rather than the three Revolutions riding atop Islam."[905]

While Plinio Corrêa de Oliveira developed these considerations, the first news was published on the construction of a large mosque in Rome, center of the Catholic Church. The mosque was inaugurated on June 21, 1995. Starting at that time, Islam unveiled its global project for the conquest of civilization, its ultimate goal not being Vienna or New York but the city of Rome, capital of Christendom. Caliph Abu Bakr al-Baghdadi, head of the self-proclaimed Islamic State, indicated Rome as

---

[904] Idem, p. 220.
[905] RRR, 27 March 1993.

the ultimate ideological goal of global Jihad and called on all Muslims to join him. If they will do so, he promised that Islam will arrive all the way to Rome and dominate the earth. However, Sheikh Yusuf al-Qaradawi, spiritual leader of the Muslim Brotherhood, had already declared in a fatwa promulgated on February 27, 2005: "Despite the pessimism in the Muslim ranks, Islam will ultimately rule and become master of the whole world. One of the signs of victory will be that Rome will be conquered, Europe will be occupied, Christians will be defeated, and Muslims will grow and become a force that will control the entire European continent."[906]

Satanism in the Fifth Revolution

Islam's entry into the scene thus coincides with the transition from the Fourth to the Fifth Revolution, the preternatural revolution par excellence, whose boundaries are still uncertain but which represents the apex of Satanism.

The devil has more than just acolytes, covens, rituals, and sacrifices. With his power as a fallen angel, he can also exercise a profound influence on the world.[907] A countless number of demons surrounds us: "...great is their multitude in the air around us, and they are not far away from us," one reads in the *Life of Saint Anthony*.[908]

As angels, demons can act not only on man's external but also internal senses: his imagination, nervous system, and the brain, which is not the organ of the intellect but the physical organ of imagination.[909] Angels, good or bad, affect external images, excite moods and feelings that favor the formation of ideas and finally incline to action. The good angels help one's common sense to know the beauty of the universe, to penetrate the world of symbols, to orient toward good, and to instill peace and tranquility in the soul; bad angels present images distinct from reality, influence the formation of bad thoughts, instill confusion and restlessness. They can alter or affect the brain by causing euphoria and depression, an effect similar to that of drugs. Thus, the battlefield of angels and demons is especially that of human imagination and tendencies.

---

[906] Cf. MAURIZIO MOLINARI, *Il califfato del terrore. Perché lo Stato islamico minaccia l'Occidente*, Rizzoli, Milan, 2015, pp. 125-129. Cf. also GIULIO MEOTTI, "Un muezzin sveglierà Roma," *Il Foglio*, March 1, 2015.

[907] Cf. *Satan*, Desclée de Brouwer (Etudes Carmélitaines), Paris, 1948; PAOLO CALLIARI, *Trattato di demonologia, secondo la teologia cattolica. Dottrina, fatti, interpretazioni*, Centro Editoriale Carroccio, Vigosdarzere, 1992; EGON VON PETERSDORFF, *Dämonologie*, Christiana Verlag, Stein am Rhein, 1995.

[908] *Vita S. Antonii,* prepared by G. M. Bartelink, Fondazione L. Valla, Milano, 1974, p. 59.

[909] *Summa Theologica*, I, III, 2-4.

Just as divine grace acts on human nature to complete and perfect it, the action of the devil requires a nature to subjugate. The human nature of Christ is the supreme degree of creation. But human nature can also exist reduced to its lowest degree, in which, as Plinio writes, "the old standards of reflection, volition and sensibility will be gradually replaced by increasingly collective forms of thought, deliberation and sensibility."[910]

This lowest degree, in which human nature is broken and dissolved, is what the devil needs in order to achieve his end: a counterfeit hypostatic union between Satan and the tribal community, which is the antithesis of the hypostatic union between the perfect human nature of Jesus Christ and His perfect divine nature.

In the dark atmosphere of nightclubs or in the excitement of rock concerts, consciousness dissolves and a shapeless collectivity offers the prince of this world a human matter suitable to be animated by his evil influence. In these ambiences, Satanism, demonolatry, finds its natural *humus*.

This satanic character becomes ever more explicit in the course of the revolutionary process.

> "We could call the Fifth Revolution mystical."[911] "The Fifth Revolution already is pure mysticism."[912] "It means the disappearance of the *lumen gratiae* [light of grace] on earth and the appearance of blackness or hellfire replacing it. It is the appearance of the devil and his imperious demand to be adored, amid temptations and noise."[913]

This irruption of the devil is an inevitable consequence of the intrinsic and profound evil of the Revolution, which has an impulse to attain its fullness, which is the anti-Church, the glorification of the devil on earth:

> "The final goal of the Revolution is the implementation of the devil's kingdom on earth, that is, of a religious and temporal order in which men worship the devil as their own God – not a devil disguised as an angel of light (there are apparitions in which the devil poses as an angel of light), but the devil appearing in his horror."[914]

---

[910] *Revolution and Counter-Revolution*, p. 158.

[911] RRR, 25 May 1991.

[912] RRR, 15 June 1991.

[913] RRR, 25 May 1991.

[914] RRR, 16 January 1988.

The Invincible Mediation of the Blessed Virgin Mary

The devil, a creature, seeks to disfigure the work of creation. Providence granted another creature the mission of restoring the whole truth and beauty of the disfigured divine order. The devil is the father of sin, chaos, Revolution. Our Lady is the Mother of all grace, order, and restoration. Devotion to Our Lady – Plinio always insisted – is a condition *sine qua non* for the Revolution to be crushed and for the Counter-Revolution to triumph.

> "Grace depends on God, but by a free act of His will He wanted the distribution of graces to depend on Our Lady. Mary is the Universal Mediatrix, the channel through which all graces pass. Therefore, her help is indispensable for there to be no Revolution, and for the latter to be defeated by the Counter-Revolution." [915]

The life of grace is nourished by the Sacraments and by an intimate union with Our Lady, Mediatrix of All Graces and Mother of the victorious Counter-Revolution. However, devotion to Our Lady is ineffective if not accompanied by an equally ardent hatred for the devil and his works. God made only one enmity – but irreconcilable, which will last until the end of time, says Saint Louis de Montfort:[916] that between Mary and the devil, between the children and servants of the Blessed Virgin and the children and followers of Lucifer. *"Inimicitias ponam."* "This sentence," Msgr. Delassus writes, "links the history of the earth with that of heaven. There took place the first salvo of a war that ends with us."[917] The fight that began in heaven between Lucifer and the Archangel Michael unfolds throughout history and is renewed during our time on earth. But its result is already written and was personally announced by Our Lady. The devil's rebellion is one of the causes, not only of the Incarnation of the Word, but also of Mary's divine maternity, and hence of her privileged role, which will be to crush the head of the devil and to bring God's plans to their perfect fulfillment.

> "Therefore, Our Lady plays a role in crushing the demon, a personal role that did not exist before her and which she exercises since her Immaculate Conception. Therefore, it is not exercised through the ministry of angels, but personally by Her. Her fight against the demon, in which she eternally crushes his head, is inserted in the eternal struggle of angels against demons. But her fight is personal, individual, and distinct from the struggle of angels against demons. So one can understand that, in

---

[915] Preface to the Argentine edition of *Revolution and Counter-Revolution*, op. cit.

[916] ST. LOUIS MARIE GRIGNON DE MONTFORT, *Treatise on True Devotion to the Blessed Virgin*, no. 52.

[917] MSGR. HENRI DELASSUS, *Il problema dell'ora presente*, It. tr., Desclée, Roma, 1907, vol. II, p. 41.

Her fight against the demon, which took place in the context of human nature, and in which Our Lord Jesus Christ has the great preponderant part, men are especially inserted – *christianus alter Christus* – not in an alliance with the whole angelic structure, but in the union with Our Lady."[918]

The Angelic Fight

In Genesis, the Lord said: "I will put enmities between thee and the woman, and thy seed and her seed: she shall crush thy head, and thou shalt lie in wait for her heel" (Gn. 3:15).   The twelfth chapter of the Apocalypse describes the infernal dragon's violent struggles against the offspring of the Virgin. The Immaculate Woman appears clothed with the sun, with the moon under her feet and a crown of twelve stars on her head; facing her stands the Dragon, reddened by the blood of martyrs, proud, fierce, and seemingly invincible but destined to irrevocable defeat (Ap. 12:1-8).

In his Encyclical *Humanum Genus*, Leo XIII recalls that after Lucifer's rebellion, mankind "is separated into two diverse and opposite parts, of which the one steadfastly contends for truth and virtue...the other for those things which are contrary to virtue and to truth."[919] Everything stemmed from those acts of fidelity and rebellion at the beginning of time.

Since then, God, the first cause of all that exists, has used angels as secondary causes to govern the universe He created.[920]   Angels are pure spirits, penetrated by the Holy Ghost. Although their number is immense, each has his own unique face. They are organized into Choirs and Orders (Col. 1:16) and their hierarchical inequality reflects well the inexhaustible beauty and variety of the Holy Trinity:

> "The angels are members of the heavenly court and live there in an eternal contemplation of God, knowing, loving, praising and serving Him face to face. This contemplation is expressed in large celebrations, which some mystics have been able to see. These are not mere metaphors. Heaven is an eternal celebration in which God shows His grandeur more and more and where the angels, along with the saints, acclaim Him with new triumphant praise that will never end...Heaven is the home of our soul and is properly speaking the order of things for which we were created, which fully meets all our aspirations. Something of the eternal

---

[918] EVP, 26 February 1978.

[919] LEO XIII, Enc. *Humanum genus*, op. cit., EE, *Leone XIII*, p. 287.

[920] Cf. *Catechism of the Catholic Church*, nos. 328-336, 391-395. Cf. also G. A. and L. S. SOLÍMEO, *Anjos e Demónios*; MSGR. A. PIOLANTI, *Dio nel mondo e nell'uomo*, Desclée, Roma, 1959, pp. 165-166; F. SBAFFONI, *San Tommaso d'Aquino e l'influsso degli Angeli*, Edizioni Studio Domenicano, Bologna, 1993.

heavenly happiness is reflected on earth. For example, in times of true faith, some of this happiness and piety is felt by pious souls and later spread by more notably pious ones as a common treasure for the whole Church."[921]

Saint Thomas says that "all physical bodies are governed by angels."[922] God, the Angelic Doctor explains, governs lower beings through higher ones, not out of inability to rule directly, but in order to generously communicate the dignity of causality to superior creatures.[923] Through the Angels, at every moment and in every circumstance of our lives, God exercises a profound and invisible action on us to lead us to our supernatural end. This is why we pray to our Guardian Angel to "rule and guide us."

The angels, however, are not mere tools for the sanctification of individual souls. They are present wherever men gather in societies, natural and spiritual families, and clusters of families such as nations; they are instruments of God's glory, not just private but public. This is why there are angels of nations, angels of peoples, angels of the Church. Saint Thomas, who is called the "Angelic Doctor" because of his doctrine on angels, which he develops in many works, and especially in the *Summa Theologica*, adds that the custody of human societies belongs to the angelic order of Principalities, or perhaps that of Archangels.[924]

The mission of Angels with nations aims above all at their protection and temporal assistance. This is why Deuteronomy says, "When the Most High divided his inheritance among the nations, when he separated the sons of men, he set the boundaries of the peoples according to the number of the angels of God" (Dt. 32:8).[925]

In Sacred Scripture the Prophet Daniel reveals that three nations, Israel, Persia and Greece, had each a custodian or "guardian" angel called the "prince" of nations (Dan. 10:13ff.), perhaps to indicate that it belonged to the highest angelic hierarchies. Through the angels the Lord sent the Law to the Hebrew people (Acts 7:53). But if even Gentile nations such as Persia and Greece were under the protection of an angel, how could one admit that Christian nations would be left unprotected after the coming of Jesus Christ?

---

[921] SD, 28 September 1966.

[922] *Summa Theologica*, I, q. 110, a. 1.

[923] Idem, I, q. 22, a. 3.

[924] Idem, I, q. 113, a. 3, resp.

[925] The author cites this verse of Deuteronomy according to the Greek version of the Pentateuch. The Douay translation has "according to the number of the children of Israel," and the Confraternity has "after the number of the sons of God," following the Hebrew version, but we have followed the Greek version so that the author's commentary retains its meaning (translator's note).

Our Lady, united to Jesus Christ, Lord of Heaven and Earth, reigns with Him above all things and is therefore revered as the "Queen of Angels," and guides the heavenly army in a battle that had already begun when God created the angels and showed them His designs. In Plinian angelology, Saint Michael the Archangel, Prince of the heavenly army and primary patron of the Church, who stands out in the assembly of angels, is also the guide and protector of the Counter-Revolution.

"We can imagine the beauty of the heavenly cohorts with all the choirs of angels, and Lucifer leading as their archetype and representing all their perfections. And suddenly Lucifer is invited by God's Revelation – as all other angels – to recognize that God would create men, whose nature would be inferior to that of angels. And that in those men – something that already irritated him – the Word of God, the Second Person of the Trinity, would become incarnate, taking human nature, and so it was not Lucifer but the Word of God Incarnate that would command all creation. A God-Man, and therefore God, but incarnated in a nature inferior to Lucifer's, would thus lead all heavenly cohorts.

"Faced with this revelation, he uttered the first cry of revolution, which reverberates to this day. He said: *Non serviam*! I will not serve! In other words, I will not obey, I will not bow before this human creature united to the Creator. I am a pure spirit, the most splendid of all angels, I will not accept this subjection."

"If Lucifer was made aware of the existence of the Virgin – also superior to him, though without the Hypostatic Union between human nature and divine nature – his hatred likely grew even more. And when he shouted, 'I will not serve!' this cry produced a huge impression on the other angels of heaven. From what the Bible says, it is certain that a considerable number of angels – we do not know how many – joined Lucifer and also cried, '*non serviam*.' And so, says Scripture, a revolution by angels who would not serve took place in heaven. The first of all revolutions.

"And a Counter-Revolution gloriously and luminously arose immediately thereafter. It is Saint Michael the Archangel, who despite being an angel from a rank lower than that of Lucifer, obeys God and raises the standard of discipline, hierarchy, obedience, against the cursed banner of disobedience, insolence, rebellion and negation of God that Satan had raised. Two armies are formed, therefore, in the celestial spaces, and these armies fight – Scripture says – a great battle: *Proelium magnum factum est in coelo,* a great war was waged in heaven. And in this war, Saint Michael the Archangel and his faithful angels – naturally favored and protected by God – were victorious. Satan and his angels were overturned and thrown into Hell forever, and the faithful angels remained alone, shining in heaven." [926]

The cosmic battle between Lucifer and the Archangel Michael relentlessly continues today. That battle and victory in heaven prefigure a battle and a victory on earth by the offspring of Mary over that of Lucifer: the victory of the Counter-Revolution:

"We should consider Saint Michael as our natural ally in our fight, for the Counter-Revolution is nothing but a group of people carrying out on a human level the same task as Saint Michael, by defending the honor of God, the glory of Our Lady, the Catholic Church and Christian civilization – but defending them as a counter-offensive in such a way as to overthrow the empire of the devil and establish the Reign of Mary on earth. So we see great affinity between Saint Michael and the Counter-Revolution, and those wishing to elect Saint Michael as their special patron are right to do so."[927]

The Irreversible Restoration of Christian Society

Plinio Corrêa de Oliveira not only made a lucid and penetrating diagnosis of the Revolution. He also was the prophet of Christian civilization, the one who announced the possibility and indeed certainty of the restoration of Christian Civilization if men fully cooperate with heavenly grace.

In the conclusion of his last book, dedicated to the *Nobility and Analogous Traditional Elites in the Allocutions of Pius XII,* he describes the ominous outcome of the long revolutionary process:

"This process has advanced relentlessly, from the waning and fall of the Middle Ages to the initial joyful triumphs of the Renaissance; to the religious revolution of Protestantism, which remotely began to foment and prepare the French Revolution and, even more remotely, the Russian Revolution of 1917. So invariably victorious has been its path, despite innumerable obstacles, that one might consider the power that moved this process invincible and its results definitive.

These results seem definitive indeed, if one overlooks the nature of this process. At first glance, it seems eminently constructive, since it successively raised three edifices: the Protestant Pseudo-Reformation, the liberal-democratic republic, and the Soviet socialist republic.

"The true nature of this process, however, is essentially destructive. It is Destruction itself. It toppled the faltering Middle Ages, the vanishing Ancien Régime, and the apoplectic, frenetic, and turbulent bourgeois

---

[926] SD, 11 August 1995.
[927] Meeting of September 28, 1966.

world. Under its pressure, the former USSR lies in ruins – sinister, mysterious, and rotten like a fruit long-since fallen from the branch.

"*Hic et nunc,* is it not true that the milestones of this process are but ruins? And what is the most recent ruin generating but a general confusion that constantly threatens imminent and contradictory catastrophes, which disintegrate before falling upon the world, thus begetting prospects of new catastrophes even more imminent and contradictory? These may vanish in turn, only to give way to new monsters. Or they may become frightful realities, like the migration of Slavic hordes from the East to the West, or Moslem hordes from the South to the North.

"Who knows? Will this actually happen? Will this be all? Will it be even worse than this? Such a picture would discourage all men who lack Faith. Those with Faith, however, can already hear a voice coming from beyond this confused and grim horizon. The voice, capable of inspiring the most encouraging confidence, says: 'Finally, my Immaculate Heart will triumph!'"[928]

These words outline a great theology of history. A human gaze resting on today's horizon can only recoil with terror. For the West there is no future, only death and decay. But another gaze falls upon this horizon, which illuminates it and turns death into life, fear into hope, and hope into confident certainty. It is the merciful gaze of the Wise and Immaculate Heart of Mary.

---

[928] *Nobility and Analogous Traditional Elites*, op. cit., pp. 130-131.

PART FOUR

THE PROPHETIC MISSION

CHAPTER I

PROPHETISM AND CATHOLIC APOCALYPTICS

Prophecy in the Old and New Testaments

The legacy Plinio Corrêa de Oliveira leaves to the spiritual and cultural school he formed is a theology of history that unveils the horizon of a prophetic mission.

In everyday language, "prophet" is one who, by intuition or sharpness of mind, predicts future events with some accuracy. Theology calls a prophet a person who speaks or acts by divine mission. Prophecies can be based on the pure capacity to reason, concatenating causes and effects, or can result from a supernatural gift if God Himself reveals messages or provides visions to elect souls. In the former case, for example, we call prophetic such documents as the *Syllabus* of Pius IX[929] and the Encyclical *Pascendi,* of Saint Pius X.[930] In the latter we refer to messages and visions received by many saints or privileged souls throughout history.[931] In the twentieth century, for example, the message of Fatima.

In the Old Testament, prophetism is characteristic of the religion of the people of Israel, where the presence of prophets is the primary tool through which Yahweh communicates with His people. Here God intervenes in history directly and in an extraordinary way, and the prophets are intermediaries of Divine Revelation with the primary mission of leading the chosen people.[932]

Saint John the Baptist is considered the last prophet of the Old Testament, while Our Lord is the first prophet of the New, the Prophet

---

[929] Cf. for example, Msgr. LUIGI NEGRI, *Pio IX. Attualità e profezia*, Ares, Milano, 2006.

[930] Cf. The third chapter of the study by ALBERTO CATURELLI dedicated to "La *Pascendi Dominici grecis*, a prophetic encyclical," in *La Iglesia catolica y las catacumbas de hoy*, Gladius, Buenos Aires, 2006.

[931] Cf. the collection of messages by Abbé J.M. CURICQUE, *Voix prophétique, ou signes, apparitions et prédictions modernes*, 2 vols., Victor Palme, Paris, 1872, and by Father AUGUSTE SAUDREAU, O.P., *Les divines paroles, ou ce que le Seigneur a dit ses intimes dans le cours des siècles chrétiens*, Téqui, Paris, 1936, 2 vols.

[932] Msgr. FRANCESCO SPADAFORA, *Profeta*, EC, X (1953), cols. 92-101.

par excellence of Whom the Old Testament prophets had been forerunners. The Church, Mystical Body of Christ, prolongs the royal, priestly and prophetic mission of her Divine Founder. It is a hierarchical institution in which there is a clear distinction between clergy and laity, the teaching Church and the taught Church, but in which every baptized person participates in the gifts of the Holy Ghost according to his own role within the Mystical Body.

Among these gifts, prophecy is a sign of the true Church, as Saint Paul teaches (1 Cor. 14). Sacred Scripture distinguishes true from false prophets, i.e., persons that improperly ascribe to themselves the title of prophet. The contest between Elias and the worshipers of Baal on Mount Carmel is an archetype of the clash between true and false prophets. Thus the Gospel says, "Beware of false prophets, which come to you in sheep's clothing, but inwardly they are ravening wolves" (Mt. 7:15). "Take heed that no man deceive you; for many will come in my name saying, I am Christ; and they will seduce many. And many false prophets shall rise, and shall seduce many" (Mt. 7:24:4-5 &11).

Christian tradition has seen a long series of false prophets, from Montanus to the Anabaptists[933] all the way to certain contemporary charismatic sects. What are their characteristics? They have no external rules, oppose the Church, her laws and traditions, and claim that inspiration of the Holy Ghost is the only rule of faith and conduct. In this way they replace the hierarchical Church with a prophetic and charismatic Church.

That distinction is irrelevant to contemporary rationalism: there can be no false prophets, because there cannot be true prophets; or if you prefer, all those said to have the prophetic spirit are false prophets. The prophet is depicted as a visionary and irrational character moved by a rather eccentric and fanciful mind.

Conversely, the true prophet is faithful to the Church and to her Magisterium. His first characteristic is prediction; even when revealed by God, this prediction always follows the laws of logic. A divine revelation, or simply the supernatural spirit that nourishes his soul, leads the prophet to understand the inevitability of an event, based on logical premises. A prophet announces a punishment, not necessarily by divine revelation but because he understands how certain human forms of behavior inevitably lead to divine punishment.[934]

---

[933] Cf. RONALD A. KNOX, *Enthusiasm. A Chapter in the History of Religion*, Clarendon Press, Oxford, 1962; FRIEDRICH RECK-MALLECZEWEN, *Il re degli anabattisti*, It. tr., Rusconi, Milano, 1971 sees the history of the Anabaptists of Münster as a precursor of the modern revolutionary utopias, with indirect allusions to Hitler.

[934] CORNELIUS A LAPIDE, *Commentaria in Scripturam Sacram – In Acta Apostolorum*, Ludovicum Vives, Paris, 1877, tome 17, p. 253.

In the *Summa Theologica*[935] Saint Thomas systematically explains the nature of this divine action, which is essentially a supernatural illumination of the prophet's intellect. The Angelic Doctor distinguishes between natural and supernatural prediction. Even angels are capable of making a natural prediction through intellectual assumptions. A supernatural prediction, instead, is directly inspired by God. God speaks by external means, dreams or images that influence the intellect, through the person's interior life, or by directly placing an idea in man's intellect, the safest form of divine intervention because it is directly inspired by God, lowering the possibility of error.

The prophet is not only an announcer of events. He generally also indicates the way to avoid their consequences. The Church does not limit herself to guarding the deposit of faith, but defends it against the errors of the age; the faithful who live according to her spirit can make a penetrating diagnosis of contemporary ills. For this end they must try to find out and interpret the "signs of the times," of which the Gospel speaks (Lk. 12:56), and which today are often misunderstood by certain theological schools.[936]

The prophet is thus the one who knows how to interpret the religious meaning of events and "knows how to read God's design in the fabric of events"[937] under the influence of the Holy Ghost. "No doubt," says Pius XII, "[the circumstances of the times] helped form and bring to light a Benedict, a Bernard, a Dominic, a Francis, and also an Ignatius of Loyola; but their spirit and the momentum of their ardor, which struck 'wherever the resistance was greater,' were not born of the circumstances but of their own hearts and minds, which drew light and boldness from the Spirit of God."[938]

Between the sixteenth and seventeenth centuries, Cornelius a Lapide[939] wrote: "In this our century the spirit of prophecy clearly shone in Saint Charles Borromeo, Saint Francis of Paula, Blessed Louis Bertrand, Saint Ignatius, Saint Francis Xavier, Gaspar the Belgian, Louis

---

[935] *Summa Theologica*, II-IIae, q. 171ff.

[936] GUIDO VIGNELLI, *Fine del mondo? O avvento del Regno di Maria?* Fede e Cultura, Verona, 2013, p. 23.

[937] FABIO CIARDI, *I Fondatori uomini dello Spirito. Per una teologia del carisma di fondatore*, Città Nuova, Roma, 1982, p. 298.

[938] PIUS XII, Speech of April 27, 1941, in *Discorsi e Radiomessaggi*, III, p. 64.

[939] Cornelius a Lapide (Latinization of the Flemish name *Cornelis Cornelissen van den Steen*: 1567-1637), was a great Jesuit exegete, professor of Sacred Scripture at Louvain, and from 1616 in Rome, at the Roman College. He commented on almost all the books of Sacred Scripture.

Gonzaga, Teresa and many others, as can be seen in their lives written by men worthy of faith."[940]

For his part, Charles Cardinal Journet observes:

"The Church…is also enlightened on the state of the world and the movement of minds. The most richly endowed of her children share her miraculous penetration. The divine light enables them to discern the fundamental tendencies of their times; they know how to diagnose the real evils, and prescribe the proper remedies….they go straight to the point with supernatural instinct. Time merely shows how just their vision was. St. Athanasius or St. Cyril, St. Augustine or St. Benedict, Gregory VII, Francis of Assisi, Dominic – these saw, as with prophetical insight, the tendency of their times and the orientation that had to be given to souls. The author of the City of God, the contemplative who eight hundred years ago founded the rule of the Carthusians, St. Thomas who three centuries before the Reformation elucidated the truths that were to be most vigorously contested on the threshold of the new era, Joan of Arc, Teresa of Avila – there you have the true prophets of the Church. They were also saints, though prophecy is distinct, even perhaps separable, from sanctity. But it always occurs, when authentic, in the wake of the apostolic revelation; and as the power of the master sustains and guides the effort of the disciples, authentic prophecies are sustained and guided by the revelation of Christ and His Apostles. 'No epoch,' says St. Thomas, 'has lacked men endowed with the spirit of prophecy, not indeed to introduce some new doctrine of the faith [ad novam doctrinam fidei depromendam], but to direct human acts [ad humanorum actuum directionem]' [II-II, q. 174, a. 6, ad 3]. Those prophets who deviate from this course are false prophets."[941]

The prophecy of Plinio Corrêa de Oliveira was manifested in his ability to interpret the events of his time in the light of the Church's principles, often predicting their developments and consequences. From the Molotov-Ribentropp Pact, made by "enemy brothers," Nazism and Communism, to the rise of Islam after the Second World War, countless of his historical and political analyses were punctually confirmed by events.

Many events predicted by Plinio Corrêa de Oliveira actually took place after his death in 1995: Islamic terrorist attacks in New York, Madrid and London; the specter of the Iranian nuclear threat; the emergence of China and its attempt to reconcile Marxism and the market; the rise of former KGB members in an expansionist and challenging

---

[940] CORNELIUS A LAPIDE, *Commentaria in Scripturam Sacram – In Prophetas Proemium*, tome 11 (1875), p. 43.
[941] CHARLES CARDINAL JOURNET, *The Church of the Word Incarnate*, at https://www.ewtn.com/library/THEOLOGY/chwordin1.htm#00.

Russia; the return of the populist left in Latin America; economic turmoil and a serious risk of depression in the West; appeals for dismantling the capitalist system and establishing a global economic governance; the spread of chaos in the world, and profound cracks opening up within the Church.

However, the prophetism we attribute to the Brazilian leader is found not only in his extraordinary ability to predict events, but especially in the task he undertook to guide them in the context of the decisive clash between the Revolution and the Counter-Revolution. Quoting Saint Thomas Aquinas,[942] Pope John XXIII recalled that "at all times there have not been lacking persons having the spirit of prophecy, not indeed for the declaration of any new doctrine of faith, but for the direction of human acts."[943] This is what characterizes persons entrusted by Divine Providence with a historic mission, as was the case, for example, with Saint Joan of Arc, of whom Plinio writes:

> "She was a prophetess not only because she predicted God's direction – to drive the English from France – but because she carried out what she prophesied: she cast out the English. She was therefore a prophetess in the order of prediction and in the order of fulfillment of what she predicted....Saint Joan of Arc...was arrested and killed, but soon afterward the French ended up by expelling the English." [944]

Plinio Corrêa de Oliveira did not develop new doctrines on faith or morals but sought to orient and direct the action of those who wanted to fight in defense of the Church in an era of Revolution. He always had a supernatural certainty of the final victory of the Counter-Revolution by direct intervention of the Blessed Virgin Mary, Mediatrix of all graces. "Reign of Mary" was the name he gave to this new triumphal historical era for the Church, with the restoration of Christian civilization.

The great theological and historical framework he outlines makes him the leading exponent of Catholic eschatology in the twentieth century.

Catholic Eschatology and Theology of the Apocalypse

Looking at the future is not something only for prophets but for all the baptized, for every Christian has the certainty not only of his own

---

[942] *Summa Theologica*, II-II, q. 174, a. 6, ad 3.

[943] John XXIII, *Radio Message to All Faithful Gathered in Lourdes for the Solemn Closure of the First Centennial of the Apparitions of Mary Immaculate*, February 18, 1959, in *Discorsi*, vol. I, II. p. 158 (pp.154-160).

[944] EXT, January 8, 1993. On the prophetic mission of the French saint, cf. J. B. AYROLES, "La vénérable Jeanne d'Arc, prophétisée et prophétesse," *Revue des Questions historiques*, LXXXIX (1 January 1906), pp. 28-56.

death but also of the end of the world. By the very fact of being a creature of God, the world necessarily tends to a conclusion and an end. "The history of mankind would be nothing but an inexplicable drama, a series of isolated facts without consistency or purpose, if it did not have, sooner or later, its end and outcome,"[945] writes one of the favorite authors of St. Therese the Little Flower, Abbé Charles Arminjon, who dedicated a suggestive book to the *End of the Present World and the Mysteries of the Future Life*.

According to the theology of Christian history, history will end with the Second Coming. The word *parousia* (literally: presence, arrival, coming)[946] is a Greek term for the second coming of Jesus Christ on earth, in the glory of the Father, to render every man according to his works. The Second Coming will mark the end of the world and the full realization of the purpose for which it was created (I Cor. 15:23-28).

Jesus declares that the time of the Parousia is unknown. "But of that day and hour no one knoweth, not the angels of heaven, but the Father alone" (Mt. 24:36). Not knowing the day or hour does not mean ignoring the imminent possibility of that moment. Just as with one's death, Saint Paul invites us to be ever vigilant and to behave "as if the day of the Lord were at hand"[947] (2 Thess. 2:1-2). That is why the Lord recommends: "Watch ye therefore, because you know not the day nor the hour" (Mt. 25:13). Scripture indicates some signs that will precede the preaching and acceptance of the Gospel throughout the world (Mt. 24:3-14; Mk. 16:15-16; Lk. 21:24; Rom. 9:25), the conversion of Israel (Rom. 11:25-27; II Cor. 3:14-15), the great apostasy (II Thess. 2:3; Mt. 24:11-12; Lk. 17:26- 30).

If a Christian does not keep this expectation alive he risks going the way of the "bad and slothful servants" or "foolish virgins" (Lk. 12:35-36) described in Gospel parables. The whole Christian theology of history hinges on this expectation. "No generation can or should exclude the prospect of living the Second Coming as a real possibility,"[948] but a Christian must actually desire it. That is why the Catechism of the Council of Trent admonishes: "Since from the beginning of the world everyone longed for the day when the Lord would take on human flesh,

---

[945] Abbé CHARLES ARMINJON, *Fin du monde présent et mystères de la vie future*, Office central de Lisieux, Lisieux, 1970, p. 12.

[946] J. J. CHAINE, *Parousie*, DTC, XI (1932), cols. 2043-2054; ANTONINO ROMEO, *Parusia*, EC, vol. IX (1952), cols. 875-882; LOUIS CARDINAL BILLOT, S.J., *La Parousie,* Beauchesne, Paris, 1920.

[947] The Fifth Council of the Lateran forbade preachers from setting a determined time for the coming of the Antichrist and the Last Judgment (*Concilius Lateranense V*, Sessio XI of December 19, 1516, in COD, p. 637).

[948] CANDIDO POZO, S.J., *Teologia dell'aldilà,* It. tr., Paoline, Milano, 1994, p. 119.

and placed their hope of deliverance in that day, so also....today we must ardently desire that second day of the Lord, waiting for that blessed hope and glorious appearing of God most high." [949]

In turn, the new *Catechism of the Catholic Church* reaffirms: "...the present time....ushers in the struggles of the last days (1 Jn. 2:18). It is a time of waiting and watching.... This eschatological coming [of Christ] could be accomplished at any moment.... The coming of the glorious Messias is suspended at every moment of history...." [950]

From this perspective, Christian life is an invocation and "expectation" of the Second Coming of Christ as described in the Apocalypse, "with power and glory" (Mt. 24:30) to install His messianic kingdom, defeating the Antichrist, and establishing the heavenly Jerusalem.

Eschatology (from the Greek *eskhaton*, last, and *logos*, study) is the part of theology dealing with the ultimate future realities not only of individual men (the so-called "four last things": death, judgment, Heaven and Hell) but of humanity and the created world. [951] While liberal Protestant theologians sought to make eschatology the very essence of Christianity by emptying it of its doctrinal content, modernists dissolved eschatology, reducing the kingdom of God to a purely moral reality. However, since the beginning of the Christian era, reflections on history and on the end of time occupied much of the writings and discussions. Saint John's book of the Apocalypse, which closes the New Testament and places a seal on Divine Revelation, casts a mysterious light on the future of humanity. [952]

One can legitimately speak of Catholic apocalyptics, if by that we mean theological speculation on the Apocalypse, which is for every Christian the prophetic and inspired book that closes the New Testament. It describes the history of the future in connection with the present, encompassing the conflict of all time between Jesus Christ and His eternal enemy, all the way to "the last persecution which, in the imminence of the last judgment, the Church shall suffer throughout all the earth, that is, the whole city of the devil shall afflict all the City of God." [953] Throughout the Middle Ages apocalyptic literature is not a fruit of lucubrations by sects or isolated intellectuals, but the expression of the

---

[949] *Concilii Tridentini Catechismus*, § 88.

[950] *Catechism of the Catholic Church*, §§ 672-674.

[951] Cf. entries dedicated to eschatology by EUGÈNE MANGENOT, DTC, V (1913), cols. 456-457; FRANCESCO SPADAFORA, *Escatologia*, EC, V, (1950), cols. 544-548; JEAN GALOT, DSp, IV (1960), cols. 1020-1059; A. LEMONNYER, O.P., (*Fin du monde*), DAFC I (1925), cols. 1911-1928.

[952] A. ROMEO, *Apocalisse*, EC, I (1948), cols. 1600-1614.

[953] ST. AUGUSTINE, *De Civitate Dei*, book XX, chap. 11.

expectation of the end of time, rooted in Christianity.[954] All the Fathers of the Church and the great medieval authors have meditated on the Apocalypse, trying to define the "age of the world," i.e., the periods of history between the Creation, the Incarnation, and the Second Coming.[955]

Cardinal Billot comments, "In fact, it suffices to open the Gospel to admit that the Second Coming is indeed the alpha and the omega, the beginning and the end, the first and last word of the preaching of Jesus, which is its key, solution, explanation, reason for being, sanction; in short, it is the supreme event to which all else reports, and without which all the rest collapses and disappears.[956]

Millenarianism and Its Deviations

Millenarianism is found among the well-known deviations from the Christian apocalyptic. Strictly speaking, Millenarianism or Chiliasm[957] is the eschatological doctrine that Jesus Christ will reign on earth with His elect for a period of one thousand years between the first resurrection of the saints, and the second, universal resurrection at the end of the world. This theory, based on a literal interpretation of a passage of the Apocalypse,[958] was supported in the early centuries of the Church by Greek and Latin Fathers such as Saint Irenaeus,[959] Saint Justin,[960] Tertullian,[961] Lactantius,[962] but was later abandoned.

---

[954] BERNARD MCGINN, "Apocalypticism in the Middle Ages: an Historiographical Sketch," *Medieval Studies*, 37 (1973), pp. 252-286; RAUL MANSELLI, "La 'Lectura super Apocalipsim,'" op.cit.; various authors, *L'attesa dell'età nuova nella spiritualità della fine del Medioevo*, Todi, 1962; ROBERTO RUSCONI, *L'attesa della fine. Crisi della società, profezia ed Apocalisse in Italia al tempo del grande scisma d'Occidente (1378-1417)*, Istituto storico Italiano per il Medio Evo, Roma, 1979.

[955] Cf. AUGUSTE LUNEAU, *Histoire du salut chez le Pères de l'Eglise. La doctrine des âges du monde*, Beauchesne, Paris, 1964; R. MANSELLI, "La 'Lectura super Apocalipsim,'" op. cit.

[956] LOUIS CARDINAL BILLOT, S.J., *La Parousie*, p. 10.

[957] On Millenarianism: cf. entries by H. LESÊTRE, DB, IV (1908), cols. 1090-1097; GUSTAVE BARDY, DTC, X (1929), cols. 1700-1763; ANTONIO PIOLANTI, EC, VIII (1952), cols. 1008-1011; JEAN SÉGUY, *Catholicisme,* IX (1982), cols. 158-166; cf. also F. ALCANIZ, *La Iglesia patristica y la Parusia,* Ediciones Paulinas, Buenos Aires, 1962; TED DANIELS, *Millennialism: An International Bibliography*, Garland, New-York-London, 1992; JEAN DELUMEAU, *Mille ans de bonheur. Une histoire du paradis*, Fayard, Paris, 1995; CARLO NARDI, ed., *Il Millenarismo. Testi dei secoli I-II*, Nardini Editore, Fiesole, 1995. L. GRY, *Le millénarisme dans ses origines et son développement,* Paris, 1904.

[958] "And I saw an angel coming down from heaven, having the key of the bottomless pit, and a great chain in his hand. And he laid hold on the dragon the old serpent, which is the devil and Satan, and bound him for a thousand years. And he cast him into the bottomless pit, and shut him up, and set a seal upon him, that he should no more seduce the nations, till the thousand years be finished. And after that, he must be loosed a little time..." (*Apoc.* 20:1-5).

[959] ST. IRENAEUS, *Adversus Haereses*, l. V, 32-35, PG, VII, cols. 1208-1224.

[960] ST. JUSTIN, *Dialoghi con Trifone*, nos. 80-81, PG, VI, cols. 663-667.

[961] TERTULLIAN, *Contra Marcionem*, l. III, chap. 24, PL, II, cols. 355-358.

The Holy Office, in a decree of July 21, 1944, stated that Millenarianism, even in its mitigated form, which teaches that "Christ the Lord, before the final judgment, whether or not preceded by the resurrection of the many just, will come visibly to rule over this world...cannot be taught safely." [963]

Old Millenarianism, not to be confused with Jewish messianism or modern Millenarianism, is a theological hypothesis that has not been supported by the consensus of Catholic Tradition and therefore cannot be taught without imprudence. Saint Augustine, who admits to having experienced the millenarian attraction, firmly rejects the system in *De Civitate Dei*,[964] as does Saint Thomas in the *Summa Theologica*.[965] Cardinal Franzelin makes a comparison between the millenarian opinion of earlier Fathers from the fourth century and the common opinion of the later Fathers. He writes that from the beginning of the fourth century and up to recent times, no Catholic author has recalled that view without criticizing it.[966] "Although Chiliasm has not been declared a heresy," Father Allo says, "the common feeling of theologians of all schools, however, is that it is an 'erroneous' doctrine to which some ancient Fathers could have been dragged by certain conditions of the early age."[967]

---

[962] LATTANZIUS, *De Divinis Institutionibus*, VII, cols. 24 & 26, PL, VI, cols. 808-811 & 813-818.

[963] SUPREMA SACRA CONGREGATIO S. OFFICII. *Responsum de millenarismo* (Chiliasm) of July 11, 1941, AAS, 36 (1944), p. 212; DENZ-H, no. 3839. "The decree therefore affirms that millenarianism (or chiliasm), whether mitigated or spiritual, according to which Christ would visibly return to earth to reign there, before the universal judgment, preceded or not by the resurrection of a certain number of righteous, is a doctrine that cannot be taught without imprudence regarding the faith" (G. GILLEMAN, S.J., "Condamnation du millénarisme mitigé," *Nouvelle Revue Théologique*, 67 (May-June 1945), p. 240 (pp. 239-241). Cf. also SILVIUS ROSADINI, S.J., *Responsum de millenarismo, Adnotationes,* Tip. Pont. Univ. Gregoriana, Roma, 1942. "*Millenarismus, qui publice a Deo revelatus praetenderetur, in Responso S. Officii describitur tamquam consistens in sententia quae tenet Christum corporaliter ante ultimum iudicium in hanc terram reversurum regnandi causa*" (*Periodica*, II (1942), p. 168).

[964] ST. AUGUSTINE, *De Civitate Dei*, lib. XX, chap. 7.

[965] *Summa Theologica*, III, q. 77, art. 1, ad. 4. Cf. also *IV Sent.*, dist. XLIII, q. 1, a. 3, sol. 1, ad 4.

[966] GIOVANNI BATTISTA CARDINAL FRANZELIN (1816-1886), *Tractatus de divina Traditione et scriptura*, S. C. de Propaganda fide, Roma, 1882, XVI, pp. 186-201; Fr. tr., *La Tradition*, prepared by ABBÉ JEAN-MICHEL GLAIZE, *Courrier de Rome*, Versailles, 2012, pp. 241-255 ; thesis XVI, no. 334 (p. 243).

[967] E. B. ALLO, O.P., *Saint Jean, L'apocalypse*, J. Gabalda et C., Paris, 1933, 3rd ed., p. 323.

Joachim of Flora and Joachimism

There has been much discussion about the Calabrian Abbot Joachim of Flora.[968] The multiplication of Joachimite studies did not help to shed light on this figure, which remains shrouded in an aura of ambiguity.[969] He developed a theology of history that distinguishes between an age of the Father, which began with Adam, an age of the Son, fulfilled with Christ, and a third age, of the Holy Spirit. In the first age, the life of profane man was affirmed; in the second age, priestly life flourished; in the third, announced by Saint Benedict, the spiritual life of monks would have its perfect flowering.

The Third Age – the Reign of the Spirit, following those of the Father and of the Son – will be a kingdom of achieved perfection established on earth, in history. However, what seems heterodox in this view of history or "posteriority" is not the Trinitarian division of history or the expectation of a "new age," but the denial, if there was one, of the unity of the Divine Persons, the perpetuity of the Gospel of Christ and of the salvific mission of the Church in that "third age."

Cardinal Journet explains: "The error is not in distinguishing the age of the Spirit succeeding the age of the Son. It is, as in the case of the Montanists and later the [Franciscan] 'spirituals' of the Middle Ages, to poorly understand when and how that succession takes place." What is needed, Cardinal Journet explains, is to understand the real meaning of the mystery of Pentecost. "The Holy Spirit comes, not to abolish the age of the Son but rather to extend its effects to the entire world. And since the purpose of the age of the Son was to bring forth with Christ the fullness of grace, so the age of the Spirit will have the purpose of making that fullness overflow to men, who will manifest their unsuspected

---

[968] On Joachim of Flora (1130-1202) and Joachimism, bibliograpy is abundant. Cf. E. JORDAN, *Le Joachimisme*, DTC, VIII/2 (1925), cols. 1437-1458 ; HERBERT GRUNDMAN, *Studien über Joachim von Floris*, Lipsia, 1927; MARJORIE REEVES, BEATRICE HIRSCH-REICH, *The Figure of Joachim of Fiore*, Clarendon Press, Oxford, 1972; M. REEVES, *The influence of Prophecy in the Later Middle Ages; A study in Joachimism*, Oxford University Press, Oxford, 1969; DELNO C. WEST and SANDRA ZIMDARS-SWARTZ, *Joachim of Fiore: A Study in Perception and History*, Indiana University Press, Bloomington, 1983; BERNARD McGINN, *L'abate calabrese. Gioacchino da Fiore nella storia del pensiero occidentale*, It. tr., Marietti, Genova, 1990, and the numerous studies dedicated by Msgr. GIOVANNI DI NAPOLI to the Calabrian abbot: "La teologia trinitaria di Gioacchino da Fiore," in *Divinitas*, no. 3 (October 1976); ID., "L'ecclesiologia di Gioacchino da Fiore," in *Doctor communis*, no. 3 (September-December 1979); ID., "Teologia e storia in Gioacchino, in Storia e messaggio in Gioacchino da Fiore," *Atti del Congresso Internazionale di Studi Gioachimiti* (19-23 September 1979), Centro di Studi Gioachimiti, S. Giovanni in Fiore, 1980, pp. 71-150.

[969] GIOACCHINO DA FIORE, *Sull'Apocalisse*, prepared by Andrea Tagliapietra, di Feltrinelli, Milano, 1994; *I sette sigilli/De septem sigillis* (edited by Alfredo Gatto), with an essay by Andrea Tagliapietra, Mimesis, Milano, 2013.

potential the more they become differentiated in space, and the longer they succeed in time."[970]

One should not confuse the thought of Joachim of Flora with Joachimism, which is a current as heterodox as it is heterogeneous and complex. Among the many scholars of Joachimism, we should mention the names of Eric Voegelin[971] and Father Henri de Lubac.[972] Voegelin sees in Joachimism a fledgling "immanentization" of Christian eschatology. De Lubac, who devoted two volumes of over a thousand pages to the influence of the Calabrian monk, states that Millenarianism is incomparably more limited than Joachimism because, unlike the latter, it does not expect a substantial transfiguration of the Church and Christianity, but only of the world, on the natural level.

Joachim of Flora enjoyed great prestige between the nineteenth and twentieth centuries, when he was re-evaluated in the context of an intellectual movement to rediscover medieval heterodoxy. Romantic philosophy rediscovered the Calabrian abbot, attributing to him the myth of the "Ecclesia spiritualis" and the "Kingdom of the Spirit," which would see the end of the current ecclesiastical order and the disappearance of the Papacy. Thus, Ernst Benz attributes to him the creation of a "Johannine Christianity" that managed to dominate minds and especially affect the Russian religious philosophy,[973] while Marjorie Reeves and Werwick Gould traced the history of those intellectuals attracted by esotericism, who saw Joachim de Flora as a prophet of the new "religion of humanity."[974]

In 1957, Norman Cohn published *The Fanatics of the Apocalypse,* in which he states that elements typical of medieval millenarianism are present in the totalitarian movements of the twentieth century, and that the way of thinking of Hitler, Rosenberg, Marx and others was eschatological and apocalyptic. The authors cited, however, run the risk of attributing to Joachimist millenarianism the paternity of all forms of Christian eschatology. As a matter of fact, Joachim of Flora was only one of many, and certainly one of the most controversial voices of Christian

---

[970] CARDINAL JOURNET, *L'Eglise du Verbe Incarné,* I, p. 290-291.

[971] ERIC VOEGELIN, *La nuova scienza politica,* It. tr., Borla, Torino, 1968, with an Introduction by A. DEL NOCE; ID., *Il Mito del mondo nuovo. Saggi nei movimenti rivoluzionari del nostro tempo,* It. tr., Rusconi, Milano, 1970.

[972] HENRI DE LUBAC, S.J., *La posterità intellettuale di Gioacchino da Fiore,* It. tr., Jaca Book, Milano, 1981-1984. Father de Lubac, who sought to trace Joachimism through the centuries, states that "for the most part, the history of Joachim's spiritual posterity is the history of the betrayals of his thought" (vol. I, p. 84).

[973] ERNST BENZ, *Evolution and Christian Hope; Man's Concept of the Future from the Early Fathers to Teilhard de Chardin,* London, 1967, p. 46.

[974] M. REEVES-WARWICK GOULD, *Joachim of Fiore and the Myth of the Eternal Evangel in the Nineteenth Century,* Clarendon Press, Oxford, 1987.

eschatology. One should note, however, that according to Gian Luca Podestà, a scholar on the Calabrian abbot, "more than in specialized literature, the idea of a Millenarianist and progressivist Joachim was established in summaries by K. Löwith, J. Taubes, and H. de Lubac with regard to the interpretations of the history of the Christian West, and centered on the nexus between apocalyptic and secularization."[975]

It is certain, however, that the fourteenth century saw the beginning of an apocalyptic that represents the antithesis of the theology of Christian history. Modern Millenarianism developed with the left wing of the Protestant Revolution, beginning with Thomas Müntzer and the Anabaptists, and proposing an earthly revolution to establish the Kingdom of God strictly in the temporal sphere. The humanist idea of "rebirth," like that of the Protestant *"Reformatio,"*[976] expresses the eschatological expectation of a new age characterized by the end of the Catholic Church and the Papacy, at times identified with the Antichrist. More than Millenarianism, it is a "Messianism" that permeates the origins of modern philosophy and flows into the French Revolution,[977] while its spiritualized version gives rise to movements as different from one other as Adventists, Mormons, Jehovah's Witnesses, Pentecostals, and the New Age.

The Trinitarian division of history produced within an immanentist philosophy is present in the theory of Auguste Comte[978] on three successive stages: theological, metaphysical, and scientific; in Hegelian dialectics on thesis, antithesis and synthesis; in Marxist dialectics on bourgeoisie, proletariat, and classless society; and on the National Socialist symbol of the "Third Reich."

---

[975] GIAN LUCA POTESTÀ, *Il tempo dell'Apocalisse. Vita di Gioacchino da Fiore*, Laterza, Roma-Bari, 2004, p. 7.

[976] On the Protestant apocalyptic, above all among the English sects of the seventeenth century, cf. BERNARD S. CAPP, *Fifth Monarchy Men: a Study in Seventeenth Century English Millenialism*, Bowman and Littlefield, Totowa, 1972; ERIC RUSSEL CHAMBERLIN, *Anti-Christ and the Millennium*, Saturday Review Press, New York, 1975; WILLIAM B. BALL, *A Great Expectation: Eschatological Thought in English Protestantism*, E. J. Brill, Leiden, 1975; PAUL CHRISTIANSON, *Reformers in Babylon: English Apocalyptic Visions from the Reformation to the Eve of the Civil War*, University of Toronto Press, Toronto, 1978; CATHERINE FIRTH, *The Apocalyptic Tradition in Reformation Britain 1530-1645*, Oxford University Press, New York, 1979; ROBIN BRUCE BARNES, *Prophecy and Gnosis: Apocalypticism in the Wake of the Lutheran Reformation*, Stanford University Press, Stanford, 1988.

[977] Cf. RENZO DE FELICE, "Note e ricerche sugli 'Illuminati' e il misticismo rivoluzionario (1789-1800)," *Storia e Letteratura*, Roma, 1960; CLARKE GARRETT, *Respectable Folly: Millenarians and the French Revolution in France and England*, John Hopkins University Press, London, 1975; REGINALD GRÉGOIRE, "Rapporti tra apocalittica medievale e messianismi laici odierni," in *Storia e messaggio in Gioacchino da Fiore*, op. cit., pp. 225-244.

[978] Auguste Comte (1798-1857), author of *Système de politique positive* (4 vols., Paris, 1851-1854), in 1848 founded a kind of church that recognized humanity as the new divinity, and himself as its high priest.

Its opposition to Catholic theology could not be clearer:[979] Christian eschatology seeks to sanctify society and history, ordering them to God; secular messianism seeks an implicit deification of man and of social structures to achieve the "Kingdom of God" on earth in its absolute perfection.

Saint Hildegard of Bingen's Glimpse of the Future

If the voice of Joachim of Flora is fraught with ambiguities and dangers, from the depths of the Middle Ages comes to us the crystalline voice of a genuinely orthodox prophetess, Saint Hildegard of Bingen,[980] whose teachings are recalled by great counter-revolutionary authors such as Father Ramière and Msgr. Delassus.

Hildegard was born in 1098 in Bermesheim, Germany, and died in 1179. She founded near Bingen two monasteries of which she was abbess, and maintained correspondence with superiors of monasteries, emperors, bishops, Pope Eugene III, and Saint Bernard of Clairvaux. Since her childhood, the Lord granted her a series of visions, the contents of which she dictated to the monk Volmar, her secretary and spiritual counselor, and to a nun. In a letter to Saint Bernard, the mystic from the Rhine confesses: "The vision fascinates my whole being: I do not see with the eyes of the body, but the mysteries appear to me in the spirit... I know the profound meaning of what is said in the Psalms, the Gospels and in other books shown to me in the vision. This burns like a flame in my heart and soul and teaches me to profoundly understand the text." [981]

The main works of Saint Hildegard are *Scivias, Liber vitae meritorum,* and *Liber divinorum operum.* In these works she describes the events of the history of Salvation from the creation of the world to the end of time, and in particular the advent of the Antichrist and the times preceding it. In the twelfth century, Pope Eugene III recognized the orthodoxy of her doctrine, and the Christian people constantly celebrated her holiness. Benedict XVI canonized her on May 10, 2012, and on October 7 of that year proclaimed her a Doctor of the universal Church,[982]

---

[979] On the modern utopia, cf. WALTER NIGG, *Das ewige Reich*, Artemis, Zürich 1954; E. GILSON, *Les métamorphoses, op. cit.*; THOMAS MOLNAR, *Utopia: The Perennial Heresy*, op. cit.; BRONISLAW BACZKO, *L'utopia*, It. tr., Einaudi, Torino, 1979

[980] MARIANNA SCHRADER, *Hildegarde de Bingen*, DSp, VII (1969), cols. 505-521; BERNADETTE VERHAGGE, BSS, III Appendix (2009), cols. 632-640; CRISTINA SICCARDI *Ildegarda di Bingen. Mistica e scienziata*, Torino, Ed. Paoline, 2012

[981] ST. HILDEGARD OF BINGEN, *Epistolarium pars prima I-XC:* CCCM 91.

[982] BENEDICT XVI, Apostolic Letter of October 7, 2012, *Insegnamenti*, VIII, 2 (2012), pp. 363-372.

asserting that her message "appears extraordinarily relevant in the contemporary world" and "serves as a guide to *homo viator.*"[983]

In her *Liber vitae meritorum,* Saint Hildegard speaks of a "feminine time"[984] in which faith will decline, drawing God's justice: "After justice has addressed its lament to the chief judge, He, accepting its words of indictment, will take revenge by judging with his righteous judgment the enemies of righteousness, and by allowing them to be plundered by their tyrannical enemies."[985]

In one of her visions, however, the Lord announces a future age in which "laws of justice and peace will be fulfilled that are so new and unknown that men will marvel at them and say they never heard of such things. And just as peace preceded the coming of the Son of God, so also will they be given peace before the day of judgment, but will be unable to fully enjoy it for fear of the future judgment; and they will invoke Almighty God to justify them in the universal faith; and even the Hebrews will be filled with joy and affirm the arrival of the One whose coming they still do not recognize. In fact, the peace that preceded the advent of the Incarnation of the Son will come to full perfection in those days, for mighty men and great prophets will appear; and all seeds of justice will flourish in the sons and daughters of men, as the prophet my servant said, fulfilling my will: 'In that day the bud of the Lord shall be in magnificence and glory, and the fruit of the earth shall be high, and a great joy to them that shall have escaped of Israel' (Is 4:2)."[986]

These prophetic visions confirm others by many souls elevated to the honor of the altars such as Blessed Catherine Emmerick[987] and Blessed Ana Maria Taïgi.[988] In his biography of Blessed Taigi, Carlo Cardinal

---

[983] Idem, p. 370.

[984] ST. HILDEGARD OF BINGEN, *Il libro delle opere divine,* prepared by MARTA CRISTIANI and MICHELE PEREIRA, Arnoldo Mondadori Editore, Milan, 2014, p. 1057 (fifth vision of part three).

[985] Idem, pp. 1058-1059.

[986] IDEM, pp. 1067-1068 (fifth vision of part three).

[987] Ana Catarina Emmerick (1774-1824), a German Augustinian nun who received the stigmata and was favored by mystical gifts, was beatified by John Paul II on October 3, 2004. From 1819 until her death, she carefully dictated her visions to the poet Clement Brentano (1778-1842), who later made a sincere conversion to Catholicism. He annotated her revelations, comparable to those of the Spanish Conceptionist nun Maria de Agreda (1602-1655), on sixteen thousand large pages.

[988] Ana Maria Taigi (Anna Maria Giannetti, 1769-1837), born in Siena, lived in Rome from age six until her death. She married Domingos Taigi and belonged to the Third Order of the Holy Trinity. She was beatified by Pope Benedict XV on May 30, 1920. Privileged by spiritual gifts and visions, including a bright sun that shone before her eyes for forty-seven years and in which she saw everything that happened in the world and the state of souls, living and dead. Her words were gathered by her spiritual director, Msgr. Rafael Natali. Some of his volumes are preserved in the archives of St. Charles Church in Rome, in the care of the Trinitarian Fathers; from those volumes Giovanna Cossu Merendino extracted a volume titled *The Mercy*

Solatti[989] recalls that "almost all the heroic souls who shone in Rome in the first half of the nineteenth century, from Venerable Pallotti[990] to Blessed Del Bufalo,[991] Venerable Clausi[992] to Venerable Canori-Mora,[993] prophesied how, after the storm forming over the Church in their time, and after the persecution afflicting the Papacy, there would come a bright, solemn and complete triumph of Catholicism.[994] Msgr. Henri Delassus collected many of these prophecies in his work, showing how the idea of a divine punishment accompanied by hope in an era of triumph and renewal of the Church has been part and parcel of Christian tradition.[995] The work of Plinio Corrêa de Oliveira fits right into this eschatolgical Catholic tradition.

of God toward His Creatures: Blessed Anna Maria Giannetti Taigi (Vatican Press, Vatican City, 2005).

[989] CARLO CARDINAL SALOTTI, La Beata Anna Maria Taigi secondo la storia e la critica (Libreria Editrice Religiosa, Roma, 1922, p.. 337). Cardinal Carlo Salotti (1870-1947) was Dean of the Pontifical Urbanian University and Prefect of the Sacred Congregation of Rites.

[990] VICENTE PALLOTTI (1795-1850), founder of the Catholic Congregation and Apostolic Society, was proclaimed a saint by John XXIII on January 20, 1963.

[991] GASPAR DEL BUFALO (1786-1837), founder of the Congregation of Missionaries of the Precious Blood, was canonized by Pope Pius XII on June 12, 1954.

[992] VEN. BERNARDO CLAUSI (1789-1949) of the Order of Minims, was a religious in southern Italy well known for his virtues and charisms.

[993] ISABEL CANORI MORA (1774-1825), mother of a family, lay member of the Third Order of the Holy Trinity (Trinitarians), was beatified by John Paul II on April 24, 1994. Cf. La mia vita nel cuore della Trinità. Diario della beata Elisabetta Canori Mora, sposa e madre (1774-1825), Libreria Editrice Vaticana, Vatican City, 1996. Cf. also Paola Giovetti, Madri e mistiche. Anna Maria Taigi ed Elisabetta Canori Mora, Edizioni Paoline, Cinisello Balsamo, 1991.

[994] CARLO CARDINAL SALOTTI, La Beata Anna Maria Taigi, p. 337.

[995] MSGR. HENRI DELASSUS, Il problema dell'ora presente, vol. I, pp. 75-76, recalls the prophetic words of Saint Catherine of Siena and Saint Hildegard on the future destiny of mankind.

CHAPTER II

TOWARD THE REIGN OF MARY

Reign of Christ and Reign of the Antichrist

A certain point of the Catholic faith is that the history of the human race will end with a universal tyranny of evil known as the Reign of the Antichrist.[996]

The Scriptures prophesy a general apostasy and the manifestation of the Man of Sin, the "son of perdition," the Antichrist, "who opposes, and is lifted up above all that is called God, or that is worshipped, so that he sits in the temple of God, showing himself as if he were God" (2 Thess. 2:3-12). The Antichrist, Msgr. Antonino Romeo says, "is the archenemy of Christ" who at the end of time will "seduce many Christians with satanic wonders and tricks" before he is annihilated by Christ in His Second Coming. The prophetic picture of the struggle between Christ and the Antichrist is contained in Chapter 12 of the Apocalypse and is part of Revelation, which was entrusted to the Church.[997]

Christian eschatologists wonder whether the Church will know an age of decadence or progress before the era of the Antichrist. Cornelius a Lapide, who can be considered the greatest scholar among the interpreters of the Holy Scriptures, and who collects all the exegetical tradition prior to the seventeenth century, believes that the end of time will not come before Christendom is not only propagated worldwide but also publicly organized to encompass the whole earth and fulfill the prophecy that

---

[996] "In the Western tradition of the philosophy of history," a well-known Catholic philosopher observes, "the end of time bears this name: dominion of the Antichrist" (JOSEF PIEPER, *Sulla fine del tempo*, It. tr., Morcelliana, Brescia, 1959, p. 113). About the "end times," cf. also ALFREDO SÁENZ, S.J., *El fin de los tiempos y seis autores modernos*, Ediciones Gladius, Buenos Aires, 1996.

[997] A. ROMEO, *Anticristo*, EC, I (1948), cols. 1433-1442; A. LEMONNYER, O.P., *Antechrist*, DAFC, I (1925), cols. 146-150; V. ERMONI, *Antéchrist*, DTC, I (1930), cols. 1361-1365; BÉDA RIGAUX O.F.M., *L'Antéchrist et l'opposition au royaume messianique dans l'Ancien et le Nouveu Testament*, J. Duculot, Louvain, 1932.

"there will be only one Church and one shepherd."[998] The Kingdom of Christ on earth will be preceded by that of the Antichrist. A theology of history very different from Millenarianism developed above all in the nineteenth century from ultramontane and counter-revolutionary thought, namely, that of the social kingship of Christ. It posits that Jesus Christ, King of History, will triumph over His enemies before the end of the world and His second coming in the Parousia.[999]

The doctrine of the social kingship of Christ emerged and developed in the wake of devotion to the Sacred Heart.[1000] This devotion appeared in the Middle Ages with veneration of the Wound made by the lance, and found in Saint John Eudes,[1001] its first great propagator. After the revelations of Paray-le-Monial, the Jesuits became its tireless promoters.[1002] In 1673, Jesus asked Saint Margaret Mary Alacoque,[1003] a Visitation sister at Paray-le Monial, to spread the devotion to His Sacred Heart throughout the Church, and indicated to her the Jesuit Claude de la Colombiere as a contributor to that work.[1004]

In an era of decadence and spiritual coldness such as the second half of the seventeenth century, the purpose of that devotion was to ignite the love of Jesus in souls, corresponding to the infinite love He has for us. "Behold the Heart that so loved men," Jesus said to Saint Margaret Mary, later promising: "My heart shall expand itself to shed in abundance the influence of Its Divine Love upon those who honor me." Thus was born,

---

[998] CORNELIUS A LAPIDE, *Commentaria in Mattheum*, cap. XXIV, 14.

[999] HENRI RAMIÈRE, S.J., *Les ésperances de l'Eglise,* Le Puy, 1862, pp. 638-641.

[1000] On devotion to the Sacred Heart, the best work is still that by Father AUGUSTIN HAMON, S.J., *Histoire de la dévotion au Sacré-Cœur*, Beauchesne, Paris, 1923-1940, 5 vols. Cf. also JEAN-VINCENT BAINVEL, S.J., *La dévotion au Sacré-Cœur*, Beauchesne, Paris, 1931; DANIELE MENOZZI, *Sacro Cuore. Un culto tra devozione interiore e restaurazione cristiana della società*, Viella, Roma, 2001. Cf. also HELVECIO ALVES, "O Escudo do Sagrado Coração de Jesus," *Catolicismo*, no. 630 (July 2003), pp. 26-35.

[1001] John Eudes (1601-1680), born in Normandy, was a disciple of Cardinal Berulle and superior of the Oratory at Caen. In 1641 he founded the order of Our Lady of Charity and in 1643 the Congregation of Jesus and Mary. He was beatified by Saint Pius X on August 25, 1909 and canonized by Pius XI on May 31, 1925. Cf. ANGE LE DORÉ, C.J.M., *Les Sacrés Cœurs et le vénérable Jean Eudes, premier apôtre de leur culte,* 2 vols., Lamulle & Poisson, Paris, 1891; Fr. VENCESLAUS JURGA, *La dévotion au Coeur Immaculé de Marie d'après et dans les oeuvres de saint Jean Eudes et l'enseignement posterieur de l'Eglise,* Dissertatio ad lauream apud Angelicum, Typis Poliglottis Vaticanis, Città del Vaticano, 1956.

[1002] On devotion to the Sacred Heart and the Society of Jesus: E. LETIERCE, S.J., *Etude sur le Sacré-Coeur*, 2 vols., Vic et Amat, Paris, 1891-1892, the second volume of which is dedicated to *Le Sacré Coeur et la Compagnie de Jésus*; and J. DE GUIBERT, S.J., *La spiritualité de la Compagnie de Jésus*, op. cit., pp. 387-396.

[1003] Saint Margaret Mary Alacoque (1647-1690), Visitation religious at the monastery of Paray-le-Monial, was canonized by Pope Benedict XV in 1920.

[1004] Saint Claude de la Colombiere (1641-1682), Jesuit, superior of the house of Paray-le-Monial, was spiritual director of Margaret Mary Alacoque. Pope John Paul II canonized him in 1992.

inspired by the saint, the feast of the Sacred Heart, giving rise to the pious practice of the Nine First Fridays of the month.

Of great importance among the heavenly messages received by Saint Margaret Mary is one she conveyed on June 17, 1689 to Mother Marie-Françoise de Saumaise, in Dijon, with instructions to send it on to the King of France, Louis XIV. In it, the Sacred Heart asked the sovereign to "reign in his palace, be painted on his standards and engraved in his arms, to make them victorious over all his enemies, casting down at his feet those proud heads to make him triumphant over all the enemies of Holy Church."[1005]

The message went unheeded, and 150 years later the French Revolution broke out. In 1792, when Louis XVI lost his throne and was imprisoned in the Temple, he placed in the hands of Eudist Father Hébert, his confessor, a vow to place his kingdom under the protection of the Sacred Heart if he were freed.[1006] That vow, which circulated clandestinely, had a profound repercussion in Catholic ambiences at the time. The Sacred Heart, embroidered next to the Bourbon fleur-de-lys, was the symbol of the Catholic and Royal Army of the Vendée, whose insurrection could hardly be understood without going to the roots of this popular piety which caused "all peasants to have, out of devotion and without anyone having ordered them, a Sacred Heart embroidered on their attire and a rosary through the buttonhole of their lapel."[1007]

Between the nineteenth and twentieth centuries the devotion of the Sacred Heart developed in the Church thanks to the impulse of souls like Blessed Mary of the Divine Heart.[1008] The Popes approved and disseminated it, especially Leo XIII, with the encyclical *Annum Sacrum*, of May 25, 1889; Pope Pius XI with his Encyclical *Miserentissimus,* of May 8, 1928; and Pius XII with *Haurietis Aquas,* of May 15, 1956.

The Reign of Christ According to Father Henri Ramière

Devotion to the Sacred Heart and the theology of the social kingship of Christ had in the nineteenth century a fiery speaker in Father Henri

---

[1005] *Vie et œuvres de la bienheureuse Marguerite Marie Alacoque*, Poussielgue, Paris, 1915, II, p. 436.

[1006] François-Louis Hebert (1735-1792), coadjutor to the Superior General of Eudists, in 1790 he succeeded, as confessor of the king, Abbé Poupart, who had sworn allegiance to the civil Constitution. Father Hebert exerted a profound influence not only on the sovereign but also on Madame Elisabeth and Madame Royale (cf. P. J. B. ROVOLT, *Les martyrs eudistes*, J. de Gigord, Paris, 1926).

[1007] *Mémoires de M.me la M.se de la Rochejaquelein*, H. Dudin, Paris, 1883, I, p. 144.

[1008] Mary of the Divine Heart (Maria Droste zu Vischering: 1863-1899), German religious of the Congregation of the Sisters of Our Lady of Charity of the Good Shepherd, promoted the consecration of the world to the Sacred Heart of Jesus, made by Leo XIII in 1899. She was beatified by Paul VI on November 1, 1975.

Ramière, SJ.[1009]   Father Ramière was director of the Apostleship of Prayer, founded by his colleague, Father François-Xavier Gautrelet,[1010] and of the newsletter titled *Messenger of the Sacred Heart of Jesus*. Beginning in 1861 he wrote a series of profound reflections in *The Reign of Jesus Christ in History*.[1011]   He argued that the social kingship of Jesus Christ had to be realized on earth before the second royal return of Christ, the Parousia. "The great law of history, that is, the supreme objective the Divine will has proposed to individuals, society and to the whole of humanity, is the establishment of the Kingdom of Christ," that is, "the perfect likeness and complete submission of individuals, peoples and all mankind to the Man-God, sovereign model of all perfections and sovereign Lord of all things."[1012]

The diffusion of devotion to the Sacred Heart was the main tool to stop the revolutionary process and establish the Reign of Christ. In the book titled *The Hopes of the Church*,[1013] Father Ramière shows the close link between the cult of the Sacred Heart and the social kingship of Jesus Christ to be established on earth by the Church. In a later book dedicated to *The Roman Doctrines on Liberalism*, he clearly defined: "By social kingship of Christ we mean the right that the God-Man possesses, and with Him the Church, which represents Him on earth, to exercise His divine authority in the moral order on societies as well as individuals, and the obligation this right imposes on societies to recognize the authority of Jesus Christ and the Church in their collective existences and action."[1014]

His colleague, Father Paul Dudon, writes about Father Ramière: "The professor at the Catholic Institute of Toulouse, director of the *Messenger of the Sacred Heart of Jesus* and editor of *Etudes*, theologian of Vatican I, preacher and spiritual director, are only one and the same

---

[1009] Henry Ramière (1821-1884), born in Castres, diocese of Toulouse, joined the Society of Jesus in 1839, was ordained in 1847, and assigned to teaching. He attended the First Vatican Council as the theologian of Most Rev. Joseph-Armand Giguoux, Bishop of Beauvais, and published in Rome a *Bulletin of the Council* (36 issues from December 16, 1869 to August 20, 1870) in which one can follow the controversy over infallibility, which he staunchly defended. On him cf. *L'Eglise catholique et les libertés modernes*, Lecoffre, Paris, 1879; *L'Ecole de la réforme sociale*, A. Mame et fils, Tours, 1875; *Le cœur de Jésus et la divinisation du chrétien*, Toulouse, 1891; *Le Regne social du S. Cœur*, Toulouse, 1895. Cf. PIERRE VALLIN, DSP, XIII (1988), cols. 63-70 ; ID. "Le père Henri Ramière (1821-1884)," in *Bulletin de littérature ecclésiastique*, no. 86 (1985), pp. 24-34; PAUL GALTIER, DTC, 13 (1937), cols. 1649-1651; Charles PARRA, S.J., ed., et al, *Le père Henri Ramière de la Compagnie de Jésus,* Apostolat de la prière, Toulouse, 1934; D. MENOZZI, *Sacro Cuore cit.*, pp. 108-169.
[1010] François-Xavier Gautrelet (1807-1886), Jesuit spiritual writer, authored a *Manuel de la dévotion au Sacré Cœur* (Lyon, 1850), which was reorganized by Father Ramière in his book *L'apostolat de la prière* (Lyon, 1861).
[1011] The book contains written notes from his course at the University of Toulouse.
[1012] HENRI RAMIÈRE, S.J., *O Reino de Jesus Cristo na História*, p. 185.
[1013] ID., *Les Espérances de l'Eglise*, Perisse, Paris, 1862.
[1014] ID., *Les doctrines romaines et le libéralisme*, Lecoffre, Paris, 1870, p. XIV.

man devoted to the reign of Jesus Christ."[1015] "No one at his time had preached devotion to the Heart of Jesus with equal enthusiasm, constancy, fullness of doctrine and success. His initiative had, so to speak, obliged Pius IX to consecrate the Catholic world to the Divine Heart."[1016]

In the same years, two laymen, Alexandre Legentil and Hubert Rohault de Fleury, took the initiative to promote a national vow to build in Paris a church dedicated to the Sacred Heart.[1017] Cardinal Joseph Hippolyte Guibert, archbishop of Paris, on January 18, 1872 approved the text of the vow and chose the hill of Montmartre as the place for building the vowed temple. On July 24, 1873, the National Assembly voted for the bill declaring the chosen place "of public interest."[1018] The mosaic in the choir of the basilica represents the homage of the Church of France to the Sacred Heart. Its base shows the inscription: "To the Sacred Heart of Jesus Christ, from penitent, devout and grateful France." The historian Daniele Menozzi emphasizes that the "goal was not to restore the monarchy or exalt a Catholic country but to establish throughout the earth a social reign directed by the Church, to which all nations of the earth, with their various political organizations, were called." [1019]

In 1874, Gabriel García Moreno[1020] consecrated the Republic of Ecuador to the Sacred Heart. For the first time a head of state and his government formally proclaimed the social kingship of Christ.

The Kingdom of Christ in Papal Teaching

The condemnation of State religious neutrality by Leo XIIII in the encyclicals *Diuturnum illud*[1021] of June 29, 1881, *Immortale Dei*[1022] of November 1, 1885, and *Libertas,*[1023] of June 20, 1888 is an implicit affirmation of the social kingship of Christ. From the beginning of his

---

[1015] PAUL DUDON, S.J., *L'homme d'Action*, in Charles PARRA, S.J., op. cit., p. 295.

[1016] IDEM, p. 379.

[1017] Cf. ALFRED VAN DEN BRULE, *Le Sacré-Cœur de Montmartre. Hubert Rohault de Fleury*, Téqui, Paris, 2000.

[1018] A. HAMON, *Histoire de la dévotion au Sacré-Cœur*, V, pp. 57-58. The first stone was laid on June 16, 1875 and the first Mass was celebrated in the cript by Cardinal Guibert on April 21, 1881. Cf. JACQUES BENOIST, *Le Sacré-Cœur de Montmartre, de 1870 à nos jours*, Les Editions Ouvrières, Paris, 1992, I, pp. 270-301.

[1019] D. MENOZZI, *Sacro Cuore*, p. 153.

[1020] Gabriel García Moreno (1821-1875), President of the Republic of Ecuador for two mandates (1861-1875 and 1869-1875), was assassinated by Freemasonry *in odium fidei* in front of the cathedral of Quito. Cf. AUGUSTIN BERTHE, *García Moreño, Président de l'Equateur, vengeur et martyr du droit chrétien (1821-1875)*, 2 vols., Rétaux-Bray, Paris, 1887, and the imposing biography in 10 vols. by SEVERO GOMEZ JURADO, S.J., *Vida de García Moreño*, Romlacio Editor, Cuenca-Quito, 1954-1971.

[1021] LEO XIII, Enc. *Diuturnum Illud* of June 29, 1881, EE, *Leone XIII*, pp. 170-195.

[1022] LEO XIII, Enc. *Immortale Dei* of November 1, 1885, EE, *Leone XIII*, pp. 330-375.

[1023] LEO XIII, Enc. *Libertas* of June 20, 1888, EE, *Leone XIII*, pp. 432-477.

pontificate, Saint Pius X adhered to the same position.   And in the Encyclical *E supremi apostolatus*[1024] he sums up his program with the motto *Instaurare omnia in Christo* (Eph. 1:10): "For other foundation no man can lay, but that which is laid; which is Christ Jesus" (I Cor. 3:11). "...Hence it follows that to restore all things in Christ and to lead men back to submission to God is one and the same aim.   To this, then, it behooves Us to devote Our care – to lead mankind back under the dominion of Christ."[1025]   The great perspective of the social kingship of Christ comes to Pius X thanks largely to the work of Cardinal Pie.[1026]

Beginning in 1921, Father Enrico Rosa, director of *Civiltà Cattolica* and a disciple and fellow priest of Father Ramière,[1027] published a series of articles on the social kingship of Jesus Christ.[1028]   He could see two opposing tendencies in the world: into the first flowed communist, socialist and anarchist movements and all those, even Catholics, who diminished the rights of Christ on society. This current was expressed in the cry *"Nolumus hunc regnare super nos"*: "We do not want Him to reign over us" (Lk. 19:14). The second current, composed of those who loved and served the Church, expressed its program of action in the motto, *"Adveniat regnum tuum,"* "Let Thy kingdom come" (Mt. 6:10), to which many Catholics added *"Adveniat per Mariam,"* "Let it come through Mary."

"Let thy kingdom come, a kingdom of truth and justice, sincerity and love," Father Rosa wrote, so that Christ may reign "not only upon individuals but over families and nations given to Him as eternal legacy: an eminent sovereignty that transcends every political motive, all earthly considerations, but is not confined only to the sanctuary of individual conscience or to the private life of the family, but is destined to shine in the bright light of civil society."[1029]

[1024] PIUS X, Enc. *E Supremi Apostolatus* of October 4, 2003, EE, *Pio X,* p. 21-39.

[1025] Idem, p. 27.

[1026] On Edouard-Louis Cardinal Pie (1815-1880) and the social kingship of Christ, cf. above all the studies by ETIENNE CATTA, *La doctrine politique et sociale du cardinal Pie*, Nouvelles Editions Latines, Paris, 1959; THEOTIME DE SAINT-JUST, *La royauté sociale de Notre-Seigneur Jésus-Christ, d'après le cardinal Pie*, Ed. Sainte Jeanne d'Arc, Chiré en Montreuil, 1988; ALFREDO SAENZ, *El cardinal Pie; lucidez y coraje al servicio de la verdad*, Buenos Aires, 1987. *"I read everything Cardinal Pie has written; he is my teacher,"* Saint Pius X said of him (cf. RENÉ BAZIN, *Pie X*, Flammarion, Paris, 1928, p. 58).

[1027] ENRICO ROSA, S.J. (1870-1938) joined the Society of Jesus in 1886, was ordained in 1900 and made his vows in 1904. In 1905 he began to write for *Civiltà Cattolica,* of which he was director from 1915 to 1931.

[1028] ENRICO ROSA, S.J., *Il regno sociale di Cristo e la restaurazione della società, Civilltà Cattolica,* year 72 (1921), II, pp. 481-493 and ID. *La sovranità sociale di Cristo e l'Internazionale cattolica,* Idem, year 72 (1921), III, pp. 97-107.

[1029] E. ROSA, S.J., *Il regno sociale di Cristo,* op. cit., pp. 481-482.

On December 11, 1925, Pius XI issued the Encyclical *Quas Primas*,[1030] which introduced a special feast to celebrate Christ the King. In it the new Pope developed the Scriptural, liturgical and theological foundation of the social Kingship of Christ by stating: "It would be a grave error, on the other hand, to say that Christ has no authority whatever in civil affairs,"[1031] because, as Leo XIII[1032] had said, "the whole of mankind is subject to the power of Jesus Christ…for all men, whether collectively or individually, are under the dominion of Christ."[1033]   The Pope also denounced "so-called 'secularism' with its errors and wicked activities" "the plague of our age."[1034]

Pius XI based the doctrine of the social kingship of Christ on the hypostatic union, through which Jesus Christ, as God and Man, has authority over all creatures.   Jesus Christ is King by right of birth, as divinity and kingship are intimately connected in Him, and by acquired right, through the Redemption of mankind.   Around the same time, the "Cristeros"[1035] rose up in Mexico on behalf of that Kingship, becoming the first martyrs of the social kingship of Jesus Christ just as the Vendeans had been martyrs of the Sacred Heart.

Pius XII took up the theses expressed by his predecessor in his Encyclical *Summi Pontificatus*[1036] of October 20, 1939, in which he outlined the program of his pontificate.   By publishing it on the eve of the feast of Christ the King, on the fortieth anniversary of *Annum Sacrum*, with which Leo XIII consecrated the world to the Sacred Heart, the Pope affirms that only the recognition of the social kingship of Christ could restore man to the degree of civilization he had enjoyed in medieval Christian Europe.   "At the head of the road which leads to the spiritual and moral bankruptcy of the present day stand the nefarious efforts of not a few to dethrone Christ; the abandonment of the law of truth which He proclaimed and of the law of love which is the life breath of His Kingdom. In the recognition of the royal prerogatives of Christ and in the return of individuals and of society to the law of His truth and of His love lies the only way to salvation."   The Pope goes on to address his

---

[1030] PIUS XI, Enc. *Quas Primas*, of December 11, 1925, *AAS* 17 (1925), pp. 593-610; It. tr., EE, Pio XI, pp. 158-193.

[1031] Idem, pp. 173-175.

[1032] LEO XIII, Enc. *Annum Sacrum* of May 25, 1899, EE, *Leone XIII*, pp. 1128-1141.

[1033] PIUS XI, Enc. *Quas primas*, cit., p. 175.

[1034] Idem, p. 183.

[1035] On the *Cristeros'* insurgency in Mexico between 1925 and 1929, also called *Cristiada*, cf. HUGUES KÉRALY, *Les Cristeros*, Dominique Martin Morin, Paris, 1986; JEAN MEYER, *La Christiade; L'Etat et le peuple dans la révolution mexicaine*, Payot, Paris, 1975, later republished as *La Rébellion des Cristeros*, CLD Editions, Paris, 2014.

[1036] PIUS XII, Enc. *Summi pontificatus de summi pontificatus munere,* of October 20, 1939, AAS 31 (1939), pp. 413-453.

greetings, thanks, and hopes that "numbers of fervent men and women of youth obedient to the voice of the Supreme Pastor and to the directions of their bishops, consecrate themselves with the full ardor of their souls to the works of the apostolate, in order to bring back to Christ the masses of peoples who have been separated from Him....These have truly placed their lives and their work beneath the standard of Christ the King; and they can say with the Psalmist: 'I speak my words to the King' (Psalm xliv, 1). 'Thy Kingdom come' is not simply the burning desire of their prayer; it is also the guide of their activity."[1037]

Plinio Corrêa de Oliveira and the Social Kingship of Jesus Christ

While liberal Catholicism denied the social kingship of Christ, all counter-revolutionary authors, faithful to papal teachings, see it as an indispensable ideal and principal remedy to the crisis of our time.[1038] Jean Ousset dedicated to it a programmatic work, *That He May Reign*,[1039] while Archbishop Marcel Lefebvre summed it up with the formula *They Have Uncrowned Him*,[1040] the title of one of his last books, subtitled "From Liberalism to Apostasy: The Conciliar Tragedy." Msgr. Delassus, to whom Plinio Corrêa de Oliveira refers, wrote that he was convinced that "the defeat of the Revolution will inaugurate the social reign of Our Lord Jesus Christ upon mankind, forming a single fold under a single Shepherd."[1041]

Plinio embraced this ideal from his youth, capturing its close connection with devotion to the Sacred Heart. In October 1939, when the Second World War had already started, he wrote in *Legionário*:

[1037] Idem, pp. 421-424, 446.

[1038] It is well to recall also the contribution of eminent Irish Catholic authors such as Fr. Denis Fahey (1883-1954) and convert Hamish Fraser (1913-1986).

[1039] JEAN OUSSET, *Pour qu'Il règne*, La Cité Catholique, Paris, 1959. On Jean Ousset (1914-1994), founder of La Cité Catholique, cf. MASSIMO INTROVIGNE, "Jean Ousset et La Cité Catholique. A cinquant'anni da Pour qu'Il règne," *Cristianità*, no. 355 (January-March 2010) pp. 9-61.

[1040] MGR LEFEBVRE, *Ils l'ont découronné. Du libéralisme à l'apostasie. La tragédie conciliaire*, Editions Fideliter, Escurolles, 1987 (Angelus Press, 1988) . Marcel Lefebvre (1905-1991), of the Congregation of the Holy Spirit, ordained in 1929, was Apostolic Vicar (1948-1955), later archbishop of Dakar (1955-1962), apostolic delegate for French Africa (1948-1959), bishop of Tulle (1962), then in Sinnada in Frigia (1962-1970), superior general of the Congregation of the Holy Spirit (1962-1969). In 1970 he founded the Priestly Society of Saint Pius X in the diocese of Freiburg in Switzerland, with the approval of the local ordinary, Bishop François Charrière. From 1974 onward a dispute with the Holy See led him to be suspended *a divinis*, subsequent to the priestly ordinations of June 29, 1976, and later, after the consecration of four bishops, to an excommunication *latae sententiae* of June 30, 1988, revoked by Benedict XVI on March 10, 2009. About him, see, among others, BERNARD TISSIER DE MALLERAIS, *Marcel Lefebvre*, Clovis, Paris, 2002; *The Biography of Marcel Lefebvre*, Angelus Press, Kansas City, MO, 2004.

[1041] MSGR. H. DELASSUS, *La conjuration antichrétienne*, vol. I, p. 68.

"The doctrine on the kingship of Jesus Christ is closely linked to the most beautiful and gracious practice of enthroning the Sacred Heart of Jesus in homes. If we enthrone an image of the Sacred Heart of Jesus in the richest and most noble place in our home, it is precisely because we recognize that He is King. However, in how many homes out there the image of Christ has been enthroned in the room, but Christ is not enthroned in people's hearts!...

"In order to make us understand His absolute authority upon us as God, Jesus Christ deigned to compare Himself to a King. However, since it is through Him that kings reign, and since the authority of kings is authentic only because it comes from Him, He is in fact the only King, the King par excellence. And kings or heads of state are nothing but humble acolytes of His, whom He deigns to employ in the work of governing the world.

"Christ is King because He is God. By calling Him King, we merely affirm His Divine Omnipotence and our obligation to obey Him. Obedience! Behold one of the concepts essentially contained in the concept of the kingship of Our Lord Jesus Christ. Christ is King, and to a King, obedience is due. To celebrate the kingship of Our Lord Jesus Christ is to celebrate His power over us. And by implication, our obedience to Him. How do you obey a King? The answer is simple: by knowing His will and fulfilling it with loving detail and accuracy. Thus, the only way for us to obey Christ the King is to know His will and follow it. From this very clear, simple and luminous notion there also follows a program of life, which is likewise clear, simple and luminous....In other words, let us be good Catholics; being good Catholics we will necessarily be apostles; and being apostles we will necessarily be soldiers of Christ the King."[1042]

In a programmatic article, which appeared in the first issue of *Catolicismo*, in January 1951, Plinio emphasized not only the individual but also the social character of the Kingdom of Christ:

"The Kingdom of God will attain its fulfillment in the next world. For all of us, however, it already begins to exist in a germinative state in this world.... And the Holy Catholic Church in this world is not only an image of Heaven, but a real anticipation of Heaven. Everything, therefore, that the Holy Gospels tell us about the Kingdom of Heaven applies most properly and exactly to the Catholic Church, to the Faith She teaches, and to each of the virtues She inculcates. This is the meaning of the Feast of Christ the King. He is above all the Heavenly King, but nevertheless a King whose rule is already exercised in this world, and a King Who, by right, possesses full and supreme authority. A king legislates, rules and judges. His royalty becomes effective when his subjects recognize his

---

[1042] "Christ the King!" *Legionário*, no. 372, October 29, 1939.

rights and obey his laws. Now, Jesus Christ has all rights over us. He promulgates laws, rules the world, and will judge mankind. Thus, it is our obligation to make His Reign effective by obeying His laws.

"This reign exists on an individual level insofar as every faithful soul obeys Our Lord Jesus Christ. As a matter of fact, Christ's Reign is exerted on our souls, and therefore each soul is under Christ's jurisdiction. The Reign of Christ will become a social fact if human societies obey Him. Thus, it can be said that the Reign of Christ becomes effective on earth, in its individual and social meaning, when men in the depths of both their souls and actions, and societies in their institutions, laws, customs, cultural and artistic manifestations, comply with Christ's Law."[1043]

Quoting Cardinal Pie, Plinio wrote in 1952 in *Catolicismo:* "The general point of convergence of the whole revolutionary work is the radical negation of the social kingdom of the Divine Savior. 'We do not want Him to reign over us!' 'We have no king but Caesar!' Therefore, in order not to desert from his faith as a member of the Church Militant, a Catholic must fight for the restoration of the Reign of Christ as the only way to restore true civilization, which is Christian civilization, the Catholic city."[1044]

The Queenship of Mary according to Popes and Theologians

In recent centuries the doctrine on the social kingship of Mary developed in a similar manner to that of social kingship of Christ. Just as the kingship of Christ is rooted in the worship of the Sacred Heart of Jesus, the queenship of Mary is closely linked to the devotion to the Immaculate Heart of Mary. The legitimacy of this cult was challenged by the Jansenists, against whom Saint John Eudes wrote a capital work, *The Admirable Heart of the Most Holy Mother of God,* showing the intimate connection between the two Divine Hearts. In his Marian doctrine, more of a Trinitarian than Christological inspiration, he attributes to Mary the title of queen not only because she "is the Mother of God, the Queen of heaven and earth, and the sovereign Lady of the universe,"[1045] but also because, as spouse of the Holy Ghost "she is the Spouse of the Sovereign Monarch of the Universe."[1046] Saint Pius X, who beatified John Eudes,

---

[1043] "The Crusade of the 20th Century," *Catolicismo,* no. 1, January 1951; also at http://www.tfp.org/who-we-are/xxi-century-crusade.html .
[1044] "Modern Legislation and the Social Kingship of Our Lord Jesus Christ," *Catolicismo,* no. 22 (October 1952).
[1045] ST. JOHN EUDES. *Le Coeur admirable de la Très Sainte Mère de Dieu,* in *Oeuvres complètes,* Paris, 1908, vol. VII, p. 657.
[1046] Idem, vol. V, p. 394.

calls him "father, doctor" and "first apostle" of this devotion, which received a heavenly seal with the Fatima apparitions of 1917.[1047]

In his Encyclical *Ad Caeli Reginam*[1048] of October 11, 1954, Pius XII, who in 1944 had extended the cult of the Immaculate Heart of Mary to the whole Church, admirably summed up the Tradition. Fathers of East and West, theologians and popes always attributed to Mary the title of queen. The Roman liturgy and also the Eastern liturgies proclaim Mary Queen of heaven, Queen of angels, Queen of the world, Queen of all saints. According to Pius XII, the reasons and foundations of the Queenship of Mary are her Divine Motherhood and association with Christ in the whole work of our salvation. Its essential constituents are royal supremacy, royal power, and effective intercession resulting from Mary's intimate union and association with Christ.

On November 1, 1954, on establishing the Feast of Mary the Queen and ordering the yearly renewal on that day of the consecration of the human race to the Immaculate Heart of Mary, Pius XII said he placed in that gesture the "great hope that a new era may arise, gladdened by Christian peace and the triumph of Religion," and stated that "the invocation of Mary's Reign is...the voice of Christian faith and hope."[1049]

Father Garrigou-Lagrange explains how royalty is attributed to Mary in the proper sense rather than metaphorical one.[1050] God alone, as Author of all things, has by His very essence universal kingship over all creatures, which He governs to lead them to their end. But Christ and Mary, the Dominican theologian recalls, participate in that universal kingship. The theological reasons, according to Father Garrigou-Lagrange, are as follows:

> a) "Jesus Christ is King of the universe, even as man, by virtue of His hypostatic union and therefore Divine Personality. But Mary as Mother of God made man belongs to the hypostatic order and shares in the dignity of her Son, for His Person is the term of her divine motherhood. Hence she shares connaturally, as Mother of God, in His universal Kingship."[1051]

[1047] PIUS X, Apost. Lett. on Blessed John Eudes, AAS, I (1909), pp. 477-482. Cf. CHARLES LEBRUN, *La dévotion au Coeur de Marie. Etude historique et doctrinale,* Lethielleux, Paris, 1918.

[1048] PIUS XII, Enc. *Ad Coeli Reginam,* of October 11, 1954, AAS, 46/2 (1954), pp. 625-640.

[1049] PIUS XII, Speech of November 1, 1954, *Discorsi e Radiomessaggi,* XVI, p. 238.

[1050] R. GARRIGOU-LAGRANGE, O.P., *La Madre del Salvatore e la nostra vita interiore. Sintesi dommatico-ascetica,* Edizioni Libreria Fiorentina, Firenze, 1943, pp. 314-334. Cf. also PIERRE-YOSHIYUKI TAKARI, PSS, *Royaute de Marie d'après l'oeuvre mariologique de saint Jean Eudes,* Dissertatio ad lauream apud Pontificiam Universitatem S. Thomae, Roma, 1964; TOMMASO M. , O.S.M., "Giustificazione dei titoli o fondamenti dommatici della regalità di Maria," *Ephemerides Mariologicae,* XV (1965), pp. 49-82.

[1051] Idem, p.318

b) "Jesus is King of the universe by His fullness of grace and by the victory which He won over Satan and sin by His humility and His obedience unto death, "For which cause God hath exalted Him...' But Mary was associated with His victory over Satan, sin, and death by her union with Him in His humiliations and sufferings. She is therefore really associated with Him in His Kingship."[1052]

c) "The same conclusion may be arrived at by considering the close relationship in which Mary stands to God the Father, of whom she is the first adoptive daughter and the highest in grace, and God the Holy Ghost, through whose operation the Word took flesh in her womb."[1053]

The Dominican theologian concludes: "Mary has a radical right to universal queenship by the fact of her divine motherhood, but the divine plan was that she should merit it also by her union with her suffering Son, and that she should not exercise it fully before being crowned Queen of all creation in Heaven."[1054]

Another great mariologist of the twentieth century, Marianist Father Emile Neubert, wrote: "The royalty of Mary is based, like that of her Son, on her participation in the mysteries of the Incarnation and Redemption, and also in her function as the Mother of all men. Mary is Mother of the Man-God, who is king; and the king's mother is Queen, participating in his sovereignty to some degree. This principle, which is true in the case of mothers of common kings, is even more true with regard to Mary. First, because in His infinite love for his Mother, Jesus made her participate in all His prerogatives to the extent they can be transmitted to a creature: Immaculate Conception, exemption from sin and concupiscence, fullness of grace, early glorification of her body, etc. Why would He not have her share in His kingship? Secondly, because Mary gave Jesus to the world to be king, according to the angel's message that 'He shall reign forever.' He depended on Mary's consent to acquire that royalty, having become king the moment He became the son of Mary, and not after his birth. For Him, this entailed a special obligation, not one of strict justice but of filial piety, to share his sovereignty with her." [1055]

Father Gabriele M. Roschini is another theologian who has devoted some beautiful pages to the queenship of Mary. He writes that the Reign of Mary is a mysterious, supernatural reality that can be understood only through the use of analogy: The term reign, like royalty, is in fact

---

[1052] Idem, pp. 318-319.
[1053] Idem, p. 319.
[1054] Idem, p. 320.
[1055] FR. ÉMILE NEUBERT, *Marie dans le dogme*, Editions Spes, Paris, 1934, p. 164 (pp. 163-169).

analogous because it can be extended to different realities, indicating the element they have in common. According to Saint Thomas, those are called king and queen who have the office of "ruling," that is "ordering the community of men of a perfect society toward the common goal."[1056] Therefore, the first analogous relationship is that between the Reign of Christ and the Reign of Mary: in both cases, reign is a moral unity with authority and subjects. In turn, this analogical relationship is based on the participation of Mary's Queenship, and the Kingship of Christ, in the supreme Kingship of God, King of Kings, Who has the fullness of kingship in the first place. The Encyclical *Quas Primas* attributes to Christ a supreme royal authority because "the Word of God, as consubstantial with the Father, has all things in common with Him, and therefore has necessarily supreme and absolute dominion over all things created."[1057]

The nature of the Queenship of Mary must be determined in the light of a twofold analogy: the analogy with the kingship of Christ and the analogy with any queen of the earth. The Kingdom of Christ is not different from that of Mary in the sense that it has the same subjects and the same intent. The true and supreme foundation of this kingship is Mary's intimate union with Christ the King. Indeed, no king was ever united to his mother as Christ the King was with Mary. But the analogy also is valid with earthly queens. In fact, the concept of "queen" applies both to Queen of Heaven and Queen of earth, although in a very different way. Consequently, "just as Jesus is incomparably more a king than all the kings of the earth, He is the King of Kings, so also Mary is incomparably more a queen than all queens of the earth, she is the Queen of Queens. The royal majesty of the kings and queens of the earth is just a shadow, a pale reflection of the royal majesty of Christ and Mary." [1058]

The thesis that "Mary is truly queen in the proper and formal sense of the term,"[1059] while still not defined *de fide*, can be considered theologically certain,[1060] Msgr. Brunero Gherardini writes in an in-depth study devoted to this subject. The Roman theologian recalls how Saint John Damascene had already expressed the foundation of this Kingship thus: "Being the Mother of the Creator, Mary is truly the Queen of all

---

[1056] ST. THOMAS AQUINAS, *De regimine principum,* L: I, c. 1.

[1057] Pius XI, Enc. *Quas Primas* @ http://w2.vatican.va/content/pius-xi/en/encyclicals/documents/hf_p-xi_enc_11121925_quas-primas.html

[1058] GABRIELE MARIA ROSCHINI, O.S.M., *Maria Santissima nella storia della salvezza,* vol. II, *Il dogma mariano,* Editrice M. Pisani, Isola del Liri, 1969, p. 490.

[1059] B. GHERARDINI, *Sta la Regina alla tua destra. Saggio storico-teologico sulla Regalità di Maria,* Edizioni Viverein, Roma, 2002, p. 147.

[1060] Idem, pp. 200-201

creatures."[1061]   Mary participates in the Kingship of Christ as Mother of God, associated with the work of the Divine Redeemer. The kingship the Creator shared with the Virgin Mary was not an abstract and vague royalty, "but fitting to a king by right of birth and by acquired right."[1062] Hence follows the triple power that characterizes the kingship of Christ. "The kingship of Christ is the mirror and paradigm of Marian queenship.... Mary is Queen because Jesus, God and Man-God, is King."[1063] Both kingships rest on the same basis but are expressed differently. "Christ is King for all eternity, while Mary became queen the moment she conceived the Only Begotten of the Father. Christ is king because he is God and Man-God; Mary is queen because she is His mother and partner [in the work of Redemption]."[1064]

Plinio Corrêa de Oliveira and the Reign of Mary

More than from theological considerations, the unshakable confidence Plinio Corrêa de Oliveira always expressed in the social queenship of Mary was born from a careful analysis, in the light of grace, of the society in which he lived. From his very early youth he was certain that modern society was going to collapse and that a Christian society had to be restored on its ruins.

In his early twenties, in a letter to José Pedro Galvão de Souza[1065] in 1929, he wrote:

"I have an ever-growing impression that we are on the threshold of an epoch fraught with suffering and struggles. The suffering of the Church becomes more intense everywhere, and the battle draws ever closer. I have the impression that clouds are gathering on the political horizon. The storm, of which a world war will be a mere preface, will not take long in coming. But this war will spread such confusion all over the world that revolutions will arise in every corner and the putrefaction of this sad twentieth century will reach its peak. Then, the forces of evil, which appear like worms when putrefaction culminates, will arise. The whole '*bas fond*' of society will emerge and the Church will be persecuted everywhere. But... '*et ego dico tibi quia tu es Petrus, et super hanc petram aedificabo Ecclesiam meam, et portae inferi non praevalebunt adversus Eam!*' As a consequence, either we will have a new Middle Ages or we will have the end of the world.... Rather than

---

[1061] St. John Damascene, *De fide orthodoxa,* IV, PG, vol. 94, col. 1158b

[1062] B. Gherardini, *Sta la Regina alla tua destra,* pp. 140-141.

[1063] Idem, pp. 141, 142.

[1064] Idem, p. 145.

[1065] José Pedro Galvão de Souza (1912-1992) was a Brazilian juridical philosopher and university professor. He founded the São Paulo Law School, which was later incorporated into the Pontifical Catholic University of São Paulo, of which he was vice-dean.

imitate the Apostles who slept on the Mount of Olives as Jesus was about to be arrested, we must 'watch and pray.' Behold our main task: prepare ourselves for the fight and prepare the Church, like a sailor who readies the ship before the storm." [1066]

In the message of Fatima Plinio found confirmation of what his intellect and faith showed him; but he found it even before that in the extraordinary predictions of Saint Louis de Montfort, who in his *Treatise on the True Devotion* speaks of a "happy time when the divine Mary will be established mistress and queen of hearts" [1067] and will rule over society through the hearts and minds of men.

It was above all from the consecration to Mary, lived according to the method of Saint Louis de Montfort, that Plinio drew the notion of the Reign of Mary as the climax of the victorious battle of the Counter-Revolution. For him, the queenship of Mary, like that of Christ, is not metaphorical; and he was convinced that before the end of the world and the Kingdom of Antichrist, history will see an era of renewal he calls the Reign of Mary: "An historical era of faith and virtue which will be inaugurated with a spectacular victory of Our Lady over the Revolution. In that era, the devil will be expelled and return to the infernal dens, and Our Lady will reign over humanity by means of the institutions she has selected for this. [1068]

In the preface to the Argentine edition of *Revolution and Counter-Revolution* he explains that the queenship of Mary, associated with that of Jesus, should not be seen as a merely decorative title: "Although she is totally submissive to the will of God, the royalty of Our Lady implies an authentic power of personal government." [1069] The Reign of Mary is nothing more than the triumph of the Church, founded by Our Lord Jesus Christ, and the apogee of Christian Civilization resulting from the merits of His Passion. This triumph is necessary in history to enable man, who has a social nature, to render to God, in time, all the glory that the angels and the blessed will give Him in eternity.

As the Angelic Doctor teaches, if man is a social being by nature, he is obviously called not only to his personal sanctification, but to sanctification in society. [1070] Indeed, the glory of God, which is the end of creation, cannot be merely individual and implicit but must be public and social: humanity should glorify God not only in its individual components but also in its collective life, because God created and redeemed man also

---

[1066] Archives of IPCO; cf. also R. DE MATTEI, *The Crusader of the 20th Century,* p. 68.

[1067] *Treatise on True Devotion to the Blessed Virgin,* no. 217.

[1068] Preface to the first Argentine edition of *Revolution and Counter-Revolution,* op. cit.

[1069] Idem.

[1070] ST. THOMAS AQUINAS, *De Regimine Principum,* I, 1.

in his social nature. Hence, peoples also, communities and States, must recognize the Kingship of Jesus and Mary. If human history should fail to attain this summit of social perfection, the glory of God, which is the ultimate purpose of creation, would be diminished.

God is always victorious, and His triumph should shine "on earth as it is in heaven," in time and eternity. Plinio writes:

> "The Reign of Mary is an order of things that we consider particularly from the temporal aspect, but whose essence is a spiritual apogee of the Holy Roman Catholic Church whereby Our Lady attains supreme power upon souls, which is the greatest glory in history after the Resurrection and Ascension of Our Lord Jesus Christ."[1071] This reign "is the full compliance of the human order with the natural order established by God and the supernatural order instituted by Our Lord Jesus Christ. The state of affairs that the devil seeks to impose is the opposite of that."[1072] Our Lady's is a "luminous, jubilant, triumphal reign full of memories of all the struggles the Catholic faithful went through, all the weaknesses that all men carry within themselves, and much more still."[1073]

Characteristic of the Reign of Mary will be the holiness of the men and institutions that compose it:

> "The Reign of Mary properly speaking is a holy society; not one made up exclusively of saints, but a society where the number of saints is exceptionally large in relation to the general flow of history."[1074]

The Reign of Mary will be the most brilliant epoch of history, but after a period of splendor, it will see decay, sin, and God's punishment. That punishment will be the end of the world and the reign of the Antichrist.

The Historical Certainty of the Revolution's Defeat

For Plinio, the certainty of God's triumph does not come from reading theologians, but from the requirements of Divine Justice facing the present state of the world and the needs of the Counter-Revolution in its struggle against the Revolution.

> "Knowing the Revolution and the Counter-Revolution, and considering this universal disorder, one could not but think that there would necessarily be a punishment and a victory of God now or at the end of the world. In this latter case we would tread a sorrowful path until the

---

[1071] CSN, 14 February 1982.

[1072] RRR, 5 May 1975.

[1073] CSN, 19 February 1983.

[1074] CSN, 30 December 1989.

sudden explosion of joy, seeing that God would no longer be offended, that His justice and mercy were drawing closer, and Judgment Day was coming.... The battle's outcome would be a triumphal one for God, although it would not be in this life.... We could die before that, but some survivors would still see God's triumph in this life."[1075]

Plinio, however, wanted a triumph of justice and mercy not only at the end of the world but for our days, for a reason at the same time theological and psychological:

"Great sins bring great punishment for peoples. Great punishments bring great amendments, and great amendments bring great reconciliations. This is the order of the economy of grace.

"Look, for example, at the expulsion from paradise, after original sin. It was a tremendous punishment, but at the same time, with the promise of the Messias. Then, after the Flood came the rainbow. The Jewish people themselves were promised a spectacular conversion at the end of the world. In other words, this is a sequence. If the end of the world does not come now, there has to be a reconciliation as great as the punishment."[1076]

Prof. Plinio presents other reasons to maintain there will be the Reign of Mary before the end of the world.

"Despite four hundred years of a diabolical conspiracy to eliminate all the remains of Christian civilization, we are astonished to see that some institutions still remain and, however much their leaderships are de-Christianized, today's nations still show a level of religious resistance no one could have imagined one could count on.

"If we compare, for example, the influence of the papacy today with what it was a hundred years ago, we come to the conclusion that all that pseudo-scientific offensive of irreligion, which raged in Europe and dazzled the nations of the New World, has disappeared. While it is true that there is an offensive by Communist atheism, and that atheism exists even among theologians, it is also true that in the contemporary world, the masses are less and less impressed by all this, and that over the last one hundred years the word of a Pope was never as able to influence events as profoundly as it is today.

"Why is the Church a force that all the governments of the earth have to reckon with even if they are anti-religious? Why is it that a hundred years ago, ungodliness openly attacked the Church and today it puts on a 'theological' mask to be able to attack the Church? It is undoubtedly because there has been a religious persistence in the world, a

---

[1075] MNF, 21 March 1991.
[1076] SEF, 6 August 1971.

faint, weak and drowsy fidelity, if you will, but in any case, a fidelity that amazes.

"Now, if God's justice is clairvoyant, it does not leave the least fault unpunished nor fail to take the smallest act of virtue in due consideration. And if His mercy is boundless for those who sin, He is *a fortiori* also merciful to those in whom He finds some good. In today's world there appears to be something that, in God's eyes, does not deserve to die but rather to survive. And this is one of the reasons why we should believe in a great tomorrow after a great punishment." [1077]

Another reason could be added:

"Never have the driving forces of the Revolution had such a small ability to drag people with them. Never have the masses been so indifferent to the noise of the Revolution. And if there is a bored indifference toward Christian civilization, there is also a bored indifference toward the Revolution. For this reason one would say that a huge mental vacuum is forming in the world today. This mental emptiness affects people whose mentality no longer has the complexity, vivacity and stridency that once existed in the struggle between the Revolution and the Counter-Revolution. It is that kind of man without ideology, temperament or conviction that we usually call 'glass man.' This void is already a proof of the weakness of the Revolution.

"It is a proof that the claws of the Revolution no longer penetrate the entire fabric of the soul of the contemporary world, and it already indicates a kind of loss of strength, which in the darkness and desolation of the contemporary situation represents a factor in the breakdown of the Revolution. Even more, we find – with much joy and consolation – that however empty the soul of the 'glass man' is, that emptiness is open to receive precisely the seeds sown by the cause of Our Lady. Accordingly, we find everywhere people whose spirit is full of that emptiness but who heed the call of the Counter-Revolution. And people in whose emptiness the seed of the Reign of Mary begins to germinate.

"Therefore you have the beginning of a change. Just as plants under the snow do not die but germinate, and when the thaw comes one sees that all nature is alive, so also at the height of this winter of the Revolution something is beginning to germinate, trying to break out of this snow crust. And this germination not only indicates that Providence will save the world, but also that the hour of mercy has come, the time of forgiveness is approaching, and a radiant tomorrow is being prepared in the bosom of today's sorrows." [1078]

[1077] Meeting 29 January 1967.

[1078] Idem. Prof Corrêa de Oliveira developed this thought following a conversation with a well-known Hungarian Catholic writer, Thomas Molnar (1921-2010), who visited the Brazilian TFP in those years.

The Reign of Mary, Fruit of an Explosion of Grace

Contemplating from his very early youth the remnants of medieval civilization, Plinio reflected about the spirit that once animated those remnants, often reduced to ruins. He saw remnants of the Middle Ages surviving in some of society's customs, institutions and traditions. What was the origin of that spirit of whose last rays of light one could still catch a glimpse?

"There was a time when the Holy Ghost greatly spread the medieval spirit – that is, the Catholic spirit – among men, giving rise to a whole series of ways of being, a fruit of grace, that impregnated peoples' customs and the general behavior of the Church and society, and were transmitted from father to son, from grandson to great-grandson, and remained alive.

"That posed a question of the utmost importance to calculate what the Reign of Mary would be like in the future: how was it possible for that whole society to be, feel and think that way at one point? And why did they successively cease being, thinking and feeling that way? By ascertaining how that spirit originated it would be possible to understand the cause of its decline, and finally, how there could be a possible restoration.

"The conclusion was that grace at one point had very deeply implanted those ways of being, thinking and acting in the souls of men as implicit principles. The Magisterium of the Church made them largely explicit, but they could never be fully explicitated because that still semi-barbarian population lacked the necessary understanding. For this reason, this whole gift that God made at a certain moment to develop the temporal life of Catholics, which is called Christendom, was born from a colossal, explosive movement of grace. It was not a contamination or osmosis but something like an explosion. This spirit had as a starting point an explosion, a phenomenon much higher than any human action."

"I deduced the explosive nature of that grace from this fact: The attitudes of fidelity to that way of being, thinking and acting were highly individual but attained such a breadth and penetrated the whole world in such a way that they could not have come from a single earthly cause. They could only have a single heavenly cause, more or less like Pentecost. That spirit came from within the Church, but not necessarily through the hierarchy. That explosion of grace, which produced that colossal fermentation, was a forerunning event of which the sanctity of the pope, bishops and priests was a component. In other words, they too were favored and motivated by it in order to serve the Church in her hierarchy, etc.[1079]

[1079] CSN, 30 June 1990.

"Cluny was the matrix of the Middle Ages; it was the institution in which the Church (here Cluny was an agent of the Church) generated this fullness of spirit which the Church has always had and passed it on to the Middle Ages. The spirit of the Middle Ages and that of Cluny are therefore identical things. Cluny should be seen as the soul of the Middle Ages."[1080]

According to Plinio, the renewed Christian civilization of the future will be born from a similar explosion of grace:

"The Reign of Mary is the fullness of holiness and order in the Church, the plenitude of the Church's mission in the world, encompassing all mankind except of course for the few who will continue the conspiracy.

"A corresponding situation of plenitude will be found in temporal society. That means a fullness of the influence of the Catholic spirit in temporal society: fullness in culture, civilization, State organization, the family, etc. Fullness of temporal society with all the elements that constitute it.

"Why is this plenitude called Reign of Mary? Because all the graces the Church receives are in proportion to its union with Our Lady, Mediatrix of all graces. Therefore, for that plenitude of graces to exist there must be a fullness of devotion to Our Lady. Wherever devotion to her is full, she is Queen, and thus it is the Reign of Mary. It is like a home with an accomplished mother whose qualities are fully recognized by everyone and they are all fully in union with her. That home is her kingdom, and this is the Reign of Mary."[1081]

The world cannot end without the Church attaining all the perfection to which she was called by Divine Providence. The Middle Ages contained the seeds of this perfection, but the principles on which it was based failed to attain their full development. The fertility of these principles remains immense, and history is still a field open to this development.

"Admirers of the Middle Ages express themselves poorly when they say the world attained its maximum development in that era. There would still be much progress to be made along the same line in which the medieval civilization was advancing. The grandiose and delicate charm of the Middle Ages comes not so much from what it accomplished but from

---

[1080] SD, 26 February 1970. The Abbey of Cluny, founded in 910 as a "free monastery" under the protection of Rome, was the center of a great spiritual renewal under the guidance of some saints, particularly Odo (927-942), Maiolo (954-994), Odilo (994-1048) and Hugh (1049-1109), who established religious supremacy on medieval Christendom. Cf. CESARE HALLINGER, EC, III (1949), cols. 1883-1893, with bibliography; and the brilliant articles in *Catolicismo* on this topic, written by Prof. FERNANDO FURQUIM DE ALMEIDA (1913-1981).
[1081] SEF, 6 August 1971.

the scintillating veracity and profound harmony of the principles on which it was built. No other civilization had the same profound knowledge of the natural order of things; none had as it did such a keen sense of the need for the supernatural and the paucity of the natural, even when fully developed within its own order; none shone with greater clarity and more sincere candor in the sun of supernatural influence."[1082]

Plinio also gives the example of the life of Jesus Christ, Who, according to Tradition, died at age thirty-three, the perfect age of man.

"Why? Because having become incarnate, He would come to the fullness of his physical, intellectual and moral development. As the Son of God, in His most holy humanity, He had to attain His fullness before dying. A Being as exalted as the human nature of the Son of God hypostatically united to the Second Person of the Trinity could not exist without completing His course and attaining perfection. That would be contrary to the wise order of things."

What is appropriate for the Head must be, *mutatis mutandis,* fitting for the Body.

"Thus the Church Militant, the Mystical Body of Christ, cannot leave this world without having attained its perfection."[1083]

The question then arises whether the Reign of Mary will be a return to the past or will open the way to a new and unpredictable future.

"The answer to both questions should be yes. Human nature has its constants, which are invariable for all times and places. The basic principles of Christian civilization are immutable as well. Thus it is certain that in its essential traits this new order of things, this new Christian civilization, will be profoundly similar or rather identical to the old one. And God willing, it will be the same in the twenty-first century as it was in the thirteenth.

"But on the other hand, the technical and material conditions of life have profoundly changed and nothing would be more inorganic than to ignore these modifications. On this specific point one must not make many plans. The founders of Christian civilization in the early Middle Ages did not have in mind the thirteenth century the way it came to pass. They simply had a general intention of building a Catholic world. For that end, each generation gradually resolved with deep insight and Catholic sense the problems that came up within its reach. As for the rest, they wasted no time with conjectures.

[1082] "Reflections on Ten Years of Struggle against Nazism," *Legionário*, no. 666 (May 13, 1945); also at http://www.tfp.org/tfp-home/news-commentary/reflections-on-ten-years-of-struggle-against-nazism.html.
[1083] SEF, 6 August 1971.

"Let us do as they did. In its general lines, the whole framework is known to us from history and from the Magisterium of the Church. As to the details, let us advance step by step without purely theoretical plans made in an office: 'sufficit diei malitia sua' ['sufficient for the day is the evil thereof']."[1084]

A "Grand Retour" to the Spirit of the Middle Ages

The Reign of Mary will contain *nova et vetera,* new and old. Plinio believes it will be a restoration, and not an innovation:

"Something that was almost dying takes revenge on its opponent, not by resurrecting but by reviving without having passed through the shadows of death."[1085]

Plinio employed the expression *Grand Retour* even before he learned about the great movement of souls that developed in France in the 1940's, with a pilgrimage to a statue of Our Lady and the Child Jesus venerated in Boulogne-sur-Mer, France, since the Middle Ages.

On December 8, 1943, Pope Pius XII consecrated the world to the Immaculate Heart of Mary, and on March 28 of the same year the French clergy confirmed the consecration of France. To reap the fruits of this consecration, four statues of "Notre-Dame de Boulogne-sur-Mer," taking four different routes, visited all the dioceses of France, including overseas territories, drawing huge numbers of faithful. That was the largest Marian visitation in the twentieth century: during sixty months, from 1943 to 1948, 16,000 parishes and eighty-three dioceses were visited. That movement of prayer, penance and renewed fervor was called *Grand Retour,* not only because of the much longed-for return of millions of French POW's still imprisoned, but above all for France's return to the Faith.

Plinio employed this French expression to call "grace of the Grand Retour"[1086] a profound spiritual restoration that Our Lady would grant her faithful children in view of the dramatic events foreseen at Fatima. He was convinced that the Reign of Mary would be preceded by an irresistible movement of grace, a "Grand Retour" of humanity to the spirit of the Middle Ages.[1087]

[1084] "Christian Society v. Mechanistic and Pagan Society," *Catolicismo,* no. 11 (November 1951).

[1085] AMC, 8 November 1989.

[1086] NOR, 6 September 1961.

[1087] During an audience to a group of Grand Retour pilgrims on November 22, 1946, Pius XII stated: "Be faithful to the One who guided you here…. The precondition for perseverance in this consecration [to the Immaculate Heart of Mary] is to capture its true sense, to make it in all its scope, to loyally assume all obligations inherent to it. Here we cannot but recall what We said in this regard on an anniversary very dear to Our heart: 'The consecration to the Mother of

In the deluge of sin of today's world, counter-revolutionary Catholics who remain faithful will receive as a prize the first fruits of this Grand Retour, which lead them to aspire for a refinement of medieval civilization:

> "What we look for in the Middle Ages…is a spirit, a mentality that showed through more in Notre Dame than in other monuments, but which did not attain as great a flourishing as our soul would want. We noticed that seed and we hope it will finally reach its full expansion in another order of things. In that new order we would not find something different, but the aroma of the Middle Ages with a more intense presence and greater beauty. That order will be nothing but the *épanouissement,* the development of that medieval seed whose manifestations we all see and are enchanted with. But of course, our souls desire something more. And this desire can be the fruit of a grace, as a prize for our fidelity in the midst of this deluge of sin, in the expectation that our fidelity will attain its apex with the Grand Retour."[1088]

Fatima and the Reign of Mary

In the message of Fatima, which he learned about many years after reading the *Treatise on the True Devotion to the Blessed Virgin* by Saint Louis Marie Grignion de Montfort, Plinio Corrêa de Oliveira found an extraordinary confirmation of the expression and concept of the Reign of Mary.

In 1917, at Cova da Iria,[1089] Our Lady entrusted to three Portuguese children a message that unveiled horizons of tragedy but also of sweet

---

God…is a total gift of self for life and for eternity; not merely a formal or sentimental surrender, but effective self-giving carried out in the intensity of Christian and Marian life'" (PIUS XII, *Discorsi e Radiomessaggi*, VIII, pp. 323-324).

[1088] CSN, 29 August 1992.

[1089] The six apparitions of Our Lady to Lucia dos Santos, ten years old, and her two cousins, Francisco Marto, nine, and Jacinta, seven, took place between May 13 and October 13, 1917, at the most crucial time of the First World War. In 1930 the Bishop of Leiria, Most Rev. Jose Alves Correira, authorized the cult of Our Lady of Fatima. In 1946 Aloisi Cardinal Masella solemnly crowned the image of Our Lady of Fatima in the presence of 600,000 pilgrims. There is superabundant literature on Fatima. The most authoritative sources are the *Fatima documents. Memoirs and Letters of Sister Lucia*, prepared by Fr. Antonio M. Martins, S.J. (1918-1997), Porto, 1976 edition, with a facsimile of the manuscripts of Sister Lucia with the original Portuguese text and the corresponding Italian and Spanish translations. The best compendium is by Antonio Augusto Borelli Machado, *The Apparitions and Message of Fatima According to the Manuscripts of Sister Lucia*. This study, published in *Catolicismo*, no. 197 (May 1967) on the occasion of the fiftieth anniversary of the apparitions, was completely revised and expanded based on the manuscripts of Sister Lucia published in 1973, and was republished by *Catolicismo,* no. 295 (July 1975). Since then the work has been published in many languages, with hundreds of thousands of copies. Recently, the Carmel of Coimbra published *A Pathway Under the Gaze of Mary: Biography of Sister Maria Lucia of Jesus and*

hope, with the promise of the triumph of Her Immaculate Heart. As Sister Lucia stated, the message of Fatima consists of a single secret in three different parts.[1090] Two of these parts were revealed by Sister Lucia herself in 1941. The first is the terrible vision of Hell, where the souls of sinners plunge; in contrast, the mercy of the Immaculate Heart of Mary is a supreme remedy God offers humanity for the salvation of souls. The second part of the secret concerns the dramatic crossroads of our time: either the world converts and obtains peace by fulfilling Our Lady's requests, or a terrible punishment would await humanity if it remained stubbornly attached to sin. The essential conditions Our Lady required to avoid the punishment are the consecration of Russia to Her Immaculate Heart and the practice of Communion of reparation on the First Saturdays of the month. Implicit in that appeal is the need for conversion, understood primarily as a re-Christianization of society and a moral restoration of its customs.

> "If they listen to my requests, Russia will convert and there will be peace; if not, it will spread its errors throughout the world, promoting wars and persecutions of the Church. The good will be martyred; the Holy Father will have much to suffer and many nations will be annihilated. Finally, my Immaculate Heart will triumph. The Holy Father will consecrate Russia to me; it will convert and a certain period of peace will be granted to the world." [1091]

Sister Lucia joined the Dorothean Sisters and was sent to Pontevedra in Galicia (Spain). On December 10, 1925 the Blessed Virgin appeared in her cell with the infant Jesus on a luminous cloud at her side and called for the practice of doing reparation on the first five Saturdays of the month.[1092] Fr. Joaquim Maria Alonso draws a parallel between the "Great promise" the Sacred Heart of Jesus made to St. Margaret Mary Alacoque and the promise Sister Lucia received in Pontevedra.[1093] The parallelism is found not only in the merciful appeal contained in the two devotions but also in the common vision of a regal triumph. While Jesus said to St. Margaret Mary that He would establish the Reign of His Sacred Heart, Our Lady announced to the shepherds the triumph of her Immaculate Heart, closely united to that of her Divine Son.

---

the Immaculate Heart, OCD. Edições Carmelo, Marco de Canavezes, 2013, which contains some new revelations.

[1090] *Memorias e Cartas da Irmã Lucia*, pp. 218-219.

[1091] Idem.

[1092] Cf. *Memórias*, p. 400.

[1093] JOAQUÍM MARIA ALONSO, *Dos grandes promesas: Paray-le-Monial y Pontevedra*, in *Cor Christi. Historia, Teologia, Espiritualidad y pastoral*, Instituto Internacional del Corazón de Jesús, Bogota, 1980.

According to Our Lady's indications to Sister Lucia, the "third part" of the message should have been disclosed in 1960 at the latest. However, not without controversy, John XXIII, the first Pope who read the text of Sister Lucia, refused to publish it. Paul VI, elected June 21, 1963, also read the message but took the same attitude as his predecessor. The secret was published by John Paul II in 2000, after a trip to Fatima on May 12-13, 2000, in which he beatified Francisco and Jacinta.

A coherent logical thread links the three parts: the first relates to the fate of individual souls; the second extends to nations; the third, quoted below, appears to refer to the entire Church:

> "After the two parts which I have already explained, at the left of Our Lady and a little above, we saw an Angel with a flaming sword in his left hand; flashing, it gave out flames that looked as though they would set the world on fire; but they died out in contact with the splendor that Our Lady radiated towards him from her right hand: pointing to the earth with his right hand, the Angel cried out in a loud voice: 'Penance, Penance, Penance!'

> "And we saw in an immense light that is God: 'something similar to how people appear in a mirror when they pass in front of it' a Bishop dressed in White 'we had the impression that it was the Holy Father.' Other Bishops, Priests, men and women Religious going up a steep mountain, at the top of which there was a big Cross of rough-hewn trunks as of a cork-tree with the bark; before reaching there the Holy Father passed through a great city half in ruins and half trembling with halting step, afflicted with pain and sorrow, he prayed for the souls of those whose corpses he passed on his way; having reached the top of the mountain, on his knees at the foot of the big Cross he was killed by a group of soldiers who fired bullets and arrows at him, and in the same way there died one after another the other Bishops, Priests, men and women Religious, and various lay people of different ranks and positions. Beneath the two arms of the Cross there were two Angels each with a crystal aspersorium in his hand, in which they gathered up the blood of the Martyrs and with it sprinkled the souls that were making their way to God." [1094]

[1094] Third part of the "secret" in Congregation for the Doctrine of the Faith, *The Message of Fatima,* at: http://www.vatican.va/roman_curia/congregations/cfaith/documents/rc_con _cfaith_ doc_20000626_message-fatima_en.html, accessed on 5/10/2016. This document reproduces the three parts of the "secret" as written by Sister Lucia, an introduction by the Secretary of the Congregation, Archbishop Tarcisio Bertone, S.D.B., and a theological commentary on the third part of the "secret" by the Prefect of the Congregation, Joseph Cardinal Ratzinger. A heated argument on the Third Secret of Fatima has been going on in traditional circles. Cf. Antonio Socci, *Il quarto segreto di Fatima*, Rizzoli, Milano, 2006 and Christopher Ferrara, *The Secret Still Hidden*, Good Counsel Publications, New York, 2008; Antonio Borelli Machado, "Some Friendly Reflections for the Clarification of a Debate," *Lepanto*, no. 174 (2007), pp. 2-24.

Beyond the disputes about the Third Secret, the truth is that the message of Fatima culminates in a tragedy that directly touches the person of the Pope and all Catholics.

The Most Important Event of the Twentieth Century

In early April 1945, as the Second World War was nearing its tragic end, Plinio Corrêa de Oliveira, in *Legionário*, saw the Fatima apparitions as the most important and significant event of the century:

> "'*De Fatima numquam satis*,' one might say. Fatima is not an event that happened only in Portugal or is relevant only to our times. Fatima is a milestone in the history of the Church. Like it or not, Fatima is the true dawn of a new era whose early lights did not shine on the battlefields…but the moment Our Lady came to earth."[1095]

References to Fatima characterized virtually every public speech by the Brazilian thinker.

> "In the midst of earthly confusion, the heavens opened and the Virgin appeared at Fatima to tell men the truth. Austere truth, of warning and penance, but rich in promises of salvation. As this sad and shameful year of confusion was almost drawing to an end, the miracle of Fatima repeated itself under the eyes of the Vicar of Christ to attest that God's threats continue to loom over men, but that the Virgin's protection will never abandon the Church and her true children."[1096]

In his introduction to the book by Dr. Antonio Augusto Borelli Machado, Plinio Corrêa de Oliveira thus presented the message of Fatima, in a great vision of the theology of history:

> "The Western Roman Empire ended with a cataclysm, analyzed and illuminated by a great doctor and genius, Saint Augustine. The decline of the Middle Ages was predicted by a great prophet, Saint Vincent Ferrer. The French Revolution, which marks the end of Modern Times, was predicted by another great prophet and Doctor, Saint Louis Marie Grignion de Montfort. The Contemporary Times, which seem on the verge of ending with a new crisis, have a higher privilege. Our Lady herself came to speak to men.

> "Saint Augustine could only explain to posterity the causes of the tragedy he witnessed. Saint Vincent Ferrer and Saint Louis Marie Grignion de Montfort sought in vain to divert the storm: men would not listen to them. For her part, Our Lady explains the reasons for the crisis

---

[1095] "Books v. Cannons," *Legionário*, no. 661, April 8, 1945. On Fatima, cf. also *Legionário*, no. 597, January 16, 1944; no. 598, January 23, 1944; and no. 611, May 14, 1944.
[1096] "Nolite timere pusillus grex," *Catolicismo*, No. 13, January 1952.

and indicates its remedy, prophesying a catastrophe if men do not pay heed.

"From all points of view, the nature of its contents, and the dignity of the One who made them, the Fatima revelations surpass all that Providence had told men on the verge of the great storms of history. For all this one can say, categorically and without the slightest fear of being contradicted, that the apparitions of Our Lady and the Angel of Peace in Fatima are the most important and most enthralling event of the twentieth century."[1097]

Therefore, the scope of the Fatima message is incalculable:

"After the Passion and Death of Our Lord Jesus Christ and of Pentecost, etc., in the history of the Church I do not know a more striking, tragic and dramatic event than Fatima, with all that followed. The present moment is the most tragic the Church has had since the time of the catacombs. It is a moment when the tragic scene is dominated by the presence of Our Lady, who appears to the little shepherds. Everything else happening in the world is in function of her: All is unleashed because Our Lady went unheeded. The refusal of the Fatima Message is the refusal of a last act of mercy that could have led to the liquidation of the Revolution and an early victory of the Counter-Revolution. Instead, we have an apex of Revolution, a strangulation of the Counter-Revolution, and Western Christian civilization is on its path to extinction."[1098]

Fatima not only announces great tragedies but prophesies the triumph of the Immaculate Heart of Mary. That would be enough to rule out an imminent end of the world. In fact, how could the end of history coincide with the historic triumph of the Immaculate Heart of Mary?

"The end of the world will not come now because it is clear from the context of Fatima that the world will continue with a triumph of her Immaculate Heart. She did not say: 'My Immaculate Heart will win,' but employed an expression with very sharp and distinct hues. There is a difference between a victory and a triumph: a triumph is an outstanding victory, a great victory, not an ordinary victory. Our Lady announces her triumph, that is, a victory with glory in which she will completely master the situation. Therefore we will have the Reign of Mary, for one does not understand that she would win without being Queen." [1099]

Prof. Plinio often insists that a triumph is not merely a victory, but one clothed in glory and splendor:

[1097] *The Apparitions and Message of Fatima According to the Manuscripts of Sister Lucia*, op. cit.
[1098] NOR, 25 November 1974.
[1099] SEF, 14 July 1971.

"A triumph of Our Lady cannot fail to be splendid, for all that God does for Mary and on her behalf is a masterpiece. He reserved for Our Lady all His greatness. Her personal triumph has to be the most marvelous triumph in history." [1100]

[1100] SEF, 29 January 1967.

CHAPTER III

THE APOSTLES OF THE LAST TIMES

Saint Louis Marie Grignion de Montfort: An Apostle for the Last Times

Plinio Corrêa de Oliveira can be considered a successor, in the twentieth century, of the prophetic mission of Saint Louis Marie Grignion de Montfort. In 1955, Plinio dedicated to the great saint, "doctor, prophet and apostle in the contemporary crisis,"[1101] three large articles in *Catolicismo* and countless comments in private meetings. He not only picks up Saint Louis Marie's spiritual heritage but broadens its horizon, deepens and develops its perspectives, and above all makes it concrete and effective.

Saint Louis Marie Grignion de Montfort was born in Montfort-la-Canne,[1102] Brittany, on January 31, 1673 and died in Saint-Laurent-sur-Sevre, Vendee, on April 28, 1716.[1103] Driven by a desire to proclaim the Gospel to the nations, he went to Rome to ask Pope Clement XI for guidance. However, Clement XI dissuaded him from going on foreign missions and assigned him to do apostolate in France. Montfort devoted his whole life to missionary work, particularly in Brittany, Poitou, and in the old province of Aunis. He preached everywhere the Cross and the

---

[1101] Cf. "Doctor, Prophet and Apostle in the Contemporary Crisis," *Catolicismo,* no. 53 (May 1955); "The Reign of Mary, Achievement of a Better World," *Catolicismo,* no. 55 (July 1955); "Exurge Domine! Quare obdormis?" *Catolicismo,* no. 56 (August 1955).

[1102] The city had this name until the French Revolution, when it began to be called Montfort-la-Montagne. Later it adopted the present name of Montfort-sur-Meu.

[1103] The best work on Saint Louis Marie Grignion de Montfort is still the one by one of his disciples and contemporaries, JEAN-BAPTISTE BLAIN, *Abregé de la vie de Louis-Marie Grignion de Montfort,* written between 1722 and 1724 and published by the Centre International Montfortain, prepared by Louis Pérouas, Rome, 1973. Cf. also CAMILO ABAD, S.J., "Biografia," in *Obras de san Luis Maria Grignion de Montfort,* BAC, Madrid, 1954; LOUIS LE CROM, SMM, *Un apôtre marial. Saint Louis Marie Grignion de Montfort (1673-1716),* Les Traditions Françaises, Tourcoing, 1946.

Rosary, the total consecration of self to Jesus through the hands of Mary, erected roadside calvaries, restored churches, statues, monuments. He founded two religious congregations: the Society of Mary and the Daughters of Wisdom. In the superficial and optimistic climate of the *Grand siècle,* which corresponded to one of the most brilliant times of France, with his extraordinary eloquence this unknown priest deeply moved peasants and villagers. The regions he evangelized were so deeply immunized against the virus of the Revolution that in 1793 they rose up against the Republican and anti-Catholic government in Paris. It is said that the uprising in the Vendee was one of his works.[1104] He died at only forty-three years of age. He was beatified by Pope Leo XIII on January 22, 1888 and proclaimed a saint by Pope Pius XII on July 20, 1947.

Plinio Corrêa de Oliveira stated:

> "Saint Louis Grignion is anti-mundane par excellence. He rose against the errors of the *Ancien Régime,* against the worldly spirit and the spirit of frivolity, immorality and skepticism already flooding the old society; he was the most emblematic opponent of that spirit. God sometimes raises up against a society a man who has all the qualities which that society appreciates, and none of its defects, and who fights that society, so to speak, on its own ground. Saint Louis Grignion....can be considered the great conservative and the great reactionary. He did not follow the flow of the Revolution at all, not even in that in which it could show some progress. He was a living morsel from the Middle Ages in the middle of the *Ancien Régime,* still keeping the rough and semi-peasant aspect of the Middle Ages. He was full reaction in its most complete and perfect sense."[1105]

Saint Louis Marie Grignion de Montfort is the author of many works.[1106] The best known among them are the *Love of the Eternal Wisdom*[1107] and the *Treatise on True Devotion to the Blessed Virgin,*[1108] but he expounds his prophetic vision inspired by Divine Wisdom mainly in three books: the *Treatise on the True Devotion to the Blessed Virgin,* where he speaks of the need for devotion to Mary (nos. 35, 46-59, 217), its nature (113-114) and its effects (217); *The Secret of Mary*[1109] (nos. 58-

---

[1104] Louis Perouas, *Grignion de Montfort et la Vendée,* Cerf, Paris, 1989; Pierre-Francois Hacquet, *Mèmoire des missions des Montfortains dans l'Ouest* (1740-1779), "Cahiers de la revue du Bas-Poitou," Fontenau-le-Comte, 1964.

[1105] SD, 28 April 1964.

[1106] The saint's complete works, published in 1966 by the Seuil publishers are: *l'Amour de la Sagesse éternelle, Traité de la vraie Dévotion, Secret de Marie; Lettre circulaire aux Amis de la Croix, Secret admirable du très saint Rosaire pour se convertir et se sauver, Prière embrasée, Cantiques.*

[1107] ST. LOUIS MARIE GRIGNION DE MONTFORT, *Oeuvres,* pp. 85- 216.

[1108] Idem, pp. 481-672.

[1109] Idem, pp. 439-480.

59), in which he deals with the practical effects of this devotion; and the *Fiery Prayer*[1110] (2, 5, 13, 15-17, etc.).

"The writings of Saint Louis Marie Grignion de Montfort represent what is most perfect, radical and categorical in each of the topics covered. Regarding intellectual formation, one cannot say anything higher than what he said in *Love of Eternal Wisdom*. Wisdom is the culmination of all virtues, especially the intellectual virtues, and about it the saint says the most radical, extreme and categorical things that can be said.

"On moral formation, you cannot say anything higher than what he said in his *Letter to the Friends of the Cross*. On Marian devotion, he wrote the *Treatise on True Devotion to Mary*, which teaches lesser known truths which are nevertheless necessary for the formation of a Catholic, and which set us on the way of all grace, holiness and virtue, which is Our Lady.

"Concerning Our Lady he also said the last and highest things that can be said. All this together leads us to consider Saint Louis Grignion de Montfort as the saint of holy extremism. On dealing with matters of the utmost importance, he says the most far-reaching truths with the most extreme language. Under these conditions Saint Louis Grignion de Montfort is for us, but also for all time, an apex, a pinnacle-saint of extreme and sublime perfection, a saint who represents the end of the road treaded by all his saintly predecessors, but who is at the same time on the threshold of the Reign of Mary." [1111]

The *Treatise on True Devotion to Mary* is considered one of the highest expressions of Marian devotion of all time. "This little treatise," Father Reginald Garrigou-Lagrange writes, "is a treasure for the Church, as is its summary which the saint made for a nun, titled *The Secret of Mary*." [1112]

"We see in the Church a growth in Mariology and devotion to Our Lady whose highest exponent is Saint Louis Marie Grignion de Montfort. I do not believe one can say about devotion to Our Lady anything higher than Saint Louis de Montfort said. It can be commented upon and developed, but cannot be added to."[1113]

Saint Louis-Marie had a legion of disciples around the world, starting from 1842, the date on which the manuscript of the *Treatise on True Devotion* was found, which had been lost after his death.[1114]

[1110] Idem, pp. 673-782.
[1111] SD, 27 April 1966.
[1112] R. GARRIGOU-LAGRANGE, O.P., *Vita spirituale*, Città Nuova, Roma, 1965, p. 254.
[1113] Symposium, 26 February 1966.
[1114] ALBERTO RUM, SMM, "Il trattato della vera devozione a Maria del beato da Montfort nel primo centenario del suo ritrovamento" *(1842-1942)*, *Marianum*, no. 4 (1942), pp. 114-121.

Perhaps no one understood him as profoundly as Plinio, not only for the countless comments made, but for the fact that Plinio lived the spirit of true devotion as few others in the twentieth century.

The Montfortian Principles on which the
Reign of Mary is Founded

Saint Louis Marie lists the reasons why God wants to unveil and manifest Mary, the masterpiece of His hands, in the historical era he calls the "century" or "reign" of Mary:

1) "Because She kept herself hidden in this world, and in her great humility considered herself lower than dust, having obtained from God, his apostles and evangelists the favor of not being made known."[1115] The words of the Gospel that he who humbles himself will be exalted (Lk. 1:52), should be read as applying mainly to Mary, just as the statement that everyone who exalts himself will be humbled and crushed into dust should apply primarily to the devil.

2) "Because, as Mary is not only God's masterpiece of glory in heaven, but also His masterpiece of grace on earth, He wishes to be glorified and praised because of her by those living upon earth."[1116] He who glorifies Her, glorifies Him. Mary is the mirror through which the Light of God is communicated to us and we contemplate the divine light.

3) "Since she is the dawn which precedes and discloses the Sun of Justice Jesus Christ, she must be known and acknowledged so that Jesus may be known and acknowledged."[1117] The Divine Legislator of the universe willed that everything that is created had a meaning referring first and foremost to God, Jesus Christ, and the Blessed Virgin. Mary is to God as the moon is to the star that rules the universe.

4) "As she was the way by which Jesus first came to us, she will again be the way by which he will come to us the second time though not in the same manner."[1118] The designs of God do not change: their stability and consistency transcend the ages. This is what has happened and will happen once again.

5) "Since She is the sure means, the direct and immaculate way to Jesus and the perfect guide to Him, it is through Her that souls who are to shine forth in sanctity must find Him. He who finds Mary finds life, that is, Jesus Christ who is the way, the truth and the life. But no one can find Mary who does not look for her. No one can look for her who does not know her, for no one seeks or desires something unknown. Mary then

---

[1115] ST. LOUIS MARIE GRIGNION DE MONTFORT, *Treatise on True Devotion to Mary*, No. 50.
[1116] Idem.
[1117] Idem.
[1118] Idem.

must be better known than ever for the deeper understanding and the greater glory of the Blessed Trinity."[1119] The Holy Trinity, God the Father, Son and Holy Ghost, is the only sun that illuminates the universe; but this sun is so dazzling that it requires a secure means to be known, loved, and served. According to the saint, knowing, loving and serving Mary is the sure way to penetrate the sublime mysteries of the most Holy Trinity.

6) "Mary must shine forth more than ever in mercy, power and grace; in mercy, to bring back and welcome lovingly the poor sinners and wanderers who are to be converted and return to the Catholic Church; in power, to combat the enemies of God who will rise up menacingly to seduce and crush by promises and threats all those who oppose them; finally, She must shine forth in grace to inspire and support the valiant soldiers and loyal servants of Jesus Christ who are fighting for His cause."[1120] This is the specific role reserved to the Blessed Virgin: She was created not only to be the Mother of the Savior, but also to be the Mother of the children of Jesus Christ, and in this caring motherhood manifest His glory, supporting them in the battles they will have to wage against the children of darkness until the end of time.

7) "Lastly, Mary must become as terrible as an army in battle array to the devil and his followers, especially in these latter times. For Satan, knowing that he has little time – even less now than ever – to destroy souls, intensifies his efforts and his onslaughts every day. He will not hesitate to stir up savage persecutions and set treacherous snares for Mary's faithful servants and children, whom he finds more difficult to overcome than others."[1121]

The saint draws the great picture of the battle clearly led by a divine inspiration.

"Holy Slavery" or Total Consecration to Mary

Saint Louis Marie speaks about a second coming of Jesus to earth through Mary, all the more "glorious and resplendent" as the first was secret and hidden, but "both are perfect because both are through Mary."[1122]

In that historical epoch, Saint Louis says, Mary's union with the souls of her apostles will reach an unprecedented intensity and she will instill her graces in the hearts of her faithful in such an abundant way as to "raise up great saints who will surpass in holiness most other saints as

---

[1119] Idem.
[1120] Idem.
[1121] Idem.
[1122] Idem, no. 158.

much as the cedars of Lebanon tower above little shrubs."[1123]   When will
that happy day arrive "when God's Mother is enthroned in men's hearts
as Queen, subjecting them to the dominion of her great and princely
Son?... That day will dawn only when the devotion I teach is understood
and put into practice. *Ut adveniat regnum tuum, adveniat regnum Mariae*:
"Lord, that your kingdom may come, may the reign of Mary come!"[1124]
   Plinio comments:

> "The Reign of Mary will be an epoch in which the union of souls
> with Our Lady will reach an intensity without precedent in history (with
> the exception, of course, of individual cases). What is the form of that
> union, which in a certain sense is supreme? I know no more perfect means
> to enunciate and achieve that union than the sacred slavery to Our Lady as
> taught by St. Louis Marie Grignion de Montfort in the *Treatise on the
> True Devotion.*"[1125]

Indeed, in his book Montfort reveals and explores the secret of true
devotion. Father Antonio Royo Marín states that no devotion to Mary
can compare to the one promoted by Saint Louis Marie in the *Treatise*,[1126]
"the Marian book" par excellence, which contains a "sublime
doctrine."[1127]
The "holy slavery" is a radical consecration because it includes not
only man's material goods but also the merit of his good works and
prayers, his life, his body, and his soul. "It has no limits," Plinio says,
"because by definition a slave has nothing of his own."[1128]   But in
exchange for his consecration, "Our Lady works in the depth of her slave
in a marvelous way, establishing an ineffable union with him."[1129]   Our
Lady's queenship will be accomplished first in the interior of souls, and
from there it will be reflected on the religious and civic life of peoples
considered as a whole.
By definition, to consecrate is to subordinate man and society to
God. The term "Reign of Mary" expresses the ideal of sacralization of
the temporal order through the mediation of Mary, which is nothing other
than Christian civilization, which the Popes have always indicated as the
goal. In this sense, Christian civilization, which is entirely submissive to
God and recognizes the supreme royalty of Jesus Christ and of Mary, is
"sacral" and hierarchically ordered.

[1123] Idem, no. 47.

[1124] Idem, no. 217.

[1125] Preface to the first Argentine edition of *Revolution and Counter-Revolution*, p. 331.

[1126] A. ROYO MARÍN, O.P., *La Virgen Maria*, BAC, Madrid, 1968, p. 367.

[1127] Idem, p. 393.

[1128] Preface to the first Argentine edition of *Revolution and Counter-Revolution*, p. 331.

[1129] Idem.

"At this point we may ask ourselves: In what does the service to Our Lady in our century consist? It is to save souls by all lawful means, notably this one: ordering everything according to this spirit and building Christian culture and civilization. For, in a sense, these are nothing but an arrangement of things so that they reflect God in this life and guide souls to eternal life. To be consecrated to Our Lady and to serve her is to support, promote and defend Christian culture and civilization against their adversaries; they are comparable to that precious pearl that man should seek, selling all his belongings. This culture and civilization are the peace on earth the angels of Bethlehem promised to men of good will: the sole peace of Christ in the reign of Mary."[1130]

"What else can the triumph of the Immaculate Heart of Mary be if not the reign of the Blessed Virgin prophesied by Saint Louis Grignion de Montfort? And what else is this reign if not an era of virtue in which humanity, reconciled with God in the bosom of the Church, will live on earth according to the Law, in preparation for the glories of Heaven?"[1131]

The Church and the divine, natural and ecclesiastical law that she teaches are the inescapable framework in which the Reign of Mary develops; the reign, which, according to Plinio and to Montfort, will be that of the two virtues most opposed to pride and sensuality, the driving forces of the Revolution:

"Purity and wisdom are the two elements of Our Lady's soul that should give the Reign of Mary all its splendor. *Cor Sapientiale et Immaculatum Mariae, opus tuum fac:* do Thy work of making Thy children like unto Thee." [1132]

The Fiery Prayer and the Apostles of the Latter Times

The fruits of devotion to Mary will be seen in the Apostles of the Latter Times, whose spiritual profile the saint describes with fiery lines in the *Treatise on the True Devotion,* but above all in his *Fiery Prayer.* Cardinal Journet is among the few who have understood the meaning of the "apostles of the latter times."[1133] Father Gebhard[1134] and Father Lhoumeau,[1135] and more recently Fathers Frehen[1136] and De Fiores,[1137] all

---

[1130] AMC, 21 September 1989.

[1131] "Hodie in terra canunt angeli, laetantur archangeli, hodie exsultant justi," *Catolicismo*, no. 84, December 1957.

[1132] EVP, 21 May 1989.

[1133] CHARLES CARDINAL JOURNET, *L'Eglise du verbe Incarné,* II, pp. 278-306, 433-434.

[1134] HUBERT M. GEBHARD, "Commento al Trattato della vera devozione a Maria Vergine," *Regina dei Cuori*, no. 5 (1918).

[1135] ALBERT LHOMEAU, *La Vierge Marie et les apotres des derniers temps d'après le B. Louis-Marie de Montfort,* Mame, Tours, 1919.

[1136] HENRY FREHEN, "Le second avènement de Jésus-Christ et la 'méthode' de saint Louis-Marie de Montfort," *Documentation Montfortaine,* no. 7 (1962), nos. 31, 98-108.

Montfortians, spiritualized the message entirely, without comprehending its historical scope, which Plinio Corrêa de Oliveira explains in a clear and exhaustive way.

The situation of the Church, which the saint from Brittany saw with providential lucidity, was characterized by two essential aspects that he describes with words of fire. On the one hand, the saint describes the advancing enemy:

> "Thy Divine Law is transgressed. Thy Gospel is ignored, Thy religion abandoned. Torrents of iniquity overwhelm the world, carrying away even Thy servants; the whole earth has become desolate; impiety is enthroned; Thy sanctuary is profaned, and abomination has reached even into the holy place."[1138]

On the other hand, our saint sees the inertia of the good and wants many champions on God's side to arise, more numerous than those siding with the devil.

Plinio comments:

> "He wants them as faithful, pure, strong, fearless, combative and redoutable as Prince of the Heavenly Hosts. He does not merely say they must be like Saint Michael but wants them to be human versions of the Archangel":[1139] 'Will almost no one cry out amid his brothers for the zeal of His glory like Saint Michael?'" "How different is this yearning (seeing the world full of apostles brandishing swords of fire) from the short-sighted, cold and maudlin and inconsistent sentimentality of many Catholics today, for whom to do apostolate is to close your eyes to the adversaries' defects, lower the barricades for them, hand over your weapons, accept their game and, after capitulating, saying you have every reason to be happy because things could have been even worse."[1140]

The background is devastation in the Church and in souls, the burning fire of corruption destroying Catholic institutions, laws and customs, and rampant wickedness even in the holiest places.

> "Whole legions of souls inside and outside the sanctuary (St. Louis Marie makes it quite clear) cross their arms worrying about their small microcosm and oblivious to the Church and her great problems.... Conversely, Saint Louis Marie was an immense soul. Placed in an obscure situation, he devoted himself entirely to saving his neighbors in the small

---

[1137] STEFANO DE FIORES, "Le Saint Esprit et Marie dans les derniers temps selon Grignion de Montfort," *Etudes Mariales* (1986), *Marie et la fin des temps*, vol. III, *Approche historico-théologique*, p p.134-171.

[1138] ST. L. M. GRIGNION DE MONTFORT, *Fiery Prayer*, no. 5.

[1139] "Exurge Domine! Quare obdormis?" in *Rivoluzione e Contro-Rivoluzione*, op. cit., pp. 268-269.

[1140] Idem, p. 269.

ambiences in which he lived. But his zeal had no borders or limits and encompassed the whole Church. He lived, throbbed, rejoiced and suffered in unison with the entire Catholic cause in the broadest sense of the word."[1141]

To St. Louis Marie it seems impossible for God not to halt the march of iniquity: "Will Thou suffer this any longer, just Lord, God of vengeance? Will the end of all be like that of Sodom and Gomorrah? Will Thou be forever silent? Must not Thy will be done on earth as it is in heaven? Must not Thy Kingdom come?"[1142]

After the inevitable punishments that await humanity, the Breton saint announces, there will be a grand triumph of the Holy Ghost Who, by divine promise, assists the Church in history. "The special reign of God the Father lasted until the Deluge, and was concluded by a deluge of water. The reign of Jesus Christ was concluded by a deluge of Blood. But Thy reign, Spirit of the Father and of the Son, continues at the present time and will be concluded by deluge of fire, of love, of justice."[1143] The Reign of the Holy Ghost will be the Reign of Mary over souls and society through the very close ties that bind the Blessed Virgin to the Mystical Body of Christ, of which she is the heart, and to the Third Person of the Holy Trinity, of Whom She is the Spouse.

> "Saint Louis Marie divides history into the kingdom of the Eternal Father, the kingdom of the Son, and the kingdom of the Holy Ghost. And he gives an interpretation of the reign of the Holy Ghost with the Reign of Mary. And reading his book you realize that he calls it the 'Last Times' from this historical perspective: Although it is very long, with triumphs, etc., it is the last era because it is the era of the Holy Ghost, the third Person of the Blessed Trinity, and of Mary because it represents the fullness of the outpouring of all heavenly graces. So the Apostles of the Last Times would be all those who worked for the coming of the Reign of Mary, would fight and see the dawn, plenitude and decline of the Reign of Mary. In this conception, today's counter-revolutionaries would be Apostles of the Last Times."[1144]

This triumph will be achieved by a congregation totally consecrated to Most Holy Mary, united and vivified by Her. This mysterious congregation, which will be

> "a congregation, an assembly, a choice selection of predestined souls, which Thou must make in the world and of the world," can only be established by a fruitful action of grace in the souls of those who will

---

[1141] Idem.

[1142] Idem.

[1143] St. L. M. Grignion de Montfort, *Fiery Prayer*, No. 16.

[1144] RST, 29 April 1967.

compose it. But to God nothing is impossible: "Great God, Thou Who out of the very stones can raise up children to Abraham, in the might of Thy Godhead say but one word to provide good laborers for Thy harvest and missionaries for Thy Church." [1145]

For centuries the just have been asking God for the founding of that congregation:

"Remember the prayers that have been offered To Thee by Thy servants for this end for so many centuries. Let their wishes, their sighs, their tears, and the blood that they have shed for Thee come into Thy presence and earnestly implore Thy mercy." [1146] Since this congregation will be Mary's, it is through her that Providence will send such a rich gift: "Remember to give to Thy Mother a new company who, through Her, will renew all things and thus, through Mary, complete the years of grace just as, through Her, Thou did initiate them." [1147]

St. Louis Marie conceived that congregation as an essentially militant society, permanently fighting the devil and his henchmen:

"There will be a mighty enmity between this blessed posterity of Mary and the cursed race of Satan. But it is a divine enmity, and the only one of which Thou art the author: I will put enmities. But these combats and persecutions that the children of the race of Belial will inflict on Thy Blessed Mother's race will only serve to show to greater advantage the power of Thy grace and the courage of their virtue and the authority of Thy Mother, since Thou hast given to Her, from the beginning of the world, the commission to curse this proud spirit by the humility of Her Heart: She shall crush thy head." [1148]

The apostles of the last days will be characterized by extreme combativeness, stemming from their Marian devotion. Indeed, they will be

"True servants of the Blessed Virgin, who, like other Saint Dominics, would go everywhere carrying the bright and burning torch of the Holy Gospel in their mouths and the holy Rosary in their hands; barking, like faithful watchdogs, at the wolves who would fain tear to pieces the flock of Jesus Christ; burning like fires and lighting up the darkness of the World like other suns. Men who would, by means of a true devotion to Mary...crush wherever they go the head of the old serpent, in order that the curse Thou placed on him might be entirely

---

[1145] St. L. M. Grignion de Montfort, *Fiery Prayer*, No. 3.

[1146] Idem, No. 4.

[1147] Idem, No. 6.

[1148] Idem, No. 13.

fulfilled: I will put enmities between thee and the Woman and thy seed and Her seed: She shall crush thy head (Gen. 3:15)."[1149]

This is the phalanx of lions that he asks God for in the final passage of his prayer:

"Arise, O Lord, why sleepest Thou? Arise: Arise, O Lord, why feignest Thou to sleep? Arise in Thy might, Thy mercy, and Thy justice, to form Thyself a chosen bodyguard to keep Thy house, to defend Thy glory, and to save the souls bought at the price of Thy Precious Blood, so that there may be but one fold and (Jn. 10:16), and that all may glorify Thee in Thy holy temple."[1150]

Plinio comments: "On the one hand, this closure of his prayer is like a culmination, and on the other hand it is a kind of compendium that summarizes it."[1151]

The latter times, in the language of St. Louis Marie, Plinio adds, are not times of the end of the world but those that will succeed our own: an era that will end with a great punishment that will start the Reign of Mary over souls and society:

"The latter times are especially the period of the Reign of Mary, and then comes the end of the world, the short time span in which the world ends. During this period the devil, realizing that it is the last stage of human history, will persecute and do all the evil he can. And Our Lady will fight him during the Reign of Mary."[1152]

Saint Vincent Ferrer, the "Angel of the Apocalypse"

God's "merciful designs," according to St. Louis Marie, were shown in prophetic visions to some chosen souls like Saint Francis of Paula, Saint Vincent Ferrer, Saint Catherine of Siena, Maria des Vallées and many others of his time.[1153] Our Lord had those souls contemplate the vision of a future age that would be the Reign of Mary:

"Hast Thou not given to some of Thy friends a prophetic glimpse of the future renovation of Thy Church? Are not the Jews to be converted to the Truth? Is not this what Thy Church is awaiting? Do not all the Saints in heaven cry out to Thee: Avenge Thyself? Do not all the just on earth say to Thee: Amen. Come, O Lord, for the time is at hand (Apoc. 22:20). Do not all creatures, even the most insensible, moan under the weight of

---

[1149] Idem, No. 12.
[1150] Idem, No. 30.
[1151] NOR, 10 June 1961.
[1152] AMP, 24 February 1987.
[1153] ST. L. M. GRIGNION DE MONTFORT, *Fiery Prayer*, No. 2.

the numberless sins of Babylon and call for Thy coming to reestablish all things? For we know that every creature groaneth (Rom. 8:22)."[1154]

Born in Valencia on January 23, 1350, Saint Vincent Ferrer, of the order of Saint Dominic, lived at the time of the Great Western Schism. In 1367 he took the Dominican habit and made his religious vows the following year. He was professor of theology and became one of the greatest theologians and preachers of his era.[1155] In 1378, when the Great Western Schism began, even great saints found themselves disoriented. Among them was Vincent, who followed the anti-pope of Avignon, Clement VII, and his successor, Benedict XIII, recognized as Pope by Spain and by the General of the Dominicans. He had already begun to turn away from the anti-pope when he fell seriously ill and had a remarkable vision. Dominic and Christ Himself entrusted him with the mission of apostolic preacher. He was to announce the imminent coming of the Antichrist and preach conversion before the end of the world.[1156] Vincent left Avignon and then traveled through Spain, Switzerland and France, preaching the coming of the Antichrist and the Last Judgment.

On September 13, 1403 he announced as a sign that would precede the end times that women would wear men's clothes and men would don feminine attire.[1157] His preaching aroused such enthusiasm that he was followed by about ten thousand people, the so-called "flagellants," also found around other great preachers of the Middle Ages such as Saint Anthony. Following their example, brotherhoods of penitents sprang up everywhere and survived for centuries. On November 7, 1415, almost dying, he was miraculously healed and returned to the pulpit, giving the famous speech known as *Ossa arida, audite Verbum* [hear the Word, O dry bones!] before Benedict XIII, cardinals, princes, ambassadors, and thousands of faithful. In November 1417, Pope Martin V was elected, put an end to the Western Schism, and restored the prestige of the See of Peter in Christendom.

St. Vincent died April 5, 1419 in Vannes (Brittany), in St. Peter's Cathedral, where his mortal remains are still kept. Countless miracles

---

[1154] Idem, No. 5.

[1155] Cf. J. M. DE GARGANTA-V. FORCADA, *Biografía y Escritos de San Vincent Ferrier,* Madrid, 1906 (life and works, with ample bibliography); SADOC M. BERTUCCI, *Vincenzo Ferrer,* BSS XII, (1969), cols.1168-1176; PIERRE-HENRI FAGES, *Histoire de S. Vicent Ferrier. Apôtre de l'Europe,* 2 vols., Picard, Paris, 1901 (the most complete biography); ID. *Notes et documents de l'histoire de saint Vincent Ferrier,* Picard, Paris, 1905; MATHIEU-MAXIME GORCE, *Saint Vincent Ferrier,* Librairie Plon, Paris, 1924.

[1156] P. H. FAGÉS, *Notes et documents,* pp. 213-224.

[1157] Cited in PLINIO MARIA SOLIMEO, "São Vicente Ferrer. Profeta e pregador, gloria da Igreja," *Catolicismo,* no. 736 (April 2012), p. 18 (pp. 16-18); ROBERTO ALVES LEITE, "São Vicente Ferrer: o 'Anjo do Apocalipse,'" *Catolicismo,* no. 557 (April 1997), pp. 21-23.

followed; the Roman Curia recognized 873 as authentic. On June 29, 1455 he was elevated to the altars by Pope Callixtus II. In the canonization bull he is likened to the angel of the Apocalypse, called to dissolve the sixth seal.[1158] He is often portrayed in paintings and statues as an angel of the Apocalypse, with wings, and holding a trumpet and a book open on the verse of the Apocalypse of John: *"Timete Deum et date illi honorem quia venit hora judici eius"* (Fear God and render Him honor, as the time of His judgment has come).

"He was," his biographer writes, "the last medieval man, the last perfect fruit from St. Dominic's tree, in full blossom during those last two centuries of wonderful fertility; he witnessed the decline of that age of faith, saw the world flee integral Catholicism, and played the same role that the Angel of the Apocalypse, of whom he was the appointed forerunner, will play in the final days."[1159]

His grandiose figure announces the disasters coming from the very fact that the Catholic people would not listen to him. "Exactly," Plinio recalls, "as a prophet of the Old Testament, announcing misfortunes to the people of God because they had not heeded His envoy."[1160] The preaching of Saint Vincent Ferrer is a model for all preachers of punishment and mercy in the latter times, and so Plinio considered it.

Marie des Vallées and the Appeal to Divine Justice

Saint Louis-Marie also came to know and spread the revelations by the "saint from Coutances," Marie des Vallées.[1161] This seer was born from a poor family in Saint-Sauveur-Lendelin, near Coutances, on September 25, 1590, and died there on February 25, 1656. After an unhappy childhood, at age nineteen she began to suffer tremendous crises, attributed to sorcery, which they vainly attempted to exorcise. During these crises she first suffered, in spirit, the torments of hell (1616-1618) and later those of the Passion of Jesus (1621-1633). She thus lived fifty years in darkness and abandonment to fulfill her vocation: suffering for

---

[1158] P.H. FAGÉS, *Notes et documents*, pp. 210 & 221; M.-M. GORGE, *Saint Vincent Ferrier*, p. 92.

[1159] P. H. FAGES, *Histoire de saint Vincent Ferrier*, vol. I, p. 329.

[1160] SD, 4 April 1966.

[1161] On Marie des Vallées (1590-1656) cf. EMILE DERMENGHEM, *La Vie admirable et les révélations de Marie des Vallées, d'après des textes inédits*, Plon-Nourrit et Cie, Paris, 1926, pp. 91-103; IRMGARD HAUSMAN, *Marie des Vallées. Ame expiatrice pour le temps de la conversion générale*, Editions Résiac, Montsurs 199; PAUL MILCENT, *Marie des Vallées*, DSp, XVI, coll, 207-212. By her, cf. the *Manuscrits* 11942-11944 and no. 950 of the Bibliothèque Nationale and the *Manuscrit Renty* in the Mazarin library. It seems that Grignion, librarian at the Seminary of Saint Sulpice, had read the "Renty Manuscript" that was found there at the time (Fr. MILCENT, *op. cit.*, 211). Cf. S. DE FIORES, "Lo Spirito Santo e Maria negli ultimi tempi secondo S. Luigi Maria da Monftort," *Quaderni Monfortani*, 4 (1986), pp. 3-48.

the destruction of sin and the triumph of Divine Justice. Marie du Saint Sacrement, a saintly nun of the Carmel of Pontoise, confirmed before her death on June 30, 1642 that in 1634 she had the revelation that a poor daughter of the people who lived in abandonment and concealment, treated as insane, halted the torrent of divine wrath that otherwise would have fallen upon France because of its sins.

The axis of her spiritual life was the total and disinterested submission of her will to the will of God. *Tres sunt qui testimonium dant in terra: spiritus, aqua et sanguis*, Saint John says (I Jn. 5:8). According to the revelations made to Maria des Vallées, Divine Justice intends to destroy sin with three floods: The first flood is that of the Father, which was a deluge of water; the second is that of the Son, which was a deluge of blood; the third is that of the Holy Ghost, which will be a deluge of fire.[1162] The world will be purified by fire, and all the sins of the earth will be annihilated. The *Fiery Prayer* echoes this prophecy:

> "When shall it come, this deluge of fire and pure love, which Thou art to enkindle in all the earth with so much strength and sweetness that all nations, Turks, idolaters, even the Jews, will burn with it and be converted? And there is no one who can hide himself from its heat (Ps. 18:7). May it be enkindled: May this divine fire, which Jesus Christ came to bring the world, be enkindled before that of Thy anger, which will reduce everything to ashes." [1163]

That great tribulation will be followed by an extraordinary outpouring of graces. The world will be converted, according to the prophecy: *"Et convertendum ad Dominum universes fines terrae."* A deluge of graces will rain upon the earth.

God allowed the secret of this woman to be known only by seven people, including two great figures of French spirituality in the seventeenth century: Saint John Eudes and the Baron of Renty.[1164] Eudes and Renty were apostles of Normandy, as was Montfort for the Vendée. The former was superior of the Oratory of Caen since October 26, 1640; the latter from 1641 was superior of the Society of the Blessed Sacrament, a Catholic secret society that gathered together the most fervent souls of France in that period. In 1641, Saint John Eudes went on a mission to Coutances, where he met Marie de Vallées and was deeply

---

[1162] Ms Renty, l. II, c. LXX, p. 199.

[1163] Idem, No. 17.

[1164] Baron Gaston de Renty (1611-1649), a leading member of the Society of the Blessed Sacrament, was directed by Father Saint-Jure, S.J., who wrote his biography. RAYMOND TRIBOULET, *Gaston de Renty 1611-1649. Un homme de ce monde. Un homme de Dieu*, Beauchesne, Paris, 1991, devotes a chapter to *Marie de Vallées, la voyante de Coutances*, pp. 332-352.

impressed. In a remarkable *Summary of the Life and States of Marie des Vallées,* he defends the sanctity of the seer of Coutances in ten chapters.

Marie des Vallées was not yet canonized by the Church, but the canonization of Saint John Eudes is a confirmation not only of her holiness but also of the truth of her revelations, which he always emphasized. The date of his first meeting with the seer of Coutances was decisive in Saint John's life. He was always grateful to her, assisted her at the point of death, and defended her against slanders and misunderstandings.

He owes Marie des Vallées the founding of his work and the beginning of his devotion to the Sacred Heart of Jesus, which he started to spread inside the small circle of people united by a prophetic bond, of which they were part; and this happened even before the revelations at Paray-le-Monial. Providence decreed that the revelations by Marie des Vallées would be known only to a select few, while those of Saint Margaret Mary were spread to the whole world; but both come together into one great devotion in which the names of Saint John Eudes and Marie des Vallées are inseparably joined to those of Saint Margaret Mary and Saint Claude de la Colombiere.

The history of holiness is also the history of intense spiritual ties in time and space. A mysterious spiritual genealogy connects Plinio Corrêa de Oliveira to Saint Louis Marie Grignion de Montfort and the latter to souls like Vincent Ferrer and Marie des Vallées, whose prophetic voices echo in the twenty-first century.

True and False Apocalyptic

Those who criticize the prospect of the Reign of Mary reject the possibility of the social kingship of Christ and of a historic triumph of the Church on earth. Yet if the Christian civilization of the Middle Ages was formed thanks to the Church, why could a civilization inspired by the same ideals not be reborn before the end of the world? For those who deny this perspective the Church should be reduced to a merely spiritual society destined to be always defeated in history.[1165] The Holy Ghost would thus be ineffective and Divine Providence would have left history to the devil's domain, reserving only a symbolic victory for Itself. This theology of history is typical not only of liberal Catholicism, which renounces sanctifying society and focus only on individuals, but as Guido Vignelli observed, presupposes the Gnostic theory of the "weakness of God" and His "historic failure."[1166] This false theology of history has

---

[1165] G. VIGNELLI, *Fine del mondo,* p. 130.
[1166] Idem, p. 131.

inspired a minimalist and "catacombal" pastoral policy in which the Church is limited to bear "prophetic witness," and renounces the conquering of the world, submitting herself to it and accepting the paradigm of the irreversibility of history.

These are consequences of a merely spiritualized eschatology that, under the pretext of rejecting a material and "carnal" vision, renounces the visible and temporal dimension of the messianic Kingdom. The myth of the "ecclesia spiritualis" has long characterized a series of heretical currents, from Donatists to followers of Wyclif and Hus, and radical sects of Protestantism.[1167] But the deniers of the social kingship of Jesus and Mary endorse precisely the unilateralism of this spiritualized vision of the Church and society. The rejection of Christian civilization and of the social kingship of Christ implies the rejection of the visibility of the Church. The Church, the Mystical Body of Christ, has a supernatural end, but in addition to being an invisible society, it is also a visible society that operates in the world, a public institution endowed with its own legal structure. While the destiny of its members is heaven, they are men composed of soul and body, living in the world, struggling against the world, who must affirm their own ideas and values in the world.

Millenarianism has nothing to do with the Reign of Jesus and Mary in history. The Millenarianism condemned by the Church consists in waiting for a millennial era before the end of the world when Jesus Christ will *physically* return to earth, establishing a kingdom similar to that of a blessed eternity in Heaven, in which all evil and suffering will disappear from the face of the earth. In this millennial reign, all men will be saints, free and equal, living as brothers in perfect harmony; therefore they would govern themselves and no longer need authorities or institutions, civil or ecclesiastical; finally, the Church with its clergy and sacraments would disappear, as God would be "everything in everyone" in an egalitarian fashion. Over time, this heretical vision was secularized and degraded into a utopian project of human regeneration that works for the coming of a *Regnum Hominis*, i.e., a "universal democracy" in which the abolition of social differences and the establishment of a common ownership of goods would ensure a final era of peace and prosperity. In this "new world" utopia are found the roots of "modern aspirations" and particularly of today's progressivism, both in its secular and Christian versions.

[1167] MARIA TERESA BEONIO BROCCHIERI FUMAGALLI, ed., *La chiesa invisibile. Riforme politico-religiose nel basso Medioevo*, Feltrinelli, Milano, 1978.

Prof. Plinio has always shown the basic difference that exists between the millenarian perspective and aspirations for the Reign of Mary.

"Millenarianism is a heresy that was born in the early days of the Church and claims that before the end of the world Our Lord Jesus Christ would visibly return to the world as He was during His earthly life, and reign for a thousand years. And so it would be an era of glory, light, peace, tranquility, because His Kingdom would be accepted by all men.

"At first glance it would therefore be a kind of Reign of Mary. In fact, it is not a Reign of Mary because they imagine that Kingdom of Jesus with men free from original sin and thus exempted from all vigilance, mortification, and moral rule. Deep down....an anarchic dream in which Jesus would play the role that a totem plays in modern structuralist concepts. This is millenarianism, obviously condemned by the Church." [1168]

Any Catholic in the least familiar with the history of Church doctrine easily understands how millenarianism is a well defined doctrine, unmistakably different from the message of Fatima and the theses of Saint Louis Marie Grignion de Montfort and Plinio Corrêa de Oliveira. Plinio clearly stated it:

"However concrete, bright and tangible the earthly reality of the social kingdom of Christ was in the thirteenth century, for example, we must not forget that this kingdom is but a preparation and prelude. The Kingdom of God in its fullness will be realized in Heaven." [1169] "The Church teaches us that this earth is a place of exile, a vale of tears, a battlefield, and not a place of delights....Thus, imagining a world without struggle and setbacks is the same as conceiving a world without Jesus Christ." [1170]

Neither sin nor struggle will be absent from the Reign of Mary:

"To imagine a Reign of Mary without struggle is foreign to the designs of Providence. Any epoch of history is a time of trial. Did the devil not enter Paradise and tempt Adam and Eve because God willed it to be so? Imagine a life completely without fight. It is no life! Struggle is necessary to the state of trial, and he who in this state does not love the fight, does not love God." [1171]

The Middle Ages was the most luminous era in history, and as such it can be considered a prefigure of the Reign of Mary; but those who think

---

[1168] NOR, 15 November 1971.

[1169] *The Crusader of the 20th Century,* op. cit., p. 255.

[1170] "Utopia and the Message," *Folha de São Paulo,* July 19, 1980.

[1171] AMC, 12 October 1989.

the Middle Ages had no dramas and tragedies are deceiving themselves. The Middle Ages knew heresies and revolts against which it was necessary to fight.

> "So also in the Reign of Mary there will be things against which it will be necessary to fight. The Reign of Mary will not be an asphalt road without obstacles. It would not be earthly, nor would it be a reign of glory, if it were a reign without obstacles."[1172]

The Revolution will be defeated, but the germ of disordered passions will lodge in every man until the end of the world with an incendiary potential, which is why the Church and the faithful cannot "lie on their laurels":

> "I have the impression that the Reign of Mary will be extremely solid, magnificent, glorious, but will have, as a punishment for men, a sword of Damocles hanging over its head. This sword of Damocles will be present in its brightest feasts and most splendid triumphs. If society caves in matters of egalitarianism, pride or sensuality, the Reign of Mary will immediately crumble. It will not gradually fall over four hundred or five hundred years like the Middle Ages, but will immediately crash to the ground."[1173]

The Certainty of the Reign of Mary

Hostility in certain social ambiences, including Catholic circles, to the perspective of a Reign of Jesus and Mary often has no doctrinal roots but rather psychological-spiritual ones. It is due to a lack of hope, a subjectivist conception of religion, and an inability to project theological truth to the current historical panorama. All this favors a certain prejudice and mistrust of a perspective deemed "triumphalist" and "theocratic." Christendom is thus relegated to a past, judged hopelessly extinct and unrepeatable, or denied as a historical possibility, reducing Religion to a factor of individual rather than social sanctification, according to a spiritual perspective of "white heresy."

This mentality reduces the Reign of Christ to its purely spiritual and individual aspect and sets it for the end of time, exiling it to the afterlife. A typical example of this mentality is manifested in certain charismatic currents widespread also in the Catholic camp. This eschatology represents the equal and opposite reaction to another mindset called "incarnationist," which reduces the Reign of Christ to its mundane historical and social aspects, imprisoning it in the earthly dungeon. A

[1172] CSN, 23 October 1982.
[1173] CSN, 9 March 1985.

typical example of this error is manifested in "liberation theology."[1174] Both of these positions are wrong for their unilateralism, the former by rejecting the historical and social aspect of the Kingdom, and the latter by reducing it to this aspect.

True, the Reign of God will attain its plenitude only in the next world, but that will happen only to the degree that this Reign already begins to take place in this world, throughout history, in the life of the Church militant. Therefore the Kingdom of God is both eschatological and temporal, otherworldly and earthly, individual and social, precisely to render glory to God in all fields and at all levels. We should therefore expect the advent of an era characterized by a revival of faith so strong as to overcome the anti-Christian Revolution and build a much more perfect, vast and lasting Christendom than the one achieved during the Middle Ages.

Moreover, if that were not so, one could erroneously believe that God is sovereign and master of eternity, but not of time; of Heaven, but not of Earth; of the spirit, but not matter; of individuals, but not societies. This may lead to believe that Divine Providence has abandoned human history to the devil's domain, reserving for Itself only a belated and symbolic final victory; or that It relinquished society, reserving for Itself only the sanctification of individuals. This reductionist mentality, of Manichean flavor, stemming from a crisis of faith and a lack of supernatural hope, is at the root of many illusions and defeats of contemporary Christianity.

The coming of the Reign of Mary is not a dogma of faith. If it were, if we had a dogmatic certainty of it as is the case with the Second Coming, we would not need to practice the virtue of hope to desire it, but only that of faith to believe in it. Waiting for the Reign of Mary requires faith united with hope: from this junction is born the confidence mentioned by Saint Thomas Aquinas[1175] in the *Quaestio* dedicated to magnanimity, the virtue of the soul that tends to greatness and is related to all other virtues.[1176]

Blessed Duns Scotus did not have a dogmatic certainty of the Immaculate Conception when he met the doctors of the Sorbonne who denied that privilege of the Virgin Mary, five centuries before it was defined as a dogma by Blessed Pius IX (1856). But he did have a moral certainty of this Marian privilege, and his confidence was based on that certainty. In later centuries preceding the dogmatic definition by Pius IX, many theologians, priests and faithful, particularly in some Spanish and

---

[1174] Cf. the excellent analysis by JULIO LOREDO, *Teologia della liberazione,* op. cit.

[1175] *Summa Theologica,* II-IIae, q. 129, art. 6, No. 3.

[1176] Idem, II-IIae, q. 129, art. 1, resp, art. 4.

Italian universities, made a vow to defend *usque ad effusionem sanguinis* – unto the shedding of their own blood – the privilege of the Immaculate Conception, even though it was still not defined as a dogma of faith, but openly denied by many prominent Catholics to the point of appearing to be a matter of opinion.[1177] Those priests and laymen were ready to suffer martyrdom in order to defend the truth of the Immaculate Conception. Their intellect was illuminated by faith, and their will strengthened in this magnanimous decision. This explains the spirit of confidence and ardent belief with which so many counter-revolutionaries struggle for the Reign of Mary around the world, comforted by the promise of Fatima.

Divine Justice

The climate in which the twentieth century ended and the twenty-first began is very different from a hundred years earlier. Even non-believers are warning that humanity is on the brink of an economic, political and moral catastrophe, for when the natural order is violated, society becomes corrupted and dies. Few, however, warn that the disaster looming over the world is a punishment that brings God's hour of justice closer.

The idea of justice, like that of divine judgment, has been removed from Catholic circles, which forget that we must seek first the Kingdom of God and His justice (Mt. 6:32), and that in the Last Judgment the angels will separate the wicked from the righteous (Mt. 13:49). Yet Church doctrine teaches that after every person's death there is a particular judgment with immediate retribution, and at the end of the world there will be a universal Judgment in which angels and men will be judged for their thoughts, words, works, and omissions. Wherefore Scripture says: *Justus es, Domine, et rectum judicium tuum* (Ps. 118:137); "O Lord, Thou art just, and upright is Thy judgment."

God is just and rewards everyone with his due. Justice, theologians explain, is one of God's infinite perfections.[1178] Divine justice is the order of things on earth and in heaven: the order by which all things give glory to God and to Him alone, and each thing has its own place in creation in reference to Him.

[1177] The University of Granada made the *votum sanguinis* in 1617. It was preceded by the University of Seville and succeeded by other Spanish and some Italian universities. Said gesture spread rapidly among religious Orders, saints, confraternities, and the faithful. This however provoked a controversy initiated by L. A. Muratori (+1750), who opposed what he called "bloody vow." He was answered by Saint Alphonsus Liguori and eminent Jesuit theologians. Cf. Julien Stricher, CSSR, *Le voeu du sang en faveur de l'Immaculé Conception. Histoire et bilan théologique d'une controverse*, Accademia Mariana Internazionale, Roma, 1959.

[1178] R. GARRIGOU-LAGRANGE, *Dieu, son existence et sa nature*, Beauchesne, Paris, 1950, pp. 440-463.

God rewards all the good and punishes all the evil done by creatures endowed with free will. What we call punishment is nothing but the natural bond existing between guilt and punishment. Guilt is in the essence of sin, and the penalty is proportionate to its seriousness. We often understand the seriousness of sin from the scope of its punishment. For example, if we did not know that hell awaits unrepentant sinners we could not understand the gravity of mortal sin, which is the only true evil of the universe.

The theology of history tells us that God rewards and punishes not only men but also communities and social groups: families, nations, civilizations. Now, while men have their reward or punishment at times on earth, but always in eternity, nations, which have no eternal life, are punished or rewarded only on earth. Pius XII teaches that "even though God often punishes private individuals for their sins only after death, nonetheless, as history teaches, He occasionally punishes in this mortal life rulers of people and their nations when they have dealt unjustly with others. For He is a just judge." [1179]

The sin of society as a whole is far more serious than sins of the individuals who compose it, for the same reason that the common good of the citizens is higher than the good of individuals. And since sins entail punishments, the theology of Christian history teaches that great catastrophes are often punishments to purge the public sins of nations. In such catastrophes, God's justice is never separated from His mercy; but God's mercy is linked to repentance, and punishment becomes inevitable when the world, rejecting contrition and penance, draws upon itself God's justice rather than His mercy. Earthquakes, famines, epidemics, wars, revolutions have always been considered divine punishments. *A fame, peste et bello libera nos Domine* [1180] – free us, O Lord, from famine, pestilence and war – is the liturgical prayer that has been repeated, through the ages, in rogations or processions that the Church holds to implore the help of Heaven, against those calamities the Christian people

---

[1179] PIUS XII, Enc. *Datis Nuperrime* on the bloody repression of the Hungarian people, of November 5, 1956, in *Discorsi e Radiomessaggi*, p. 864 (pp. 863-864).

[1180] "You know, beloved children, the mysterious knights mentioned in the Apocalypse. The second, third and fourth are war, famine, and death. Who is the first knight on the white horse? 'He that sat thereon had a bow, and there was a crown given him, and he went forth conquering that he might conquer' (6:2). He is Jesus Christ. The Evangelist seer looked not only at the ruins caused by sin, war, famine and death; he also saw Christ's victory in the first place. Indeed the journey of the Church through the centuries is a way of the cross, but in every time it is also a triumphal march. The Church of Christ, men of Christian faith and love, are always those who bring light, redemption and peace to a humanity without hope. *Iesus Christus heri et hodie, ipse et in sæcula* (Heb 13:8). Christ is your guide, from victory to victory. Follow him." (Pius XII, Speech of September 12, 1948 to the Youth of Catholic Action, *Discorsi e Radiomessaggi*, X (1948-1949), p. 212.

have always seen as punishments. But the blind forces of nature are hidden behind God's designs, mysteries sometimes of justice, sometimes of mercy.[1181]

The announcement of divine punishments for humanity characterizes the principal Marian revelations of the nineteenth and twentieth centuries, from La Salette to Fatima, and is echoed by the prophetic voices of all saints. On November 16, 1905, three years before the Messina earthquake of December 28, 1908, Saint Annibale Maria di Francia, in a sermon preached in the cathedral, announced to his fellow citizens that Messina was under the threat of God's punishment: "We need a punishment that will shake us, frighten us, wake us up! And such is an earthquake when it's really strong and exterminating!"[1182] The earthquake, Saint Annibale concluded, "while terrible, has this good aspect: it brings general conversion! It is a great missionary. People resist sermons. But when we feel the ground shaking...." While these words may seem too strong, they were uttered by the man whom Don Orione called the greatest living saint in Messina.[1183]

How can one forget Saint John Bosco's prophetic dreams and predictions of punishments?

On the eve of the second session of Vatican Council I, January 6, 1870, Don Bosco had a vision in which it was revealed that "war, plague, famine are the scourges with which men's pride and malice will be struck." Thus spoke the Lord: "You, O priests, why do you not run to weep between the porch and the altar, calling for the suspension of the plagues? Why do you not take the shield of faith and go upon roofs, into homes, in the streets and squares, even in all inaccessible places to take the seed of my word? Do you not know that this is the terrible two-edged sword that strikes my enemies and unleashes the wrath of God and men?"[1184]

For his part, Saint Thomas Aquinas thus speaks about God's "revenge" upon sinful humanity:

> "When the whole multitude sins, vengeance must be taken on them, either in respect of the whole multitude, as in the case of the Egyptians who were drowned in the Red Sea while they were pursuing the children

---

[1181] Cf. on these points R. DE MATTEI, *Il mistero del male e i castighi di Dio*, Fede e Cultura, Verona, 2011.

[1182] St. ANNIBALE MARIA DI FRANCIA (1851-1927), *Appunti di predica*, November 15, 1905, in *Scritti*, s. d., Curia Generalizia dei Regazionisti, vol. 55, doc. 2005, pp. 34-35.

[1183] St. Annibale Maria di Francia (1851-1927) was born and lived in Messina. He founded the Congregation of Daughters of the Holy Zeal (1887) and the Rogationists (1897). With the foundation of the former he was helped by the seer of La Salette, Mélanie Calvat, with whom he remained spiritually connected. He was canonized by John Paul II on May 16, 2004.

[1184] Cf. *Memorie biografiche del venerabile don Giovanni Bosco. Raccolte del sac. Salesiano Giovanni Battista Lemoyne*, edizione extra commerciale, vol. IX, Tipografia S.A.I.D. Buona Stampa, Torino, 1917, p. 782.

of Israel, and also in that of the people of Sodom were entirely destroyed; or as regards part of the multitude, as may be seen in the punishment of those who worshipped the calf. Sometimes, however, if there is hope of many making amends, the severity of vengeance should be brought to bear on a few of the principals, whose punishment fills the rest with fear; thus the Lord (Numbers, 25) commanded the princes of the people to be hanged for the sin of the multitude. On the other hand, if it is not the whole but only a part of the multitude that has sinned, then if the guilty can be separated from the innocent, vengeance should be wrought on them: provided, however, that this can be done without scandal to others; else the multitude should be spared and severity foregone. The same applies to the sovereign, whom the multitude follow. For his sin should be borne with, if it cannot be punished without scandal to the multitude: unless indeed his sin were such, that it would do more harm to the multitude, either spiritually or temporally, than would the scandal that was feared to arise from his punishment." [1185]

John Paul II, in his catechesis on Tobias (13:2-18) of August 23, 2003 states that

"Throughout the Canticle of chapter 13 of Tobit this firm conviction is repeated often: the Lord 'afflicts, and he shows mercy;... will afflict us for our iniquities; and again he will show mercy.... He will afflict you for the deeds of your sons, but again he will show mercy to the sons of the righteous' (vv. 2, 5, 9). God's punishment is a way to make sinners who are deaf to other appeals turn back to the right path. However, the last word of the righteous God remains a message of love and of forgiveness; he profoundly desires to embrace anew the wayward children who return to him with a contrite heart." [1186]

Benedict XVI, at the audience of May 18, 2011, recalling the biblical episode with Abraham and his prayer of intercession for the wicked cities of Sodom and Gomorrah (Gen. 18:16-33), insists that the punishment is not unjust but "a destruction paradoxically deemed necessary by the prayer of Abraham's intercession itself. Because that very prayer revealed the saving will of God: the Lord was prepared to forgive, he wanted to forgive but the cities were locked into a totalizing and paralyzing evil, without even a few innocents from whom to start in order to turn evil into good."[1187]

The Plinian school develops this fundamental notion of Catholic theology. The Revolution is a long system of causes and effects that have

---

[1185] *Summa Theologica*, IIᵃ-IIae, q. 108 a. 1, ad 5.
[1186] JOHN PAUL II, General Audience of August 13, 2003, at https://w2.vatican.va/content/john-paul-ii/en/audiences/2003/documents/hf_jp-ii_aud_20030813.html (accessed on May 16, 2016).
[1187] Benedict XVI, general audience of May 18, 2011, at http://w2.vatican.va/content/benedict-xvi/en/audiences/2011/documents/hf_ben-xvi_aud_20110518.html (accessed on May 16, 2016).

their origins in original sin, their archetype in the angelic sin, and their outcome in a new terrible sin that renews the great sins of history. The revolutionary process is a pattern of offenses against God, which, constituting a chain over centuries formed a single, immense, collective sin that led to the apostasy of peoples and nations. Today the Divine Law and the natural law are transgressed not only privately by individuals but above all publicly and in a systematic and organized manner.

No historical study is required to understand that today mankind is immersed in sin, justifies sin, and lives in a greater state of sin than has ever been seen in history.[1188] The greatest scandal is that entire nations have morally defected:

> "Moral corruption is not a sin only of individuals but of society. It is publicly practiced and has entered the habits of society. This multitude of sins are sins of nations. Nations that are rejecting God and find themselves almost at the end of their apostasy... The end result: these nations have to be punished on this earth. Even more, the punishment must be proportionate to the sin."[1189] "Somehow, justice will be done *in diebus nostris*, in our days.[1190] Our soul longs for these days not to end without justice being done."[1191]

It is an understatement, for example, to say that homosexuality is a mortal sin. In Plinio's last few years this violation of the natural and divine law began to be institutionalized by Western nations:

> "It is of one of the sins that Catholic doctrine defines as sins against nature which cry out to heaven – says the Catechism – and clamor to God for vengeance. Sodom and Gomorrah were destroyed because they practiced homosexuality. This is the reason; the Bible itself says so.[1192] Why? Because it is a sin that attracts God's wrath. Nations where homosexuality becomes generalized march toward complete disintegration."[1193]

Twenty years after these words the apostasy of European nations was expressed in the referendum of May 23, 2015, with which the Irish people approved the introduction of so-called "same-sex marriage" in their legislation.

More generally, however, we now live a sin that is that of rebellion against the Church and Christian civilization: the sin of the Revolution.

[1188] MNF, 21 March 1991.

[1189] SEF, 6 August 1971.

[1190] From the Introit to the Mass of the Machabeans: *Da pacem, Domine, in diebus nostris quia non est alius qui pugnet pro nobis, nisi tu Deus noster.* "Give peace, O Lord to our days, for there is no other person but Thee, our God, that fights for us."

[1191] SEF, 6 August 1971.

[1192] Gn. 19:4-11.

[1193] NOR, 14 July 1971.

This sin calls for intervention by divine justice because a supreme sin deserves a supreme punishment: "Accordingly, one can say that the whole world is heading for one of the most furious clashes with God that history has ever known."[1194]

Plinio also notes how great catastrophes in history remain suspended above the culprits for a long time. The greater the delay, the more terrible the punishment. If the punishment is late it does not mean that it will not come, but that it will be terrible.[1195] The more the allotted time is longer, the more severe will be the punishment if there is no repentance. The harshness of the punishment is proportional to the seriousness of the sin but also to the length of time God grants people to convert. God is in no hurry (Wis. 12:1-10): He waits for the times to be fulfilled and carries out His designs (Is. 46:11). Infinitely patient, He often delays punishment to give the wicked time to repent and gain merit.

The Flood (Gn. 6:5; 9:17) was a supreme punishment because of all mankind, only Noah and his family were saved; but it was also an act of mercy because during the punishment, as Saint Peter attested (1 Pt. 3:19), many who otherwise would have been lost converted before dying. The worst of evils is not death but sin; and death can sometimes be a grace.

The Bagarre

Bagarre is a French word that indicates a state of confusion due to a dispute or brawl. Plinio Corrêa de Oliveira employs it as a metaphor to describe the punishment that awaits humanity: a moment of supreme justice but also of supreme mercy, because that is when God will intervene in history to destroy the Revolution and establish the Reign of Mary.[1196] The Bagarre is not the punishment of the times of Antichrist but a prefigure of it. It will be, according to Plinio, "one of the most majestic and tragic events in world history."[1197]

To prefigure means that one thing can represent another, to be its "figure." Plinio gives this example: a painting representing a rose is the figure of the rose that the painter wants to depict. But a prefiguration is a figure that precedes the thing represented. If a representation of the rose precedes the existence of the rose, one can speak of a prefiguration. From this standpoint, by anticipating an event the prefiguration is a prophetic event, as would be a painting done before the rose existed. In this sense

---

[1194] RRR, 5 May 1995.

[1195] SD, 3 April 1970.

[1196] The custom was born of a conversation in France in 1952 with then young Dr. Luiz Nazareno Teixeira de Assunção Filho (1931-2009), who became his closest disciple. Since it refers to a major event, we will always capitalize it.

[1197] SD, 29 June 1966 & 31 August 1985.

the fall of Jerusalem is a foreshadowing both of the Bagarre and of the end of the world; and the Bagarre is a prefigure of the end of the world and the coming of the Antichrist,[1198] which Cornelius a Lapide describes as characterized by "very serious riots, wars, famines, pestilences, earthquakes, false christs."[1199]

The Bagarre is a supreme chastisement for the gravity of the sin it punishes. It can be defined as the synthesis of all the punishments with which God always punishes humanity: wars, epidemics, famine, natural disasters.[1200] To these misfortunes today is added a more serious one: psychological and moral chaos, which leads to the loss of reason and a profound suffering of the soul. It will be a universal convulsion, that will bring an upheaval in the world's disorderly situation, which will be followed by a fullness of order and holiness in the Church and in the world. It will be a convulsion not only in human order but in the meteorological and cosmic order, a supernatural and preternatural punishment which will lead to the liquidation of today's world, the conversion of survivors, and the establishment of a new Christian civilization: the Reign of Mary, a triumphant era for the Holy Roman Church, and a prodigious increase in the action of the Holy Ghost in her life.[1201]

As a consequence of this punishment, unrepentant and irreducible sinners will be wiped from the face of the earth; many sinners will convert and perish, while others will be converted and saved, regenerated by grace. Many of the just will die, while others will be saved and build the Reign of Mary.

The days of Bagarre will be days of avenging anger that restores violated justice and purifies and sanctifies the earth, as happened at the time of the Flood.[1202] The Bagarre will be started and ended by the angels. If it is true that "all corporeal things are governed by the angels,"[1203] they will be the tools God will use to accomplish His designs.

But Our Lady's ardent devotees, the apostles of the latter times of whom Saint Louis de Montfort spoke, will play a role in it.

> "Marie des Vallées speaks about the great punishments and says the instruments of divine justice will be some men, very weak and soft before the chastisement, but who during it will receive an action of the Holy Ghost that will transform them into men of extraordinary fortitude. She gives them two titles: God's increpators and avengers. In other words,

---

[1198] SD, 29 September 1990.
[1199] CORNELIUS A LAPIDE, *Commentaria in Mattheum*, cap. XXIV, 6.
[1200] SD, 6 April 1966.
[1201] SD, 22 January 1971.
[1202] SD, 11 April 1970.
[1203] *Summa Theologica*, I, q. 110, a. 1.

they should have two purposes: 1) reproach the world for the sins it committed and into which it fell, to try and save part of humanity; and 2) they must be avengers, that is, strike blows of divine justice against those committing the sin of Revolution at its peak, who were plotting against the good in order to wipe them out from the face of the earth and virtually eliminate the children of Our Lady."[1204]

"To increpate is to accuse someone of a certain transgression, describing it with sovereign eloquence and nobility. Hence the difference between increpating and simply accusing. The increpator rises to the zenith of the principles on whose behalf he makes the accusation. He is, as it were, an embodiment of the principles in whose name he accuses. He rises up to accuse. In his person, nobility and elevation of soul he is the embodiment of the principles he avenges against the increpated one. And if these principles are unheeded, he threatens."[1205]

The Bagarre will be the historic hour in which the Counter-Revolution will wage the final battle.

"Either the world ends – and it will not – or a Counter-Revolution has to come that dominates the world, and this is inescapable. How does this Counter-Revolution win? Through a great chastisement that crushes the power of evil, and through the fight of the good, who win in the name of Mary. What is the end result? It is predicted that a handful of good people will fight even in the worst of times and circumstances, and will raise the standard of Our Lady during the fight. For now these good ones are still very few in view of the immense mass of the Revolution, but the course of events is on their side because evil marches to its own death and annihilation. This is because the nature of evil is such that it inevitably destroys itself. Evil is like a disease: when allowed to run its course, it kills the patient. But by killing the patient, it also dies. Cancer kills the cancer patient; but the patient's death kills the cancer, as both die together."[1206]

The Bagarre will not be the end of the world "because Our Lady will obtain a postscript in world history to establish Her Reign. Then there will be an entirely exceptional reign, in circumstances we cannot entirely predict."[1207]

For Plinio, the certainty of these events is based on the fact that a punishment is always an act of supreme mercy. Mercy can ward off punishment, as happened to Nineveh, but if there is no repentance, punishment is logical and necessary. If we are convinced that the moral degradation of humanity is the result of a long revolutionary process we

---

[1204] AMP, 20 July 1973.
[1205] Idem.
[1206] SEF, 14 July 1971.
[1207] MNF, 20 June 1979.

cannot but expect a purifying punishment: only that extraordinary punishment will make the world understand the seriousness of the sin of Revolution.

The certainty of the Bagarre is a logical consequence of the undeniable existence of the Revolution. Indeed, the dynamic of evil has its own irreversibility:

> "In the moral order, vices are nourished by their own effect. For example, addiction to alcohol or compulsive gambling. The individual gets drunk because he is intemperate, the cause was intemperance; but drunkenness, which is the effect, feeds its own cause, which is intemperance. Result: the individual sinks into drunkenness. The same could be said of a thousand other vices. For example, addiction to games, sensuality, or anger. All vices are like that: they are nourished by their own effect.

> "No moral defect is irreversible, for grace can interrupt the corruption process. But the more a sinner becomes mired in vice, the rarer is the intervention of grace. This is natural, for it is much harder for an individual at the height of addiction to receive a grace to convert, something that is less difficult at the beginning of his addiction. So in the final stage of addiction there is, as it were, an irreversibility. It is not irreversibility properly speaking, as an intervention of grace is always possible, but there is something like irreversibility, a quasi irreversibility.

> "If we switch from the general moral case to the concrete fact, we know that the Revolution has reached a pinnacle of pride and sensuality worldwide, making it almost impossible, or rather impossible without a spectacular miracle, for these vices, which bring with them all others, not to cause humanity to explode. Why? Because, when it attains its fullness, disorder causes complete breakdown. This is the cause of death. It would be like a clock that works: if disorder is progressively introduced in its mechanism, at some point the clock stops.

> "Now, sensuality and pride are on the verge of attaining a fullness – the fullness of disorder – and therefore they have *a priori* to cause an explosion, that is, wars, revolutions, agitation etc. Therefore, the Bagarre is certain, as it were!" [1208]

The Bagarre is therefore a terrible punishment, but one that also has a dimension of forgiveness and mercy.

The theology of history shows that from the Creation of the universe until the end of the world there have been and will be immense sins followed by immense acts of divine mercy. The history of the universe opens with a supreme sin, the revolt of the angels, but from that moment the role of the Virgin Mary, Queen of Angels, called to crush the head of

---

[1208] SEF, 6 August 1971.

Satan and of the rebellious angels, begins to emerge in history. The sin of Adam's descendants corrupts humanity, which decays until the Flood, and is followed by God's covenant with the chosen people. The chosen people are stained with the sin of Deicide, but the Passion of Christ redeems mankind, and from the pierced side of Christ the Church is born; and from the Church is born the Christian civilization of the Middle Ages. The sin of Revolution, which halted the development of Christian civilization for many centuries and led to the spiritual and moral ruin of our day, cannot but arouse a reaction which, supported by divine grace, will lead to the historical realization of the great plan of Divine Providence.

Plinio Corrêa de Oliveira explains:

> "The whole theory of the Bagarre is based on the idea that under the normal and even extraordinary ways of grace, when great apostasies occur, from a certain moment the possibility of real conversion no longer exists. Theoretically, conversion is possible because God can do whatever He wants, but this is entirely out of His habits. Therefore, one must act as if it were not likely, while not excluding the possibility that in the present world's worthless disorder, recoverable elements can be found to prepare a worthy order after the Bagarre." [1209]

"Residuum revertetur"

The history of the Church is one of great apostasy and great punishments, but also one of great revivals that always begin with a small group of faithful. Indeed, God wishes to use the weak in the eyes of men to confuse and defeat the mighty. This principle is expressed in the formula *residuum revertetur*.

This formula is part of Catholic theology. An eminent biblical scholar, Msgr. Salvatore Garofalo,[1210] devoted an in-depth study to *The Prophetic Notion of the 'Remnant of Israel'*"[1211] in which he shows that this concept is a cornerstone of the prophetic tradition. He recalls that God never fails in His promises and continues to assist the chosen people even when they betray Him and persecute Christ. The story of the prophet Elias (3 Kings 19:10, 14-18) is a testimony to the fact that "in the midst of the general apostasy, God reserved a *remnant* of faithful unknown even to the discouraged prophet; so also at the time of the apostles, in the midst of

---

[1209] RRR, 4 September 1976.

[1210] Salvatore Garofalo (1911-1998), ordained in 1933, was a professor of Biblical exegesis and later dean of the Pontifical Urbaniana University, and participated in the Second Vatican Council as a *peritus*.

[1211] SALVATORE GAROFALO, *La nozione profetica del "Resto di Israele,"* Lateranum, Roma, 1962. Cf. also R. DE VAUX, O.P., "Le 'Reste d'Israel' d'après les Prophètes," *Revue Biblique*, no. 42 (1933), pp. 526-539.

a hardened and unfaithful nation, He raises up a chosen minority, a 'remnant,' a 'remainder,' attaining the end unfulfilled by the masses."[1212]

The figure of Elias is at the center of this tradition. When religious syncretism corroded the soul of Israel, Elias suddenly hails from a wild gorge on Mount Carmel in the presence of a huge crowd. After the "prophets" of Baal frantically pleaded their lord to no avail, he turns to Yahweh Who, answering the cries of his prophet, incinerates both the victim and altar in an immense fire (3 Kings 18:16-40). God then reveals to Elias the continuity of the covenant, and the fortunes of Israel are entrusted to a small remnant thereof, a faithful remnant chosen and watched over by the Lord, among whom the privileges of the first-born people are summed up and endure.[1213] The Lord cannot allow His people to face the same end as Sodom and Gomorrah, so He saves a small remnant. "And there shall be still a tithing therein, and she shall turn, and shall be made a show as a turpentine tree, and as an oak that spreadeth its branches" (Is. 6:13) because the God who uprooted and tore down will build up and plant (Jer. 31:28).[1214] The doctrine of the remnant presents the twofold aspect of a threat of punishment and a promise of salvation.[1215] Indeed, God does not punish to destroy, but to purify.

Msgr. Garofalo comments:

> "According to the earliest formulation of the idea, especially deserving of divine providence are those who did not bow their knees to Baal (3 Kings 19:18). The Remnant essentially is a *holy seed* (Is. 4:2 ff: 6:13, cf. 35:8), a gathering of the righteous (60:21), for only the good escape from the divine scourge (Am. 9:10; Is 33:14-16; Jer. 35)."[1216]

Scripture tells us that God in His Justice, "seeing that the wickedness of men was great on the earth, and that all the thought of their heart was bent upon evil at all times," decreed the Flood (Gen. 6:5-7). But in the midst of all the wicked men was Noah, a "just and perfect man who walked with God" (Gen. 6:9). God showed mercy and ordered him to build an ark (Hebrew "Tebah" = "ark"), or rather a house with four walls that rose above a large and sturdy raft. God told him: "I will bring the waters of a great flood upon the earth, to destroy all flesh...[but] will establish my covenant with thee" (Gen. 6:17-22).

The Covenant with Noah was to save him and his family (eight people in all) plus all animals of each species. God used Noah and his

---

[1212] SALVATORE GAROFALO, *La nozione profetica del "Resto di Israele,"* p. 5.
[1213] Idem, p. 49.
[1214] Idem, p. 210.
[1215] Idem, p. 192.
[1216] Idem, p. 211.

family to rebuild the alliance after the Flood; and when the chosen people fell into infidelity He used the remnant of Israel to found the Church.

Plinio recalls:

> "Our Lord did everything for the country of Israel, showing goodness, wisdom, power, working miracles etc. But everything ultimately came down to this point: taking the faithful or convertible remnants of Israel to prepare His Kingdom with them. This is also the policy of the Counter-Revolution:...from the moment when a certain ideological institution becomes a pole of thought it gradually exercises a certain effect on those who do not agree with the dominant revolutionary situation and occasionally produces conversions. For example, that was the role the Church played in the Western Roman Empire: She had grown so much that she became a pole of thought and later ordered paganism to end." [1217]

In this age of self-destruction in the Church, the Lord will use a little remnant of faithful Catholics, not to re-found the Church but to renew her customs and restore her perennial doctrine. Fidelity to the Roman Catholic and Apostolic Church, to her doctrine and laws, is a distinctive note of the Plinian mission, which adds nothing to Divine Revelation. "After all, for us the Church is everything, absolutely everything on this earth." [1218]

There is a line of continuity throughout history from Elias the Prophet to the Apostles of the Latter Times through Saint Louis de Montfort and many other saints. It is the continuity of those who fight for the triumph of the Church against her enemies. This legacy is prophetic, because those who receive it play the role of leading and guiding souls.

> "Reading Saint Louis de Montfort's *Fiery Prayer* asking for missionaries for his Society, we have the moral profile of the perfect devotee of Our Lady. Reading the life of Elias one realizes that his whole life corresponded to that moral profile. Founder of the first existing religious family in the world devoted to venerate Our Lady from the start, the Carmelites; man of fire in a tremendous struggle against Baal, false idols, and the defects of the people of Israel. Prophet who prophesied the coming of the Messias and His death; prophet who will still fight to the end of the world as a true heel of Our Lady to crush the head of the serpent. Elias was a Saint Louis de Montfort of the Old Testament, and Saint Louis de Montfort was an Elias of the New Testament." [1219]

> "Elias is one of the Apostles of the Latter Times. For as we know, he should return in the last days of human history to fight against the

---

[1217] RRR, 4 September 1976.
[1218] EXT, 27 February 1966.
[1219] NOR, 29 March 1967.

Antichrist. So we consider Elias at the same time a forerunner of our apostolate and the one with whom the struggle in which we are engage will culminate."[1220]

A handful of good counter-revolutionaries will fight in the worst situations created in history; they will raise Our Lady's standard and have her at their side during the events. "The remnant are those who were faithful. A small, insignificant number that valiantly and imperturbably continue to fight."[1221]

This unshakable fidelity characterizes Plinio's vocation. On Christmas in 1946, turning to Jesus in the crib, he wrote in *Legionário*:

"Who are we? We are those who do not bend even one knee to Baal. Those who have Thy Law written on the bronze of our souls and do not allow this century to write its erroneous doctrines on this bronze that Thy Redemption made sacred. Those who love the immaculate purity of orthodoxy as the most precious of treasures and refuse to make any pact with heresy, its works and infiltrations. Those who have mercy on the repentant sinner but also implore Thy mercy for ourselves, so often unworthy and unfaithful but who do not spare insolent and proud impiety, vice parading with pride and mocking virtue. Those who have pity on all men but especially on the blessed who are persecuted for the sake of Thy Church, oppressed throughout the earth for their hunger and thirst for virtue, abandoned, scorned, betrayed and reviled because they remain faithful to Thy Law. Those who suffer while contemporary literature forgets to exalt the beauty of their sufferings: a Christian mother today who prays alone before the manger in a home abandoned by her children, who profane Thy Christmas Day with orgies; an austere and strong husband who, out of fidelity to Thy Spirit has become misunderstood and disliked by his own; a faithful wife who bears the hardships of loneliness of heart and soul while the levity of customs dragged to adultery he who ought to be the stalwart of her home, her beloved half and 'other self'; a pious son or daughter who during Christmas, while Christian homes celebrate, feels more than ever the icy atmosphere with which selfishness, the thirst for pleasure and worldliness have paralyzed and killed family life in his own home. The student abandoned and scorned by his colleagues because he remains faithful to Thee. The master detested by his disciples because he is not complicit with their errors. The parish priest or bishop who feels rising around him a dark wall of incomprehension or indifference because he refuses to allow Church doctrine, entrusted to him, to deteriorate. The honest man reduced to poverty because he did not steal. These are, Lord, the ones who at this

---

[1220] SD, 14 June 1967.
[1221] SEF, 14 July 1971.

moment, dispersed, isolated, not knowing one another, approach Thee to offer their gift and present their prayer." [1222]

Plinio Corrêa de Oliveira picks up the abandoned flags of the Crusades, Lepanto, the Counter-Reformation, and the Counter-Revolution. Referring to all current or potential counter-revolutionaries struggling throughout the world and facing the Revolution in its various aspects, he stated:

"We represent everything which the Revolution gradually destroyed and Our Lady would want to continue living in us. In us live the remnants of all the past glories of Christendom. Through enraptured, enthusiastic, tender and nostalgic admiration in us live the heroism of the martyrs, the grandeur of doctors, the strength of confessors, the splendor of Cluny, the magnificence of Chivalry, the sacral audacity of the Crusades, the force of the Counter-Reformation, the fire and perspicacity that characterized so many champions of the Counter-Revolution in the nineteenth century and, in our days, the anti-modernist zeal of a Saint Pius X, the courage of a Garcia Moreno. Men reject all that even when placed at the highest and most splendorous echelons of the Holy Roman Catholic and Apostolic Church.

"Historically, we are a remnant. Our Lady did not want those values to disappear form the Earth, and thus she chose us. If historically we are a remnant, the remnant is worth all that it represents." [1223]

[1222] "Beside the Creche," *Legionário,* no. 750, December 22, 1946.
[1223] RRR, July 26, 1975.

CONCLUSION

Vir totus catholicus et apostolicus, plene romanus

Now at the end of this work, I cannot hide the sense of dismay that struck me facing the obvious impossibility of fitting into a small volume a teaching that fills hundreds of thousands of pages, but which, above all, is so rich and varied that in order to be properly expounded, it would require the work of many scholars from different theological, philosophical, and historical disciplines. I hope that this may happen in the future, and for my part I will be happy if I have at least managed to convey the spirit that animated the *Crusader of the Twentieth Century*. A man whose supreme point of reference was always the Church, of which he said he was even unable to speak without emotion. That was not a passing attitude, as he confided:

> "This is my attitude every day, every minute, every moment: to gaze at the Catholic Church in order to be imbued with her spirit, to have her inside me, and to be entirely inside her. And if the Church were abandoned by all men, to the extent that would be possible without her ceasing to exist, I would want to have her entirely inside of me. To live only for her so that upon dying I may say: 'I truly was a Catholic and fully apostolic man, Roman, Roman and Roman!'" [1224]

Vir totus catholicus et apostolicus plene romanus. This inscription, on the tomb of Plinio Corrêa de Oliveira in the Consolation Cemetery in São Paulo, not only sums up the meaning of a life, but also provides the key to understanding the prophetic mission that he passes on to his school of followers in the twenty-first century.

Some might think that the term "crusade," which I employed to define Plinio's life, objectively corresponds to the nature of his great battle, while the term "prophecy," projecting his mission onto a future still to come, is uncertain and questionable, and as such unsuitable for use by a historian.

The same objection, however, could be made to those wishing to study a prophecy intimately linked to the Brazilian master and certainly

---

[1224] Introductory words by Prof. Corrêa de Oliveira, answering a tribute to him by his spiritual sons on the occasion of the sixty-ninth anniversary of his baptism, June 7, 1978.

unfulfilled, that of Fatima.[1225] The fact that it has not been entirely fulfilled does not mean that it cannot be the subject of study, and even less that it is false. God alone knows the times and ways in which the Fatima message will be fulfilled, but Our Lady gave the three seers the great mission of announcing it to the world precisely to interpret the times and guide future action. After all, a person with a historic mission lives to fulfill it, not because he knows its outcome but because he knows that the realization of his vocation depends on his correspondence to grace. This applies to Plinio Corrêa de Oliveira and to those who continue his work today, having received his cultural and spiritual heritage.

Did his death on the threshold of the twenty-first century mean that his mission failed? To answer this objection I will close these pages by recalling two episodes of Plinio's life directly related to this issue.

Expiatory Victim?

Since the years when Brazil lived through a tormented season of terrorism, the Brazilian leader had been wondering what would happen to his work if he died:

> "I wondered: what if I die? If they shoot me, what will the future of the Counter-Revolution be? I do not know, but because of the order of the universe I know there will not be a world without someone who is fully counter-revolutionary, and that at least one very faithful counter-revolutionary must exist. Therefore, if I die another will come perhaps better than me and will better accomplish the task for which I will not have been worthy. But I expire in peace because God will not abandon His work." [1226]

Plinio then asked himself another question, which he already had in mind in his youth after reading St. Therese the Little Flower's *Story of a Soul* and Dom Chautard's *Soul of the Apostolate*:

> "Would it not be better to offer myself as an expiatory victim? In other words, I die but my death serves to pay for a large number of situations that it was not possible to overcome, or that I was unable to overcome. Is that not the will of God?"[1227]

The tradition of the Church has recorded the existence of victim souls who offer their life in atonement for the sins of the world.[1228] It is a

---

[1225] "We would be mistaken to think that Fatima's prophetic mission is complete," stated Benedict XVI on May 13, 2010 during a visit to the Fatima Shrine. *Insegnamenti*, VI, 1 (2010), p. 699 (pp. 696-700).

[1226] MNF, 21 March 1991.

[1227] Cf. also "Expiatory Victim," *Legionário*, no. 790, September 28, 1947.

[1228] GIUSEPPE MANZONI, *Spiritualité victimale,* DSp, XVI, cols. 531-545; MARCEL DENIS, SCJ: *La spiritualité victimale en France,* Studia Dehoniana, Roma, 1981; LORENZO PREZZI,

high calling that can only come from a special inspiration of the Holy Ghost, to which the soul corresponds with self-sacrifice and generosity. The Cistercian monk Dom Vital Lehodey, who sees a victim's vow as an extension of self-abandonment, conceives it only in the event of an indisputable divine call.[1229] But many are the souls that made this radical vow,[1230] from Saint Veronica Giuliani,[1231] who offered her life in atonement for the sins of the world, to Saint Mariana de Jesus,[1232] who offered her life to save the city of Quito from divine punishment; from Saint Gemma Galgani[1233] to Saint Therese of the Child Jesus, who on June 9, 1895 offered herself in holocaust to the merciful love of Jesus.

Plinio Corrêa de Oliveira, seeking to be a saint and do so in the most perfect way, wondered if God was asking him to make that supreme act of offering his life. Yet he felt an inner resistance, which did not arise from a lack of generosity and self-sacrifice, but from the growing awareness that Providence had reserved another mission for him.

The inner voice of grace that spoke to his soul led him to embrace the counter-revolutionary struggle. It was as if a prophetic flash had blown away the clouds obscuring his future: he should not die but live to fight.[1234]

> "In spiritual matters, when uncertain between two paths, one should prefer the most unpleasant. And I was horrified at this expiatory path of Saint Therese the Little Flower. Not that I did not admire that path, I did admire it profoundly, but I was horrified to have to follow it, as my whole makeup was opposed to that. Even worse, it implied renouncing some inner voices calling me to the counter-revolutionary fight, in which I found my joy, support and consolation. And it sufficed for me to place

---

Spiritualità oblativa riparatrice, EDB, Bologna, 1989; CLAUDE AUGER, "La spiritualité victimale au Canada français. Étude de dix congrégations de religieuses au service du clergé," *Claretianum*, No. 46 (2006), pp. 361-412.

[1229] DOM VITAL LEHODEY (1857-1948), Abbot of La Trappe Bricquebec, *Le saint abandon*, part I, chap. 10.

[1230] Let us recall among many victim souls, Mother Marie de Jésus (Emilie d'Oultremont, 1818-1878), founder of the Société de Marie Réparatice; Blessed Maria Deleuil Montigny (1841-1884), assassinated by an anarchist, founder of the Daughters of the Heart of Jesus; Blessed Maria Alexandrina da Costa (1904-1955); Blessed Blandina Merten (1883-1918) of the Order of St. Ursula, all victims of atonement for the sins of the world.

[1231] Saint Veronica Giuliani (1660-1672). A Poor Clare Capuchin favored by mystical graces, she was abbess at Città di Castello. In her virginal heart were found carved emblems of the Passion as she had drawn and described by order of her confessor. She was canonized by Gregory XVI on May 26, 1839.

[1232] Saint Mariana de Jesus de Paredes y Flórez (1618-1645), a Third Order Franciscan, was proclaimed a saint by Pius XII on July 9, 1950. She is the first canonized saint of the Republic of Ecuador, where she is known as the "Lily of Quito."

[1233] Saint Gemma Galgani, (1878-1903), favored by supernatural gifts, lived in union with the sufferings of the Passion of Jesus and was canonized by Pius XII on May 2, 1940.

[1234] CSN, 23 March 1985.

myself outside the perspective of those inner voices, and in the perspective of an expiatory victim, that everything would dry up." [1235]

"Hesitant, I then decided to take a path taught by Saint Therese the Little Flower, which consisted in never asking Our Lord for anything and never refusing anything, accepting all that would happen without making the divine request: *Si fieri potest, transeat ad me calix iste.* [1236] 'None of this *fieri potest*, don't take away the chalice, drink it as soon as it presents itself, and drink it to the end, consuming your sacrifice.'

"But at the same time this produced in me such a prodigiously unnatural effect that it was a real torment. In spite of it I stopped asking Our Lord and Our Lady for anything. I asked for nothing. And a whole number of things were happening, proper to cause apprehension, and many others to cause an appetite and stimulate desire; therefore they were things I wanted, but I would not ask for anything." [1237]

Every fiber of Plinio's soul yearned to fight in defense of the Church and of Christian civilization, a struggle that did not exclude the possibility of death. He would be happy to die fighting, and his soul was repugnant to a death that excluded the fight:

"Dying is beautiful. The martyrs died, the victims of the French Revolution died. Offering oneself as a victim is beautiful! A bed-ridden patient can offer himself as a victim: Saint Therese of the Child Jesus offered herself as an expiatory victim. But fighting has a special beauty!" [1238]

"The beautiful thing is not to say, 'I would love my vocation so much if it did not require the fight,' but to say the opposite: never is my vocation as beautiful as when I fight. This is where the fight appears in all its grandeur, for it has the character of an affirmation of the absolute, and God visits the soul of the fighter. He who fights feels, so to speak, God's absolute touch on his soul, and in this he is a hero even if he is crushed to death." [1239]

Here he is not talking about the physical and bloody struggle as faced, for example, by the Crusaders, but of a cultural and moral struggle against the enemies of the Church, characteristic of the era in which he lived.

Plinio did not ask God, like some victim souls, to die in atonement for the sins of the world, but to fight to the death against the sins of the world and especially against the sin of Revolution, which is the greatest

---

[1235] CSN, 16 July 1994.
[1236] "My Father, if it be possible, let this chalice pass from me. Nevertheless not as I will, but as thou wilt" (Mt. 26:39).
[1237] CSN, 16 July 1994.
[1238] SDS, 3 August 1974.
[1239] RRR, 23 September 1974.

possible offense to the Lord. In this spirit he faced the prosaic struggle of everyday life like a knight engaging in battle.

> "I am not offering my blood but my life. That means hours and hours of attention, effort, application and earnest commitment – a whole man's life! – that I sacrifice so that the cause of the Counter-Revolution may effectively have a great advantage in every specific move.

> "I do so with the forward thrust of soul with which a Crusader would advance in battle. And this gives me the courage to do it because I do not see it as a complicated little role, difficult to play; I do not look at it as one more little thing of every day life. I see everyday life in a supernatural way, projected to a much higher and more beautiful level, and there I see the beauty of what I am doing." [1240]

> "If I were given the choice I would like to die especially glorifying Our Lady and fighting despite my age, combating to defend, for example, an image of hers. How I would like to have my mortal remains buried in a church next to an altar so that when the priest celebrated Mass he would be stepping over my body!"[1241]

It is God, not man, who chooses our vocation, and Plinio Corrêa de Oliveira said he was willing to accept whatever God had in store for him. But God heeded the most pure and profound longing of his heart: He gave Plinio the struggle for which he yearned, with all its bitterness and satisfactions, sorrows and consolations that this kind of struggle entails.

The Inner Grace of Genazzano

In his life as a Christian combatant, Plinio Corrêa de Oliveira always asked himself, as every Catholic should, if he had entirely corresponded to what Providence wanted of him. Indeed, for a Catholic there is only one real failure: to have missed holiness, which is full correspondence with God's plan for the soul of each of us. In his long life, Plinio had many experiences: he was a congressman, journalist, university professor, Catholic Action leader, congregant of the Sodality of Our Lady; but only in 1960, when he founded the TFP, did he conclude that he had achieved what Providence asked of him. Struck precisely in those years by a serious form of diabetes, he questioned his conscience as each of us must do at life's crucial moments. He then suffered one of the deepest interior trials of his life.

In 1967 he found himself in a hospital room when a TFP member brought him from Italy a print of Our Lady venerated in the Shrine of Genazzano. Contemplating the image, Plinio was touched and had the

---

[1240] EXT, 11 October 1990.
[1241] EXT, 21 August 1992.

impression that Our Lady was looking at him with a particularly maternal and smiling expression. His soul was deeply touched and his spiritual trial suddenly ceased. His health gradually began to improve and he was fully able to resume his activities.[1242] It was not a miracle but a great spiritual grace that gave him the inner certainty that he would bring his mission to completion.[1243]

The inner grace of Genazzano added to the promise of Fatima and the historical and theological certainties he drew from a historical and philosophical analysis of his time. Plinio then had an unshakable certainty: one day, the Counter-Revolution would be victorious.

> "God would not drag me in vain to a desert into which I was venturing alone, trusting only His word (He would have the right to do so). But since He instilled in my soul the hope that I would work on this – as the Jewish people worked, at least during certain phases, for the coming of the Messias and the establishment of the Biblical order of things – He would not give me this certainty as a means and source of strength to do all of that if He wanted the opposite from me. From this thought I drew a singular certainty: come what may, the establishment of a Marian order of things would also take place." [1244]

"The Voices Did Not Lie!"

Plinio Corrêa de Oliveira nourished the hope that he would be able to witness the defeat of the Revolution, but that was above all the expectation of his disciples, who could not imagine the dawn of the Reign of Mary without the living and visible presence of the one who had opened their hearts to that hope. Providence decided otherwise, calling Plinio's soul on October 3, 1995, the feast day, on the old calendar, of Saint Therese of the Child Jesus, who, on her deathbed, turning to her Superior, whispered: "Oh, no, I would not be afraid of going to war. For

---

[1242] Cf. the statement by Prof. Corrêa de Oliveira published in the journal of the Sanctuary of Genazzano, *Madre del Buon Consiglio* (July-August 1985), p. 28: "That print [of Our Lady] came to me at a moment of spiritual trial that made me suffer much more than physical infirmity....When I gazed at her I had the unexpected impression that Our Lady's image, while not changing at all, expressed an ineffable and maternal sweetness that comforted me and filled my soul – I do not know how – with the belief that the Most Holy Virgin promised me that I would not die without having done the work required. That infused great suavity in my soul. To this day I keep that same conviction intact. And with Our Lady's favor, this work has admirably prospered, authorizing the hope that it will attain its goal."

[1243] "And the mission was that of, for lake of better, Our Lady resigning herself to have me as leader of the counter-revolutionary effort. And she would be content with this out of mercy and kindness, and would actually lead me to its fulfillment" (CSN, 16 July 1994).

[1244] MNF, 23 March 1995.

example, at the time of the Crusades, with what happiness would I leave to fight the heretics."[1245]

On January 26, 2011 Benedict XVI decided to recall the profound influence Saint Therese received from another great French saint, Joan of Arc: "In the context of a completely different life, spent in the cloister, the Carmelite of Lisieux felt very close to Joan, living in the heart of the Church and participating in Christ's suffering for the world's salvation. The Church has brought them together as patronesses of France, after the Virgin Mary."[1246]

The two patronesses of France also were, in a sense, patron saints of Plinio's soul. He saw in them a blend of two virtues especially dear to him: purity and heroism. But a more mysterious and profound affinity bound him to the life, and especially the death, of the warrior maiden of Orleans.

In the bull canonizing Saint Joan of Arc, Pope Benedict XV thus acknowledged the divinity of her mission before the whole Church:

> "The eyes of all Christians turn to the new Saint who, to fulfill divine orders, abandoned her family, left female occupations, took up arms, and led soldiers into battle: she therefore feared no death threats or the unjust sentence that condemned her to the stake. Aware that she was innocent and no heretic, witch, apostate or relapsed, while surrounded by flames she offered prayers and supplications and repeated having done everything by the will of God, until, finding strength at seeing the cross, she gave up her spirit. But the justice lacking in her judgment through men's inconsiderate passion was not long in coming, and soon the Supreme Pontiff was able to completely restore the reputation of Joan of Arc, whose example should stand before the eyes of all those who endure unjust suffering, that they may serenely await reparation by the just and eternal Judge."[1247]

The condemnation to the stake seemed to belie her prophecy about the expulsion of the English from France. Yet, to the very end, the Maid of Orleans denied that she had been a victim of illusions, claimed the divine inspiration of her mission, and even as her hopes of seeing the fulfillment of her mission seemed to dissolve into the flames she cried out to men and to heaven: "The voices did not lie! The voices did not lie!"[1248]

[1245] ST. THERESE OF THE CHILD JESUS, *Opere complete*, Libreria Editrice Vaticana, Città del Vaticano, 1997, pp. 1054-1055.

[1246] BENEDICT XVI, General audience of January 26, 2011, *Insegnamenti*, vol. VII, 1 (2011), p. 142 (pp. 137-142). For a parallel between the two saints, cf. OLIVIER RIOULT, FSSPX, *Jeanne d'Arc. Histoire d'une âme*, Clovis, Paris, 2010, pp. 563-582.

[1247] BENEDICT XV, Apostolic Exhortation *Divino disponente,* of May 16, 1920, BELLOCCHI, vol. VIII, *Benedetto XV*, p. 350 (pp. 339-351).

[1248] MNF, 26 December 1994.

Her appeal comes all the way to our days:

> "It is possible she had on her mind a temptation to doubt, but then at a certain moment they heard her shout from inside the fire: 'The voices did not lie! The voices did not lie!' It was the ultimate message she left to men. And for perpetual memory until the end of time, she cried out to the future: 'The voices did not lie! The voices did not lie! The voices did not lie!' Would that her cry would reach all the way to the depths of darkness in which we will enter, and may we understand that we can go through situations every bit as harrowing and distressing as hers, but that 'the voices do not lie'! We hear no voices but have the graces we feel and the appeal of our souls. If we stand very firm on this conviction I think we can march on unimpeded, and even enter the threshold of death without trembling."[1249]

The voices had not lied. As the Maid had predicted, after her death the British were expelled from the city of Paris, then from Normandy, Aquitaine, and from all over France. About 120 years later, Calais, the last English city in France, fell, and the reconquest of French territory ended. But the mission of the French heroine was not only to expel the English from France. Msgr. Delassus devoted a book to the *Posthumous Mission* of Saint Joan of Arc, in which he recalls that the ideal of the social kingship of Our Lord is what the saint tried to instill in France and the world: "Renewing faith in the God-Man, supreme sovereign of heaven and earth, in the minds of kings and peoples, rejuvenating it with her words, and bearing witness by her miraculous life and works, was and will be the culminating point of her mission."[1250]

Likewise, the culminating point of the mission of Plinio Corrêa de Oliveira was the supernatural confidence that he inspired in the triumph of Our Lady over the Revolution.

The voices did not lie, graces received do not deceive, he repeated to the end. As happened with Saint Joan of Arc, the promise will not go unfulfilled.

> "My eighty-six years are a formidable argument in favor of the devil, that I will not see the Reign of Mary before closing my eyes. And I must confide in Our Lady that it will not be so. That is because of the grace of Genazzano, but also because of this inner light. It goes so far that if I were to die in these conditions, I would die in peace, saying: 'The voices did not lie.'"[1251]

[1249] EXT, 11 October 1981.

[1250] MSGR. H. DELASSUS, *La Mission posthume de sainte Jeanne d'Arc et le Règne social de Notre Seigneur Jésus-Christ*, Editions Jeanne d'Arc, Villegenon, 1983, p. 421.

[1251] MNF, 26 December 1994.

Plinio Corrêa de Oliveira always had the certainty of the triumph of the Immaculate Heart of Mary. However, he never ruled out the possibility of dying before that historic moment.

> "I saw very clearly – that is something I did not make explicit to myself entirely because I lacked theological self-assurance, study, etc. – that this vocation was clearly given by God and that I would have the strength to fulfill God's calling as long as He gave me the conviction that everything would finally work out right. God did not ask me to passively accept the collapse of everything over me, and the collapse of these hopes, but He nurtured in me the hope that I would see His Kingdom on this earth."[1252]

However, his mission was to defeat the Revolution rather than personally attend its demise. The extreme sacrifice that Divine Providence asked of him to complete his mission was to renounce the consolation of seeing the Reign of Mary. But his life and death were the seed of this future triumph of the Counter-Revolution.

At his last "Clippings' Meeting," on August 19, 1995, Plinio said, as if to seal his earthly mission:

> "What will happen after this meeting? I do not know. I am certain of only one thing: in five, fifty or a hundred years from now, someone may proclaim: Our Lady has won, won, won!"[1253]

> "We should tell ourselves: 'There is a risk that you die without seeing the Reign of Mary....On the other hand, there is something like a promise that it will not happen to you. But if it does happen, will you die peacefully without entering the promised land, as happened to Moses?'"[1254]

A few months before being called by God, he sensed that he would die and announced it to a disciple. In the last months of his life he suffered profoundly, not because of death or the fear of not having fulfilled his mission, but with the knowledge that many of his disciples would be unable to continue fighting without his visible leadership and would look for another "Moses" to lead them to the promised land.

Our Lord's deepest suffering during His Passion certainly was spiritual rather than physical, and perhaps caused by concern over the salvation of souls that would not respond to His redeeming mercy. The abandonment of their vocation by many of his sons was perhaps the greatest cause of pain to Plinio Corrêa de Oliveira, to which he replied with increasing acts of love for the Blessed Virgin Mary, in the certainty

---

[1252] MNF, 23 March 1995.
[1253] RRR, 19 August 1995.
[1254] AMC, 4 May 1989.

that he had accomplished his mission, because other faithful sons would bring his work to completion.

I dedicate these pages to his old and new faithful sons spread all over the world.

Rome, May 31, 2015, Feast of the Queenship of Mary.

Index of Names and Authors Cited

S

T